The Best of The Humanist
Humanist Philosophy 1928–1973

The Best of The Humanist
Humanist Philosophy 1928–1973

EDITED, WITH INTRODUCTORY ESSAYS, BY
CHARLES MURN

Humanist Press
Washington, DC

© 2018 Humanist Press LLC
1821 Jefferson Place NW
Washington, DC 20036
www.humanistpress.com

Charles Murn
The Best of *The Humanist*: **Humanist Philosophy, 1928-1973**

All rights reserved. No part of this book may be reproduced in whole or in part without written permission from the publisher, except in the case of brief quotations embodied in critical articles and reviews; nor may any part of this book be reprinted or reproduced or utilized in any form or by any electronic, mechanical, or other means, now known or hereafter invented, including photocopying and recording, or in any information storage or retrieval system, without written permission from Humanist Press, LLC.

Published by: Humanist Press LLC
Cover Design: Sharon McGill

Printed book ISBN-13: 978-0-931779-77-0
Ebook ISBN-13: 978-0-931779-78-7

Table of Contents

NOTE FROM THE PUBLISHER	I
INTRODUCTION	1
CHAPTER 1 **Some Essentials of Humanist Philosophy**	5
Naturalism, Pluralism, Contingency, Relativism, and Emergence in Humanist Philosophy	5
Humanistic Naturalism *Harold H. Titus*	14
What Is Meant by Cosmic Purpose? *Edwin Ewart Aubrey*	22
Value is Relative to Man: The Case for Naturalistic Humanism *Paul Kurtz*	26
Faith in What? A Sociologist's Answer *Robert A. Harper*	36
CHAPTER 2 **Types of Humanism**	42
New Naturalistic Religious Marxist Evolutionary Ethical Behaviorist Rationalist Existential Secular Scientific Materialist Planetary Humanism	42
Neo-Humanism—What Is It? *A. Eustace Haydon*	51
Scientific Humanism: A Formulation *Lloyd Morain and Oliver Reiser*	53
Humanism and Atheism *Miriam Allen deFord*	59

The Best of The Humanist

Sartre or Russell—Why Not Both?   61
  G. William Domhoff

Evolutionary Humanism—Part I   65
  Julian Huxley

The Basic Characteristics of Marxist Humanism   74
  Mihailo Marković

Humanism and Behaviorism   87
  B. F. Skinner

CHAPTER 3   95
The Source and Nature of Humanist Values

Modern Humanist Values
Have Always Been Progressive   95

Science and the Reconstruction of Value   102
  Van Meter Ames

Science in a Time of Moral Confusion   112
  Erwin W. Fellows

A Theory of Metamotivation   119
  Abraham H. Maslow

The Meaning of Humanism   123
  Corliss Lamont

Scientific Humanism   129
  Read Bain

The Social Implications of Humanism   138
  Curtis W. Reese

CHAPTER 4   145
Scientific Method and Scientific Knowledge in Humanist Philosophy

The Meaning of Salvation for Scientific Naturalism   154
  Horace J. Nickels

Commitment to Humanity — 161
R. Buckminster Fuller

The Theology that Obstructs Science — 177
Horace S. Fries

Humanism and Positivism — 185
Harold Buschman

CHAPTER 5 — 188
Humanism Explores the Unknown and Defines the Uncertain

Fear and Loathing (Not) in
Mid-Century Humanist Philosophy — 188

Mysticism or Mystery — 193
Gerald Barnes

Humanism and Peace — 209
Dr. Linus Pauling

The Vanity of Wisdom — 220
Alfred G. Smith

Probabalism: A Hardy Foe of the Absolute — 226
Ted Brameld

CHAPTER 6 — 231
Religious Humanism as Nontheistic, Naturalistic, and Instrumental

The Legacy of Modern Humanism's Origins — 231

Humanism as Religious Instrumentalism — 236
Harold Scott

Humanism and Ethical Culture — 241
Jerome Nathanson

The Best of *The Humanist*

Humanism Has Its World View,
Techniques and Ideals   245
  A. Eustace Haydon

Humanism as a Religion   249
  Roy Wood Sellars

CHAPTER 7   254
The Roles of Emotion and Spirituality in Humanism

Two Taboos in Humanism?   254

Emotional and Intellectual Humanism   259
  Barbara J. Bates

Definitions of Humanism: Reason with Compassion   261
  H. J. Eysenck

Natural Mysticism   265
  Kenneth L. Patton

CHAPTER 8   270
Working Out Humanist Morals and Ethics

Humanism's Struggle With
Remaking Morals and Ethics   270

Ethics, Human Needs, And Individual Responsibility   275
  Rollo Handy

Rationality in Sexual Morality   288
  Albert Ellis

Why Can't A Woman ... ?   304
  Helen Mayer Hacker

Searching for the Roots of Moral Decisions   316
  Lester A. Kirkendall

CHAPTER 9
Humanistic Psychology and Freedom   325

Humanistic Psychologists to the Rescue   325

On Getting Values Out of Science   329
Priscilla Robertson

Peak Experiences in Education and Art   337
A. H. Maslow

A Therapist's View of the Good Life   347
Carl R. Rogers

Freedom of Choice   359
Corliss Lamont

The Relationship of Science and Morality   365
Harold A. Larrabee

CHAPTER 10
Humanism, Science, and the Arts and Humanities   373

Not Just a Shotgun Marriage   373

Of Thee I Sing   378
Frank Lloyd Wright

One Humanism, Not Two   383
John M. Morris

Science and Humanities:
Two Branches of One Trunk   385
Lucile W. Green

Escape into Reality   393
Isaac Asimov

The Best of *The Humanist*

CHAPTER 11   **401**
**Humanism Comes to Value
Other Life Forms and Nature**

Early Evolution of Humanist Environmental
Consciousness   401

Can Humanism Meet Man's Spiritual Need?   405
  Algernon D. Black

Conservation Of Man Together With Nature   419
  C. E. Busby

The Furtherance of All Life:
A Vision To Broaden And Strengthen Humanism   425
  Eleanor Woods

INDEX   **432**

NOTE FROM THE PUBLISHER

The essays reproduced here are in substantially their original form, except for the correction of a few obvious typographical errors.

One result of this decision is that there are numerous inconsistencies of style from article to article, and between the articles and the form preferred by today's Chicago Manual of Style, which we normally follow. The word "church," for example, is capitalized in places where today it would not be.

More serious than the peccadillos of style is the frequent use of gendered terminology that is no longer used by *The Humanist* or other AHA publications. There are hundreds of instances of "mankind," "man," "he," "himself" and other masculine words that demean the dignity of women. We had multiple options for dealing with this:
- Ignore the issue altogether, with a brief mention in the introduction that "Articles are reproduced in their original form for historic accuracy purposes, without regard to contemporary sensibilities."
- Attempt to correct all the instances, ignoring the value of historic accuracy. This is much more easily said than done, especially when the article itself quotes an earlier source using similar language – e.g., the Declaration of Independence, which says that "all men are created equal." Even the Humanist Manifesto I uses the term "man."
- Correct the "easy" cases, and leave the "hard" ones alone.
- Disqualify every article that uses gendered language, or is otherwise offensive in any way, notwithstanding the merit the remaining 99 percent of the article might have.

The problem becomes even more complex when you recognize that the sexism here extends beyond the mere use of language. Changing every single masculine word in an article would still not change the fact that the author may cite only men, no women, as authorities. Congratulating ourselves that we've done something special by making lots of changes to "he or she" would be self-deluding.

Much of the use of gendered language prior to the 1970s results from the fact that this was considered proper English form at the time. That's what I was taught in grade school, by women. If I had turned in a paper saying "himself or herself," I would have gotten it back with big red X and a lower grade. Even some of the women authors whose articles appear here use terms like "man" rather than "humanity."

But the problem runs deeper than that. When Paul Kurtz, writing (as many authors here do) of "man," asks "Why exacerbate his guilt complex, and his sense of sin, and why exalt feminine acquiescence?", he betrays a repugnant sense of feminine inferiority.

Nor is sexism the only embarrassment in these pages. For example, it is unlikely we would use the word "retardates" today, as another author here does.

Deviating from historicity would create its own problems. This is a book for serious research, not for light beach reading. A researcher who is interested in how sexism and other issues changed over time inside a movement that prides itself on sensitivity should be given the raw materials with which to do so. Sanitizing our history, instead of reproducing it warts and all, makes us look better than we really were.

Humanism is a process of trying to live our lives better. The authors whose work is reproduced here were not perfect. When we reach the twenty-second century, folks may well shake their heads about how insensitive and backward we were back in 2018, about something or other. The decision we have made is to reproduce the articles as they were written, but with more than just a perfunctory reference to their flaws. Reproduce them instead with a sincere attempt at a thoughtful acknowledgement that they contain quite serious defects, and a firm commitment to try to do better in the future.

I do not expect everyone to agree with this solution. If we all agreed, we wouldn't be humanists, would we? We generally do agree, though, on the value of trying to do better, which is what this editorial thought process represents.

Luis Granados
Humanist Press

INTRODUCTION

This volume is a collection of essays on early modern humanist philosophy. As its title suggests, this volume includes selected essays from *The Humanist* (*TH*) magazine through the "Humanist Manifesto II" (HMII),1 published in 1973 (*TH* 33:4). One thing that the title leaves out is that this volume also includes essays on the same subject from the predecessor to *TH*, discussed below. Each chapter starts with an essay by the editor commenting on the included archival essays, as well as referencing other essays not included for lack of space.

The predecessor to *TH* was a publication called *The New Humanist* (*TNH*). *TNH* was first published on mimeograph in April 1928 by The Humanist Fellowship in Chicago. *TNH* had a run of nearly nine years, monthly for the first two years, then every other month. The publisher of *TNH* switched from the Fellowship to several individuals and then to the Humanist Press Association. *TNH* published the "Humanist Manifesto" (HMI) in 1933.2 The last issue was August-September 1936, Vol. 9, No. 4. *TNH* was primarily focused on humanism as a religion, although as discussed in Chapter 2, it also published secular views of humanism that would become dominant later.

TH began with a Spring 1941 issue, and was published quarterly. In 1950, publication of the *TH* switched to six issues per year, where it has remained ever since. As American Humanist Association (AHA) President Roy Speckhardt pointed out during the planning of this collected essays project, the early *TH* was dominated by philosophers. The extent of that domination is anecdotally evident in the list of presidents of the American Philosophical Association who at some point published essays in *TNH* or *TH* up through 1973. That list includes John Dewey, Roy Wood Sellars, Brand Blanshard, Ernest Nagel, Sidney Hook, Van Meter Ames, and Herbert Feigl.

Speckhardt also pointed out that after humanistic psychology began developing, *TH* starting in the mid-1950s developed a strong focus on writings about that new field. Two presidents of the American Psychological

Association who wrote for *TH* during the period were Carl R. Rogers and Abraham H. Maslow.

Throughout this volume, the acronyms, "*TH*" and "*TNH*," are used to reference the two publications.

Due to space limitations, discussion of the precursors of modern humanist philosophy are limited to situations where it is relevant to the essay or issue under consideration.

The idea for this volume was sparked during a discussion with Roy Speckhardt and Luis Granados in 2011. A response to my interest in volunteering for the AHA was to produce an edited volume of collected *interviews* from *TH*. I countered with the idea of a volume of collected *essays* from the magazine. Roy suggested that I could do a collected volume of essays, and while combing through the archives, flag the interviews along the way. Thus, a separate volume of collected interviews under separate editorship may yet also result from, in part, the research for this volume. In addition, the quantity of worthy essays proved sufficient to fill this volume solely from the period from 1928 through 1973. Future publication of a volume of subsequent essays may be a matter of time.

The publication of this project could not have happened but for Roy's commitment to it. In addition, three AHA staffers, Meghan Hamilton, Cynthia Lee, and Meredith Thompson, deserve credit for the tedious scanning of the collected essays. Following up on their work, AHA staffers Meredith Thompson and Jessica Xiao deserve thanks for converting the selected articles into electronic data files. Equally, I thank Fred Edwords for reading the manuscript and Humanist Press director Luis Granados for proofing the data files for conversion errors and final editing of my commentary essays in this volume. Finally, I gratefully thank my wife, Jacqueline Ganem, who endured the task of first edits on all of my commentary essays in the volume.

My motivation for undertaking this volume is the too oft-heard charge that humanist philosophy is still not sufficiently refined. The charge includes the idea that humanist philosophy is too fragmented, has too many versions, and has only a partial narrative on how the world works. More problematic, some critics argue that humanism does not sufficiently address the questions facing people in their daily lives.

Similar problems cropped up in trying to select which essays to include. First, many writers simply discussed philosophy without connecting it to humanist philosophy per se. Generally, I did not select these articles for that reason alone. Second, and more challenging, the great majority of essays that do talk about humanist philosophy, including those selected for this volume, range far beyond philosophy as well. I could have placed most of the essays in this volume in multiple chapters despite the limited range of subjects in those chapters. In the end, I placed a few where I did simply to balance the number of essays in each chapter. Accordingly, you may find a few essays do not necessary focus on the issue covered in the chapter in which the essay is included. They nonetheless still serve the overall goal of remembering the best essays in the magazines on early modern humanist philosophy. The essays are included in the order in which they are mentioned in the introductory material for each chapter. Not surprisingly, copyright issues kept at least one essay out of this volume.

One final problem was the limited pool of essays from which to choose. Naturally constrained by the subject and time parameters of this volume, the essays reflect the fact that most essays about philosophy were written by white men. Women and people of color wrote essays on individual values too numerous to include, and on politics and culture that were outside the philosophical subject of this volume. Likewise, Sidney Hook, a white male philosopher who was on the AHA board and *TH* editorial board, did not, by my reckoning, write a single philosophical essay in *TH* through 1973.

Nonetheless, my hope is that pulling these essays from *TNH* and *TH* will help show the initial lines as well as subsequent trends in thought on what humanist philosophy is. Both magazines maintained focus on excessive religiosity in public institutions and government. Certainly, between 1928 and 1973, humanism trended strongly away from religion toward secularism. The biggest difference between *TNH* and *TH* is that *TH* more directly, albeit gradually took on more of the issues of the day. The rise of communism, fascism, and imperialism forced a lot of discussion about how humanism is different from each. After World War II, those discussions were joined by concern about McCarthyism and the Cold War, humanism internationally, and new ideas about individual and group psychology. In 1968, the editor declared that *TH* would from then on become more activist, debating new issues and adapting to new perspectives. Thus, in the 1960s and early 1970s, the various social movements brought in many new issues that had not been part of the debate. Those many issues, along with the secularization of the humanist movement, no doubt prompted the process resulting in the HMII.

A comparison of the original HMI and HMII is left to the reader. But the mere existence of these two statements of humanist values, a mere forty years apart, illustrates the most fundamental conclusion that the reader must take from this volume. Conventional religions generally have a virtually immutable canon of written rules and principles. Humanism, by contrast, reflects human understanding of reality. Just as that understanding changes, humanism changes. That in fact is the foundational tenet of humanism: everything changes. That humanism itself changes is not only the result of human design, but is also the natural result of the nature of the reality that it mirrors. Humanism by nature incorporates changes in human understanding of reality. All the other elements of humanism truly concern either (1) what it means to humans that everything changes, or (2) what actual past, present, and future changes mean to humans.

Charles Murn, Editor
dialogue@cmurn.com

Notes

1. https://americanhumanist.org/what-is-humanism/manifesto2/
2. https://americanhumanist.org/what-is-humanism/manifesto1/

CHAPTER 1
Some Essentials of Humanist Philosophy

Naturalism, Pluralism, Contingency, Relativism, and Emergence in Humanist Philosophy

From its naming at the start of the twentieth century, writers have generally agreed on certain fundamental characteristics of the philosophy of humanism. The elements of humanism covered in this chapter are most fundamental to it, although by no means its only fundamental elements. Others are set forth in later chapters, with a few made the subject of a chapter.

In her 1971 essay in Chapter 2, Miriam Allen de Ford defined humanism as "a philosophical system based on the concept that the universe, life, and consequently mankind are the result of natural evolutionary processes alone." Rollo Handy, in prefacing an essay in which he distinguishes himself somewhat from the mainstream of humanism, quoted Corliss Lamont's definition of humanism from his book, *The Philosophy of Humanism*: "To define twentieth century Humanism in the briefest possible manner, I would say that it is a philosophy of joyous service for the greater good of all of humanity in this natural world and according to the methods of reason and democracy" (*TH* 27:1). In what may be the shortest summary, Roy Wood Sellars said that humanism "deals with the estimation of mankind and his situation" (*TNH* 6:6).

Taking another angle, B. F. Skinner, in his essay in Chapter 2, defines a "humanist" as a person "who, because of the environment to which he has been exposed, is concerned for the future of mankind."

As humanists are an argumentative lot, humanism comes in many types. Elements specific to a type of humanism are covered in Chapter 2. This chapter sets forth elements argued by at least some writers in *TNH* or *TH* to be characteristic of all philosophical humanism.

Scientific Naturalism, Not Supernaturalism or Purpose

In his essay in Chapter 2, A. Eustace Haydon asserts that a humanist "takes his naturalism straight." The second clause of Haydon's run-on sentence in his last paragraph sets forth the idea that humanism gets its knowledge through testing reality with the scientific method, without any dilution by supernaturalism. Thus, from the first year of publication of *TNH*, 1928, the idea that naturalism is essential to humanism had a proponent in Haydon.

His early statement that humanism is naturalistic reflects that this strain of thought began developing prior to the 1933 HMI. The HMI does not use any form of the word, "naturalism." Like Haydon, one of the signatories of HMI, Sellars, was specifically arguing months before publication of HMI that religious humanism was inherently naturalistic (*TNH* 6:3). In the second affirmation, it states that "man is a part of nature." In the fifth, that even religious humanism "must formulate its hopes and plans in the light of the scientific spirit and method." Sellars saw the references to "nature" and "naturalness" as all directly summoning naturalism as a philosophy, now referred to as metaphysical naturalism. His references ground humanness in nature. In so doing, they harken back to the original discussions about "nature" and the nature of humans in the Sophist period of ancient Greece.

Writing later than that essay by Sellars, Harold H. Titus approaches humanism from the scientific naturalist perspective in his essay in this chapter. He names several types of naturalism, in order to distinguish his humanistic naturalism from earlier scientific naturalism focused on physics or pre-scientific naturalism focused on poetry. In doing so, he equates scientific humanism with humanistic naturalism. Lamont notes in his essay in Chapter 3 that John Dewey, who was key to bringing the scientific method into naturalism, preferred to call himself a "humanistic naturalist," rather than a humanist. Around the same time,

Humanist Philosophy 1928 – 1973

E. Burdette Backus wrote in *TH* that the philosophy of humanism is naturalism (*TH* 6:3). Paul Kurtz, in his essay in this chapter, lists three main contributions of naturalism to humanism. They are the ways in which humanism is indebted to naturalism under the consensus view of humanist scholars. Essays asserting differences between scientific naturalism and scientific humanism are the subject of Chapter 4.

The HMI and HMII both do not use the word "truth." It is not one of Kurtz's three key contributions of naturalism, either. But Kurtz does point out that truth is central to humanism, as does Robert Harper in his essay in this chapter and Priscilla Robertson in Chapter 9. That centrality, too, comes from scientific naturalism.

Titus juxtaposes humanistic naturalism to "literary humanism," an elitist form of classical humanism, and to materialism. But he notes that humanism, like materialism, does not see evidence of dualism, the asserted "bifurcation of nature." Indeed, the third affirmation in HMI says as much even for religious humanism. Humanism thus rejects others' distinctions between the "sacred" and the "secular," as well as between "nature" and other concepts, such as "art," the "supernatural," "experience," the "transcendent," and "man." Indeed, he points out that nature encompasses "reality." But Titus rejects the mechanistic nature of materialism as incompatible with humanism, although he seems to implicitly assume all materialism is reductionist and rejects emergence, discussed below.

Humanists agree with Titus that nature is not teleological. That is, humanism sees no evidence of purpose in nature. Lamont pointed out that humanism does not see evidence of a mind in the universe, whether divine or otherwise (*TH* 8:2). It is not monist in that sense. Rather, nature in the form of the universe is indifferent to human existence and concerns. Interestingly, Titus uses the word "qualitative" to describe differences of experiences and processes. That is a good word for explaining an aspect of pluralism covered below.

The essay in this chapter by Edwin Ewart Aubrey concurs with Titus and Lamont on the lack of purpose in the universe in humanist understanding of reality. Aubrey effectively dissects the requirements for a teleological universe and briefly discounts them. Aubrey argues instead that the evidenced purpose in the human realm is that which humans themselves decide on.

By the same token, as noted in HMI, rejection of supernaturalism is a settled element of humanism. Nonetheless, some humanists consider humanism to be a naturalistic religion. Essays on that topic are the subject of Chapter 6.

Humanism and Pluralism

The monist character of humanism discussed above pertains to the issue of whether the human mind is separate from the human body. Humanism, seeing the two as an integrated whole, is therefore what philosophers call monist in that sense.

But the word "monism" has another meaning relevant to the discussion of humanism. This meaning pertains to the idea of a mind in the universe. As Lamont explained, this notion views the universe as some sort of unified whole. Humanism is not monist under this definition. Lamont and, in his essay in this chapter, Paul Kurtz assert a more tenuous interconnectedness without unity or wholeness.

Horace J. Nickels presents the alternative view in his essay in Chapter 4, which is pluralism. Pluralism is central to humanism. Rather than asserting a mind in the universe, humanism as pluralistic generally understands that while, however attenuated, a given thing *can* affect a great many other things, nothing *substantially* affects anywhere near everything. The vastness of the universe makes this impossible.

By extension, humanism accepts the evidence that each thing affects some things more than other things. While what happens on the nearest star to our solar system, four light years away, can and, certainly to one extent or another, does affect what happens on Earth over huge timespans, what happens on our solar system's Sun has a far greater and more frequent impact on what happens on Earth. Less abstractly, the people in your life affect you generally more frequently and substantially than any particular person on the other side of the Earth.

Pluralism comes down to Earth, too. In their essays in Chapter 8, Albert Ellis and Helen Mayer Hacker touch on how pluralism leads humanists to accept different views of morals and ethics in human life. Humanism advocates reasonable freedom to enrich the desirable parts and reduce the occurrence and negative effects of the undesirable parts of human life. Accordingly, humanist philosophy compels exploration and appreciation for a plurality of ideas about human existence. Pluralism is thereby a prerequisite for the relativism in humanist philosophy discussed below.

Contingency and Change in Humanism

An element of relativism is the notion of "contingency." In his essay in Chapter 9, Lamont discusses this important concept, which too many people do not still understand today. The term applies to the fact that scientific laws are highly conditional. Those laws are typically stated in greatly oversimplified form that makes them far more elegant and poetic than they are.

Lamont uses the example of the law that liquid water freezes at thirty-two degrees. The conditions that would have to be added in order to fully define this law are far more extensive than the simple statement portends. In the first place, thirty-two is an arbitrary number on a scale devised by humans. So even the measuring stick is contingent—upon human history and, indeed, which scale, in this case Fahrenheit, for measuring temperature that humans have devised is being used. More significantly, simply the altitude on earth at which the water is cooled has a huge effect on the relevant number of degrees on the chosen scale at which liquid water will freeze. Far more significantly, the environment in which the water is cooled is a giant set of conditions for the so-called law, including: the gravitation of the planet earth, which is contingent upon the formation of the earth itself, as well as the composition of its atmosphere, again equally contingent, as well as the density of its atmosphere producing the ambient pressure at the particular altitude. Indeed, it is not an overstatement to say that the "law" as applied on earth is also contingent upon the formation of a planet exactly like earth (in its solar system and galaxy)!

By the same token, when a person has particularly good luck or bad luck, the sheer number of conditions necessary for that occurrence is huge. Lamont touches on this insight. While theologians have explained these in terms of "acts of God" and the like, they come down to the fact that in the laws of nature, if something *can* happen, it almost certainly eventually *will* happen somewhere. Once it happens, the odds are no longer relevant to the reality of the occurrence.

As a logical result of the acceptance of contingency, Lamont appropriately sets forth the humanist arguments against determinism. Determinism, along with mechanism, generally asserts the analogy of the universe as a running clock. Not only the motions and reactions of inanimate objects are pre-determined like clockwork by all that came before. Determinism also views the thoughts and actions of humans as being similarly determined. In contrast, humanism asserts that humans have evolved with capacities both: (1) to react quickly and mechanistically to something like a threat, and (2) to reason, which is the ability to choose among options based on consideration of relevant perceptible factors. Lamont connects the latter ability to the view that humans have free will and the power to choose.

The contingent nature of reality corresponds to another aspect of contingency, as understood in humanism. As Julian Huxley's essay included in Chapter 2 posits, change is inevitable. That is, a particular set of facts on the ground are themselves contingent. The seasons are an obvious example. Another more recently perceived example is the level of the oceans on earth. From antiquity until sometime in the modern era, humans generally understood that the sea level does not change (except in tales of deity-induced floods). But we now know that the sea level changed for one reason or another. Indeed, the present climate change challenge requires limiting human production of greenhouse gases to limit the change in sea level for the benefit of human civilization around the globe.

Humanist Philosophy 1928 – 1973

Issues similar to the threat of climate change are the reason why even human progress is contingent. Humans must act to prevent regression of human society, in order for even the current mixed state of civilization to persist. Even if humans manage that, they remain dependent on their environment for conditions conducive to their flourishing.

Humanism and Relativism

Whether relativism is a fundamental element of humanism is more controversial among humanists.2 Kurtz's essay in this chapter argues that humanist values are relative to humans and what humans find "to be worthwhile." For purposes of clarification, it is worth pointing out that Kurtz in his doctoral dissertation stated it more specifically as "relative to the strivings or valueings of individual[s]."[3] Humans are the source of human values. Accordingly, Kurtz says that humanist values are subject to criticism and modification. He briefly lays out the good values that humanism has adopted. But he does not use the term, "relativism" in the essay. Of course, the difficulty is in the details, which Kurtz does not dig into.

E. Burdette Backus distinguished humanism from philosophical naturalism in this realm (*TH* 6:3). He accepted that humanism is a naturalism, but unlike metaphysical naturalism, it is relativistic. Of course, more recently, pragmatic naturalists have come around to consider aspects of relativism in their metaphysics, although it seems fair to say that they have yet to embrace it to the extent that humanists have.

The result of those details is that, as Harper puts it, "relativism is hard work." It requires resolving each situation one experiences in light of the multiple personal and social factors he outlines. He suggests that this difficult nature is the root cause of religious liberalism's losing its way. Relativism is a thought process for finding the highest value possible at the time. Unlike absolutist ideologies such as canonized religion or communism, relativism requires thinking things over, and maybe thinking them over again. It requires accepting truths wherever they may lie. Algernon D. Black, in his essay in Chapter 11, says the same thing in different words.

Of course, absolutist theologians and other critics try to paint all relativism as nihilistic. That is no doubt why, for example, Kurtz did not use the term, "relativism." Nihilism posits no basis for comparing anything. But writers in TH have acknowledged that humanism requires coming up with a source of values.[4] As for the nature of humanist values, see Chapter 3.

Emergence in Humanism

Kurtz notes that most naturalists are not reductionists, as he defines the term. Close examination suggests Kurtz was talking about ontological reductionism. While certainly humanists reject supernatural explanations of reality claiming one substance makes up all reality, that does not preclude a scientific conclusion that all that exists is a form of photonic energy.

Titus as well as Sellars in another, contemporaneous essay (*TH* 13:2) likewise criticize reductionism as not compatible with humanism. Their discussions suggest they were referring to methodological reductionism. That kind of reductionism sees the fundamental laws of physics as the basis for all that exists. Methodological reductionism has been used by religionists and theologians in attempts to paint all atheists, secularists, and skeptics as having no values. To do so, they obviously must extrapolate the limited reductionism that has gotten much attention to the idea that all people who accept the laws of physics as fundamental somehow are reductionists. On that assumption, they claim that methodological reductionists therefore cannot explain how the laws of physics result in, say, the evolution of humans.

Humanists generally reject methodological reductionism, like its ideological sibling, materialism. Writings giving either one shrift in *TNH* and *TH* are hard to find. But the discussion of the alternative was not robust, either.

Instead, Titus argued that humanism accepts what he terms, "continuity," now generally known as "emergence." Sellars described the emergence of humans and other higher life forms from the evolutionary process, referring to it as "emergent organization." That makes sense because evolutionary theory depends on the notion of emergence. Emergence illustrates how different and new combinations of organic molecules can emerge under proper conditions as stable, unique life forms. In fact, the second affirmation in HMI says that humans "emerged as the result of a continuous process."

More generally, "emergence" refers to the characteristics of complex systems of energy and matter that emerge from specific combinations of simpler systems devoid of those characteristics. For Titus, continuity includes intellectual or mental processes in the realm of the complex. Humanism considers both intellectual and physical or biological systems to be equally natural. Of course, the matter is not scientifically settled, and some present-day humanists and secular thinkers suggest even today that the mind has a source outside the physical body, despite extensive evidence to the contrary. Nonetheless, emergence, in Titus' and Sellars' discussion, is thus the property of matter and energy explaining why subatomic particles in the right combination can reason. On those grounds, emergence is essential to humanist thought.

Notes

1. For a history of the first "Humanist Manifesto," see Edwin H. Wilson, *The Genesis of a Humanist Manifesto* (Amherst, NY: Humanist Press).
2. For the view, however briefly stated, that humanism is not compatible with relativism, see, e.g., Nathanson's essay in Ch. 7.
3. Kurtz, Paul, *The Problems of Value Theory* (NY: Columbia U., 1952), p. 120.
4. See Kluckhohn, Clyde, "Science as a Possible Source of New Moral Values," TH 14:5, p. 211 et seq. (1954).

Humanistic Naturalism

Harold H. Titus
The Humanist, January-February, 1954

The term "naturalism" stands over against the term "supernaturalism," or "otherworldliness." It takes nature as the whole of reality, but "nature" is interpreted in many different ways. The dictionaries of philosophy1 give many different uses of the term "nature" in philosophical discussions. When the term is used to designate a point of view, it is necessary to use some adjective to make the meaning clearer. For example, there are the logical or structural or realistic naturalists who look to mathematics and physics for their orientation. There are the poetic naturalists like George Santayana. There are the humanistic naturalists who stress the social studies, the welfare of man, and the universal applicability of the empirical, experimental methods of the natural sciences. In this section we deal with humanistic naturalism.

Humanistic Naturalism Defined

Humanistic naturalism is a philosophy which places emphasis upon man or upon human interests and affairs. It has also been called humanism, the new humanism, evolutionary naturalism, empirical naturalism, and scientific humanism. The differences which exist between them are largely matters of emphasis.2 A definition by two contemporary humanists is as follows: "Scientific humanism is the doctrine that men, through the use of intelligence, directing the institutions of democratic government, can create for themselves, without aid from 'supernatural powers,' a rational civilization in which each person enjoys security and finds cultural outlets for whatever normal human capacities and creative energies he possesses."3

Humanistic naturalism is to be distinguished from two other movements of thought. First, it is not to be confused with mechanistic materialism. Materialism is a way of thinking that is constructed on the basis of a rigid determinism and mechanism and that tends to reduce everything to the terms and the laws of the physical sciences. In contrast, humanistic naturalism places its main emphasis upon the social studies and seeks to do justice to the organic and to human interests and aspirations. It acknowledges that which is unique in man, and its defenders claim that it is as sensitive as idealism to man's interests and welfare.

In the second place, humanistic naturalism is to be clearly distinguished from the humanism of the Renaissance although it has been called "Renaissance humanism modernized and brought up to date." The humanists of the Renaissance admired the Greeks especially for their reasonable balance of life, and they placed emphasis upon the classics. The movement was a literary one, although there was a new confidence in man and in human reason. There was a revival of classical, as opposed to ecclesiastical, studies. A modern movement, known as "literary humanism" and led by Irving Babbitt, Paul Elmer More, and Norman Foerster, supports a classical type of liberal education and opposes the present vogue for vocational education. This movement should not be confused with humanistic naturalism.

Humanistic naturalism has much in common with the "Religion of Humanity" of Auguste Comte in the nineteenth century, and with the pragmatism of William James and the instrumentalism of John Dewey. While a few of the humanistic naturalists are realists, many of them are pragmatists. In 1933 a group of thirty-four college professors, ministers, and other "progressive thinkers" issued "A Humanist Manifesto" summing up their convictions in fifteen brief propositions.4 In 1941 the American Humanist Association5 was founded. It publishes a bimonthly journal, *The Humanist*.

The Method

The humanistic naturalists have a profound respect for modern science and they accept its assumptions and postulates at face value. However, they are more particularly interested in biology, psychology, medicine, and the social studies, since their attention is centered upon man and his welfare. Science is viewed not as a transcript of reality but as a human construct to secure control over the world. The "laws" of nature are recognized as based on hypotheses which are man-made structures.

The ultimate court of appeal is to empirical facts or to man's verifiable experience. All distinctions between a "sacred" and a "secular" disappear. Humanistic naturalism is thus a philosophy based on the empirical scientific method and interested in hypotheses and experimentation for the purpose of human control.

Writing under the title Naturalism and the Human Spirit6 members of a group who call themselves empirical naturalists emphasize the universal applicability of the methods of experimental inquiry. This method, they claim, is self-correcting and indefinitely progressive. It does not need to be checked or tested by some "higher" or nonexperimental principles. This emphasis upon the universal applicability of scientific method rules out the intuitions of the mystics, a priori principles, the primacy of spirit, and all systems of thought that accept or imply a bifurcation of nature.

Until the nineteenth century, man and his various experiences had usually been set over against nature and had been interpreted independently. The theory of biological evolution and the application of scientific methods to all areas of existence put man and all his powers and activities in the nature over against which he had previously been placed. Basic to experimental naturalism is the view that nature is the whole of reality. Naturalism is "opposed to all dualisms between nature and another realm of being to the Greek opposition between nature and art, to the medieval contrast of the natural and the supernatural, to the empiricist antithesis of nature and experience, to the idealist distinction between natural and transcendental, to the fundamental dualism pervading modern thought between nature and man. For present-day naturalists 'nature' serves rather as the all-inclusive category, corresponding to the role played by 'being' in Greek thought or by 'reality' for the idealists."7 Whatever man encounters in any area of experience or in whatever way is regarded as "natural."

Humanistic naturalists stress the principle of continuity. There is no sharp distinction between intellectual, biological, and physical processes. There is, they assert, continuity between the less complex and the more complex. Intellectual processes "grow out of" organic or biological processes and organic processes arise from physical processes without being identical with them. This is a methodological postulate and is in no sense an attempt to "reduce" one to the other. The naturalist thus insists upon continuity of analysis in the sense that all phenomena must be interpreted by the experiential methods of verification as used by the special sciences. There is continuity between the "human" and the "physical," between the "logical" and the "biological," and the method of inquiry in each of these areas must be experiential and objective.

The humanists contend that the richness of human experience and the great variety of natural phenomena can neither be "explained away" nor "reduced" to something else. This opposition to reductionism separates this form of naturalism from the older materialism. The world is what it is in all its qualitative variety and its different kinds of activity. Empirically there are numerous qualities and different types of activity. The new naturalism can accept physical and intellectual (mental) processes at their face value. It finds some processes to be mechanical and some to exhibit teleology or purpose. It accepts all these as experimental facts. The new naturalism thus attempts to avoid the oversimplification of nineteenth-century naturalism, which attempted to explain away the richness of human experience.

The Humanist World View

Humanistic naturalists regard the universe as "self-existing and not created." They have abandoned all conceptions of a supernatural and all forms of cosmic support. The world beyond man is not interested in his weal or woe. Consequently, man must give up all teleological conceptions and realize that the world order is nonpurposive and neutral in its relation to human values. Life is dependent on a physicochemical order. It is likely that "life is a local and episodic phenomenon in the cosmos at large."8 The quest for an understanding of the ultimate origin, nature, and goal of the universe is felt to be futile.

That the universe is an objective order which goes its own way without regard to the human venture has been forcefully stated by M. C. Otto: "It is thus a constructive social suggestion that we endeavour to give up, as the basis of our desire to win a satisfactory life, the quest for the companionship with a being behind or within the fleeting aspect of nature; that we assume the universe to be indifferent toward the human venture that means everything to us; that we acknowledge ourselves to be adrift in infinite space on our little earth, the sole custodians of our ideals."9 Thus humanists support an "unreservedly naturalistic" view of the universe and of life.

In the new naturalism the categories of "matter" and "motion" have been replaced with the categories of "events," "qualities," and "relations." That is, nature operates in terms of "processes." Existence is not to be interpreted in terms of indestructible atoms in motion. All ranges of existence are now considered complex, fluid, and interactive. The naturalism which emphasizes events is not committed to any single hypothesis regarding the nature of the qualities and relations which are found by observation or experience. To experience change or process is to be aware of differences of the kind called "qualitative." The naturalists insist that they are not committed to any one interpretation of the nature of anything. Neither the theory of levels nor the principle of reduction is used. Observation merely indicates that some existents differ sharply from one another and some differ less sharply. An explanation is acceptable when it is supported by the observed evidence. Scientific knowledge is not limited to any field of subject matter; it may deal with the processes of history, with values, with the fine arts, and with the experiences of purpose.

Man and Human Society

The Humanist Manifesto states that humanists hold an "organic view of life"; reject the "traditional dualism of mind and body"; and believe that "man is a part of nature and that he has emerged as the result of a continuous process." Man with all his faculties is a part of one all-embracing natural order. He is the highest product of the creative forces of the universe, with "nothing above or beyond him" but his own aspirations.

While man is a part of nature, that does not mean that there is nothing distinctive about him. "Evolutionary naturalism does not sink man back into nature. It acknowledges all that is unique in him and vibrates as sensitively as idealism to his aspirations and passions. Its claim is that its canvas is larger and its perspective truer."[10] Nature must be interpreted so as to make a place for man.

The humanistic naturalists stress the worth of every human being. They claim that they are gaining a new sense of human values. The values of life are the products of human relationships. A realization of this fact can bring a new human confidence. Men are now able to look to the future with a new spirit of progress, of adventure, and of courageous conquest. Our task, as men, is to appropriate the instruments which science has given us and to co-operate in building a more satisfactory life on earth. We need to naturalize the spiritual values of life and to humanize the mechanical world of things. The humanists have a strong faith in the possibility of improving human life and in the essential unity of mankind.

The humanistic naturalists stand for human freedom—freedom of choice and the civil liberties. They are opposed to determinisms of every kind. They are also exponents of democracy, education, peace, and international co-operation. Most of them oppose an acquisitive society and favor a socialized and co-operative social and economic order. "The goal of humanism is a free and universal society in which people voluntarily and intelligently co-operate for the common good. Humanists demand a shared life in a shared world."[11]

Humanism and Religion

Many of the humanists retain the word "religion" and give it a new meaning. Some of them would prefer to drop the term "religion" for "the humanist way of life."[12] There is a complete abandonment of the orthodox or traditional conceptions of religion. Religion is viewed as a social product. It is loyalty to the values of life and the co-operative human quest for the good life.[13] The religious or the spiritual is not something alien to man or imposed from without. It is a quality of man's life which is grounded in his own human activity. The spiritual in man is man at his best fighting loyally and courageously for the values of life. It is co-operating for human welfare, projecting ideals and struggling to attain them, and making room for sympathy and love. "Any activity," says John Dewey, "that is pursued in behalf of an ideal and against obstacles and in spite of threats of personal loss because of conviction of its general and enduring value is religious in quality."[14] The essence of religion is interpreted as the integration of the human personality around loyalty to some high ideal. It is "a religion without God," but the humanists claim that it meets the needs which religion has always met in that it unites men in devotion to human interests and values. The humanists hope to integrate scientific, social, and religious thought into one unified philosophy which aims to realize the best life that is possible for men.

Footnotes and Bibliography

1. See James Mark Baldwin, Dictionary of Philosophy and Psychology, rev. ed. The Macmillan Company, New York, 1901-1905; The Dictionary of Philosophy, edited by Dagobert D. Runes, Philosophical Library, New York, 1942.
2. In this section no attempt is made to distinguish between these terms. They are used as different expressions for the same general approach.
3. Oliver L. Reiser and Blodwen Davies, Planetary Democracy, p. 212. Creative Age Press, Inc., New York, 1944. Used by permission of the publishers.
4. See The Christian Century for July 7, 1953, pp. 743-745. In recent years a number of similar statements have been published. For example, see the "eight central propositions" of the humanist philosophy in Humanism as a Philosophy, by Corliss Lamont, pp. 19-21, Philosophical Library, Inc., New York, 1949; "Ten Premises for a Humanist Philosophy of Life," by Rudolph Dreikurs, in The

Humanist Philosophy 1928 – 1973

Humanist, Spring, 1949. See discussion, "Humanist Manifesto—Twenty Years After," Vol. XI, The Humanist, 1953, Nos. 2 and 3.
5. Actually the AHA dates from 1928 when the New Humanist was first published. Several forms of organization preceded incorporation in 1941.
6. Naturalism and the Human Spirit, edited by Yervant H. Krikorian, Columbia University Press, 1944. Used by permission of the publishers.
7. Ibid., p. 357.
8. Edwin A. Burtt, Types of Religious Philosophy, rev. ed., p. 341, Harper and Brothers, New York, 1951.
9. Max C. Otto, Things and Ideals, p. 289, Henry Holt and Company, New York, 1924. Used by permission of the publishers.
10. Roy W. Sellars, Evolutionary Naturalism, p. 343, The Open Court Publishing Company, La Salle, Ill., 1922.
11. "A Humanist Manifesto," part of point 14.
12. The "Humanist Manifesto" of 1933 uses the term frequently. Corliss Lamont in "The Meaning of Humanism," The Humanist, Vol. II, No. 2, pp. 41-45, deplores the use of the term. See discussions in succeeding issues of The Humanist.
13. A. Eustace Haydon, The Quest of the Ages, pp. ix and iff, Harper and Brothers, New York, 1929. See also Haydon's Man's Search for the Good Life, published in 1937.
14. John Dewey, A Common Faith, p. 27, Yale University Press, New Haven, 1934.

What Is Meant by Cosmic Purpose?

Edwin Ewart Aubrey
The New Humanist, June, 1930

The process of definition of terms is popularly regarded as a pedantic occupation; but it has vindicated itself so often in the interest of progress in thought that no apologies need be offered in the present instance. As in most issues in the controversy between science and religion the correct definition of terms is subordinated to their use as battle cries. Who can fight a man when he is trying to understand him? Who can fight off an idea at the same time that he is trying to clarify its bearings?

In current debate between what Dr. Fosdick recently termed the alternative between theos and chaos, it is assumed that the world either expresses a divine personal intent or is a chaos of meaningless events. Hence the conflict is stated as one of mechanism versus purpose: not necessarily a true antithesis. The more familiar form, the argument from design, is an oversimplification.

What does purpose involve? Obviously we cannot tackle the problem of teleology till this is known. The term "purpose" connotes four items all of which in their logical order are requisite. The first of these is *order*. But order has also various meanings each of which is used as a point of departure by different debaters. Order may be regarded as a subjective arrangement of impressions after the manner of radical skepticism, as in Hume, or it may be referred to objective categories which condition our observation, whether in the Kantian or the Realist manner. Again, order is used to mean simply a sequence of events in repetition by some; while others take it to mean a sequence of events in uniformity throughout the universe.

But to order must be added the idea of *result* if we are to move in the direction of teleology. Result, again, is viewed as a causal connection of a sequence: A does not merely follow B, it results from B. Put differently, and with a slight shift of import, B is said to be the culmination of a process A. Indeed, it may even be inferred by some from this that B was implicit in the process from the beginning.

Humanist Philosophy 1928 – 1973

Now the scientist will as a matter of evidence accept the first statement: that B follows A. He may, however, despite repetitions of the A-B sequence be loth to admit causation, (indeed the term "cause" has become a word to conjure with in the philosophy of science). Still less inclined will he be to say that B is the culmination of A, while to say that B was implicit in A and A's antecedents is to him meaningless.

Yet the teleologist cannot stop even here. He must demonstrate not only order and result but also *design*. At this stage in the development of the argument a pattern of events appears in which we have order with a focus. A complex variety of forces have converged upon a particular resultant. This resultant may be regarded as a creation of the synthesis (or concatenation) of forces, and called an emergent. The term "creative synthesis" will be used. Yet the word "design" also carries a subtle overtone of meaning, viz. that the emergent represents the real direction of the complex of trends, that it reveals the "function" of the synthesis. Accordingly a complex of events with one particular event as the focus is treated as an evidence of design.

But "design," or even "synthesis," carries its overtone of meaning through awareness to another step in the logic of teleology. To order, result and design is added the crucial implication of intent. Here for the first time, "purpose" comes into its own in the debator's thought; but it comes so imperceptibly out of the other concepts that the thinker assumes all too readily that it is proved when they are proved. Witness the time honored arguments from design still in use.

Now science observes "orderly sequence," frames hypotheses of "result," is chary of "design" and doubts "intent." So far as experimentation and observation of sense data go, science does not find conscious intent outside of the animal realm. Science cannot affirm that functional behavior in non-human organisms connotes a will operative within the organisms. Science is unable to formulate any unified objective as observable among its data. (It is pure assumption that man is the objective of organic evolution.) Furthermore, any perfectionist conception of a cosmic plan must confront the difficulties inherent in the vast wastefulness of the evolutionary plan and the maladjustment of innumerable forms.

Common ground may be found, however, for the teleologist philosopher and the non-teleologist. This is the fact that human purpose is a reality. The necessary intelligence for the construction of ends is here. That organization of means to ends which gives purpose to processes is here visible. Further, ends are here envisaged before means are found or fully de-veloped, and hence intent is established. But purpose cannot be ascribed to the processes except as their significance is seen, (it should be noted that a result may all too easily be "rationalized" as a purpose.) We cannot here digress upon the related question of human free-will, except to say that human action is regarded as purposeful even when the purposive significance is not that willed by the actor. "Divine overruling" is often made to account for unintended benefits of human conduct.

After all, what has been the religious significance of belief in cosmic purpose? Has it not been a threefold assurance: (1) that the world is "going somewhere;" (2) as a corollary, that the human quest, individual life, and moral conduct "count for something;" and (3) that man can, by active effort, achieve a unity and harmony with the universe that shall reinforce his own attempts at goodness with the forces beyond himself. Is it possible to secure these assurances apart from the difficulties that attend the traditional teleology?

The clue would seem to lie in the word that has come from biology into religion to supplant such theological inheritances as "submission," "communion," "atonement." This is the word "adjustment." It is a companion word of "organism," and "function." Out of an illimitable variety of possibilities a particular combination appears. This may be viewed either as determined by the constitution of elements, as in mechanism; or as directed toward the synthesis which serves, as it were, to evoke the combination (see holistic views such as those of Smuts and Whitehead). Creative synthesis thus becomes a fact of great value for the control of ourselves and our world.

Humanist Philosophy 1928 – 1973

It is just at this point that the conception of purpose takes on a new meaning: purpose becomes adjustment of behavior in perspective. Any event becomes purposive in terms of the larger whole of which it is a constituent part. Its purpose is furnished by its context. Thus purpose in nature shifts its meaning from external agency using natural events with some intent, to internal meaning of natural events in their relation to one another. Consequently the most comprehensive meaning of a process is our basis for estimating its purpose; and this is a problem of our relating it to the widest area of its reference.

After all, adjustment in the widest perspective is the aim of any conception of purpose. This is what religion has meant by "finding the will of God." It means the search for the fullest meaning in any event, the acceptance of that meaning as a basis for the direction of our effort, and the underlying faith in the meaningfulness which is nurtured only by adventuring with our activity in our cosmos. This is the quest of religion. It is also the quest of science. Speculation may go one step farther and seek the largest unified significance of the total process; to satisfy our desire for comprehensive integration of experience. When this is assumed to be known, philosophy may even call it God. When theology personalizes this meaningfulness into a divine intent it introduces a factor beyond the purview of scientific evidence.

Edwin Ewart Aubrey was a Professor of Christian Theology, University of Chicago.

Value is Relative to Man: The Case for Naturalistic Humanism

Paul Kurtz
The Humanist, November-December, 1964

This article is a critique of orthodox theism and an analytic restatement and defense of non-theistic naturalistic humanism.

Theistic religion has been widely interpreted as referring to "some unseen, transcendent, and divine power controlling human destiny and entitled to worship and obedience." Generally this involves some faith, commitment or belief in the existence of God or of gods.

The issue is clear: How can the theist support his cognitive claim that a divine being exists independently of himself? We have witnessed in the modern world the erosion of the classical religious system and its "eternal truth." Among the conflicts have been those between its cosmology and natural science; between the theistic picture of human nature, with man higher than the beast but a little lower than the angels, and the Darwinian theory of evolution; between the literal interpretation of the Bible and the higher Biblical criticism. Today theism conflicts with the criticism by social, psychological and behavioral sciences destructive of any privileged status to the religious "soul," or to the special claims of any one religion to be universal. Thus most philosophic naturalists and scientific humanists find that theistic religion has not supported its assertion that God exists and they suspect that it will probably be unable to do so.

Theism: Unproved

Indeed, skepticism goes further today than in previous ages by showing that the whole theistic question itself verges on meaninglessness: there usually has been little or no clear conception of precisely what was to be demonstrated or proved. In other words, the term or concept "God" appears to be devoid in most of its uses of literal, cognitive, or empirical significance. This does not mean that the symbol or idea is unimportant, morally or emotionally, to people—only that it has not been clearly defined. Thus before we can determine whether and to what extent the claim is true, we must know what we mean. And the analysis of the uses of religious terms in ordinary language, as far as I can tell, has not clarified but only confused the issue with a new form of apologetics. That is why so many contemporary scientific philosophers and logicians would not care to be labelled "atheists," since they do not know exactly what they are alleged to be denying; nor "agnostics," since they are not sure that a genuine cognitive question is being propounded. Rather they are simply skeptics or "ignostics" (that is, ignorant) about the whole matter.

Religion: Quality in Experience

This analysis does not necessarily mean that all critics of theistic religion are indifferent to reli-gious values. In fact, many take religious values so seriously that they resent the attempt by the theist to preempt the field. Many naturalistic humanists, for example, consider themselves to be religious although they mean something different by religion from what the theist means. Religion for the humanist refers primarily to a *quality in human experience.* It is centered around man and his concerns. It is, as Tillich suggests, the expression of our "ultimate concern," the basic ideal ends to which a person is committed—the confession of which may call forth a stutter, a smile, or a blush. Thus we have a "religious experience" when we are aware of our basic values and aims.

In what way does this differ from philosophical awareness? Philosophy is cognitive and rational, religion affective and attitudinal. Science describes for us, religion profoundly moves us. A philosophical position is converted into a religious position only when the philosophy is given the strength of passionate devotion and conviction. Religion thus goes beyond thought to stir our irrational natures. Under this definition the communist would be religious in his devotion to the aims of dialectical materialism, as would the Epicurean, the Buddhist, the Taoist in their devotion to other ideals. Here faith does not involve belief in an alleged reality of a being unseen which is independent of, or contrary to reason and expedience; but it is a conviction that an ideal can be achieved. Religion in this sense is a serious and compelling commitment to a way of life; it gives direction and form to our energies and activities.

There are thus two main characteristics to this humanistic definition of religion: (a) its reference to fundamental and basic ideals and values, and (b) its reference to *attitudes* and feelings. One's values, however, are not held in isolation from one's general cognitive beliefs about the world and our place within it. Indeed, one's world-view, whether naturalistic or theistic, has some effect upon the general attitudes and responses that one takes towards the world in general and other human beings. Yet it is the prescriptiveness and the expressiveness that a system of beliefs may arouse that is the distinctive religious quality of experience. So far as persons are aware of their basic values, and as these have some controlling emotive power in their lives, they may be said to be "religious." When one becomes concerned attitudinally with his ultimate principles, he is functioning religiously.

Three Main Principles of Naturalism

The naturalistic humanist has his own basic ideal values which are related to his outlook of the world and of his place within it. And to the extent that he is religious, he may feel rather deeply about them. But let me state what I take to be the main principles of naturalistic humanism.

First, naturalism is committed to certain methodological principles, primarily to scientific and empirical methods as the most effective way to arrive at reliable knowledge. Thus to be warranted, a descriptive belief (a) must be experimentally verified, (b) it must be logically consistent, internally with itself and externally with our other beliefs, and (c) it may be judged convenient in part by its role in inquiry and its relation to the situations in which it arises.

A descriptive belief is considered by the naturalist to be (d) fallible and tentative. It is (e) an hypothesis open to revision, and it must be (f) capable of some public and objectively repeatable tests by a community of inquirers. But this method itself is (g) self-corrective and open to revision should new techniques be discovered. These methodological first principles of naturalism are not articles of faith; they have been gradually elaborated in civilization and have been found to be the most effective means for furthering the aims of inquiry. The empirical method requires that we should be skeptical and suspend judgment wherever there is insufficient evidence; and this involves some skepticism concerning its own first principles.

Second, naturalism provides not only a logic of inquiry, but an account of the generic traits of the world as it is encountered and a reflective commentary on the human scene. Using the empirical method, naturalism rejects any easy bifurcation between nature and super-nature. It is dubious of the notion of cosmic teleological purpose and of a transcendental realm lying beyond all rational and empirical interpretation. But the naturalist does not deny that there are aspects of the universe which now (and perhaps in the future) are beyond his investigation; nor does he exclude the trans-empirical on *a priori* grounds. He only maintains that any claims to a non-natural realm must be examined objectively and in the light of the evidence. Nor does the naturalist callously dismiss the reports of religious experience which the mystic claims. But he looks upon these reports as events to be explained and interpreted, much the same as other data which are experienced. Such events he finds can be parsimoniously explained by reference to an alleged transcendental reality. In any case, he asks that all claims to knowledge be open to a responsible examination of the grounds under which they are supported; and he does not consider the evidence referred to by the mystic as conclusive.

Third, the naturalist takes man as part of nature, a product of evolution, and capable of being explained scientifically by reference to causal conditions, which operate in other parts of nature as well. This means that there is no break between the human mind or consciousness and the body, no special status to personality or "soul," and no privileged place in the universe for human existence. All eschatological claims to immortality, for example, are held to be an expression of wish fulfillment, a reading into nature. Nature, for the naturalist, is indifferent and blind to human purposes and ideals. This does not mean that man does not possess some characteristics not found to the same extent in other species, for example, man's ability to respond to symbols, to build culture, or to destroy himself. But his symbolic, socio-cultural dimensions and other differentia are in principle capable of empirical explanation; at least, no *a priori* demonstration has been made concerning a limitation to such inquiry.

Most naturalists, however, are not reductionists. While the naturalist maintains that matter, mass and energy, or the laws of physics and chemistry, in some way are basic to and present in all processes, he recognizes the multiplicity and plurality of natural things, their variety and richness. Indeed, the naturalist is reluctant to use the term "nature" in a universal sense; for he is not convinced that nature is a monistic block system, or an interconnected whole. Rather the naturalist notes that his experience shows there are many different kinds of qualities, properties and relations that things manifest; and he consequently looks to descriptions which allow for the full contextual characteristics of processes. Indeed, there may very well be many different levels in nature, or at least it is convenient to treat the varieties of things on their own levels, as we encounter them, without explaining them away.

Here the naturalist, unlike the classical materialist, maintains that the human being can only be fully understood in his own terms. Human experience and history are after all human and not to be reduced solely to non- or extra-human terms. Thus the naturalist takes seriously the diverse qualities encountered in human experience: in art, religion, morality, science, philosophy, and ordinary life. Man is a knowing being, but he is also a passionate being immersed in the immediacy of enjoyment (of love, joy, suffering and fear); and he is a dynamic being, entering into the world and changing it. In classical terms, the naturalist wishes to give full play to the "human spirit"; that is, to our developed and civilized natures, moral, aesthetic, and intellectual. The naturalist thus does not debase man, nor ignore the existence of man's higher creative talents. On the contrary, he emphasizes that the highest human excellences are achievable by the full realization of our creative capacities, but he insists that these creative talents are fully describable as natural processes.

Naturalistic Humanism

The contemporary naturalistic humanist, I believe, accepts the above three points of naturalism but he goes on to emphasize another. This fourth point I shall label humanism. The humanist is not primarily committed to a logic of inquiry, nor does he simply describe the world and man's place within it. He recommends a set of ideal values, a way of life. That is, he provides a basic view of the good life. And here a philosophical point of view is translated into a religious position.

Humanism's basic prescriptions concern man and his works. The problem for man is to discover the good life, which is achievable in human terms: as joy, pleasure, happiness, satisfaction of our needs, self-realization, fulfillment of our powers, productivity, creativity, love, friendship, reason, harmony and justice. The point is that value is relative to man and to what he finds to be worthwhile. The standard is not to be found outside of human life, but within it. This, I assume, is what Aristotle, Spinoza, the Renaissance man, the man of the Enlightenment, Nietzsche, Marx, Bentham, Mill, Freud, Fromm, Santayana, Russell, Dewey, Sartre, and the Zen Buddhist—to name some humanists if not naturalists or naturalistic humanists—all share in common. Here there is confidence in the powers of man to find within himself the sources for the good life, and here is an affirmation that life is worth living. Most naturalists and humanists (such as Dewey) believe that in some sense the methods of empirical inquiry and reason can be applied to human values and that some degree of objectivity is possible. Thus values are not merely capricious or emotive but are given to intelligent criticism and modification.

The naturalistic humanist is an uncompromising critic of the established orthodoxies, of theistic and authoritarian religion. For such religions have frequently ignored Jesus' claim that "the kingdom of God is within thee," and they have often suppressed the best human instincts. They have been dishonest concerning man's right to truth; and they have frequently censored and blocked free and responsible intellectual inquiry. The humanist, on the contrary, asks that we, as human beings, face up to the human condition as it is. We should accept the fact that "God is dead" (according to Nietzsche); that we have no way of knowing that He exists; or even of knowing that this is a meaningful question. We should accept the fact that human existence is probably a random occurrence existing between two oblivions, that death is inevitable, and that there is thus a tragic aspect to our lives. A free thinker, too, is capable of some stoic resignation.

Hope for the Living

Yet matters are not hopeless, for with a proper recognition of the human estate, there must also come an awareness of the challenges and of the possibilities that await us; and there may be a source of genuine confidence and optimism, not despair and cynicism. For while there is death and failure, there is also life and success. And with life come great and bountiful promises: these are the joys of human love and shared experience, the excitement of creativity, the power of reason, the possibilities that we as human beings have some control over our destinies. We can, for example, alleviate distress and suffering and help to create an equitable society. If we grant that not all human sorrows and evils can be avoided, still the human situation is not totally irremediable; and with some confidence in our powers, particularly of thought and intelligence, we may help to build a good life. Scientific intelligence in this regard is a great instrument, though it is not an omnipotent open sesame to salvation or certainty.

The theist has not always allowed man to be himself. He has looked outside of nature or human nature, and has created idolatrous religions, worshiping graven images. He has often frustrated and thwarted independent self-assertion. He has thus contributed to the alienation of man from himself and from nature. Man is made to feel himself dependent upon God, a "sinner" who must renounce and suppress his pride. But the more he exalts God, as the Father image, the more he demeans himself. Surely man is dependent upon external forces, some of which are beyond his control (such as death), but why worship or submit to them, and why belittle or weaken man? Why exacerbate his guilt complex, and his sense of sin, and why exalt feminine acquiescence? Man needs to be himself (says Fromm). He needs to affirm his manhood, to develop the courage to persist in spite of all the obstacles that would destroy him, indeed to exceed himself by creating a new life *for* himself. The challenge for the free man is to realize his potentialities, and to create new ones, not to cower in masochistic denial, nor to withdraw in fear, anxiety and trembling, nor to look outside of man for a false help that is not there.

Humanism thus looks to the ennoblement and enrichment of human life as the end whether in individual terms, as each man satisfies his desires and fulfills his ideals and dreams, or in social terms, where we seek to develop rules and norms of justice (to solve, for example, the arms race, the population explosion, or contribute to the uplifting of the underdeveloped areas, or to enrich enjoyment of leisure). Humanism claims that man is rooted in the soil (nature), that it is the flesh (life) that gives him satisfaction, but that it is in social harmony and creative fulfillment (the spirit), that he finds his deepest significance.

"God" for the humanist is only a symbol of man's aspirations, the ideals which stimulate him to devotion and action. Where one takes "God" to be a hidden or transcendental being, he only confuses the issue of life and does not face death. Some humanists (Tillich) are willing to retain the classical symbols of theistic religion, but they wish to demythologize them and to reinvigorate them with new meaning appropriate to our age of science and world revolution. Thus the dramatic symbols of mythological and miraculous revelation are to be reinterpreted to arouse concern for man as man. The symbol "God" thus is not of one who speaks to man from on high, but is an expression of man's deepest longings, man speaking to himself.

Other humanists are dubious of the attempt to translate all such symbols into naturalistic and humanistic terms—myself included—and would instead build new sets of symbols and beliefs appropriate to the present age, symbols better able to dramatize the aspirations of humanity. Sartre has said that there are no absolute values or norms independent of what man chooses. Instead, man is condemned to make man; we alone are responsible for what we are or what we do. Perhaps this is an overstatement of the case for freedom; at least the humanist asks that man begin to shed the chains of illusion that bind him, and assert himself. What man needs is not renunciation, but affirmation; not resignation, but confidence; above all, not blind piety and faith, but honesty and truth.

The *scientific* humanist, as distinct from others, is cautious and tentative in his judgments, and he is even skeptical about his own naturalism and humanism, recognizing their limitations. He knows that it is difficult to find absolute standards, or categorical imperatives. Yet he suggests that although the human animal finds himself thrust into existence without asking to be put there, he can to some extent define himself and determine who he is and what he shall be. Man can achieve a satisfying and authentic existence here and now. But the first essential for this is that he cease deluding himself about what is and is not in store for him. The humanist recognizes the rich variety, diversity and relativity of value, and the fact that there are alternate paths which men may take to achieve the good life. He merely claims that it is we who are to choose, whatever we choose, and that we should not shirk our responsibility to so choose, or escape to a world of dogma and myth.

There are other aspects of humanism—such as a moral commitment to social co-operation, shared experience, and even democracy—which many humanists have strongly supported. But I have not emphasized these, since some humanists might not accept them. Instead I have highlighted what I take to be the central doctrine of humanism: that *value is relative to man.* What the humanists today suggest as a minimum doctrine, as I see it, is that mankind has reached the age where it is mature enough to choose its own way of life, and that the soil, the flesh, and the creative spirit, as thoroughly human and natural ideals, are the best that we have.

As an aid to the non-specialists in philosophy, we present the following glossary of terms that may not be self-evident to all. If readers like this, please let the editor know.

Glossary

1. *Cognitive.* A cognitive question is a meaningful question of literal significance, as distinct from a meaningless or pseudo-question.
2. *Apologetics.* Theological argumentation designed to justify religious belief and commitment to divinity.
3. *Affective.* Involving emotion, attitude, feeling.
4. *Prescriptiveness.* The guiding or directing of action, especially by moral rules and principles.
5. *Expressiveness.* Evoking and arousing feeling, emotion, passion.
6. *Teleological.* Proof for God which claims to find purpose and design in the universe, and attributes this to an intelligent being.
7. *A priori.* Rationally presuming that something is the case antecedent to inquiry.
8. *Eschatological.* Pertaining to the doctrine of last or final things, as death, immortality, and resurrection.
9. *Reductionist.* The simple reduction of nature to one kind of "stuff" or "reality," whether of mind, matter or something else.
10. *Exacerbate.* To render more violent or bitter, to irritate or accentuate.
11. *Demythologize.* The attempt to purge religious theology of its mythological aspects.

Faith in What? A Sociologist's Answer

Robert A. Harper
The Humanist, October, 1949

Psychologists, psychiatrists, sociologists, and theologians seem to be in pretty general agreement about at least one thing: modern man's lack of a faith lies at the core of many of his personal and social maladjustments. Lack of an integrating faith we can see in abundance all about us in war, mental illness, crime, psychosomatic maladies, racial conflict, and other personal and social corruptions. A large void in faith is obvious. It is in answer to the question of how to fill this void that we encounter widely differing opinions, many conflicting values. The various answers to the questions of a contemporary faith seem to fall, however, into two general categories: absolutism and relativism.

The absolutists may be subdivided into the old and the new schools. The older variety are those who unquestioningly accept orthodox religions of one variety or another. The old-school absolutist has his whole cloth of faith measured out in standard form by tailors of other times and other places. Each such garment of faith includes blinders that prevent his observing the inappropriateness of the faith-fit for contemporary social conditions. His is not a faith that is attractive to a person who is searching for truth, looking for ever better answers to the problems faced by himself and others.

The new-school absolutist doesn't differ too much from the old-school variety. The cut of his clothes is of a little later period, but it is no less the product of standard production and carries a similar set of blinders. The new-school absolutist makes the same unthinking act of faith in relation to some predetermined absolute. But the new-style absolute is usually couched in economic or political rather than theological terms. He becomes a communist or a fascist or a Ku Klux Klanner or a Coughlinite and just as unthinkingly attaches his destiny to a fixed fundamentalism as does the hard-shelled Baptist, the Missouri Lutheran, or the Jehovah's Witness.

Humanist Philosophy 1928 – 1973

The quite evident difficulty with any sort of absolutist faith, especially under contemporary social processes of rapid change, is that the faith is very apt to render us decreasingly effective in coping with ourselves and our environment. We are dedicated by absolutism to a faith of stagnancy. While we are anchored to our faith, the world about us changes and makes islands where there were seas, and seas where there were islands. Truth is an ever-changing and ever-receding goal; the pursuit of it is a process. Whenever our faith provides us with a product instead of a process, with a final answer or a closed system, we have cut ourselves off from life-giving powers. Such a faith is our death, not our salvation.

Thinking, questing people have turned to a faith of relativism. Many have failed to find it. One reason that many of us who cut ourselves from fundamentalist faiths get lost in the mire of no-faith is that the demands of a relativist faith are more exacting. We must continue to think; we must search for and be open to the truths about us. The lost liberal in religion is the one who, finding that no answer of faith is permanent and final for all situations, gives up in the ever-demanding, ever-challenging responsibility of finding the right answer for each specific situation.

To find a faith of relativism is hard work. Each life experience can reveal to the religious relativist the best answer in the light of the time, the place, his own stage of understanding and ability, and the welfare of the other parties to the experience, providing he is willing to seek, with flexibility, for that best answer. But the best answer for that experience is not at all certain to be the best answer for the next one. The lost liberal decides that since answers change, any answer is good enough and that no answer matters. The true religious liberal has faith in truth as a process, not a product, in specific, not absolute, right solutions.

Right must be judged in terms of the history of the society and the individual. Thomas Jefferson kept slaves; Grover Cleveland didn't. Neither man as a democrat or a Democrat may be judged more or less favorably than the other on the issue of slavery, for the personal and social aspects of slavery changed greatly in the time elapsing between Jefferson and Cleveland. For my mother, with her conditioning, to smoke cigarettes would be immoral; for my wife, with hers, it is not. What is right depends on the social setting and the personal participants, but it is precisely at this point that the lost liberal becomes lost. He points to such variables as Jefferson, Cleveland, changed attitudes on smoking, variables in sex morals, and the like, and says: "Since there is no fixed answer, what's the difference?" All the difference in the world. Your decisions, and mine, must be made in terms of what now exists in the environment and what exists in us. The fact that these inner and outer conditions vary, in no way relieves us of the responsibility of making our decisions on the basis of what appears to us at the time to be the highest value, the best possible course of action. This, I believe, is the heart of a faith that fits contemporary reality: what, for me now, in this particular circumstance, is the best way of behaving for the welfare of society and myself? If we make our decisions on our best judgments, we have, I think, acted on a sound faith.

This brings us to another factor destructive of faith: the current confusion of ends and means. Even the most alert of us occasionally get sucked in on wrong actions because of this issue. The people that usually confuse us are the absolutists. The absolutists are convinced that a certain fixed goal is important, so important that it doesn't matter how we get there, so long as we arrive. The communists, for example, point out the injustices of the profit system and are willing to use any means that are expedient to arrive at the socialized state, where, presumably, injustices would be fewer. But what such absolutists fail to realize is that the use of wrong means, such as the liquidation of enemies, the sacrifice of the democratic process, or alliance with those seeking different ultimate goals, will render the end—in this case a socialized state—something worse than the present society. The same goes double, I should hasten to point out, for the absolutist opponents of the communists who wish to use whatever means are available to wipe out the threat of communism.

The relativist gets caught very often between the grinding wheels of two conflicting absolutisms. He is told by the communist, for example, that he is a reactionary unless he goes along fully with the current communist program. He is called a communist by the absolutist reactionaries if he fails to support their expedient means for fighting the communists. He finds himself at variance in some ways with part of his fellow liberals or relativists. He is, at this point, apt to join the lost liberals; he is apt to decide that his choice is either-or so far as "practical" action is concerned. He has been sucked in by the absolutists, then, on one side or the other, for he has lost perspective—the perspective of religious relativist faith that informs him that his responsibility is one of means more than ends.

Especially in so complex and dynamic a society as ours, no individual can really feel himself responsible for the full achievement of desirable objectives. There are too many unknown and uncontrollable and variable factors involved in even the simplest goals. But he can be and must be, if his faith is to function positively, responsible for his means.

The Scandinavian philosopher Kierkegaard had, in my opinion, his own susceptibilities to absolutes, but in his series of essays that have been translated into English by Douglas Steere under the title *Purity of Heart Is to Will One Thing*, he has much wisdom to impart to the ever-seeking religious relativist. On our issue of means and ends, he speaks:

> The individual is not ... eternally responsible for whether he reaches his goal within this world of time. But without exception, he is eternally responsible for the kind of means he uses. And when he will only use or only uses those means which are genuinely good, then in the judgment of eternity, he is at the goal. If reaching the goal should be the excuse and the defense for the use of illicit or questionable means—alas, suppose he should die tomorrow. Then the clever one would be caught in his own folly. He had used illicit means, and he died before reaching the goal. For reaching the goal comes at the conclusion; but using the means comes at the beginning. Reaching the goal is like hitting the mark with his shot; but

using the means is like taking aim. And certainly the aim is a more reliable indication of the marksman's goal than the spot the shot strikes. For it is possible for a shot to hit the mark by accident. The marksman may also be blameless if the shell does not go off. But no irregularities of the aim are permissible. ... Conscience is ... the "blushing innocent spirit that sets up a tumult in a man's breast and fills him with difficulties" just because to conscience the means are without exception as important as the end.

It is our own consciences that we must follow in living in accordance with a faith of relativism that fits the demands of life under the exacting gauge of contemporary society in transition. Because we are changing day by day as persons and because our society is altering as often, we should expect that the specific demands of our consciences will vary in and between ourselves. But because all changeth does not mean that we are freed from the demands of the best in us for the welfare of ourselves and others as of yesterday and today and tomorrow. The faith of the right, the good, as it appears to the individual in his time and his place is the one unalterable law in the relativism of the life process.

Faith in what? Faith in the way of life that says to us that we follow the most enlightened judgment obtainable for what we may think and feel and do in the ever-present now in light of the inescapable past and the always forthcoming future. With a look toward our neighbors for stimulation, not decision-making, with ear open for thought-provocation, not answer, what may we now do that will best further the steadiness of our aim toward that which we believe to be right and good?

We turn again to the Kierkegaard of *Purity of Heart Is to Will One Thing* for our reminder that

> Here, too, the speaker has his own life, his own frailties, his own share of doubleness of mind. Oh, that the talk might not seem to wish to judge or accuse others. For to wish to judge others instead of one's self would also be double-mindedness. Oh,

that the talk might not seem to press demands that are binding upon others but that exempt the speaker, as if he had only the task of talking. For this, too, is double-mindedness, just as it is hidden pride to wish to offer comfort to others but not to be willing to let oneself be comforted.

Increasingly, it seems to me, those of us who reject religious fundamentalism or absolutism on the one hand and drifting liberalism on the other must learn to sharpen our information and broaden our wisdom for making decisions as to what is good in specific situations and then to act in relation to those good goals with good means. It is our responsibility as religious relativists to aim straight, even if we feel rather certain that in our lifetime we shall not see the shot hit its mark. In what direction, for example, lies international peace, racial equality, world government, economic as well as political democracy, mental and physical health for everyone, greater educational opportunities, and other good goals? What methods are available to us aimed directly toward such ends? Then, regardless of how inexpedient or immediately unpromising these means may seem, we are obligated, as religious persons, to employ them.

CHAPTER 2
Types of Humanism

New Naturalistic Religious Marxist Evolutionary Ethical Behaviorist Rationalist Existential Secular Scientific Materialist Planetary Humanism

Chapter 1's discussion of basic elements of humanism noted that humanism comes in a number of types. This chapter briefly examines the main types of humanism discussed in *TNH* and *TH* through 1973 and still relevant today.

Whether something is humanism must be answered in accordance with reference to the essential elements of humanism set forth in Chapter 1, as well as a few more primary principles set forth elsewhere in this volume. More specifically, then, this chapter highlights the elements that distinguish types of humanism from one another.

Logically, a type of humanism must be describable in terms of "x humanism," where "x" is an adjective delineating the "type." That is because a "humanistic x" does not clearly refer to something that fully incorporates all the basic elements of humanism. For example, "humanistic religion" is excluded, because, while it may subscribe to values in the humanities, it may nonetheless ascribe those values as originating from a deity. Accordingly, this chapter only considers "x humanisms."

One final prefatory note is that the title to this chapter lists more versions of humanism than the following text covers. The included types represent those earnestly discussed in published essays still salient today.

Neo-Humanism or New Humanism

Some early humanists of the modern philosophical movement, including A. Eustace Haydon in his 1928 essay included in this chapter, talked about "Neo-Humanis[m]" or "The New Humanism."1 And of course, the pre-cursor to

Humanist Philosophy 1928 – 1973

TH was named *The New Humanist*. While some discussed modern humanism as being rooted in ancient Greece, or the Enlightenment, others viewed the humanism arising early in the twentieth century as a new version. Hence, the insertion of the word "new" in that name. However, there was a problem, in that the much criticized2 anti-scientific "literary humanism" briefly discussed in Harold H. Titus' essay in Chapter 1 and Corliss Lamont's essay in Chapter 3, was also known as "new humanism." Thus, the adjective became anathema to modern humanists, and avoiding that association is why "new" was dropped when *TH* began to be published in 1941.3 Accordingly, humanism denoted as "new" did not receive lots of attention in *TH* through 1973.

Naturalistic Humanism

As noted in Chapter 1, key principles of scientific naturalism were incorporated into the earliest statements of modern humanist principles. But the phrase "naturalistic humanism" came later. In his 1942 essay in Chapter 3, Corliss Lamont equated "scientific humanism" and "naturalistic humanism," distinguishing it from "religious humanism." Roy Wood Sellars used "naturalistic humanism" to refer to religious humanism in a 1953 essay (*TH* 13:2). Paul Kurtz, in his 1964 essay in Chapter 1, describes the general aspects of naturalistic humanism, while distinguishing scientific humanism from that more general category. In 1971, Lamont defined naturalistic humanism as that which "rejects all supernaturalism, pantheism, and metaphysical idealism, and considers man's supreme aim as working for the welfare of all humanity in this one and only life, according to the methods of reason, science, and democracy" (*TH* 31:5). In 1973, the HMII referred to naturalistic humanism as encompassing five types in a manner that appears intended to be a comprehensive list of the kinds of modern humanism. Thus, over time, "naturalistic humanism" came to serve as an umbrella term for modern humanism generally.

The Best of *The Humanist*

Scientific Humanism

As noted in the next section, the phrase "scientific humanism" was not used in the 1933 HMI. In their essay in this chapter, Lloyd Morain and Oliver Reiser set forth a good description of this type of humanism. A number of essays advocating scientific humanism were a reaction to the religious nature of humanism in HMI. Like some other proponents of scientific humanism in that period, Morain and Reiser do not consider scientific humanism to be a religion. Unlike some, though, they do leave space for a "religious spirit." Humanism's take on spirituality is treated in Chapter 7. Scientific humanism flowed naturally from the naturalistic nature of the humanism of HMI.

In his essay in Chapter 1, Harold H. Titus quotes another definition of "scientific humanism" from around the same time as Morain and Reiser's. Kurtz, too, distinguishes the "scientific humanist" from humanists generally, but his view at that point was that humanism was a religion.

In her 1971 essay in this chapter, Miriam Allen deFord gives her definition of scientific humanism. The HMII in 1973 listed "scientific" as one of the five types of naturalistic humanism. Its growing acceptance led to a proliferation of writings about the details of scientific humanism through 1973, to which Chapter 4 is devoted. Its importance had already grown sufficiently at that point that deFord argues that an atheistic scientific humanism is the only coherent kind of humanism. Not surprisingly, scientific humanism has evolved in subsequent decades into secular humanism, the predominant version of humanism outside religious traditions.

Religious Humanism

"Religious" is the only adjective used before the word "humanism" in the 1933 HMI. HMI sets forth the principles of humanism as a religion. Humanism as religion is today propounded by such organizations as the American Ethical Union and its affiliates and the Unitarian Universalist Humanist Association.

Humanist Philosophy 1928 – 1973

A few humanists argued in *TNH* and *TH* through 1973 that humanism cannot be religious or a religion. For example, Corliss Lamont wrote in 1936 that HMI should not have asserted that humanism is a religion (*TNH* 9:3). He argued a few years later that the definition of "religion" in the HMI is so broad as to include any human endeavor. He thereby implicitly sought to undermine HMI's assertion that humanism is a religion (*TH* 2:3). His 1942 essay in Chapter 3 says the same thing, while noting the "Catholic Humanism" or "Christian Humanism" hailed by Jacques Maritain. In 1962, Julian Huxley's assertion that evolutionary humanism, discussed below, is a new religion (*TH* 22:1) drew a rebuttal.4 By 1971, deFord was arguing that "religious humanism … is … merely a contradiction in terms."

Be that as it may, advocates of religious humanism give it several distinguishing characteristics that put it on the periphery of what might be considered a religion. Essays on its distinguishing elements are the subject of Chapter 6.

In contrast with HMI, HMII treats religious humanism as only one of five types of naturalistic humanism. By 1973, then, "naturalistic humanism" had replaced "religious humanism" as the umbrella term in the modern US humanist movement. That fact reflects the US tendency toward secular humanism, which looks at humanism and religion as mutually exclusive. Of course, subsequent developments post-date the period of essays covered in this book.

Planetary Humanism or Panhumanism

Morain and Reiser, though focusing in their essay on scientific humanism, take the humanist principle of advancing knowledge and perspective to suggest the notion of "planetary humanism." Their concept is a humanism bringing together dualities such as "reason" and "emotion," and "science" and "morality," to form a more coherent humanist understanding of the entirety of human experience. Thus, it is a refinement of scientific humanism.

A year later, in 1944, Carl J. Friedrich called for a humanism that reflects not only the reason predominant in Western culture, but also the more spiritual values of

Eastern cultures. Writing in *TH*, he called this "organic humanism" or "panhumanism" (*TH* 4:4).

World War II was undoubtedly a major impetus behind the broader thinking of these writers. While they did not expand upon these notions, their formulations were taken up by others decades later. An interim development that was probably related to the adoption of their concept was new awareness of environmental conservation, discussed in Chapter 11.

Existential Humanism

World War II inspired another kind of humanism. Jean Paul Sartre's book arguing that existentialism is a humanism[5] generated several responses over the years from writers in *TH*. Most writers opposed the idea of existentialism as humanism. The essay by G. William Domhoff summarizes the distinctions between the humanism of Bertrand Russell and that asserted by Sartre. In doing so, Domhoff lays out significant differences that capture many of the points set out by other writers. He suggests that the value of existential humanism is that it forces us to remember the dark side of human nature and the danger it presents to human progress. That is one reason that he accepts Sartre's existentialism as compatible with humanism in the US. His view is echoed by Curtis Reese in his essay in Chapter 3 and Erich Fromm in TH (*26*:4). Of note, others have come to the opposite conclusion on similar evidence.[6]

Evolutionary Humanism

Julian Huxley's included essay calls for a new religion of evolutionary humanism. His definition of religion is discussed in Chapter 6. The latter part of his essay concentrates on the details of this type of humanism. A companion essay in *TH* expanded on this formulation (*TH* 52:6).

Huxley was a central author using the formulation, "evolutionary humanism," in *TH*. However, Harold Buschman, in his 1929 essay included in Chapter 4, used the phrase "evolutionary naturalism" in advocating religion similar to Huxley's.

Huxley not only centers on the principles of evolution, as does Buschman; he also sets out the role of humans in shaping future evolution of their species and other life forms. He includes in evolution the psychology of humans, echoing humanistic psychology.7

Socialist or Marxist Humanism

In 1936, Corliss Lamont compared humanism with Marxism, concluding that "in a general sense Marxism can be classified as a *form* of humanism, though certainly not as *religious* humanism" (*TNH* 9:3). In his 1942 essay in Chapter 3, Lamont still refers to dialectical materialism, rather than Marxist humanism. Over subsequent years, certain writers advocated a Marxist version of humanism.

Shortly before the issuance of the HMII, the relationships between Marxism and Marxist humanism, as well as between humanism and Marxist humanism, were explored at length. Three "Marxist/Humanist Dialogues" were held: in Vienna, September 1968;8 in Herzog Novi, Yugoslavia, August 1969; and in Boston, August 5-8, 1970 (*TH* 31:1).

Erazim V. Kohak described in *TH* a prevailing paradox of the time (*TH* 31:1):

> On the one hand, social developments brought about by the industrial and the scientific-technological revolutions have made Marxism by far the most available conceptual framework for the articulation of humanist ideals. On the other hand, wherever Marxism became the official ideology of a state, the exigencies of power displaced its humanist intent.

A well-known participant advocating a Marxist humanism was Mihailo Marković. His 1969 essay in this chapter acknowledges that Marxist humanism had already been roundly criticized as obsolete, as had humanism generally.

Marković points out that certain forms of Marxism are not humanist and argues that Marxist humanism shares the emphasis on democracy, nontheism, and freedom in liberal humanism. He argues that Marxist humanism differs from the liberal form in its additional emphasis on social phenomena. However, his characterization of liberal humanism is a little skewed away from social concern, which HMI already expressed in 1933. In that respect, his definition of liberal humanism is lacking. As a result of it, his foil sounds more like the short-lived nineteenth century inward-looking, individualistic "literary humanism" of Babbitt and More discussed in Harold H. Titus' essay in Chapter 1 and Corliss Lamont's essay in Chapter 3.

Nonetheless, Marković's critique was part of a growing chorus of voices calling for more concern for the social implications of humanism. He argues that, in contrast to the Marxist humanist vision, liberal humanism lacks a universal vision. Nonetheless, liberal humanism has since made substantial progress in achieving such a vision. That said, substantial work remains to be done. Thus, in view of subsequent developments in humanism, starting with HMII, his view of Marxist humanism was partly vindicated. At the same time, Marxist societies, including Marković's own, utterly failed to vindicate the Marxist humanist vision.

Addressing the far side of Marxist humanism, various writers in *TH* argued that humanism is incompatible with communism. Huxley gives a typical view on why.

Behaviorist Humanism

One of the last types of humanism propounded before the 1973 issuance of HMII was "behaviorist humanism." Several writers squared off on whether behaviorism can be humanism in one issue of *TH*. Floyd W. Matson, a humanistic psychologist, argued that the two are incompatible (*TH* 31:2). Other authors argued against his position, and he published a rebuttal in the same issue. In the next issue of *TH*, B. F. Skinner added a brief response, later publishing the longer essay included in this chapter.

As the essay puts it, the structures and contingencies that individuals face in the environment of their daily lives should replace morals and ethics. In this view, the goal is to change socially acceptable behavior in particular interactions, rather than abstract social norms in the form of morals and ethics. Doing so consists of structurally precluding unacceptable behavior in those interactions, such as monitoring a caregiver to an incapacitated person in a manner that prevents the caregiver from abusing the incapacitated person without suffering punishment as a result. The point, then, of behaviorist humanism is to focus on obtaining moral and ethical outcomes reflecting humanist values by making effective structural changes in interactions.

Anecdotally, behaviorist humanism does not seem to have had large numbers of supporters. While its emphasis on structural changes to induce behavior changes has its uses, humanism's concern for civil liberties renders difficult the devising of structural bases for changing behavior. The structural changes may not overburden individual freedoms and privacy. For example, a surveillance state enforcing humanist values might be effective at limiting unhumanist behavior, but humanism would not accept, among other things, many aspects of the loss of personal privacy. Accordingly, not only Matson argues that behaviorism is not humanism at all. So do humanist psychologists Abraham Maslow, as stated in his essay in Chapter 9, and Carl Rogers (*TH* 24:2).

Notes

1. See, also, R. Lester Mondale, "The Second Generation Humanists," *TNH* 5:4, p. 1 et seq. (1932); and Herbert W. Schneider, "The New Humanism," *TH* 13:1, 31 et seq. (1953).
2. See, e.g., *The Critique of Humanism; a Symposium*, ed. by C. Hartley Grattan, Essay and General Literature Index Reprint Series (Port Washington, N.Y: Kennikat Press, 1968) (reprint of 1930 original).
3. Wilson, Edwin H., "The Origins of Modern Humanism," TH 51:1, p. 9 et seq. (1991), p. 28.
4. See Barnes, Harry Elmer, & Herbert T. Rosenfeld, "Is Humanism a New Religion?" *TH* 22:4, p. 127 et seq. (Jul/Aug 1962).
5. Sartre, Jean Paul, *Existentialism Is a Humanism*, Carol Macomber, trans. (New Haven: Yale U. Press, 2007), originally published in essay form in 1945.

6. See, e.g., Tonne, Herbert A., "Humanism and Tillich's Existentialism," *TH* 20:6, p. 346 et seq. (Nov./Dec. 1960).
7. For writings on humanistic psychology, see Ch. 10.
8. In addition to Marković's essay included in this chapter, see Paul Kurtz, "Humanism and the Freedom of the Individual," *TH* 29:1, p. 14 et seq. (1969).

Neo-Humanism – What Is It?

A. Eustace Haydon
The New Humanist, Summer, 1928

It is difficult to believe that there is anything profound or disturbing in New Humanism; yet only rarely do its critics touch the heart of it or apprehend its reason for being. Some seem to think that it is simply another rationalization of the traditional ideology leaving out the precious consolations and guarantees which make earlier rationalizations meaningful. Some interpret it as a new form of social service and claim that it is not really new to any wide awake Christian. Some call it a revival of Positivism which would seem to be the most unkindest out of all. One critic says it is not humanistic enough because it has not solved all the problems of our tangled social complexity. Some would call themselves humanists and add the adjectives "Christian" or "evangelical." That might be possible but not in the manner of their books. Some feel that the New Humanism does not adequately deal with moral values, which is perhaps the most serious misunderstanding up to date. Some say it has no motive power to keep men at the task of creative achievement. One critic is sure that it can only be acceptable to the intellectual elite and could never be made comprehensible to the lowly people. The most recent comment claims that no humanist has over been a Roman Catholic or a teacher of philosophy. If true, that would be just too bad. The implication of the first charge may be that a Roman Catholic would never stray quite so far from the faith of his fathers; of the second, perhaps, that a philosopher should have a tidy system and could never dare the adventure of life unless "The belly-band of the universe were tight." Unfortunately for the critics none of these charges strike home.

The reason for them lies probably in the fact that there have been so many who claim to be humanists who have not yet been really born again and yet are vocal, while the men who carry the torch of the movement do not like to be labelled and must be recognized by the discerning. It would be a fine thing if a fund could be raised to present a copy of Professor Otto's beautiful and persuasive book, "Things and Ideals," to each of the critics as they appear.

At any rate it ought to be made clear that the Neo-Humanist is one who takes his naturalism straight; that he works with the method of science in all realms and is not in quest of anchorage in absolutes or finalities; that he feels rather comfortable and secure in being an earth child and a terminal thrust of the cosmic life; that he prefers to depend upon human loyalties and intelligent purpose rather than upon faith or fate for the actualizing of his ideals; that he is not a dogmatist regarding what is still beyond human experience for the material of the sciences, natural, social and religious; that his primary interest is the age-old quest of the human race for the realization of a good life in a good world, and his blatant optimism lies in the fact that he dares to bellow that today, if man will himself assume the responsibility, he can make that ancient dream come true.

Scientific Humanism: A Formulation

Lloyd Morain and Oliver Reiser
The Humanist, Spring, 1943

The term "scientific humanism" is now coming into popular use. The label seems to have sprung up spontaneously in several quarters. But what does it mean? And what is its program? Here is one statement of the meaning and program of scientific humanism.

    1.   The scientific humanist holds that man is a natural creature living in a natural universe. Evolved from star-dust by cosmic processes, man has emerged from the creature who *adapts* himself to nature, into the self-directive agent who *recreates* that nature to serve the needs of his own progressive enlightenment. There are in this universe not gods and men, masters and slaves, but human beings in various stages of development, all born of the earth-womb.

    2.   The scientific humanist is global in his background and outlook. He draws his strength not from a transcendental heaven, but from the untold resources of the planet: the invigorating rhythms of the seasons, the vibrant zest of the northlands, the ecstasy of the fertile prairies, the lush familiarity of the tropics, the rimming expanses of the inland waters, the cadences of the seven seas, and the configurations of the drifting continents.

    3.   The scientific humanist is a spearhead of social progress. Pioneering along the frontiers of social change comes natural to him. He is committed to the challenging adventure of becoming ever more globalistic, of constantly striving to be a time-binder as well as a space-conqueror of our planet. But he realizes that the symphony of the continents cannot be a one-author recording. Thus far only a few overtones have been caught; only a few themes have been written.

In writing new scores, in even the simplest new melodies, we have to face factors and issues which disturb old habits of thinking and ancient evaluations. More attention must be given to technique, for harmonies require global notation. And it is no longer permissible to regard global issues from individualistic frameworks; the limited perspectives of social introverts, whether in business, economics, politics or religion, are manifestations of psychological isolationism and provincialism.

4. The scientific humanist is no dogmatist who believes that he knows all the answers to all the questions. He sees, however, that there are some things in this universe we must accept as basic, brute fact. An uncreated universe—the space-time-matter trinity, or the cosmic movement-continuum—is one such brute fact. Not everything can be proved and not everything can be defined in verbal terms.

The scientific humanist insists that we have not the solution to some of our "problems" because not every combination of words ending with a question mark poses a real problem. Some problems are not only unsolved, but forever insoluble, just because they are meaningless problems. Wisdom in life consists in asking the right kinds of questions, formulating our problems in such ways that they yield answers. For example, scientific humanism holds that there is no "riddle of existence" and no antecedent "meaning of life" which is to be sought for and found—the "meaning of life" is not something we discover, but create.

5. The scientific humanist always recognizes that every "thing" or "event" exists or happens within a context or environment, here on earth within a planetary framework, and thus guards against the fallacy of the "absolute individuality of the subject of predication." He sees that no scientific "law" expresses everything about that part of nature or society it abstracts and pretends to describe. Therefore no man, not even the scientist, ever knows or tells "all" about anything. However, while there are no absolute certainties, we can make adjustments on the basis of probabilities. Predictability and a real feeling of assurance are possible, even in terms of the process-character of the universe, or cosmic movement-continuum.

6. Since the scientific humanist is constantly seeing things in terms of contexts and frames of reference, he is forever reminding himself that every event is multi-causational and that we can't change things without regard to backgrounds. There are no panaceas, except in terms of the broader changes of supporting patterns. Since "scientific laws" are tentative statements, useful only so long as they

enable us to describe and predict within the framework of human experience, we should not be bound too rigidly by existing notions of what is considered to be "possible" or "impossible." Man is a real agent in determining the future course of events in society and in nature. The future of our earth will be determined in part by the role which humanity is to play in the remaining acts of this as-yet-incomplete drama.

7. The humanist is a semanticist, concerned with communication across the world-whole. The humanist is trying to discover how each man may speak to all men in friendliness. He stands for the application of scientific method to all problems; for him scientific method simply democracy in thinking.

Scientific humanists believe that our "intellectual abstractions" and their verbal equivalents should always be subjected to semantic analysis. We now know that our difficulties and misunderstandings frequently have a linguistic basis. It is one aim of scientific humanism and basic semantics to provide a common platform for human standing and cooperation. There are those who stigmatize global thinking as "globaloney" and semantics as "social evasion"; but the fact remains that the starry-eyed makers of maps of territories-to-be (blueprints of non-existent worlds) more frequently provide the motives and the goals for social progress than the retrogressive bleary-eyed "realist."

Planetary humanism (basic semantics and world planning) protests against the present separation of "reason" and "emotion," of "facts" and "values," of "science" and "morality," as harmful, individually and socially. Just as individually we must commit ourselves to "total living," so socially we must overcome the schisms which separate us as groups. Science can no longer escape social evaluations. And science must accept a greater measure of responsibility for controlling the social impacts of inventions and technology. Scientific humanism frankly accepts the social responsibilities of scientific research and discovery.

8. Scientific control of the world has reached a stage where our society could, if properly organized, produce

enough food, shelter, clothing, and medicine for all mankind. Economic security is not a vain dream, if we organize for an economy of abundance. Cynicism, defeatism and escapism result from an inadequate comprehension of the vast potentialities of social reform, when guided by social intelligence.

Scientific humanism holds that human nature is characterized by wide flexibility, and this provides a plastic basis for social progress. Present difficulties are surmountable, but the broad background of social causation is world-wide in scope and no simple remedy will cure all our ills. By the humanized and socialized application of scientific methods and results it will be possible to guarantee peace and security to all men.

But to accomplish this requires some fundamental changes in our political and economic systems. This means, within a more restricted area, that the problems of labor and capital, unemployment, and the like, should be solved in terms of human well-being rather than by reference to the profit motive as the dominant concern. And on a broader scale, new ideas about "money," "debts," international trade, access to "raw materials" and outlets for "surplus commodities" are called for. Indeed, our loyalty to the principles of the Atlantic Charter require this. A World Federation of United Nations is one medium for international planning. Global thinking applied to the fabrication of new economic-political-ideological structure is therefore essential.

9. Morality needs no supernatural sanctions or motivations. It is not heaven-sent; it is man evolved. The socializing (moralizing) process begins with the smaller social units and progressively extends to the more inclusive; from the family through the tribe, the city-state, the nation-state, to the most inclusive world-community. Genetically one merges one's self with humanity through the immediate community therefore a world federation of friendly cultures is merely the globalized projection of the smaller circle of friendliness. In the past morality has frequently been a matter of latitude, longitude, and even altitude; but in the future we need to adjust ourselves through techniques of international living expressing a

universal morality. Obviously, in such a universal ethics, "racial" discriminations (e.g., anti-semitism) and color distinctions stand condemned.

10. In the coming planetary civilization of a world-embracing humanism those "religions" that obstruct social advance must be subordinated. In the world of scientific humanism "religion" will be obsolete; but the "religious spirit"—the sense of awe and reverence in the presence of a majestic universe—will constitute a wholesome ingredient in the economic-political-reflective synthesis. Fragmentation in society must give way to integration—the unification of economic, political, religious, scientific and artistic impulses, interests and activities.

11. Scientific humanism holds that all groups working for the improvement of the world through the cultivation of good will and social intelligence should seek means for cooperation. In order that the benefits of the quest for the good society may be made to serve universal humanity rather than the more limited ("selfish") interests, it is imperative that knowledge be made available to all. Through education, "science" as well as "politics," "religion," "art," "economics," and the rest, must be socialized and humanized within an international framework. This places a heavy responsibility upon "philosophy," which should serve as a cultural universalizer for the planetary pattern of a world-encircling civilization.

12. The scientific humanist finds his courage as well as his challenge arising from the fact that man's scientific progress is commensurate with his means and media of locomotion. He sees, in retrospect, that in successive order man has conquered solids, liquids, and gases from the land, sea and air he moves on to more subtle media. As he thus triumphs over space and time he is uniting his planet into a technological unity which cries out for a parallel political intellectual unity. The radio, airplane and television are giving us mastery over distance and time, and the further conquests of our air-age global technics must either result in a vast enslavement of mankind, or the air-age technology will be used by free peoples everywhere to build their own planetary civilization.

The scientific humanist labors so that the era of air-age inter-communication shall break over the artificialities of national boundaries, racial demarcations, exclusive religious frameworks, and political economic barriers into a topology of human relationships that overshadow the old principles of exploitation and transcend the relative values of wealth, caste, race and nation.

Scientific humanism, first and last, aims at global orientations, global symbolisms, and global techniques for doing things. Let us catch more and more of the human overtones of mankind the world round. Let us hear the emerging melody of all the peoples of the earth, who can now be satisfied only to the extent that they share in the solution of their common problems, world-wide in scope and perplexity. Humanism affirms that men will become most human when men go "all out" for "total living"—and thus create a federation of friendly peoples on this planetary abode of all mankind.

Humanism and Atheism

Miriam Allen deFord
The Humanist, July-August, 1971

It is perhaps unfortunate that the term "humanism" was ever adopted for a humanity-centered philosophy; the word had already had a long and honorable career as denominating the renewed interest in the ancient classics and the humanities that came with the Renaissance. "Rationalism" or "secularism" would have would have been much more precise. Either of them, of course, would have barred the religiously oriented, but that, in my opinion, would have been desirable rather than disadvantageous.

My own tentative general definition of humanism would be that it is a philosophical system based on the concept that the universe, life, and consequently mankind are the result of natural evolutionary processes alone, and hence that our view of them must be monistic. In other words, there is nothing in in existence except random, fortuitous forces that eventually — in the manner of the famous example of the monkeys pounding typewriters who finally emerge with the works of Shakespeare — bring together consonant elements from which, under favorable circumstances, galaxies, planetary systems, bacteria, and human beings gradually issue and evolve.

Ethical humanism can best be defined in the words of an anonymous pre-Confucian Chinese philosopher of the 10th century: "Man must look in his own heart to know what he must do." Or, to quote Robert G. Ingersoll, "The accumulated experience of the world is a power and force that works for righteousness. This force is not conscious, not intelligent. It is a result." It is the task of humanism to show that ethics is a by-product of human experience, not of some supernatural mandate. Man must either learn to exercise a high ethical policy toward the earth on which he lives, toward the multitudinous plants and animals inhabiting it with him, toward his fellow humans — yes, and toward himself as well — or cease to survive.

Scientific humanism in my thinking is humanism; the general definition I have given above predicates a scientific approach to every philosophical, ethical, and intellectual problem. This is not 19th-century mechanistic materialism; there are many aspects of proved or provable reality (for example, extrasensory perception) that we do not yet understand, but that are still phenomena susceptible to investigation and understanding.

Religious humanism (*pace* the "liberal religionists") is to me merely a contradiction in terms. Religion in its strict meaning implies belief in nonhumanistic systems, entities, or explanations. A philosophy founded on the agreement that "man is the measure of all things" can have no room for belief in the intervention of nonmaterial postulates. Conceivably, one might say that a person who believes that nothing exists but spirit is as much of a monist as a person who believes that nothing exists but natural, material phenomena. The one thing that an adherent to either faith cannot be is dualist, and religion by any definition is necessarily dependent on a dualistic order.

To put it bluntly and undiplomatically, humanism, in my viewpoint, must be atheistic or it is not humanism as I understand it. At the age of 13 I concluded that there is sufficient evidence that there are no gods, there is no "soul," and there is no survival of personality after death. That was 70 years ago, and I have never heard any arguments since to cause me to negate that conclusion. I presume, in view of the wide orbit of belief among humanists, that this makes me a heretical humanist; nevertheless, as long as the orbit remains wide enough to include me, I shall still claim humanist allegiance.

Sartre or Russell — Why Not Both?

G. William Domhoff
The Humanist, July-August, 1963

Both Jean-Paul Sartre and Bertrand Russell consider themselves humanists. Yet many American Humanists seem to consider it necessary to make a "choice" between Sartre and Russell. 1 would like to suggest that Sartre and Russell agree on the intellectual point basic to American Humanism—a non-supernatural personal philosophy—and that their humanistic differences are in the realm of personal or emotional preferences, i.e., psychological characteristics.*

Sartre and Russell are both outspoken atheists, with no hope of personal immortality, and with no penchant for redefining the word "God" and slipping the concept in the back door. The interesting point is their disparate reactions to atheism, a difference which Russell himself anticipates in his essay "On Catholic and Protestant Skeptics." Russell confronts a godless world with a stiff upper lip:

> I believe that when I die I shall rot, and nothing of my ego will survive. I am not young, and I love life. But I should scorn to shiver with terror at the thought of annihilation. Happiness is nonetheless true happiness because it must come to an end, nor do thought and love lose their value because they are not everlasting.

How does Sartre react? With anguish, abandonment, and despair, as any good Frenchman should. To understand the Sartrian meaning of these terms, it is important to realize that Sartre bases his entire outlook on his reaction to atheism. At one point he defines his brand of existentialism as "nothing else but an attempt to draw the full conclusions from a consistently atheistic position" ("Existentialism is a Humanism," in Walter Kaufmann's *Existentialism From Dostoevsky to Sartre)*.

By "abandonment," then, Sartre means only that God does not exist, and that man is therefore without excuse, without justification. "Despair' means that everything we do has an element of uncertainty; to paraphrase Sartre: I hope that my friend will arrive on the evening train, but there is only a certain probability that the train will ever arrive. Indeed, it is only a probability that my friend will not die before the train arrives. This truism causes Sartre much despair. "Anguish," the most slippery of the three terms, is the realization that man must constantly choose, not only for himself but for all men. Sartre here contends that each man realizes in his depths that he has the "complete and found responsibility" of choosing for all mankind.

It can be seen that Sartre is presenting concepts that are not completely strange to the Humanist in America. Science has long taught us that we live in a world of probabilities; that life is contingent upon many unknown and uncontrolled variables is something of which we are all painfully aware. That God does not exist and that we are without "excuse" — these are conclusions that every atheist has reached, even if he does not constantly dwell upon them in an obsessional fashion.

Hair Shirt of Freedom

I would dispute Sartre's contention that "anguish" is due to the fact that man realizes that he is deciding "for the whole of mankind" whenever he makes a choice or decision, but the exact cause of anguish is not crucial to this particular discussion. What matters here is to note the different roads that Sartre and Russell have taken in reacting to atheism. Sartre feels abandoned and lost without Father. He likes to tell everybody what it's like to be without help, wearing his atheism like an itchy hair shirt. Russell, on the other hand, also realizes that there is anguish and despair, and we are abandoned—anyone who reads *A Free Man's Worship* can convince himself of this. But he does not find this "embarrassing," as Sartre does. Instead, it gives him a sense of freedom and personal worth. Russell enjoys standing alone without excuse.

Russell's attitude towards a world without God seems to annoy philosopher William Barrett. He calls it "urbane," and claims that it "presupposes the existence of believers against whom he can score points in an argument and get off some of his best quips." Barrett continues: "The atheism of Sartre is a more somber affair ... Sartre relentlessly works out the atheistic conclusion that in a universe without God man is absurd, unjustified, and without reason ..."

I believe that Barrett's implied criticism of Russell is intellectually meaningless, a purely personal choice. In a world without believers, Russell would find new fall-guys for his barbs, probably the existentialists (he uses them occasionally even today in our world full of believers—cf. *Wisdom of the West*). Sartre is not somehow a better atheist because he is more somber and hysterical about it. In a world without excuse, why does Russell need an excuse to laugh? As a psychologist, I believe that Sartre and Russell are telling us about their own character structure, as all men must when they express themselves. There is no "right" way to be an atheist.

Having suggested that the humanistic differences Sartre and Russell are of a psychological nature, what of their value to American Humanism? I think Sartre can be read with profit by those who live in a world of sunshine and roses— Fromm's terms, by those who see the world as a huge breast. Sartre brings home the message that need is real. For those who have not yet taken the trip to the depths of despair, (or have long-since forgotten its emotional terrors), Sartre is a reliable and courageous guide. As he says: "happiness begins on the other side of despair." Of course, Russell's partisans will recall that he wrote in 1903, two before Sartre's birth: "happiness must be built on the rocks of despair."

But what about *after* the trip to the depths? Are we to stay there and drink from the cup of bitterness? Or are we to harken to Russell, on the other side, who has been to the depths and gone on to laugh and sing and fight with even more gusto, a true Absurd Man in Camus' sense of the term? (Unless Russell has read Camus *The Myth of Sisyphus*, he probably will not appreciate being called absurd!) Of the two, I think Russell is the best guide once on the other side. Sartre's emphasis on pre-nothingness, Russell's is post-nothingness, although neither denies the other aspect. Russell cuts through prejudice and intellectual doubletalk to suggest a reasonably satisfying existence within the framework of society. He accepts the reality of sex and aggression, and seeks acceptable outlets for them. These qualities, plus his great wit, make him the more enjoyable companion than Sartre.

Yet I conclude that we need Sartres as well as Russells within American Humanism, just as we need such stark figures as Nietzsche and Freud and Camus to complement the personalities and outlooks of such great Humanists as John Dewey and Erich Fromm. American Humanism must encompass diverse humanist personalities, as well as diverse humanist ideas, if it is to appeal to a wide range of non-theists.

After all, without God and Sartre, who would Russell have to jab with his pen? For that matter, without Russell and his particular brand of humanist ethics, who would there be to play Gadfly to American Humanists?

It is true that they differ on the question of the feasibility and value of a scientific ethic, but on this point Russell is also in disagreement with such valued American Humanists as John Dewey and Erich Fromm; I shall not try to deal with this larger problem in such a short essay. Also, this essay in no way implies that Sartre and Russell agree on other philosophical issues. They don't. For example, Sartre believes Descartes "I think, therefore I am," basic. Russell considers it to be, as he puts it, "muddled."

Evolutionary Humanism – Part I

Julian Huxley
The Humanist, September-October, 1952

A NEW RELIGION NEEDED

The present age takes an almost abnormal interest in religions. By religion I mean not only religions in the narrow sense—established churches and sects, new versions of old theologies—synthetic creeds, but also I include in the term religion, the organized pseudo religions like militant communism, fascism, and other versions of nationalist or racial devotion. I include movements that attempt to utilize man's capacity for mystical experience—and also the host of superstitions like astrology and numerology that cater to our love of magic and try to provide something to take us out of the oppressive routine of the ordinary.

There have been many periods which have shown such a heightened concern for religions. Ours differs from the others in various ways. In the first place, our thought has a scientific background. Science has revealed itself as the one universal faculty of man. And scientific thinking has become evolutionary. Whether in cosmogony or in biology, in history or in individual psychology, we are forced to think in terms of change and development. Secondly, the world has suffered a great and general disillusionment. Gone are all ideas of rapid inevitable progress. The last twenty years have revealed depths of human wickedness, new and sinister combinations of horrors, as well as reversions to ancient cruelty and ruthlessness.

There has been disillusionment about science, too. What we had hoped would bring only benefit has brought also new methods of mass enslavement of minds. Science should be free and open; yet more and more scientific work is being done in secret, in the interests of one nation as against those of another. Great hopes were cherished about planning; but many of our plans have gone awry.

On the other hand, disillusionment has been accompanied by a new hope—the hope of the backward and underprivileged peoples, which has led to their demand for a better standard and a fuller life. This hope may be exaggerated, but it is a fact, and one which is already affecting the course of events. Moreover, knowledge has increased to an almost embarrassing extent. We know of hundreds of different cultures, hundreds of religions of different character. We are the first generation of mankind to have knowledge of the main kinds of art that have flourished in the world's history. We are confronted with a relativity of working codes of morality that would have bewildered our ancestors, accustomed to the simple absolutes of "right" and "wrong." Our knowledge of history has revealed an apparently endless recurrence of the rise and fall of peoples and nations; and the last segment of history, which we have lived through, has caused many people to relinquish a belief in any kind of progress. And, finally, we are beset by irreconcilable ideologies stridently competing for our allegiance.

"WHEN I SAY RELIGION..."

Yes, the world is undoubtedly in need of a new religion. And when I say religion, I do not mean a theology involving belief in a supernatural god or gods; nor do I mean merely a system of ethics, however exalted; nor only scientific knowledge, however extensive; nor just a practical social morality, however admirable or efficient. I mean an organized system of ideas and emotions which relates man to his destiny, over and above the practical affairs of every day, transcending the present and the existing systems of law and social structure. Such systems of ideas and emotions about human destiny have always existed and will always continue to exist. They certainly include the theistic religions; and I believe we have nothing to lose by using the word "religion" in the broadest sense to include nontheistic formulations and systems as well. Otherwise, we shall run the risk of sterilizing the ideas we put forward, by implying that our systems are not so full or satisfying or compelling as those of the theistic or supernaturalistic religions.

The prerequisite today is that any such religion shall appeal potentially to all mankind, and that its intellectual and rational side shall not be incompatible with scientific knowledge, but, on the contrary be based on it. I do not think that any attempt to produce a synthetic system out of the common elements of the main existing religions of the world can succeed; their conflicting formulations need to be by-passed. I am sure that purely ethical systems, albeit necessary, will not alone fill the bill. There is at the moment a well-marked revival of Christianity; but this, with its supernaturalistic theology, cannot satisfy the humanist, while its claim to the possession of absolute truth and the special features of its theology are bound to put it in conflict with other traditional religions and to invalidate its claims to be a universal system.

"THE HUMANIST CANNOT ACCEPT COMMUNISM . . ."

Communism, on the other hand, can be regarded as a serious candidate for the title of world religion. It makes, in theory, a world-wide appeal; it is expressly concerned with man's destiny; and it is professedly allied with science. There is no question that to many people it has the appeal of a religion; furthermore, it can be utilized by politicians and parties for political and economic ends in the same sort of way that other religions have been utilized in the past.

For many reasons, however, the humanist cannot accept communism as satisfactory. It is dogmatic; it is totalitarian and subordinates the individual to the state; in its present form at least, it cannot do without the idea of an enemy—the bourgeoisie, capitalism, idealism, and now, internationalism—and so vitiates its own potential universality.

Meanwhile, ideas like democracy are too limited and too political to fill the bill. They lend themselves to use in diametrically opposite senses in different countries— witness the People's Democracies as against the idea of democracy in North America. And "the American way of life," however valuable as a central rallying point for the United States, cannot by its nature have a similar appeal to the rest of the world.

We Humanists would not call ourselves Humanists unless we were dissatisfied with official and traditional creeds and philosophies. Moreover, we cannot be content with a negative attitude; we must have a constructive aim. And this, in my view, involves religion. We must believe that some sort of Humanist religion could and should eventually arise. We must begin exploring how it might take shape and the possibilities; for its development. This does not mean that we could even attempt to proclaim such a religion now. Religions are not to be deliberately constructed overnight. They grow and develop, though sometimes particular incidents may crystallize the slow march of ideas and lead to a decisive step. But we can begin to explore the conditions for such a religion to develop. We can formulate some of the points on which we agree, the lines along which exploration should continue, and the methods by which the Humanist movement might be organized in the future.

COMPONENTS OF RELIGION

In the first place, let us utilize the knowledge gained by scholars and ask whether there is any basic element common to all religions. The answer is unequivocal. All religions are bound up, somehow or other, with the sense of the sacred. This may appear in many guises. Sometimes it is predominantly tinged with the element of fear or horror, sometimes with mystery or awe, sometimes with joy or transcendent significance; but the quality which we call sacredness is always at the core of true religious emotion. Religions are always concerned with the individual, with his personal life, and with the relation between the two. This, in turn, implies a concern with human destiny. Here, again, the way in which concern is expressed varies enormously from one religion to another. The external powers may be approached with propitiation, prayer, submission; magic may be employed, or semi-magic symbolism, or the ritual of worship. A Humanist approach would be compounded of wonder, respect, and a desire for clear-eyed understanding.

As regards the individual, the sense of guilt may be stressed or, conversely, the sense of righteousness and certainty. Sometimes religion provides a feeling of solidarity with the group, while in other cases the individual seeks his religious consolation in solitude. Some religions stress salvation, whether by works or faith; others emphasize morality; some, legalistic acts. Orgiastic self-expression or self-transcendence is a feature of some religions, but frowned on by others. The attainment of mystical states of consciousness is sometimes a goal, while elsewhere repentance or self-discipline or even self-torture is stressed. The degree to which and the methods by which the psychological burden of guilt is projected on to others varies enormously.

Of course, there is immense variation in what may be summed up as the theological side of the religious picture. The flow of sacred force or *mana*; the crude anthropomorphic or zoomorphic polytheism of various ancient religions; the concept of monotheism; the doctrines of Karma, of non-attachment; the idea of merging with an ineffable power behind appearances—all these ideas, often contradictory, have played a part in religion.

All this and much more has emerged from the comparative study of religions, that new branch of anthropological science which has done so much in the last fifty years to clarify our understanding of the role that religion has actually played in human life. A major generalization to which it has led is that all religions, including their gods as much as their rituals or their moral precepts, are human creations —organs of man in society for coping with the overall problem of his destiny. This does not mean that there is no reality underlying the assemblage of gods and spirits brought into existence by man, any more than that divinely enjoined moral commandments have no correspondence with real social needs. Every supernatural figure represents, with a greater or lesser degree of accuracy, some real fact or set of facts, such as the power of sun or storm, the existence of evil or suffering, fertility, or the emotional power residing in places, in people, or in certain ideas. But the form of that representation is given by human minds and is often a distorted one.

THE BEST OF *THE HUMANIST*

RELIGIONS CORRELATE WITH CULTURES

The other general conclusion to be drawn from the science of comparative religion is one of great practical importance: namely, that the organization of religious systems stands in some correlation with the cultural level of the times. This is perhaps most obvious for the level of scientific knowledge and its applications. It is impossible for anyone acquainted with modern science to practice the propitiation of a goddess of fertility, to believe in the Mosaic account of the Creation or the Fall, to formulate the intellectual component of his religion in terms of polytheism, or to believe in augury and the art of divination by omens. But it applies also to the moral and practical sides of religion: human sacrifice, ritual cannibalism, temple prostitution, the *lex talionis* in its crude form—such things simply cannot exist in the atmosphere of an advanced civilization.

On the other hand, once ecclesiastical organization and theological formulation have crystallized out in certain forms, they exhibit a resistance to change which may produce a serious time-lag in adjustment; or even a persistence of religious concepts and activities quite unadjusted to the real needs of society. Since ideas and organization may have powerful social effects, this time-lag may give rise to serious results in practice. The sanctity of cows in India and the theological objections of the Roman Catholic church to birth control are two obvious examples from the present day. Christianity has been much more successful than most theistic religions in its capacity to adjust itself to changing conditions, partly because of the Humanist element it contains, in the shape of the doctrine of the Incarnation, partly because of its comprehensive quality in assigning importance to works as well as faith, to learning as well as to ritualism, to practical virtues as well as to asceticism and mysticism. This has allowed a frequent shift of emphasis and has permitted reformations and new formulations (though at the expense of sectarianism). But to many it seems that the time has now come when further fundamental adjustment is impossible and new formulations are required, which in their turn will lead to a radically new system or movement with its own novel methods of organization and working.

ELEMENTS OF A HUMANIST VIEW

What are the main elements which must be taken into account today in formulating a Humanist view of man's destiny, in expressing man's relations with the facts and problems of existence in a religious way, yet one which does not do violence to reason and science or to our accumulated knowledge about the past?

In the first place, I would put the facts and principles of evolution. Man—the human species—is a product of perhaps two thousand million years of biological evolution. He has, almost certainly, an equal or greater period of time before him, during which changes as radical as those which transformed the predecessor of the amoeba into human shape are possible. The human species is the latest dominant type to arise in evolution. In a strictly scientific sense, man is the highest type known to evolutionary biology. Furthermore, man has available a new mechanism for effecting change. In addition to physical heredity, he possesses the capacity for social transmission, which acts as a basis for cultural heredity. And in addition to being subjected to purely automatic operations like that of natural selection in the biological sphere, or that of economic determinism in the social sphere, he has the possibility of guiding change by means of conscious purpose in the light of rational experience. He could, if he so desired, use conscious purpose in the biological sphere to change his genetic nature or to adjust the quantity of populations, as well as in the social sphere to alter the organization of cultural or economic life.

MAN, THE AGENT OF EVOLUTION

Thus, in the broadest view, man's destiny is to be the agent of the evolutionary process. The possibility of any further real advance, of any major novelty, of any large-scale continuation of evolutionary progress lies in his hands. Here in man's evolutionary position and function is the extreme long-term component of any Humanist religion. Secondly, if we take a comprehensive view, the developed individual human personality emerges as the highest product of evolution. This implies that only in promoting the development and dignity of individuals shall we find a criterion of further advance or accomplish our destiny in a satisfactory way. The state and the community must not be exalted at the expense of the individual. This does not imply mere laissez-faire individualism. The community provides the framework within which individual development is possible and the means by which individual satisfaction and fulfillment may be attained. And sometimes the individual or some of his interests must be sacrificed to the continued welfare of the community. But the development of individual personalities remains the paramount objective of the process.

IMPLICATIONS OF PSYCHOLOGY

The next point is clearly that, if we want to promote the right or full development of personality, we must take account of the facts and principles of psychology. How can harmful repressions be overcome or split personalities be avoided? How can we prevent the projections of guilt onto others without impairing our own confidence? Most important, how can we help to promote the growth of rich and unified personalities and permit fulfilment in place of frustration? Is it possible to develop and make widely available communicable techniques for attaining satisfying kinds of mystical experience, such as are recorded for yoga, without impairing personality and without begging theological questions or professing particular theistic religions? Can we tap the reserve forces of the psyche that in most men lie latent? Can we unlock the forces that in most men remain imprisoned in conflict?

From a slightly different angle we need a thorough exploration of the possibilities of fulfillment and expression open to people of different psycho-physical types and of the techniques for realizing them. Eventually, the concept of fulfillment, of the better realization of individual human possibilities, might well become the central ideal of

Humanist Philosophy 1928 – 1973

Humanism. Such an ideal could be capable of exerting greater influence than other competing ideals, such as material prosperity, security, nationalism, or military or political power.

"SCIENCE . . . INDISPENSABLE . . ."

Another point to be taken into account is the indispensability of science in the broad sense of the word. Science is indispensable, first, as providing knowledge in understanding of the world and, secondly, as the basis for the better control of the processes of nature, including those of human nature. From the standpoint of religion, however, it is primarily a tool and neither an end in itself nor a substitute for a religious system (though the acquisition of knowledge and understanding represents one of the ways in which human possibilities can be realized and through which individuals can find fulfillment). Thus, any Humanist religion must be based on a proper understanding of the nature of science and the scientific method. Science is opposed to dogma in that it is constantly revising its conclusions as well as discovering new facts. But it is not merely—as some of its opponents would have it—a changing body of opinions and ephemeral ideas. It never provides complete knowledge, but it is always providing more knowledge. It leads to limited, but increasing, certitude. Its very incompleteness is the guarantee that it will constantly be making new discoveries, including new discoveries about human possibilities. This is a further reason why any Humanist ideology or religion must itself be an evolutionary system, capable not only of adjustment but of real novelty and progressive change.

The Basic Characteristics of Marxist Humanism

Mihailo Marković
The Humanist, January-February, 1969

I

The growth of humanist theories and movements has usually been a symptom of an increased readiness to resist various alienated social forces such as church, market, state, ideology, and technology. Great humanist writers have invariably expressed revolt against those social structures in which man has been degraded or belittled. The recent universal surge of humanist literature can be accounted for only by the deeply rooted anxieties of a generation that had to survive not only the Nazis' atrocities but also the Stalinist purges and the brutal slaughtering in Vietnam.

And still "humanism" is one of the most ambiguous and most misused of terms. Even some of those who have never shown in practice any real concern for human freedom and dignity sometimes like to play one of those humanist verbal games that is so easy to learn and even easier to repeat.

A natural reaction to this is a desire to dismiss the very notion of humanism. For example, Herbert Marcuse, in his paper read at the Korcula Summer School in Yugoslavia (August 1968), expressed the view that humanism in general, including socialist humanism, is obsolete and belongs to the culture of a society that has already been overcome. Then he continued by expounding a plea for a new type of man, with new needs, values, and aspirations; this plea was clearly nothing else but again a demand for a humanist qualitative change.

II

If misleading concepts and misuses cannot and need not be fought by dismissing important and well-entrenched terms, some necessary distinctions must be made. One of them is the distinction between *descriptive* and *normative* concepts of humanism. The former refers to common features of various historically given forms of humanism. Humanism in this sense can be defined as a general concern for man while approaching all theoretical or practical problems. This means rejection of any transcendental and supernatural conception of the world. Our picture of the universe is contingent upon our sensory powers, language, capacities for thinking and imagination, and instruments and habits of our practical activity. Our theory of knowledge and logic depends on the historically given level of the human conceptual apparatus and accumulated experience. All values are relative to human needs, feelings, and preferences. The meaning of human life and striving is created by man himself. Many philosophical trends are humanistic in this sense, even those that do not have any explicit theory of man and do not pay much attention to anthropological, ethical, esthetic, and political problems. Such is the humanism of Ferdinand C. S. Shiller (1864-1937), who in opposition to abstract and depersonalized formal logic elaborated a theory of knowledge and logic relative to practical human experience and existing human language.

Humanism as a normative concept is a projection of a possible ideal future of man and of society. It is the expression of some specific values and, at least implicitly, a program of practical action. Humanism in this sense varies from one trend to another: it has a definite meaning just in so far as it challenges or even excludes all other humanistic philosophies. That is why some Marxists two decades ago made considerable effort to show that existentialism is not humanism. That is why there are always some bourgeois philosophers who try to show the lack of humanism in Marxism. That is why Professor Kurtz in his paper "Humanism and the Freedom of the Individual," after expounding four principles that are accepted by most humanists, goes on to say: "Surely, aside from anything else, a basic principle of humanism must be a defense of personal freedom. Any humanism that does not cherish the individual, I am prepared to argue, is neither humanistic nor humanitarian." And further: "Any humanism worthy of the name should be concerned with the preservation of the individual personality with all of its unique idiosyncrasies and peculiarities."

By insisting on this "must" and "should," Professor Kurtz tries to build up a specific normative concept of humanism that he labels "liberal" or "democratic" and opposes to Marxist humanism in the following ways: "There is, however, an important difference in contemporary humanism between those, such as Marxist humanists, who believe that the problem of man is essentially social and those, such as liberal democratic humanists, who emphasize the need to enhance the qualities of individuality."

That this distinction is rather simplified becomes obvious from the rest of the paper. Professor Kurtz quotes several texts in which Marx also insisted on the freedom and full development of each individual as the basic principle. And, even more important, Professor Kurtz himself points out the contrast between "democratic Marxism and other forms of Marxism."

III

Marxism today is really a whole cluster of opposite orientations and tendencies, some of which can hardly be classified as humanism in any sense. And although all these various orientations would really clash with "liberal humanism" precisely on the issue specified by Professor Kurtz, the reasons for disagreement would be vastly different.

Some contemporary forms of Marxism disregard the problem of individual freedom because they are ideologies of backward or fairly developed but bureaucratic societies. In the former case, the whole society still faces the tasks of the capitalist epoch; accelerated industrialization and urbanization require centralized methods and considerable sacrifices from individuals; the general level of education and culture is still low, etc. Under such conditions there can be no question of superseding "liberal humanism." In the latter case, society remains below the level of already historically possible individual freedom. Disregard for personal freedom is, in both cases, clearly the consequence of internal weaknesses of such societies, which are still rather far from completing a socialist revolution.

However, those variants of Marxism that follow Marx in projecting the possibilities of an already developed industrialized and democratic society are opposed to the classical bourgeois liberal humanism from an entirely different point of view: The problem is not to proclaim the principle of individual freedom and full personal development in an abstract, purely theoretical, ahistorical, acritical way. The problem is: How to realize this principle practically? In which concrete form can it be materialized under existing historical conditions? Which existing social structures and institutions must be abolished in order to make room for a freer and richer life for all individuals?

IV

Individual freedom in the economic sphere in every society based on commodity production means unlimited private initiative and consequently growing social differentiation. Herbert Spencer merely drew all the logical consequences from the laissez-faire conception when he condemned any governmental intervention. Poverty, according to him, is a natural result of inefficiency, stupidity, and weakness of character. Therefore intervention to favor the particular group of the poor is unfair because it negates the fundamental law of equal freedom. In addition, state intervention is always in the interest of a particular group and against the interests of other groups. This is true: state intervention in the conditions of the market economy leads inevitably to bureaucratization. Thus, liberal humanism has to choose between the inhumanity of laissez-faire capitalism and the antiliberal bureaucratism of state capitalism. Or perhaps something should be done about the assumption of commodity production? But what? And how—within the framework of liberal humanism?

Intellectual freedom is freedom of thought and inquiry, freedom of speech and publication, the freedom to teach, preach, and advocate, etc. Other conditions being equal, the very proclamation of these freedoms would constitute an enormous achievement in the process of human emancipation. But other conditions are not equal. Funds for scientific research are alienated from the research worker. The mass media of communication are either possessed or fully controlled by those who have nothing to say, especially nothing heretical. And the vast majority of mankind, anyway, has not the slightest chance to enjoy any intellectual activities, free or not.

Political freedoms—the rights of opposition, election, petition, recall, the right of assembly—are really *conditio sine qua non* of every democratic society. However, the mere proclamation of these freedoms means little, practically, in every society in which there are one or more political parties with their bureaucratic party machines, enormous funds, and developed techniques for the manipulation of individuals.

Self-management and various forms of participation of individuals in social communities in which they live and work might, under certain conditions, be a decisive step towards abolition of alienated labor. To be sure, participation in a private enterprise is, at best, a palliative measure only. Self-management within scattered, atomized, disintegrated enterprises, still subordinated to bureaucratic structures at the level of the global society, must be taken as only the first important step in the process of workers' emancipation. If this step is not followed by the next ones, if the permanently developing, integrating system of self-management does not gradually replace the organs of the state and professional politics, the principle itself might be compromised and reduced to one more of the sweet nothings of contemporary social life.

V

The difference between traditional liberal humanism and the democratic contemporary form of Marx's humanism is not, therefore, the fact that the former is concerned primarily with the human individual and the latter primarily with the totality of social phenomena. The real issue is whether radical individual emancipation is feasible without radical change of the whole social structure. The real issue is: how and in what sense would it be possible for an individual to be really freer, more capable of expressing all his potential powers, of developing a need for satisfying the needs of other members of his community, if he continued to produce commodities for the market, if political power remained alienated in the form of the state and political parties, if a monopoly on the mass media survived, if factories of ersatz culture continued their production of ever cheaper and increasingly more worthless magazines, television programs, comic books, etc.? The real issue is whether humanism remains a pure theory, satisfied with verbal declarations and abolition of existing alienation in thought, or becomes a theory that immediately implies a program of practical disalienation.

VI

Marxism is essentially a humanism of praxis, a philosophy that tends towards as complete a unification of theory and practical action as possible. This unity by all means affects both theory and practice. Theory assumes the role of a permanently vivid and concrete critical self-consciousness—thus it becomes a major historical force. Practice becomes enlightened on the one hand by a global vision of an ideally possible future, and on the other hand by a critical understanding of the existing historical situation and its inherent possibilities for change.

Thus Marxist humanism is opposed to all those trends that see the meaning of philosophy in the analysis of positive knowledge, in passive wisdom, in understanding and explanation that lead only to adjustment or to powerless intellectual revolt. In particular, it is opposed to a pragmatic, existentialist, and Stalinistic conception of human practice. Pragmatism lacks a universal, humanist vision. Also it neglects the role of prior theory. Man as presupposed by pragmatism is an atomized, isolated individual with his particular interests, an individual who has not yet become a social being, who remains enclosed within the boundaries of his given and reified world. This activity is irrational and utilitarian.

Human activity remains irrational also within the framework of existentialist philosophy. If man has no definite structure of his being, which is the product of all previous history, a structure that thus precedes any act of choice and engagement and determines the limits of the possible, then everything is equally possible and no theoretical knowledge about the past can be relevant for the future. Our activity is, therefore, purely voluntaristic. Only *a posteriori* shall we know whether the goals have been really possible, and only then will our activity acquire a definite meaning.

This view is not without merit as the expression of revolt against the conformism of the majority of intellectuals who fully conform to what is given and to what prevails. Existentialist humanism rejects this rationality of "great numbers" that avoids any radical change and any risk, and that loyally serves the existing social order. An existentialist in action refuses to be burdened by knowledge, refuses to be realistic and wise—because uncritical knowledge and conformistic wisdom lead only to unessential improvements and reforms, never to radical transformations. By refusing to admit any boundaries, any conditioning by the past, he achieves a good deal of freshness and spontaneity of behavior; he acquires a possibility of creating something really new—on the margin between the possible and impossible. But this novelty could arise only by chance. An enormous number of such blind choices and a tremendous waste of human energy are needed in order to create something really new and really important in this way. Such an activity of atomized individuals, if transferred from the field of poetry and the arts and play to politics again leads to the rule of "the law of great numbers." Various uncoordinated individual actions cancel each other and the historical process remains determined by the unknown blind forces. All spontaneity and originality of behavior of isolated authentic personalities remain only a hardly observable embellishment on the margin of great impersonal historical streams of events. These streams can be modified and redirected only by coordinate activity of large social collectives that get engaged in order to materialize a real, though maybe not very probable, possibility.

The Marxist approach to the problem of the praxis of an individual is superior to existentialism in at least two respects. First, it eliminates the utterly simplified view that all knowledge is a source of conformism. Critical knowledge, in difference from positive or technical knowledge, provides information about negative, destructive forces within a system (i.e., Marx's law of decreasing rate of profit in capitalism). Thus it allows the discovery of hidden real possibilities of radical change. Second, while existentialism overestimates the possibilities of spontaneous individual actions, Marxism realizes that an individual can influence the course of history decisively only in so far as he succeeds in expressing and articulating the real needs of the whole social group to which he belongs.

VII

With respect to both these points an ideological mystification typical of the bureaucratic abuse of Marxism must be avoided. Bureaucracy also proclaims a readiness to change the world and, as positive science does not suffice for that purpose, it wants to supplement it by a "revolutionary theory." On the other hand, bureaucracy keeps repeating that only the broad masses, especially the workers, can make history.

However, by "the change of the world" bureaucracy does not mean a real supersession of existing forms of alienation, including institutions of professional politics, but only small improvements and reforms. "Revolutionary theory" tends to be as militant and uncompromising as possible only with respect to the external capitalist world; with respect to the initial forms of socialism it is utterly conservative and apologetic.

Bureaucracy still tries to play the role of the workers' avant garde, but instead of expressing the real needs and interests of workers it expects the workers to follow loyally all the twists and turns of its policy. If workers ever rebel they are labeled "mob," "underground," or "the weapon of the class enemy." The rule of bureaucracy rests on a double basis: on the one hand sheer brute force, and on the other hand an ideology that tries to rationalize its policy and its whole social position.

VIII

The rationality implicit in Marxist humanism is fundamentally different from both ideological rationality and from the rationality of positive science. For ideological rationality an effort is characteristic to express the interests and needs of a particular social group in the form of mutually linked, systematized, indicative statements whose main function is to mystify real social relationships and to create the appearance of a universally valid *Weltanschauung*. In order to demystify this kind of apparent rationality it is necessary to show not only that seemingly factual statements are often only value judgments in disguise but also that these value judgments express not universal but particular interests and needs.

For the rationality of positive science, on the contrary, a characteristic tendency is to exclude all value judgments as irrational. However, in this way the question about the fundamental goals of human activity gets removed into a sphere of irrationality. Rationality is thus reduced to the rationality of means and consequently to technological rationality. No matter how irrational and inhuman are the goals, maximum efficiency in the process of their realization would signify also the maximum of rationality. And this best shows the absurd character of such a limited concept of rationality.

The Marxist notion of rationality includes both fact and value, knowledge and ideal. But in difference from positivism the idea of an integral, critical knowledge is assumed by Marxism. In difference from any ideological axiology, which projects the interests of a particular social group into an ahistorical, transcendental sphere of being, Marxian rationality presupposes a universal ideal of possible emancipation, solidarity, and fulfillment in a concrete historical form.

IX

The concepts of "science" and "theory" have a fundamentally new meaning in Marxist humanism. This is the consequence not only of an ever present practical orientation but also of the application of a new method of thought—dialectics.

The scientific theory that one finds in *Das Kapital* is neither empirical in the ordinary sense nor purely speculative. It is not a mere description and explanation of actually given phenomena but a study of possibilities. This study is based on ample empirical evidence—thus the possibilities in question are projections within a real historical situation. However, the projections are strongly colored by a philosophical vision. The starting point of inquiry is not just a mass of empirical data but an elaborated anthropological theory and a critical examination of all relevant previous theoretical knowledge.

The essential part of building up a new theory is the creation of a new conceptual apparatus. These concepts have both explanatory and critical functions. Dialectics is essentially a method of criticism, of discovery of inner limitations, tensions, and conflicts. Contemporary historicism, which is primarily interested in diachronic aspects of social formations, and structuralism, which pays attention only to synchronic aspects, are only partial moments of Marx's method. According to this method scientific theory tends to examine whole structures, totalities—not isolated events. But a structure becomes meaningful only when it is conceived as a crystallization of the past forms of human practice, and with respect to historically possible futures. On the other hand, what is historically possible can be established only by taking into account the structural characteristics of the whole situation. To be sure, structural characteristics are constituted not solely by the static factors that preserve the stability of the system but also by dynamic factors that lead to dysfunction and destruction.

Thus the role of science is not only to provide positive knowledge and to secure maximum efficiency within the framework of a given social system. It also discovers other possibilities of the system that correspond better to human needs. Thus critical science shows not only how man can best adjust to the dominating historical tendencies within a given social framework but also how he can change the whole framework and adjust it to himself.

X

Marxist humanism, like any other humanism, presupposes a conception of man and human society. The problem is not so much to expound this conception in detail but to clarify its theoretical nature. According to Marx the form of a genuine human society, the end of the present prehistory and the beginning of a real historical process, is Communism. It presupposes such a high level of development of productive forces that there will be an abundance of material goods; and most of our time will become free from imposed, alienated labor, free for praxis—a creative, spontaneous activity with definite esthetical qualities. Production would become a process in which the individual objectifies his potential sensual and intellectual powers, affirms his personality, and satisfies needs of other individuals. Material products and labor would no longer be commodities; consequently there would no longer be money, market, exploitation, professional division of work, state, professional politics, ideology, religion, and all other forms of alienation. Such a society would be a genuine community of free individuals. Association of producers would control and direct exchange with nature in a way most rational and most adequate to human nature. Individuals would work in such a society according to their abilities, and they would be remunerated according to their needs. Their freedom and complete self-fulfillment would be a condition of freedom and true historical development of the whole society.

This whole vision rests upon a normative concept of man. According to Marx, man is fundamentally a being of praxis, which implies a potentially free, creative, social, rational being, able to develop further his nature, powers, and abilities. Obviously this concept and the whole idea of Communism are not simple extrapolations of a necessary historical course; they are not inductive generalizations on the basis of empirically established laws.

The course of history is not constituted by any reified, linear necessity. Empirically we can only establish existence of various crisscrossing opposite tendencies with ever new deviations from established regularities. In contemporary society there are both the tendencies of fast technological progress, with obvious liberating effects, and increasing use of new technology for the purpose of destruction; there is the tendency of the reproduction of market economy in socialism and of its infringements in capitalism; also there are now tendencies in socialism of abandoning rigid planning and introducing a new social polarization, whereas in capitalism planning is increasing and social differentiation tends to be reduced.

These various tendencies open a specter of possibilities. The character of human practice depends upon which of these possibilities will be realized. The character of this practice cannot be predicted with anything approaching certainty because human behavior and development is lacking in any certainty.

All preceding history presents a picture of opposite tendencies of human behavior: craving for freedom but also escape from responsibilities; a striving for universality and internationalism but also class, national, and racial egoism; need for creativity but also powerful, irrational, destructive drives. Faced with such contradictions, we cannot be satisfied with simple extrapolations; even less can we attribute to them a scientific character in the same sense in which the empirical scientist makes his predictions in a limited, well-explored field. To assert, therefore, that Marx's anthropological theory and humanism are part of empirical science and a necessary consequence of our knowledge of social laws, would amount to an ideological mystification.

On the other hand, the humanistic ideal of Marx is not a pure *Sollen* of idealist axiology, nor a matter of arbitrary individual choice, nor only the expression of utopian hope. Values implied by this ideal are those historical possibilities that correspond to human needs; and needs are something real, historically determined, given in a practical, immediately sensory form. The most difficult problem here is how to distinguish among genuine, authentic needs and artificial needs that are the result of manipulation and enforcement of certain patterns of behavior. Any attempted solution could seek support (1) in the old humanist tradition; (2) in the existence of a widespread feeling of revolt against prevailing social habits; and (3) in actual preferences in everyday human behavior.

> (1) There is a very high degree of agreement among great humanist thinkers of the past that man should be free, able to live in peace, creative in activity, united in solidarity with other people, etc. This agreement does not prove anything but shows a universal human character of the corresponding anthropological considerations.
> (2) Marxist philosophical anthropology is a strong expression of revolt against the human condition in capitalist society. Capitalism and some initial forms of socialism have shown that privatization of individual, class, national, and racial egoism, one-sided obsession with technology, material possessions, and political power degrade man, develop destructive instincts, and eventually make human existence empty and meaningless. Marxist humanism is a radical negation of a society in which man is so deformed and in which possibilities of a fully developed life are so reduced.
> (3) This negation has a democratic character. The humanist ideal implicit in this negation expresses certain deeply rooted, basically assumed preferences. This could be empirically established by investigating which among rival norms of behavior large masses of people would follow, all other conditions being equal.

But in a way this has already been practically established. Marxist humanism is nowadays the main spiritual inspiration for very broad liberation movements. To be sure, these movements have sometimes been used for selfish and inhuman ends. And still their very existence shows that Marx's humanist ideal is not only the continuation of a great tradition and not only the expression of revolt against all that is inhumane in the present-day world but also a dream that might come true.

Mihailo Marković, noted Marxist author, is professor of philosophy at the University of Belgrade, Yugoslavia.

Humanism and Behaviorism

B. F. Skinner
The Humanist, July-August, 1972

There seem to be two ways of knowing, or knowing about, another person. One is associated with existentialism, phenomenology, and structuralism. It is a matter of knowing what a person is, or what he is like, or what he is coming to be or becoming. We try to know another person in this sense as we know ourselves. We share his feelings through sympathy or empathy. Through intuition we discover his attitudes, intentions, and other states of mind. We communicate with him in the etymological sense of making ideas and feelings common to both of us. We do so more effectively if we have established good *interpersonal* relations. This is a passive, contemplative kind of knowing: If we want to predict what a person does or is likely to do, we assume that he, like us, will behave according to what he is; his behavior, like ours, will be an expression of his feelings, states of mind, intentions, attitudes, and so on.

The other way of knowing is a matter of what a person *does*. We can usually observe this as directly as any other phenomenon in the world; no special kind of knowing is needed. We explain why a person behaves as he does by turning to the environment rather than to inner states or activities. The environment was effective during the evolution of the species, and we call the result the human genetic endowment. A member of the species is exposed to another part of that environment during his lifetime, and from it he acquires a repertoire of behavior which converts an organism with a genetic endowment into a person. By analyzing these effects of the environment, we move toward the prediction and control of behavior.

But can this formulation of what a person *does* neglect any available information about what he *is*? There are gaps in time and space between behavior and the environmental events to which it is attributed, and it is natural to try to fill them with an account of the intervening state of the organism. We do this when we summarize a long evolutionary history by speaking of genetic endowment.

Should we not do the same for a personal history? An omniscient physiologist should be able to tell us, for example, how a person is changed when a bit of his behavior is reinforced, and what he thus becomes should explain why he subsequently behaves in a different way. We argue in such a manner, for example, with respect to immunization. We begin with the fact that vaccination makes it less likely that a person will contract a disease at a later date. We say that he becomes immune, and we speak of a state of immunity, which we then proceed to examine. An omniscient physiologist should be able to do the same for comparable states in the field of behavior. He should also be able to change behavior by changing the organism directly rather than by changing the environment. Is the existentialist, phenomenologist, or structuralist not directing his attention precisely to such a mediating state?

A thoroughgoing dualist would say no, because for him what a person observes through introspection and what a physiologist observes with his special techniques are in different universes. But it is a reasonable view that what we feel when we have feelings are states of our own bodies, and that the states of mind we perceive through introspection are other varieties of the same kinds of things. Can we not, therefore, anticipate the appearance of an omniscient physiologist and explore the gap between environment and behavior by becoming more keenly aware of what we are?

It is at this point that a behavioristic analysis of self-knowledge becomes most important and, unfortunately, is most likely to be misunderstood. Each of us possesses a small part of the universe within his own skin. It is not for that reason different from the rest of the universe, but it is a private possession: We have ways of knowing about it that are denied to others. It is a mistake, however, to conclude that the intimacy we thus enjoy means a special kind of understanding. We are, of course, stimulated directly by our own bodies. The so-called interoceptive nervous system responds to conditions important in deprivation and emotion. The proprioceptive system is involved in posture and movement, and without it we could scarcely behave in a coordinated way. These two systems, together with the exteroceptive nervous system, are essential to effective behavior. But knowing is more than responding to stimuli. A child responds to the colors of things before he "knows his colors." Knowing requires special contingencies of reinforcement that must be arranged by other people, and the contingencies involving private events are never very precise because other people are not effectively in contact with them. In spite of the intimacy of our own bodies, we know them less accurately than we know the world around us. And there are, of course, other reasons why we know the private world of others even less precisely.

The important issue, however, is not precision but subject matter. Just what can be known when we "know ourselves"? The three nervous systems just mentioned have evolved under practical contingencies of survival, most of them non-social. (Social contingencies important for survival must have arisen in such fields as sexual and maternal behavior.) They were presumably the only systems available when people began to "know themselves" as the result of answering questions about their behavior. In answering such questions as "Do you see that?" or "Did you hear that?" or "What is that?" a person learns to observe his own responses to stimuli. In answering such questions as "Are you hungry?" or "Are you afraid?" he learns to observe states of his body related to deprivation and emotional arousal. In answering such questions as "Are you going to go?" or "Do you intend to go?" or "Do you feel like going?" or "Are you inclined to go?" he learns to reserve the strength or probability of his behavior. The verbal community asks such questions because the answers are important to it, and in a sense it thus makes the answers important to the person himself. The important fact is that such contingencies, social or non-social, involve nothing more than stimuli or responses; *they do not involve mediating processes*. We cannot fill the gap between behavior and the environment of which it is a function through introspection because, to put the matter in crude physiological terms, we do not have nerves going to the right places. We cannot observe the states and events to which an omniscient physiologist would have access. What we feel when we have feelings and what we observe through introspection are nothing more than a rather miscellaneous set of collateral products or by-products of the environmental conditions to which behavior is related. (We do not act because we feel like acting, for example; we act *and* feel like acting for a common reason to be sought in our environmental history.) Do I mean to say that Plato never discovered the mind? Or that Aquinas, Descartes, Locke, and Kant were preoccupied with incidental, often irrelevant by-products of human behavior? Or that the mental laws of physiological psychologists like Wundt, or the stream of consciousness of William James, or the mental apparatus of Sigmund Freud have no useful place in the understanding of human behavior? Yes, I do. And I put the matter strongly because, if we are to solve the problems that face us in the world today, this concern for mental life must no longer divert our attention from the environmental conditions of which human behavior is a function.

But why have we attached so much importance to our feelings and states of mind, to the neglect of the environment? The answer seems to lie in the immediacy and the saliency of the stimuli. Many relevant events in our personal history pass without notice. For one thing, the behavior to which they will eventually prove relevant has not yet occurred and cannot contribute to contingencies that would lead us to notice them. And if we have noticed them, we may quickly forget. But our feelings, "ideas," "felt intentions," and so on, often overlap the behavior to which they seem related, and they usually occur in just the place that would be occupied by a cause (on the principle of *post hoc, ergo propter hoc*). For example, we often feel a state of deprivation or emotion before we act in an appropriate way. If we say something to ourselves before saying it aloud, what we say aloud seems to be the expression of an inner thought. And if we say something aloud without first saying it to ourselves, it is tempting to suppose that we must be expressing a nonverbal thought.

This apparent causality lodged within the private world within a skin, together with the organization imposed upon it by the fact that all its determining conditions have occurred in the history of one person, generates a "sense of self." We feel there is an "I" who knows what he is going to do and does it. Each of us is aware or conscious of at least one such self, which we learn to manage more or less effectively.

Since the only selves we know are human selves, it is often said that man is distinguished from other species precisely because he is aware of himself and participates in the determination of his future. What distinguishes the human species, however, is the development of a culture, a social environment that contains the contingencies generating self-knowledge and self-control. It is this environment that has been so long neglected by those who have been concerned with the inner determination of conduct. The neglect has meant that better practices for building self-knowledge and self-management have been missed.

It is often said that a behavioristic analysis "dehumanizes man." But it merely dispenses with a harmful explanatory fiction. In doing so it moves much more directly toward the goals that fiction was designed, erroneously, to serve. People understand themselves and manage themselves much more effectively when they understand the relevant contingencies.

Important processes in self-management lie in the fields of ethics and morals, where conflicts between immediate and deferred consequences are considered. One of the great achievements of a culture has been to bring remote consequences to bear upon the behavior of the individual. We may design a culture in which the same results will be achieved much more efficiently by shifting our attention from ethical problem-solving or moral struggle to the external contingencies.

We may move from an inner agent to environmental determinants without neglecting the question of values. It has been argued that behaviorism is or pretends to be value free, but that no value-free science can properly deal with man *qua* man. What is wrong in the traditional argument can be seen in the expression "value judgment." An inner initiating agent is to *judge* things as good or bad. But a much more effective source of values is to be found in the environmental contingencies. The things people call good are positive reinforcers, and they reinforce because of the contingencies of survival under which the species has evolved. Until recently, the species could survive famine, pestilence, and other catastrophes only if its members procreated at every opportunity, and under such contingencies sexual contact became highly reinforcing. Sex is not reinforcing because it feels good; it is reinforcing *and* feels good for a common phylogenic reason. Some reinforcers may acquire their power during the life of the individual. Social goods, such as attention or approval, are created and used to induce people to behave in ways that are reinforcing to those who use them. The result may be good for the individual as well as for others, particularly when deferred consequences are mediated.

The values affecting those who are in charge of other people supply good examples of the importance of turning from supposed attributes of an inner man to the contingencies affecting behavior. There are five classical types of human beings who have been mistreated: the young, the elderly, prisoners, psychotics, and retardates. Are they mistreated because those who are in charge of them lack sympathy, compassion, or benevolence, or have no conscience? No, the important fact is that they are unable to retaliate. It is easy to mistreat any one of these five kinds of people without being mistreated in turn. The recent confrontation between humanists and Catholics at the LaFarge Center in New York City failed to make clear that the *sources* of conscience are not to be found in psychological realities but in punitive sanctions.

An environmental analysis has a special advantage in promoting a kind of value concerned with the good of the culture. Cultures evolve under special contingencies of survival. A practice that makes a culture more likely to survive survives with the culture. Cultures become more successful in meeting contingencies of survival as they induce their members to behave in more and more subtle and complex ways. (Progress is not inevitable, of course, for there are extinct cultures as well as extinct species.) An important stage is reached when a culture induces some of its members to be concerned for its survival, because they may then design more effective practices.

Humanist Philosophy 1928 – 1973

Over the years, men and women have slowly and erratically constructed physical and social environments in which they have come closer to fulfilling or actualizing their potential. They have not changed themselves (that is a genetic problem which has not yet been solved); they have changed the world in which they live. In the design of his own culture, man could thus be said to control his destiny.

I would define a humanist as one of those who, because of the environment to which he has been exposed, is concerned for the future of mankind. A movement that calls itself "humanistic psychology" takes a rather different line. It has been described as "a third force" to distinguish it from behaviorism and psychoanalysis; but "third" should not be taken to mean advanced, nor should "force" suggest power. Since behaviorism and psychoanalysis both view human behavior as a determined system, humanistic psychologists have emphasized a contrast by defending the autonomy of the individual. They have insisted that a person can transcend his environment, that he is more than a causal stage between behavior and environment, that he determines what environmental forces will act upon him—in a word, that he has free choice. The position is most at home in existentialism, phenomenology, and structuralism, because the emphasis is on what a person is or is becoming. Maslow's expression "self-actualization" sums it up nicely: The individual is to fulfill himself—not merely through gratification, of course, but through "spiritual growth."

Humanistic psychologists are not unconcerned about the good of others or even the good of a culture or of mankind, but such a formulation is basically selfish. Its development can be traced in the struggle for political, religious, and economic freedom, where a despotic ruler could be overthrown only by convincing the individual that he was the source of the power used to control him. The strategy has had beneficial results, but it has led to an excessive aggrandizement of the individual, which may lead in turn either to new forms of tyranny or to chaos. The supposed right of the individual to acquire unlimited wealth which he is free to use as he pleases often results in a kind of despotism, and the Hindu concern for personal growth in spirituality has been accompanied by an almost total neglect of the social environment.

Better forms of government are not to be found in better rulers, better educational practices in better teachers, better economic systems in more enlightened management, or better therapy in more compassionate therapists. Neither are they to be found in better citizens, students, workers, or patients. The age-old mistake is to look for salvation in the character of autonomous men and women rather than in the social environments that have appeared in the evolution of cultures and that can now be explicitly designed.

By turning from man *qua* man to the external conditions of which man's behavior is a function, it has been possible to design better practices in the care of psychotics and retardates, in child care, in education (in both contingency management in the classroom and the design of instructional material), in incentive systems in industry, and in penal institutions. In these and many other areas we can now more effectively work for the good of the individual, for the greatest good of the greatest number, and for the good of the culture or of mankind as a whole. These are certainly humanistic concerns, and no one who calls himself a humanist can afford to neglect them. Men and women have never faced a greater threat to the future of their species. There is much to be done and done quickly, and nothing less than the active prosecution of a science of behavior will suffice.

B. F. Skinner, considered the world's foremost behavioristic psychologist, is Professor of Psychology at Harvard University and author, most recently, of Beyond Freedom and Dignity. He is recipient of the Humanist of the Year Award for 1972. Preparation of this paper was supported by the National Institutes of Mental Health, Grant No. K6-MH-21, 775-01.

CHAPTER 3
The Source and Nature of Humanist Values

Modern Humanist Values Have Always Been Progressive

Harold Buschman's essay in Chapter 4 notes that humanism is not positivist. So humanist values are not simply what some humanist says they are. A handful of statements of humanist values have been published over the years. Thus, in order for humanism to not be positivist, those values must come from somewhere other than the minds of the persons writing and publishing those statements. Consequently, humanist values have to have another source. But where humanist values do come from was the subject of a range of arguments by writers in *TNH* and *TH* up to 1973.

Roy Wood Sellars defined a "value" as "a thing or goal or a human condition valued, more or less adequately ... by human beings" (*TNH* 6:6). A person's "valuations are expressions of his [or her] life in relation to his [or her] surroundings, expressions of what he [or she] hopes to admire and hopes to accomplish." While his definition flows naturally from his view that humanists see humans as rooted in nature, it suffers from being tautological. More helpfully, Rollo Handy defined "value" in *TH* as that which satisfies a human need. He defined "need" as "an event or condition that aids the human to function adequately" (*TH* 27:1). While other philosophers have offered different definitions, Handy's will suffice for the present discussion.

The philosophical terminology of value is at times not intuitive. Philosophers use the term "value" in its positive sense. When referring to the opposite characteristics, the proper term is "disvalue." However, when talking about aspects of "values" like their origin or acquisition, both "value" and "disvalue" may be encompassed.

Humanists give central importance to values. Arthur E. Morgan argued in TNH that intelligence, or reason, has its limits, and character, or values, are essential to the continued advancement of society (*TNH* 7:1). So while this chapter focuses on values generally, humanism relies ultimately on the individual to determine his or her own values. Chapter 8 provides a broad discussion of humanist morals and ethics for self-determination of one's own values.

Sources of Humanist Values

The first issue regarding humanist values, then, is their origins. In this chapter, Van Meter Ames sets forth the notion that humanist values originate in human life. Paul Kurtz' essay in Chapter 1 repeats that notion. This formulation is broad enough to reflect a consensus view of writers in *TNH* and *TH*. Particularly, it excludes sources external to humans, especially supernatural ones.

While Kurtz does not elaborate on how values are found in human life, Ames offers that values develop in situations of human experience. Value must be "embedded in what men [and women] actually do and think and care about." Given that what people think and care about changes, so do values. This contingent nature of values is also a consensus view of humanist thinkers. In their own ways, both Kurtz and Ames generally reflect John Dewey's view,[1] echoed elsewhere in *TH*, such as in an essay by E. Burdette Backus (*TH* 6:3), that values arise from the purposive nature of humans.

In that vein, Horace J. Nickels' essay in Chapter 4 asserts that human values come from solving problems and creative action. Gerald Barnes states in Chapter 5 that "there is much evidence that we can give [life] meaning, here and there ... ." Erwin W. Fellows insists in this chapter that one of the chief bases for "a modern system of morals" must be each human's nature "as a biological, psychological, and social organism." He provides a good example, in how unfounded beliefs about race unjustifiably undergirded racial discrimination, bias, and persecution.

Humanist Philosophy 1928 – 1973

H. J. Eysenck starts in Chapter 7 from the premise that reason cannot provide values. Humanists must instead root their values in compassion. He asserts that doing so can help reduce the reputation of humanism as being too rationalistic. Compassion is arguably the core formulation in an essay by Horace S. Fries from 1932. Fries argued that the best values are those most conducive to the total long-run welfare of all people affected, where welfare is defined as an ethical hedonism (*TNH* 5:4).

Abraham Maslow's essay in this chapter sets forth the idea that, unlike in Dewey's purposive origin of all values, some values are intrinsic. For Maslow, intrinsic human values are a part of human nature and thereby instinctoid. They constitute the value life that includes the spiritual, religious, philosophical, and axiological. But he argues that those values are on a continuum with lower "animal values" that humans also hold.

Science and Nature as Sources

As elaborated in Chapter 4, humanist philosophy fundamentally values the scientific method and conclusions based on scientifically tested evidence. In cases such as the evolution of life forms, Kurtz points to humanist values deriving from knowledge gained scientifically. In essence, those values consist of valuing outcomes of science applied to nature and human life.

The expanding realm of technology also consists of scientific outcomes. Linus Pauling argues in Chapter 5 that technologies force us to adopt values about their use. Fellows advocates democratizing scientific methods and outcomes. But these values are values *about* scientific methods and outcomes. Whether science can itself provide values is a different question. Among humanists' viewpoints on this question, the most common is that expressed by Ames, Eysenck in Chapter 7, and Abraham Maslow and Harold A. Larrabee in Chapter 9, holding that science cannot provide any values. Nonetheless, Fellows demonstrates that value choices must take science into account. His example of race shows how science proving the identical nature of humans of different races has eliminated any reasonable basis for racism.

In summary, nature or the universe provides humans things to value or disvalue. Science is a tool that serves to reveal more such things. For example, the pluralism, contingency, relativism, and emergence discussed in Chapter 1 are things that humanists value about nature and the universe that humans using science have discerned. Even science as a natural process is provided by nature. Humanists may change or add new values as scientific knowledge increases.

The Nature of Humanist Values

Between 1928 and 1973, writers in *TNH* and *TH* often delved into public issues with references to values. The best of the multitude of essays on individual issues could fill a separate volume. Most such articles did not make an explicit connection with humanism. Implicit was the editor's view that those values were worthy of discussion by humanists. Nonetheless, by no means were all authors in the magazines humanists. Accordingly, articles considered here are either by humanists or concern values elsewhere advocated by humanists.

As noted above, humanist values are dynamic or contingent, changing with new knowledge. Accordingly, statements of humanist values have changed through the years. Two widely subscribed statements of humanist values, the HMI and HMII were published in 1933 and 1973, respectively. The changes between those manifestos evidence the evolving, contingent nature of humanist values.

That multiple individuals signed HMI and HMII suggests that they represent humanist values only as far as those signers collectively mirrored the extent of thought about humanist values society-wide. Furthermore, HMI and HMII were necessarily brief, no doubt to avoid reservations by signatories on a wealth of more specific issues.

Thus, the manifestos left room for additional value conceptions. Other statements of humanist values were published in articles in TH signed only by one or two individuals. Eminent humanists, such as Lloyd Morain and Oliver Reiser in Chapter 2, undertook to make such statements. Corliss Lamont's essay in this chapter from 1942 set out five principles of humanism. In another essay twenty-nine years later, he set out twelve principal values of naturalistic humanism (*TH* 31:5). Those values are remarkably similar to HMII.

Altogether, the manifestos and statements exemplify the efforts of writers in *TNH* and *TH* through 1973. They comprise an overlapping, differing patchwork of priorities, foci, and subjects. Fellows explains that this amalgam is the natural consequence of the plurality of humanism. Humanists have differing notions, because they freely choose their values. But the various statements have some basic commonalities worth exploring in the remainder of this essay.

Progressivism in Humanism's Roots

HMI and early statements established generally progressive values that were subsequently developed. In several of its theses, HMI sets forth a progressive vision.

On a basic level, the Fifth thesis insists that values are determined by applying human intelligence in relationship to human needs. Fries' egalitarian standard specifies those needs are of all affected humans. Thus, humanists advocated progressive solutions for social issues in the period from 1928 through 1973, such as ending the arms race and war itself (Pauling); devoting technology to human progress;[2] establishing race (Curtis W. Reese's included essay) and gender equality, and national health insurance;[3] and regulating pollution (see Chapter 11).

Addressing the socio-economic level, the Fourteenth thesis of HMI states that a radical transformation of capitalist society to a socialized, cooperative economic system is necessary, with an end of equitable distribution of wealth. Bain, too, attacks economic inequality resulting from an undemocratic economy. Ames notes that one person's right to material goods cannot trump another's right to sustenance and life. Morain and Reiser extend this globally, arguing for a planetary, progressive humanism that prioritizes human needs over human wants.

Bain's essay says that humans think about experience, formulate values, and act to achieve them within the limits of nature. These activities imply an ability to envision new purposes and new courses of action to achieve them. The statements of humanist values discussed in the previous section reveal an essential inclination in humanism to advance human society in ways that recognize new knowledge as well. Given that human knowledge is constantly improving, humanism supports change in values justified by new evidence and understanding. That approach in its essence is also at the heart of progressivism.

Democracy and Action

One humanist value deserves specific mention. Hector Hawton argued in *TH* that humanism considers freedom of thought "an essential condition of civilized life." He suggested freedom of thought is only possible in democracy (*TH* 11:6). It is essential to the realization of other humanist values. George R. Geiger wrote in *TH* that "the essence of the democratic idea is to be found in its reliance on the possibilities of human nature, above all in its faith in human intelligence." Not surprisingly, Geiger argued that "[h]umanism and democracy are thus almost interchangeable" (*TH* 8:1). He may overstate this union in his enthusiasm, yet democracy is centrally important to humanism. As Nickels points out, authoritarianism robs many of their potential.

Another humanist value arising from a democratic orientation is action. In 1946, Backus listed it as one of three fundamental characteristics of humanism. Reese starts with broader value statements like those in HMI and derives some humanist principles of public policy. He points to the notion of action as an essential part of humanism. Acting in the democratic realm requires having views on public policy, and Reese's essay covers a number of essential public policy topics of concern to humanists. Especially noteworthy in that regard is his support for the recommendations of the 1948 report by the Commission on Civil Rights.

Lamont offers humanism as a philosophy of action covering the full span of human life. His fifth principle calls for a far-reaching program of social cooperation for peace and democracy. Likewise, Reese shows how humanism has been an early, strong supporter of progressive causes. Julian Huxley called for concerted social action to advance human opportunity and achievement by individuals (*TH* 12:6). Nickels posits that naturalistic humanism calls for action because only human, rather than divine, agency will improve the human condition. Pauling argues for a philosophy of humanism is whose primary aim is striving for the mutual happiness of humankind.

Suffice it to say, then, that humanism has always embodied progressive change, because it recognizes change not only in the universe, but in the course of human evolution, both physical and cultural. The final extension of that recognition is that we humans are natural agents of change in the universe. Humanism calls for humans to strive for, among others, changes that improve the lot of all human beings. Accordingly, humanist philosophy is the proper basis for the progressive political viewpoint.

Notes

1. See Dewey's *Theory of Valuation*. (Chicago: U. of Chicago Press, 1939).
2. Kraft, Julius, "Technics and the Spirit of Our Age," *TH* 1:2, p. 49 et seq. (1941).
3. Kurtz, Paul, "For a National Health Insurance Plan," *TH*, 30:6, p. 5 et seq. (Nov./Dec. 1970).

Science and the Reconstruction of Value

Van Meter Ames
The Humanist, Spring, 1945

That science in its own terms cannot pronounce anything good or bad except as an efficient or inefficient means to an end established on non-scientific ground, is a common contention. The usual implication is that science could become morally decisive only by joining traditional morality and religion in presuming to declare from outside and on high what should be done. Whether such presumption can ever be justified or not, science does not pretend to it or need to. The method of science is not designed to work in a vacuum, but in the stuff of life-situations where moral problems crop out of associated living. It is there that solutions must be found by science, experimenting to see what happens in varying circumstances.

Within the family, it is easy to see what is good and what is not. The objection is that what one member finds good may be harmful to others. How can his good be proved bad to him? Because the others resent it, not only impulsively but reflectively. There is no other reply, though he may not see it. It is the same when the evil is in the despot's notion of good or in the indoctrinated attitudes of an aggressor-nation. It will be said that there is no way to convince a person or minority that it is wrong to hurt others unless appeal can be made to an outside standard. But the person or group regarded by others as in the wrong can also appeal to an external source. If a fascist leader can persuade people to side with him, he will be justified in their eyes. If he cannot win a following he will simply be considered a dangerous fanatic to be locked up or done away with.

The rest of society may condemn the followers of such a man, but social disapproval would disappear if the followers could seize enough power to dominate the world, subjugating and liquidating all opponents. That might happen. Under Hitler it came frightfully close to happening. Over large areas it did happen with horrible thoroughness. Sufficiently strong opposition to fascism

Humanist Philosophy 1928 – 1973

fortunately was aroused in time to wage a successful though terrible war against it. The name of God was invoked on all sides, though least by the magnificent Red Army. But if the United Nations are right only because they have gathered the power to win, then Hitler was right so far as he won, and he might have won altogether. In the kind of world which would have resulted he would have been right, at least for a long time, and that is exactly what made the prospect of his ultimate victory inadmissible: what led the free people of the world to make it inadmissible. Otherwise only his victims, and only to the last gasp, would have condemned his order; just as he to the end could be expected to denounce the democracies and appeal to his intuition, even to God.

Having no stomach for the possibilities spread out by this line of thought, many people have sought an infallible guarantee against their occurrence. What such people hate as unspeakably evil they say must not for a moment be allowed to masquerade as good. Devotees of scientific method can sympathize with that viewpoint, and instead of seeking comfort outside the world in some standard imagined to be superhuman, they advocate the development of intelligent control within the world. There is no guarantee that intelligence, however shared, trained and equipped, can absolutely prevent a revival of Hitlerism. But neither can the vaunted absolutes of otherworldliness be sure to prevent anything. At most they can repeat in solemn tones that what men should hate is hateful, what they ought to love is lovely; which may inspire them to act but cannot keep them from disagreeing about what to do or where to stand.

It is manifestly good to produce more wholesome food and to make it more available, as well as to benefit by the many achievements of science. And when the good life, the moral or religious life, is said to lie beyond the sphere touched by science, most men would prefer to stick with science. This or that is not manifestly good except as people find it so; and it may be said that they will not continue to find it so unless it really is so. Certain goods may be stable at one time and not at another. Even though science can reveal things which are good everywhere at all times, it will be contended that science cannot discover the right to them or the obligation to foster them. But to hold that the good is a matter of discoverable facts and procedures, while the right must remain a mystery, whether established by preternatural agency or not, is an artificial embarrassment. If it can be doubted that men ought to promote what is found to be good, there may be no logical way for science to overcome the doubt.

For common sense it will seem enough to say that men feel entitled to what is good for them, and that there is no reason why they should not have it, if really good, so far as it can be made available and sharable. The right to goods scarcely exists when they are scarce, but as science makes them more abundant it thereby increases the right to them; for the right to them is simply the recognition that, being there, they could be had if not held by greed or antiquated social arrangements. The right to goods cannot seriously be challenged except as the value of life is questioned, since goods first enable men to have life and then to have it more abundantly. It is not the right to goods but the denial of it that would have to be established. And as men share a right they have the obligation to respect it in other persons—claim and recognition of claim being two sides of the same shield.

Those who question whether science can make more than a minor contribution to the structure of rights and obligations, deprecate the goods which science provides, by contrasting them with absolute goods expected of religion. Attention is thus diverted from what science does to what it has not done and perhaps cannot do: get rid of death, the horror of war, and all the limitations of being human. It is overlooked that science can postpone death and reduce many of war's horrors; also that war might have been abolished if what is known had been applied. There is no guarantee that science can get rid of war and make life lovely. But science does not need guarantees. It only needs a chance, which it has not sufficiently had in a world still largely ignorant of science or warned against it, though already girdled by its influence. Perhaps in order to establish peace and good will science would not need for thousands of years the chance traditional religion has had. In extenuation of religion it may be said that it has never really been tried. But when the same is said of science the difference is that with the help of science men have reached a point where they cannot go forward without relying more and more on science; whereas it seems unlikely that religion and moral teaching can continue to exercise much influence except as they become scientific.

The scientific method, to be fully adopted, calls for a freedom of inquiry and cooperation which in its very exercise promotes the common understanding essential to democracy and peace. Even to wage war men have gone a long way toward peace by rationalizing production, rationing and planning everything requisite to the welfare and efficiency of people, not only in one nation as a whole but in a block of nations. It is hardly worthwhile any more to ask whether men are free to choose and plan, since they are planning more and more. The problem of free will has been deflated by science to a purely academic question. If one enjoys that sort of thing it is still possible to ask how men could be free in a situation depriving them of freedom. But for science that situation does not exist except as a stage of social development. Science no longer describes a world in which men are tied by metaphysical restraint. They are seen rather to be hampered by political and economic disabilities, by poor representation, inferior food and housing. The problem for science is not whether men can be free, but how by changing their environment and relationships through means increasingly at hand, to free them from ignorance, illness and fear. The question of freedom becomes that of how men can organize to get and to multiply the benefits offered by science. In much traditional thought morality has been a name for the realm of freedom supposed to float somehow apart from the sphere of science which was that of necessity. With science used as the key to freedom, the scientific and the moral coalesce.

The opponents of science commonly assume that the ends of life, the goods or values, are fixed and independent of the means used to reach them. In such a view the means become morally neutral, and this "idealism" is unfortunately true to life in our society. Idealism has ironically discredited ideals by holding that they are out of the actual situation. The discrepancy between "is" and "ought" is blessed by the double-teaching that men should not forget higher things but that on the other hand "business is business, men are not angels, the flesh is weak," and so on.

Before the development of modern science, economy of scarcity gave some excuse for this attitude. With an insufficiency of substantial goods, services and opportunities, it was convenient to say these were material things and not to be compared with spiritual things of which there could be no dearth. But spiritual things have tended to be monopolized by the same people who had the lion's share of everything else, unless the term spiritual were defined so narrowly as to omit education, art, philosophy, association with cultivated persons, and the necessary leisure therefor. The medieval church did make its spiritual life available to many who individually could not have afforded it; but for most people the presence of otherworldly ideals could not prevent enthusiasm for the improvement through science.

One might say that there is no need to choose between the benefits of science and those of supernatural religion, when both can be had. Countless people have continued to enjoy both, though with increasing difficulty as they learn the incompatibility of the underlying assumptions. What seems more troublesome is to maintain in a scientific age the morality which went with the old religion. Science has so drastically altered the conditions of work and play and all the associations of men, that problems continually arise in employer-labor relations and on the international scene for there is no answer except in vague generalities, in the sacred their books or the pulpits. Little is gained by exhorting men to keep their faith in God. In addition to the need to cooperate with believers in different gods, there is the practical difficulty of interpreting and applying the will of God to current affairs. There seems no prospect of converting all men to the same religion. One might take the short cut of assuming that all the great religions really worship the same God, and still not have the answer to economic and political questions. One may say that aside from the supernatural element in various religions they agree in urging the brotherhood of man, in teaching something like the Golden Rule. A survey would help to ascertain this. But how are conflicting demands to be settled? How is a peace to be established which can and should last?

If traditional morality and religion do not provide all the guidance needed today, there is the possibility that science may succeed where they fail. In favor of science is the growing realization that its procedure is the only one upon which all men can agree. Revelations, myths, mystical intuitions, conflict. As fast as men are able to understand scientific method they agree upon it: most clearly in astronomy, physics, chemistry, electro-dynamics. Here men do not fight to find the answers: they cooperate in study and experiment. The results are never final. They can always be improved, but only by building upon what has been done and extending the same method, not by scrapping it and going back to some pre-scientific practice.

Scarcely anyone doubts that this is the way to proceed in engineering problems. The method is clearly hypothetical and tentative, subject to constant check by experience. Pursuit of that method has produced machines and weapons of marvelous power and efficiency: as means to ends, without a break where means stop and ends begin. What men want to do is suggested and qualified by the available ways of doing it. The purposes of transportation and communication are not merely served but also projected by new facilities. Going round the world in 80 days was a fantasy before the possibility of doing it was at hand. Now the goals men have in mind are governed largely by changes science has wrought in the relationships of peoples who must learn to get along together instead of indulging in mutual ignorance as they once could.

Natural science and its applications, which have been thought to deal primarily with non-human phenomena, introduce cultural change. To understand and direct that change in spite of and on account of prejudice requires a comparable development of social science. Social techniques have been somewhat vitiated by the attempt to model them after obsolescent conceptions of natural science, as if it impartially described laws holding regardless of choice and preference but unamenable to them. But with recognition that physical formulas are hypothetical and tend to take the form of predicting what will happen if certain steps are taken, if certain conditions are set up, the outlook is quite different. Dewey has made clear that science, instead of reporting what would be the case in this or that field apart from human participation, is rather a set of predictions depending for fulfilment upon what men decide and do. Science, instead of merely uncovering unalterable laws, lays out in more or less general fashion plans of action which will lead in one direction or another. Predicted results depend at least upon having an observer at a certain place at a certain time, with specified instruments and readiness to perform requisite operations. Even the precise occurrence of an eclipse can be foretold only upon condition of something being done about it. Elaborate arrangements must be made. All the libraries, laboratories and equipment of science show that it depends upon what men do in interaction with what happens. If men had no desires or drives, did not venture and experiment, science would dry up. Science is addressed not to a world empty of men but to one in which men are actively trying out various courses of action, testing materials and methods for their possibilities, developing new powers.

Although it is admitted that science as pure observation disappeared in the time of Galileo, it may be argued that any interference in nature will produce satisfactory results only if the interference arrives at a natural principle. It will be said that prediction and control are the test of a principle but not the definition of it. Then human purposes must be patterned after scientific knowledge instead of merely using it as their tool. This knowledge is prior to value in a way, yet human aims retain a priority too. Investigation enables men to meet their needs and also modifies them or suggests new ones in accordance with what is found to be the situation. Men would not engage in science if it did not satisfy desires and it continues to be instrumental to them while determining what satisfactions can legitimately be sought. Science is indeed no less useful in showing what wishes it is possible or feasible to fulfil than in fulfilling them.

Science is thus continuous with conduct: the laboratory opens on to the field of action and any human activity may be an extension of research. The supposed divorce between pure and applied science does not hold. Nor is there a gulf between human nature and the rest of nature. As the ideas of all science turn out to be working principles for the direction of human effort, as well as summaries of phenomena untouched by human minds, the difference between natural and social science dwindles. Both consist of hypotheses steadily being tried out. Any that cannot be used or cannot be squared with the body of knowledge, lose their status. It is but another step to consider all ideas, beliefs and standard hypothetical formulations of conduct to be confirmed, rejected, reconstructed as they are used in the world as known. Then even the idea of God and other religious ideas become ways of controlling behavior in view of what is known: ways which may be improved or discarded for more satisfactory ones.

This whole approach is attacked by people who fear that it will discredit everything dear and sacred. The reply is simply that here is the promise of retaining and developing the appreciation of value in the modern world. Unless value can be found in contemporary experience, embedded in what men actually do and think and care about, cynicism is inevitable. Value is not vanishing as long as men act purposefully, think constructively, and care. Only through understanding value in terms of what is sought and cherished is it possible to see how the good things of life can be increasingly selected, secured and enhanced. Then it can be understood how science becomes the guide.

Now that the fruitfulness of regarding ostensibly non-moral and non-religious ideas as instruments is hardly doubted, the hypothesis of considering the beliefs, ideals and standards, of religion and morality as working hypotheses grows more convincing. To test an hypothesis is to act upon it, try it, see how it works, in the relevant situation. The great advantage of doing this in the field of value is the promise of overcoming the conflicts in modern culture among various traditions; and between tradition in general on one hand, science and technology on the other. When what have appeared to be incompatible attitudes can be got together in the same outlook, there will be enormous riddance of tension.

As long as people try to keep their values in rigid timeless categories while their daily work and relationships go forward on a basis progressively scientific, there will be bewilderment. What men actually live by naturally gains their confidence, but when their living basis appears to be at odds with inherited loyalties there is uneasiness, a sense of guilt and loss, or of exaggerated pride and power-lust. Psychiatrists are kept busy, and commanders, dealing with inner and outer conflict. Old ideals become hollow while functioning standards are not clarified and criticized as they could be if avowed and recognized for what they are. The resultant tendency is to condemn modernity wholesale from behind an unyielding position, whether it is sincere or for the sake of intrenched interest; or to take up what is new, whatever it is, just because it does not seem to be dated, or because of selfish calculation. What is wanted is a vantage from which to compare old and new so that a common denominator, bridging the felt cleavage of sacred and profane, hidebound and emancipated, can be found for general welfare.

Here science is well qualified to serve in social and biological as well as physical problems. Beliefs and institutions, like animals and rock formations, when found to have histories, come out of their final differentiated shape as from a shell and creep in reverse motion back to their beginning in a common process of development. By investigating the origins of morality and religion and studying the stages through which they have passed, it is easy to loosen up their apparent stiffness and see them grow. Their tentative and relative character comes out. They fall in with the rest of human experience and become amenable to a kind of interpretation which is applicable to life and the world as a whole.

Enemies of science, put on the defensive by its advance into the territory of morality and religion, maintain that the heart of this value-field is inaccessible to science. But to minimize what the light of science can find is to put whatever is obscure in morality and religion more and more into the dark. The main excuse for sequestering moral and religious sanctions is that if they are dragged out in the open with everything else there can be no criterion of right and wrong. It is claimed that without a hidden standard guaranteed by God above human wisdom, there would be no authoritative morality, and that without outside authority there would be no morality at all. But after Hume it has been hard to strengthen morality by invoking a God beyond experience. Whatever morality there is, a God, like a man, must himself be governed by it to have moral authority. For science effective morality and religion are relative to cultural development; and when science becomes decisive in culture, morality and religion will lose ground except as they become partners with science and learn from it to guide society.

Every notion of a source or frame of morality and religion becomes occult and mystifying except as interpreted in terms of man's own experience of what is good and bad—and such interpretation must be added in any case if men are to have guidance. Experience is limited and fallible, always more or less confused. But men find in science a method of pushing back the limit and reducing the confusion, while keeping frankly within experience. When morality and religion at their best are seen to be scientific and science at the full is found to be moral and religious, the question comes up as to the relation between a science-guided life and the good life envisaged by previous forms of morality and religion, especially as they linger to claim allegiance. Any formulations of the good must, from the standpoint of science, be considered as hypothetical. As the natural scientist has sifted and tested pre-scientific versions of the typical world so the social scientist must study pioneer moral and religious beliefs: not to dismiss them out of hand as antiquated but to find what was or still is usable in them when they are taken as hypotheses by which men have sought to organize and interpret experience.

Science in a Time of Moral Confusion

Erwin W. Fellows
The Humanist, March-April, 1952

It is a commonplace to refer to the present as a time of moral confusion. Not only are conflicting concepts of right and wrong found in different members of the population, but considerable ambivalence and uncertainty seem to exist within individuals where standards of conduct are concerned. Further, if we consider overt behavior rather than verbal expressions of judgment, there is frequent disparity between what people do and what they generally say is "correct" behavior. The Kinsey report provides evidence of one striking instance of such a discrepancy: The sexual behavior of many people simply does not conform to their own expressed ideas of what is "right."

To be sure, there is never complete agreement—in any society or any period of history—on standards of value. Nor do all people live up to the standards they profess. It seems quite likely, however, that the present extent of disagreement is much greater than has usually prevailed. From historical and anthropological evidence, one would expect more conflict about values in a complex, large-scale civilization than in a small, undifferentiated society; more in a time of rapid social change than in one of stability; more in a time of political or military conflict than in a period of peace. At any rate, the testimony of students of behavior seems to be virtually unanimous in characterizing our age as one of moral conflict and uncertainty. This conflict is reflected in juvenile delinquency (the values of the delinquent do not correspond with those of the larger society), in various forms of racketeering and gambling (which are apparently "right" to the substantial number of persons engaged in them, but condemned by much of the rest of the population), in mental illness (much of which has its origins in conflicts between values or between values and behavior, and resulting feelings of guilt or insecurity), in disputes over censorship (a problem not likely to arise where fundamental moral agreement exists), and in many other problem areas of contemporary society.

Humanist Philosophy 1928 – 1973

The existence of such a state of affairs is not to be accounted for in terms of any single explanation. The situation is undoubtedly a result of a complex combination of factors which have been at work for a long period of time. We can mention only a few, but they are among the most important.

In the past, people have usually looked to two major sources for standards of morals and ethics: tradition and religion. (For present purposes, morals and ethics are synonymous: either has to do with problems of what is "good," "right," or "valuable.") Justification for present behavior and guides for future conduct were sought in the actions and expressions of preceding generations, as accumulated in folklore, and in the principles embodied in a set of religious beliefs. The answer to a question of why a way of behaving was right, might be that, "It's always been done that way," or that it is prescribed by religious authority.

In the twentieth century, many people have questioned the accuracy or adequacy of these two sources. Whether this questioning is logically warranted, is not here considered. Justified or not, the dissatisfaction and skepticism are there—not expressed directly in any neat logical statement, perhaps, but evident in divergent standards of behavior and in the psychological uncertainty so often felt where moral judgments of approval or condemnation are concerned.

Some of the reasons for this skepticism of traditional bases of value are not far to seek. Recent generations have seen a rapid growth of the physical and biological sciences. The world view of these sciences has differed from traditional ideas on the universe and man's place in it. The achievements of these sciences (especially in technology and medicine) have been of such great influence that even persons who understand little of the basic nature of scientific inquiry have come to accept something of the world view of science (the theory of biological evolution, for instance) and to doubt older ideas.

More recently, the development of the social sciences has introduced an additional source of doubt. Their evidence has shown that there are many different ways of living, many forms of religion, many varieties of moral belief. Neither the sincerity nor the intelligence of persons following these diverse patterns of living can always be questioned. There seems to be no "natural" way of life, no universal standard of right and wrong.

The work of psychologists has revealed a picture of man much different from the traditional view of him as a rational seeker of his own best interests, or a creature unique in his relationship to the rest of the world. He is seen to be an organism who learns almost all of his ways of behaving from the society of which he is a member. Seldom does he question the desirability or appropriateness of this behavior; seldom, indeed, is he aware of how he has acquired his basic habits and beliefs. These discoveries accentuated the suspicion of values once regarded as obvious and absolute, and contributed to the development of moral uncertainty.

Besides the direct effect of scientific knowledge on human beliefs, science has also operated less directly to bring about a period of moral confusion. It has led to problems of the use of leisure time, the distribution of large quantities of goods and services, the tremendous destructive power of modern weapons. To some extent, these problems have existed for a long time. But only in modern times has it been possible to produce sufficient economic goods with such a small expenditure of human energy that leisure time existed for a large part of the population. The productivity of technology has become so great that, except when much of it is devoted to destructive purposes, distribution of its products presents one of our great social problems. And never in the past have military weapons been so powerful as to threaten civilization in all parts of the world. Previous beliefs have not provided ready solutions to such problems as these, and therefore the beliefs have been examined and questioned.

One additional aspect of the relationship of science to this problem deserves mention. A basic characteristic of scientific inquiry involves willingness to question all assumptions, to view all ideas critically, to regard all authorities skeptically. So far as this attitude exists, it may conflict with attitudes customarily held towards moral issues—attitudes of unquestioning faith, respect for tradition, reverence of authority. We are not suggesting that these attitudes must always be held where moral questions are involved, but only that they have generally been held.

Some of the causes for this period of moral confusion, then, are to be found in the scientific conception of the universe and of man, in social problems which science has been instrumental in producing, and in the critical attitude associated with scientific investigation. If early sources of value are no longer regarded as satisfactory by a significant portion of the population, what then? Some measure of agreement on fundamental values is probably necessary if the members of a society are to cooperate with one another, and cooperation is necessary for survival in a society with a high degree of division of labor. A greater degree of value agreement than presently exists may be necessary if destructive world conflict is to be avoided. This is the reason for the urgency of the problem. Ideological differences (which are primarily differences over what is "good" or "right") aggravate power conflicts and make it difficult to establish any effective international organization. These differences exist not only in the obvious authoritarian-democratic conflict, but also in differences between capitalism and socialism, among major religious systems, and between general "Western" and "Oriental" philosophies of life. Reduction of these ideological differences will surely contribute to a more peaceful world. How may greater agreement be obtained?

There is never a shortage of persons who advise a revival of former religious beliefs or a return to the standards and practices of previous generations. Their advice is generally impractical and ineffective, partly because they fail to recognize the reasons for the weakening of these traditional sources of value. A "return to religion," at least of any strongly authoritarian or supernatural type, is not likely to occur in a society where the basic trends seem to be increasingly secular; nor is a return to the values of an earlier agrarian society to be looked for so long as people respond favorably to technological advances produced by science. If it is unlikely that people will return to these older sources of value, new sources must be looked for. Science itself may contain some such sources. Specifically, some values may be associated with scientific knowledge, scientific method, and the social organization of science. Each of these will be briefly discussed. There are surely other potential sources—in art particularly.

Whether "values," as such, can be "discovered" in the world by the process of scientific inquiry, has been a topic of much philosophical speculation. One can safely say that any value system which is to be accepted in the modern world must take account of scientific discoveries. From scientific inquiry, we have come to realize that man is a biological organism with certain fundamental needs. These needs include those for food, for activity, for sexual expression, for some sort of group membership and approval. Any system of values must recognize these needs and provide for their satisfaction. To deny any of them, or to advocate its constant suppression, is to deny the facts of human existence. Effectiveness in satisfying these needs may serve as a basic criterion of the moral worth of a society. Man's use of speech makes it possible for him to think of things not in his immediate environment, to study the past and plan for the future, to formulate alternatives and choose between them. Recognition of this capacity suggests the falsity of beliefs that human history is determined by forces outside of human behavior. A modern morality must recognize man's potentialities for planning and his responsibility in creating the conditions which surround him. Thus, it is in the nature of man, as a biological, psychological, and social organism, that one of the chief bases for a modern system of morals must be found. Any judgment of value based on assumptions about the nature of man which have been demonstrated to be erroneous must be viewed with suspicion. As an example of an unwarranted assumption which is embodied in some current value systems, we might mention the belief that some races are biologically superior to others. The best available evidence does not support such a belief; therefore any behavior or practice (discrimination, segregation) based on such a belief should be discarded.

Some moral standards, then, may be derived from scientific knowledge of the nature of man and his world. Another source of values is found in scientific method.

Humanist Philosophy 1928 – 1973

By this is meant the way in which a scientist approaches a problem. He endeavors to settle controversy by referring to experience, rather than consulting authority or tradition. He exhibits a willingness to consider all relevant facts, a critical, questioning attitude towards existing beliefs and assumptions, an attempt to eliminate personal bias or prejudice. Incorporation of these attitudes and practices into questions involving moral judgments would have important consequences. It would mean a greater willingness to experiment, to change in the light of new evidence. Indeed, an extension of the scientific approach to questions of values would represent one of the most fundamental changes in human history.

The way in which scientists strive to work together provides an additional potential source of values. As George Simpson has pointed out, in a recent issue of the *Philosophy of Science* journal, the social organization of scientific activity offers clues for the organization of society as a whole. Some of Simpson's specific points are as follows:

FIRST, science is a cooperative and collective undertaking. The body of scientific knowledge is a product of a large number of persons, each of whom recognizes that his own contributions are built on the work of others and will be superseded by the work of others.

SECOND, freedom of expression is essential for scientific advancement. The findings of any scientist must be available to others. True, science has made possible modern urban society, with powerful mass media of communication and bureaucratic organization; and these conditions may operate to restrict freedom. So far as this restriction exists, however, it is also a limitation on science and may lead to the destruction of science. If science is to continue to develop, freedom for the discovery and communication of truth must prevail.

A THIRD trait of the social structure of science is equality: equality of opportunity to achieve truth. Social inequalities of income, status, and educational opportunity violate the morality of science, as Simpson puts it, by making the opportunities for achieving truth unequal.

(This surely suggests a relationship to many points which are currently matters of political controversy.)

FOURTH, science is thoroughly international. Scientific activity is not limited by political or cultural boundaries.

This sketch of the moral character of the social organization of science suggests a number of criteria for a good society. In so far as these characteristics are generalized to the rest of society, a way of life will exist which will be conducive to the further development and application of knowledge. It would be a basically democratic and reasonable way of life.

It should be recognized that this picture of scientific activity is an ideal one. The individual scientist does not always exhibit the behavior implied in these values. Outside his field of specialization, he sometimes shows behavior quite different from that appropriate to science. Science, after all, is usually taught in specialized departments, in such a way that the nature and applicability of its general approach are not realized. No one is likely to suggest that men should always try to be scientific in attitude; science is primarily a way of inquiring, of solving problems, and men are not always engaged in problem-solving. But an extension of this attitude to problems of morality is one of the suggestions made in this essay. A society having the characteristics of the social organization of science, further, would allow for a maximum of individual expression in activities other than problem-solving.

If the outcome of the present moral confusion is to be other than destruction or a retreat to an irrational absolutism, the values inherent in scientific activity and organization, and compatible with scientific knowledge, must receive all possible development.

A Theory of Metamotivation

Abraham H. Maslow
The Humanist, May-June, 1967

It is theorized that self-actualizing individuals, those more matured, more fully-human persons who are already suitably gratified in their basic needs, are now motivated in other higher ways which we will call "metamotivations."

All such people are devoted to some task, call, vocation, beloved work "outside themselves." In the ideal instance, inner requiredness coincides with external requiredness, "I want to" with "I must." This ideal situation generates the feeling of good fortune and good luck. At this level the dichotomizing of work and play is transcended, and "pay" must be defined at a higher level.

Such mission-loving individuals tend to identify with their work and to make it into a defining characteristic of the self.

The tasks to which they are dedicated seem to be interpretable as embodiments or incarnations of intrinsic values, rather than as a means to ends outside the work itself, and rather than as functionally autonomous. The tasks are loved because they embody these values. These intrinsic values overlap greatly with the B-values, and perhaps are identical with them, which means that the self has enlarged to include aspects of the world. Therefore, the distinction between self and not-self (outside, other) has been transcended.

Less evolved persons seem to use their work more often for achieving gratification of lower basic needs, of neurotic needs, as a means to an end, out of habit, or as a response to cultural expectations, although it is probable that there are differences of degree. Perhaps all human beings are metamotivated to a degree.

The full definition of the person or of human nature must include intrinsic values, as part of human nature.

These intrinsic values are instinctoid in nature. They are needed to avoid illness and to achieve fullest humanness or growth. The "illnesses" resulting from deprivation of intrinsic values (metaneeds) we may call metapathologies.

The "highest" values, the spiritual life, the highest aspirations of mankind are proper subjects for scientific study and research because they are in the world of nature.

The metapathologies of the affluent and indulged young come partly from deprivation of intrinsic values, frustrated "idealism," from disillusionment with a society motivated only by lower or animal or material needs. This value-starvation comes from external deprivation and from our inner ambivalence and counter-values.

The hierarchy of basic needs is prepotent to the metaneeds, but the metaneeds are equally potent among themselves. On the average, I cannot detect a generalized-hierarchy of prepotency. However, in any given individual, they may be, and often are, hierarchically arranged according to idiosyncratic talents and constitutional differences. It looks as if any intrinsic or B-value is fully defined by most or all of the other B-values. Perhaps they form a unity of some sort, with each specific B-value being simply the whole seen from another angle.

The value life (spiritual, religious, philosophical, axiological, etc.) is an aspect of human biology and is on the same continuum with the "lower" animal life rather than being in separated, dichotomized or mutually exclusive realms. It is probably species-wide, supracultural, even though the values must be actualized by culture in order to exist. Pleasures and gratifications can be arranged in hierarchy of levels from lower to higher. Hedonistic theories also can be seen as ranging from lower to higher, i.e., metahedonism.

Since the spiritual life is instinctoid, all the techniques of "subjective biology" apply to its education.

B-values, seem to be the same as B-facts. Reality, then, is ultimately fact-values or value-facts.

Not only is man part of nature, and it part of him, but also he must be at least minimumly isomorphic with nature in order to be viable in it. His communion with what transcends him, therefore, need not be defined as non-natural or supernatural. It may be seen as a "biological" experience.

The B-values are not the same as our personal attitudes toward these values, nor our emotional reactions to them.

The B-values induce in us a kind of "requiredness" feeling and also a feeling of unworthiness.

The vocabulary to describe motivations must be hierarchial, especially since metamotivations (growth-motivations) must be characterized differently from basic needs (deficiency-needs).

The B-values call for behavioral expression or "celebration" as well as inducing subjective states.

There are certain educational and therapeutic advantages in differentiating the realm (or level) of being from the realm or level of deficiencies, and in recognizing language differences at these levels.

"Intrinsic conscience" and "intrinsic guilt" are ultimately biologically rooted.

The ultimate religious functions are fulfilled by this theoretical structure.

B-VALUES

I have found it most useful to differentiate between the realm of being (B-realm) and the realm of deficiencies (D-realm)—between the eternal and the practical. Simply as a matter of the strategy and tactics of living well and fully, and of choosing one's life instead of having it determined for us, this is a help.

It is so easy to forget ultimates in the rush and hurry of daily life, especially for young people. So often we are merely responders, simply reacting to stimuli, to rewards and punishments, to emergencies, to pains and fears, to the demands of other people, to superficialities. It takes a specific, conscious, ad hoc effort, to turn one's attention to the intrinsic things and values—seeking actual physical aloneness, exposing oneself to great music, to good people, to natural beauty. It is only after practice that these strategies become easy and automatic so that one can live in the B-realm without wishing or trying.

I have found this vocabulary useful also in teaching people to be more aware of values of being, of a language of being, of the ultimate facts of being, of the life of being, of unitive consciousness, etc. The vocabulary is clumsy and sometimes grates the sensibilities, but it does serve the purpose and has proved to be operationally useful in planning research.

Dr. Abraham Maslow received the Humanist of the Year Award on April 27, 1967. His complete thesis of metamotivation will appear in a book on humanist ethics to be published later this year by Prentice Hall. Selections in the book, which is being edited by Paul Kurtz, will be from the "Humanist Ethics" series in The Humanist. *Excerpts from Dr. Maslow's address will appear in that series in subsequent issues of the magazine. Presented here is Dr. Maslow's resume of his address and his statement explaining the term "B-values."*

The Meaning of Humanism

Corliss Lamont
The Humanist, Summer, 1942

As I write these lines in the spring of 1942, almost the entire civilized world is caught in the seething flames of war and the present agony of humanity approaches an appalling climax. Yet it is surely altogether fitting and worth-while that we human beings living during the course of these inhuman events, but always possessing in spite of everything the priceless faculty of reason, should take thought and attempt to work out a general philosophy of life that can be applied to the unprecedented problems that face mankind at present and as far as we can look into the future. Indeed, precisely *because* we are passing through a period of great storm and stress, we need to think more deeply and more clearly than during less critical days.

If philosophy is worth anything, it should be able to bring men and nations some measure of poise, steadfastness and wisdom in exactly such a tumultuous epoch of world history as this first half of the twentieth century. A people without a conscious and clear-cut philosophy is to be a people weak in morale; it will falter in a serious crisis because it is confused about the basic issues or has no supreme loyalty for which it is willing to make supreme sacrifices. Even a country that renders whole-hearted allegiance to an obviously false and perverted philosophy of life is stronger than a country that renders allegiance to no philosophy at all. And I am convinced that for individuals as well as peoples almost any philosophy is better than none.

If a philosophy of life is to fulfill its proper role, it must be a philosophy of living, a philosophy to live by, a philosophy of action. Philosophy at its best is not simply an interpretation or explanation of things. It is also a dynamic and developing enterprise that aims to change the world in the direction of those ends and values and standards that it sets up as supremely worth-while and desirable. The total way of life, the complete philosophy of existence, most appropriate for this modern age is in my opinion humanism. Here is a philosophy that is not only intellectually sound, but which provides the individual a significant and central purpose that emotionally integrates the various strands of his personality and gives meaning to his earthly career.

Humanism of course has roots going far back into the past and deep into the life of civilizations pre-eminent in their day. As the American historian, Professor Edward P. Cheyney, says, humanism has meant and means many things. "It may be the reasonable balance of life that the early humanists discovered in the Greeks; it may be merely the study of the humanities of polite letters; it may be the freedom from religiosity and the vivid interest in all sides of life of a Queen Elizabeth or a Benjamin Franklin; it may be the responsiveness to all human passions of a Shakespeare or a Goethe; or it may be a philosophy of which man is the center and sanction. It is in this last sense, elusive as it is, that humanism has had perhaps its greatest significance since the sixteenth century."

And it is in this last sense of humanism that we are primarily interested in this article. But this meaning is not necessarily "elusive." In fact, the five principal propositions in the humanist philosophy, as I see it, are both simple and understandable. They are:

First, a belief, based mainly on the sciences of biology, psychology and medicine, that man is an evolutionary product of the nature that is his home and an inseparable unity of body and personality having no possibility of individual immortality.

Second, a metaphysics or world-view that rules out all forms of the supernatural and that regards the universe as a dynamic and constantly changing system of events which exists independently of any mind or consciousness and which follows a regular cause-effect sequence everywhere and at all times.

Third, a conviction that man has the capacity and intelligence successfully to solve his own problems and that he should rely on reason and scientific method to do so.

Fourth, an ethics that holds as its highest aim the this-earthly happiness, freedom and progress, both economic and cultural, of all humanity, regardless of nation or race, religion or occupation, sex or age.

Humanist Philosophy 1928 – 1973

Fifth, a far-reaching social program that stands for the establishment throughout the world of peace and democracy on the foundations of a cooperative economic order, both national and international.

These five points embody humanism in what I believe is acceptable modern form, which can be more explicitly characterized as Naturalistic or Scientific Humanism. Supporting this position in general at the present time are a number of leading figures in various fields of endeavor. These include philosophers such as John Dewey, Edwin A. Burtt, R. W. Sellars, M. C. Otto, and John H. Randall, Jr.; scientists such as Albert Einstein, J. B. S. Haldane and Julian Huxley; authors such as Thomas Mann, H. G. Wells and Lin Yutang; educators such as Robert Morss Lovett, Max Lerner and Harry Elmer Barnes; and clergymen such as John H. Dietrich, Charles Francis Potter and Edwin H. Wilson.

Definitely in the Humanist category, broadly considered, are the followers of Karl Marx, who are to be classified under Marxist or Socialist Humanism and who are to be found in every country on earth. Likewise closely related to the humanist movement are the miscellaneous varieties of contemporary Freethinkers and Rationalists. It is significant to note that J. A. Hobson, in his "Rationalism and Humanism" called upon British rationalists to move on to humanism as "the next step," an affirmative one, following what had been an essentially negative and iconoclastic attack on traditional religious concepts and practices. In any case the precise relationship of all these groups to humanism requires a great deal of careful study.

Of primary importance is the Religious Humanism advocated by a number of Unitarian ministers and other progressive intellectuals in America. It was this group that issued in 1933 the vigorous *Humanist Manifesto*, comprehensively summing up their viewpoint in fifteen brief propositions. This interpretation of humanism is fundamentally the same as the Naturalistic or Scientific Humanism that I have already outlined. But its supporters insist, mistakenly in my opinion, on calling humanism a "religion." In view of the widespread association of religion with the supernatural in some sense, the religious humanists need, far more adequately than they have yet done, to justify their use of the term "religion" for the humanist way of life.

In the field of professional philosophy there are numerous individuals who are in essence humanists, though they may prefer to be known under some other name. I think particularly of the members of the Columbia Philosophy Department which, under the leadership of John Dewey and the late F. J. E. Woodbridge, has developed a strong school of naturalism. Today that Department includes Irwin Edman, Horace Freiss, Ernest Nagel, John H. Randall, Jr., and Herbert W. Schneider – all philosophers of outstanding ability. Professor Dewey, in spite of his having signed the *Humanist Manifesto*, chooses to identify himself as a Humanistic Naturalist. And the Marxists like to use the forbidding phrase *Dialectical Materialism* to describe their philosophy, though they often talk in a general way about the "Humanist" civilization of Soviet Russia and Socialism. Where all those who are in essence humanists, no matter what their terminology, can find common ground in the United States today is in the recently organized American Humanist Association, founded in 1941 with its quarterly journal *The Humanist*.

Humanism is such an old and excellent word that it has been currently adopted by several different groups that have little or no right to use it. Thus even the Fascists have occasionally referred to the "civilization" they claim to be creating as "a new humanism, a rebirth of moral values." Then there is Catholic or Integral Humanism whose leading exponent is the French neo-Thomist Jacques Maritain. In his article "Christian Humanism" in *Fortune* magazine of April, 1942, Professor Maritain talks of this philosophy as "theocentric." This indicates how far removed it is from the type of humanism I am presenting, though there are certain broad ethical aims on which we can agree with Maritain. Of less importance and admittedly on the decline at present is the Academic or Classical Humanism founded in the early nineteen-thirties by two American critics, Professor Irving Babbitt and Dr. Paul Elmer More. This brand of humanism stresses a literary and educational program with reactionary and supernaturalistic tendencies.

Humanist Philosophy 1928 – 1973

Yet another version of humanism is that put forward at the beginning of the century by the late Oxford Don, the brilliant but erratic F. C. S. Schiller. While Professor Schiller was a legitimate humanist in the sense of making man the central object of his interest, he made certain compromises with supernaturalism and concentrated on developing his own British variety of William James' pragmatism. Unfortunately he emphasized precisely those subjective, will-to-believe elements in James' theory of knowledge that are most questionable and then baptized his strange amalgam by the name of humanism. Recalling this inauspicious introduction of humanism as a technical term into contemporary philosophy, we can readily understand why some philosophers are still inclined to shy away from the word.

This discussion ought to have already made clear that the choice of words, in the realm of philosophy as elsewhere, is a most important matter. Philosophers cannot afford to neglect the social and psychological realities of language. "Naturalism" well expresses the world-view in which nature and natural law are everything and enough; but as a word it is somewhat cold and abstract and does not imply in itself any a great concern with human affairs. "Materialism" of course denotes much the same attitude toward the universe; but it has been popularly understood, at least in the English-speaking countries, less as a world-view than as a low-minded ethical philosophy which stresses the merely physical things of life to the neglect of the higher spiritual values.

On the other hand, "Humanism" is a warm, understandable term that on the face of it indicates a paramount interest in man and a corresponding lack of interest in the supernaturalist preoccupations of former times. Out of it flows naturally the implication that the great ethical end is to strive for a better life for all humanity here and now. Admittedly, humanism is ambiguous in the sense that it has been and is interpreted in diverse ways, but that is a qualification which holds true of any good word. And the fact remains in my opinion that this term humanism constitutes the most accurate, the most appealing and the most universal philosophic battle-cry around which men of intelligence and good will can rally in this turbulent age.

In our own country of America it is obvious that the real spirit of the people is becoming more and more humanistic. There is the definite decline of supernatural religion and of church-going; there is the growing secularization of all phases of living and the constant spread of science and invention; and there is the American ideal of democracy, which means equal opportunity for all individuals and groups to share in the material and cultural goods of this life. In other words, while the American people do not as yet clearly realize the direction in which they are moving and while a large proportion of them still render lip-service to outworn religious forms, their every-day pattern of existence and their highest aims implicitly embody the philosophy of humanism.

The humanistic spirit, while finding wider and more conscious formulation than ever before in modern times and in the more developed nations, has been inherent and struggling for expression in the race of man since man first he appeared upon this earth. So humanism sums up not only the current tendencies of mankind to build a more truly human world, but the best in men's aspirations throughout the age-long history of human thought and endeavor.

Scientific Humanism

Read Bain
The Humanist, May-June, 1954

Scientific Humanism relies on science-guided intelligence to attain a better integration of personal and social life. Science replaces revelation and tradition as the source of knowledge and the means of using it. Hence, complete agreement on postulates, values, and programs is alien to scientific Humanism because scientific knowledge is always subject to revision. Scientific Humanism renounces the communion of the saints and fosters the communion of free men in a free world society. It believes love and cooperation are more powerful than hatred and conflict, that science-based intelligence is more powerful than wishful and fearful fantasy, and that man can greatly improve his personal and social life. It is a positive, creative ideology regarding man's place and possibilities in the universe.

A natural-science view of the universe prohibits fixed and final theories of physical, biological, and human nature. One of man's most revolutionary ideas is the discovery that social phenomena are natural phenomena that can be studied by the methods of natural science and can be controlled, within limits, by its findings. This new knowledge is rapidly closing the schizoid hiatus in man's experience which emerged in prehistoric animism, magic, and all forms of supernaturalism.

These considerations, and others, lead scientific Humanists to assert that man is the only known being capable of thinking about thinking, formulating purposes and values, and acting so as to achieve them within the limits imposed by nature—which, of course, includes human nature. These limits are not yet fully known and probably never will be, but the scientific Humanist believes man's fate depends upon his ability to manage his own affairs. He can make some rational and effective choices in this indeterminate, but causal, universe. In the past, he has learned a great deal about manipulating his physical, biological, and cultural environments for his own welfare.

He will learn a great deal more in the near future, if he is spared from cosmic catastrophe.

Scientific Humanism asserts the dignity and the responsibility of man in his endless struggle to master his destiny. It calls upon man to honor himself by honoring and aiding his fellows; to assure all men equal opportunities; to renounce irrational, servile dependence on hypothetical supernatural beings which are the childish fantasy hopes and fears of protohumanity. All the sacred ideas of the scientific Humanist center around the sacredness of human personality and its maximum rational development.

Every human being is unique, both in his potentialities and in his achievements. The scientific Humanist not only recognizes this, he values and cherishes it because change, novelty, uniqueness, are necessary for growth, adaptation, and survival. Because there is relative stability and similarity in some energy-systems, and in his own biosocial structures in particular, order and interdependence can exist. Behavior based on symbolic communication is minded behavior; selves are aspects of other selves; social interaction and interdependence are the necessary and essential qualities of culture. "No man liveth unto himself alone." Psychosocially, we are members one of another. There can be no life and no growth without uniqueness, but there can be no survival, no cumulative order and organization, without relative similarity and stability, without co-operation and mutuality. Hence the Humanist values both unity and diversity, relative though they be. He values the collective behavior of unique individuals who must fuse with other similar individuals, and transact with them, to attain and maintain their own uniqueness.

The scientific Humanist finds himself faced with the age-old dichotomies of love and hate, life and death, co-operation and opposition. Since he recognizes that these are relative, not absolute, terms, he can deal with them rationally. He fosters all forms of acting, thinking, and feeling which to the best of his knowledge and experience promote humane life and make it most abundant, enduring, and satisfying; he opposes all things which prevent the greatest long-run good of the greatest number. Thus he is committed to the this-worldly values of Christianity and the other great world religions, their virtues of love, brotherhood, and mutual aid. He opposes their vices of supernaturalism, miracles, fears of death, contempt for reason and intelligence, condemnation of the flesh, and derogation of man's ability to solve his problems and master his animal impulses and primitive cultural beliefs and practices.

The scientific Humanist is committed to the integration of life for all men through a harmonious balance of scientific, ethical, and esthetic experience—the truth, beauty, and goodness of the philosophers. He proposes to attain this by democratic means; by physical, biological, and social science and its applications; by education in cultural perspective and technique and the development of creative ability in the sciences and the arts; by political organization that gives all men security of person and property.

Such goals require the rational solution of many pressing problems. I will name a few in what, for me, is roughly a hierarchy of evils. They are too interconnected to be overcome in the order named. They must be attacked continuously on all fronts. New evils will surely rise as old ones are destroyed: "New occasions teach new duties. Time makes ancient good uncouth." At present, there is a growing consensus among Humanists and all intelligent men of goodwill that there are great evils that gravely endanger the movement toward an integrated and humane civilization.

This rather grisly list should not lead anyone to think Humanists see nothing but evil and think our culture is wholly bad. On the contrary, we have made great progress toward the good life, especially during the last century. Were this not so there would be little point to attacking the evils which still confront us. We believe that by taking proper thought and action, man can add many cubits to his stature as a humane being. This list of evils, then, is a challenge, a call to intelligent thought and action. Humanists do not minimize the great advances in economics, politics, education, and medicine. We hail them but regard them as something to be surpassed; we are unwilling to place limits on man's further achievements.

The first and greatest evil is war. Its elimination requires an effective world government, the destruction of paranoid nationalism and the myth of absolute sovereignty. Perhaps the United Nations will evolve from its present gaseous nebulosity into an orderly system of government under which war will go the way of cannibalism, human sacrifice to the gods, and chattel slavery.

Second is the undemocratic nature of the economic system. To remedy this, work must be redefined as a privilege and a joy, instead of being considered a necessary evil. To do this, we must have a drastic reduction in the inequality of wealth and income, the abolition of inheritance, and the development of an industrial order in which all men shall have equal opportunity to produce goods and services according to their ability and shall enjoy a healthy and decent standard of living with security and dignity. In any type of economic system, maximum production requires that all men shall have a personal stake in what they do, shall feel that they are working for themselves and the community, not for their bosses or their wages. The businessman must become a professional man intent upon providing the most goods and services of the highest possible quality for the least possible cost of labor and raw materials. A professional businessman's chief motive and greatest reward are the satisfactions that come from a socially useful job well done. Great private wealth is a great evil so long as hundreds of millions lack a healthy and decent mode of life.

Third is the evil of poorer medical and psychiatric care for millions than is necessary with our present scientific knowledge and skill. It is a disgrace that some doctors are more interested in their pay than in their patient. Their Hippocratic Oath has become a hypocritic oath and their fat incomes are wet with human blood. There is too much emphasis on therapy and not enough on prevention. Self-diagnosis and self-medication are promoted by drug-mongers whose profits are enormous—and red. Quackery, druggery, and sculduggery pervade the field of medicine. The press and the air are malodorous with pill peddlers, toothpaste peddlers, and unctuous pitchmen dressed like doctors and dentists.

Humanist Philosophy 1928 – 1973

Fourth are the shortcomings of education. There are still many, many more illiterate than literate people in the world. Even in the United States, close to a quarter above age fifteen can write scarcely more than their names and grocery lists, and read little more than headlines and comics. Teachers are poorly paid and little honored. The ablest persons enter other professions or go into business and advertising. We are confused both about what to teach and how to teach it. Higher education is becoming lower and lower, and general education is becoming more and more concerned with *what* to think rather than with *how* to think. Irresponsible, opinionated "self-expression" has largely replaced rigorous, factual, critical, and creative thinking in the schools. This is inevitable when all controversial matters are systematically barred from the classroom. Where there are no real problems, there is no thinking. Fantasy imagination is encouraged and factual imagination is frowned upon. Rote-learning is prized and sugar-coated in every conceivable way. Busy-work extracurricularity has almost eliminated the idea of school *work* which tends to be regarded as a necessary evil by students and teachers alike.

Education is said to be the bulwark of democracy, but actually it is class-bound, rank with rank and titles, oppressed with fear and insecurity, and opulent with million-dollar buildings filled with two-bit teachers and reluctant, resistant students. It is oriented toward the past rather than toward the present and future. It fosters timid minds obsessed with "getting by" rather than with "getting on." The backward-looking and word-juggling humanities, the fine arts, and the vocationally oriented studies dominate the social sciences and the cultivation of creative intelligence, while infantile extracurricularity dominates everything.

Fifth is the persistence of undemocratic ideals and practices. It has a thousand morbid manifestations. The Great-Man Myth still flourishes in both high and low places and the demagogic leader is still a mystical symbol. Private wealth is an accepted evidence of superior intelligence and the justification for special privileges. Many occupations are derogated even though they are socially indispensable; others are highly honored although they are socially parasitic or seriously detrimental. Sports heroes and movie stars receive more honor and more pay than teachers, ministers, and scientists. Manual labor and nonwhite-collar jobs are held in low esteem. Races, "lower" social classes, some religions, and many types of immigrants are objects of contempt and victims of discrimination. Politics is full of name-calling, overt lies, and covert innuendo. Guilt by association and "trial" by the press and Congressional committees have perverted the ideal of justice and made a mockery of due process of law and other Constitutional safeguards to the liberty of the individual. Mass media of communication are used to corrupt and debase the human mind, to promote special interests, and to stimulate hysterical fear and hate. Men are afraid to disagree; reason and fact are ridiculed and ignored; criticism of the *status quo* is equated with subversion and treason. Over all, the ideology of Mammon spreads its poisonous fumes: "every man has his price"; "what is good for Big Business is good for the country"; "labor leaders should be stood up against the wall and shot."

One could go on with the dreary tale. Most specific evils are related to these interconnected Great Evils. Among them are such things as universal military training and the increasing dominance of military men in government, industry, and education; infringement of freedom of speech; infiltration of schools and governments by those whose first allegiance is to some undemocratic economic, racial, religious, or social class ideology; the debasement of art and recreation for private profit; the graveyard complex; the slum evil; the danger and nuisance of dogs; opposition to sex education, birth control, and rational management of marriage, divorce, and penal treatment; the commercialization of sex, mainly in theatre and advertising; death and maiming on the highways; the increasing intemperate use of alcohol; waste and exploitation of natural resources for private profit; the tragic plight of increasing numbers of the aged; and the corruption of public officials by private businessmen and professional criminals.

Most Humanists and other intelligent men of goodwill unite to attack these evils and many others that could be mentioned. How shall they do it? Shall Humanists organize local groups and action committees, co-operate with other similar organizations, and try to fuse them into a world-wide movement which has been called "the Sixth Religion?" This is a noble and inspiring goal, but I see no great future for it.

If it takes the form of a religion with a creed, or manifesto, or statement of principles, regular meetings in specialized buildings under paid leaders, it is likely to be even less successful than the Unitarians and Ethical Culturists, and much less successful than the Christian Scientists and Mormons. It cannot have much mass appeal because it minimizes ritual, uniformity in belief and action, and denounces all absolutism, supernaturalism, and mysticism. It fosters the free play of intelligence in all fields. It is more like a science seminar than an institutionalized religion.

Scientific Humanism should make its appeal to all men who want to work for a sane, humane, science-oriented civilization and pay little attention to formal organization. There should be many local groups for fellowship and discussion, but they should never become formally structured like the units of a religious denomination. The AHA should remain largely a paper organization whose main function is publishing, speaking, and counseling. It should have a few highly paid speakers and representatives but it should remain more like an educational agency than a church. It should avoid the odor of sanctity and specialize in the intellectual breath of life.

The main reason why scientific Humanism cannot become "the Sixth Religion" is what Max Weber called "the disenchantment of the world" and what sociologists call secularization. Supernaturalism in all its forms is dying out. Science has been slowly destroying it for over three hundred years, with rapid acceleration during the last century. Its final stronghold is in the psychosocial realm. During the last fifty years the social sciences have made great strides toward becoming natural sciences and most of the former psychosocial mysteries have become matters of rapidly developing scientific knowledge.

The Christian myth is taking its proper place among other primitive mythologies. Despite the injunction of Jesus that men should not put new wine into old wineskins, men still do it. They love old forms and thrill to the magic of words long after such forms and words have lost their meaning. Most men can entertain new ideas only by rationalization, which is a sort of intellectual and emotional "face-saving." The wine-skins leak and sometimes blow up in their faces, but this is part of the price we pay for change. This rationalization, symbolization, and esthetic revaluation has gone a long way for most educated Christians. They are often confused and foolish, but they are going our way. Men love a parade, whether it be circus, military, academic, or ecclesiastic. They love pomp and circumstance, bright robes, stained glass, sacred music, and the stately language of liturgy. Most of them always will, and will remain faithful to their churches, after their fashion, even after the old meanings have changed and a new dispensation of grace has come.

The only vital gospel is the social gospel; the only vital values pertain to this world; and man is the only maker of values. There are psychiatrists and social workers on the staffs of many churches. Ministers are trained family counselors and community leaders. Many sermons and lectures in many churches would please most scientific Humanists. When shorn of supernatural verbiage and outworn theology, the teachings of modern Christianity and the other great world religions do not differ much from scientific Humanism. Probably most Christians would agree that most of the evils listed above are evils and would also agree on the general methods of remedying them.

The secularization of religion is largely a result of the growth and dissemination of natural science. It will go on at an accelerating rate whether Humanism flourishes or not. However, the rapid development of scientific Humanism will hasten the process. People who know and apply science tend to become more rational and thus have fewer irrational fears and less need for the crutch of supernaturalism. One of the major functions of scientific Humanism is to be a catalyst for the secularization of all religions.

The secularization of animistic fantasies has not progressed beyond rationalization for most people. They still have to use the old conceptual wineskins, leaky though they be. Though millions of men have killed each other over the meaning of words, they are gradually learning not to quarrel too bitterly over the words if their meanings are clear. It is folly to suffer martyrdom for a semantic quibble.

When ancient words and rituals are given symbolic meanings, we enter the realm of art where rigorous scientific terminology does not apply. When rationalization has served its transitional function, connotative terms are supplanted by more denotative terms, and irrationality gives place to reason. Then more rigorous and accurately communicative discourse becomes possible.

All varieties of supernaturalism are decadent and moribund. In the near future, possibly within a couple of hundred years, animism will be a vital myth only to the extremely ignorant and the mentally deranged. Men will use their science-guided intelligence to solve what problems they can and to adjust themselves to unsolved and unsolvable problems with what grace and dignity they may. Death may be regretted, but it will not be feared or sought unconsciously because of primitive fantasies regarding what may come after death.

Man will stand on his own feet, living a sane and healthy life, employing all his powers in the joyous pursuit of truth, beauty, and goodness while enjoying the pleasures of love, art, recreation, friendly fellowship, and socially useful work. He will create a world society of humane beings worthy of the respect and love of humane and rational men.

Read Bain is professor of sociology at Miami University, Oxford, Ohio, and poetry editor of The Humanist. *He has published over 100 articles in both popular and professional journals.*

The Social Implications of Humanism

Curtis W. Reese
The Humanist, June, 1948

An address delivered at the Annual Meeting of the American Humanist Association, February 1948, by Dr. Curtis W. Reese, vice-president of the AHA. Dr. Reese depicts the social causes which demand the humanist's devotion, especially in the field of race relations, without commitment "even by implication to laissez-faire capitalism or dialectical communism."

The social implications of Humanism depend for each humanist on his understanding of the nature of Humanism. Like all free and liberal movements of the human spirit, Humanism is difficult to define. The varieties and fashions in Humanism are numerous and their lines of demarcation are not sharply drawn. This is as it should be in any non-authoritarian movement.

But in order to be vital at all, a movement must be capable of being at least described so that it can be recognized as distinct from other movements heading in the same general direction. Humanism is capable of such general description.

Let me first state briefly what I take to be the general position of Humanism, and then we can see what appear to be its social implications.

1. STATEMENT OF THE HUMANIST POSITION

The humanist position involves, first, the centering of attention on man as man and for mankind's sake. This implies belief in man's inherent worth and capabilities, and the testing of all things by their contribution to the life of man. There is a sense in which all religions give attention to man, but not man as man. Their major interest has been centered on things cosmic and on man only as he is related or is a reflection of an over-world. The logical conclusion of this attitude found expression in the classic creedal statement: "The chief end of man is to glorify God and to enjoy him forever."

Humanism is interested in man as man, with worth that is inherent and not derived, with value that is in and of his nature and not conferred. Too much emphasis could hardly be placed on this point, A program of fellowship based on the family pattern wherein men are brothers only because they are children of a common Father can hardly stand the strain of sibling rivalry in the complexity of international life.

The humanist position involves, in the second place, an attitude of inquiry toward the mystery that envelops man and his world. I am increasingly convinced that for most people religion is basically a pious attitude toward mystery. And that as mystery disappears religion tends to disappear with it. This is unfortunate, for religious attitudes are most needed in the areas where inquiry has pushed back the veils of mystery and revealed possibilities of controlling and directing events toward desired ends.

The humanist is convinced that as a result of inquiry the areas of knowledge can be expanded without set limits, and he is cautious that no particular fund of knowledge be regarded as final. In this the humanist is in accord with the whole liberal tradition, for the one thing which above all others distinguishes the liberal is the attitude of inquiry. The humanist, like the liberal, may get unsatisfactory replies, he may be baffled by the mystery that envelops us all, but he will never cease to inquire, and he will find little comfort in a peace that passes understanding.

In the third place, the humanist position involves the conviction that the purposes of man can be built into his world with the result that an increasingly satisfactory life can be effected on this planet for all men. In this respect, at least, Humanism is in agreement with existentialism, a cardinal doctrine of which is that man can build his values into his universe.

The humanist feels reasonably sure that in building his world he is not dependent on plans drawn long ago, nor on a pattern kept on some eternal mount, nor on the cyclic swing of the epochs of history, nor on an immutable cosmic will. He is persuaded that by taking thought he can add stature to the measure of man.

It is in the light of these general observations that I inquire into the social obligations of Humanism.

II. SOCIAL IMPLICATIONS OF THE HUMANIST POSITION.

1. The first and in many respects the most important social implication of Humanism is that in any given situation social value| must be available to man as man without discrimination based on racial, national, or other distinguishing origins.

Of all the social implications of Humanism, of liberalism, democracy, of religion, of mature civilization, this is the most neglected. Of all the biases that infest the fevered brain of the fanatic and that corrode the consciences of good people, prejudice based on origins has the least basis in fact. Of all injustices, bias based on origin and related to merit is the worst. Attitude toward race is the acid test to whether one understands the implications of Humanism, of liberalism, of democracy, of religion, and of mature civilization.

Fortunately we do not have to live up in the clouds with this issue. The President's Commission on Civil Rights has given us a documented bill of particulars and a concrete program of recommendations related to the legal structure of the society in which we live.

The Supreme Court has sustained the right of all to equality of educational opportunity, and now faces the issue as to whether "separate" can be "equal." The Supreme Court has denied the right of governmental units to require restrictive areas; and now faces the issue as to whether private persons can by covenants do what governmental units are enjoined from doing. Fair employment practice is a current political issue. The right to vote and to security of life and limb are issues that press for settlement.

These are all issues on which the implications of Humanism are clear and unmistakable. Social values must be available to all men without regard to race. On this issue Humanism must be forthright and clear beyond dispute.

Humanist Philosophy 1928 – 1973

2. A second social implication of Humanism is that all systems of societal arrangements must be measured and judged by their actual contribution to a satisfactory life for man.

Dogmatic adherence to a preconceived and final pattern of socio-economic arrangements is not consistent with the inquiring mind. A faith once for all delivered is as fatal in economics as in religion. This is not to say that one's thinking can be free of presuppositions and unguided by postulates; but it is to say that presuppositions and postures should be consciously held subject to change in the light of widening experience and growing knowledge.

The test of any system is how it works in meeting human needs, and its ability to adjust itself to the changing and shifting demands of a free people. With the increasing complexity of modern life, social inventiveness is of primary importance; and social inventiveness is best fostered in a society free from final commitments of an ideological nature.

Humanism cannot be committed even by implication to laissez-faire capitalism or dialectical communism. The economic implications of Humanism would seem to me to be identifiable with experimental democracy where men are free to mix their economic drinks and to test the results both by the exhilaration of the moment and by the state of the societal head the morning after the night before.

Humanism should be in alliance with all the forces that move realistically in democratic directions, and dead set against the forces of dictatorial totalitarianism.

3. A third social implication of Humanism is that the process of building values into the social order is of major concern to every individual person and is a prime responsibility of everyone.

Social orders are devices invented by man and they will contain only the values that man puts into them. I have said man, but I mean men; man is only a shorthand method of speaking of people—of individual persons. Here again Humanism is at one with democracy with its emphasis on citizen participation. The things that happen all the way from precinct politics to world statesmanship are things initiated and fostered by persons. Informed and active people can make of society what they want it to become. They cannot do it by fiat nor overnight. But I see no reason to set limits, other than those inherent in the natural order, to the extent to which man can control and direct the social order which he creates and sustains.

To fulfill this purpose requires effective action. True, ideas have consequences and may be effective action. But the action of which I am now speaking is action that implements ideas. It is not enough to wish for the fulfillment of good causes. It is not enough to talk about high resolves. The implementation of ideas, wishes, and high resolves by personal, cooperative, and corporate doings is required.

Techniques are as necessary in getting results as are the thought processes that precede their use. And techniques do not operate automatically. They must be manipulated by persons.

Too many people think they have acted when they have merely talked. Participation in the processes of democracy requires the wearing out of shoe leather in the menial tasks of precinct activity.

It should not be forgotten, however, that the clinkers of burnt-out values must be pried loose and cleared away before the fires of new values can be fanned into flame. There is a continuing function for the forces of destruction and revolution if they are guided by intelligence and enlightened by wisdom. Humanism must not make the mistake of traditional liberalism in being too tolerant to attack and too proud to fight. A David with his sling and consummate skill need not fear Goliath in all his armour. We need a fighting Humanism—a Humanism enraged over injustice, a Humanism that carries the battle into the sanctuaries of superstition, and that places the flag of human values above the altars of the unknown gods.

4. A fourth social implication of Humanism is that the social order should sustain and enhance all aspects of man's being. The kind of social order that Humanism envisages is one in which the physical and biological interests of mankind in this world are given a good solid priority over concern about the state of disembodied spirits in a world to come. For some strange reason conventional religion has tended to disparage physical well-being and to

frown upon biological functions. Consequently, religious institutions have not been alert to throw the mantle of their blessings over movements designed to provide a more abundant life in terms of food and shelter and clothing. And expansion of freedom in sex has called down upon itself the curse of the most high. Humanism is concerned over the meeting of physical needs, the understanding of biological urges, the promotion of the health of the human animal, and the enactment and enforcement of laws relating to these matters. It will take seriously such basic studies as the Kinsey Reports, and such practical health plans as the Blue Cross and Blue Shield.

The concern of the humanist will also carry him into crusades for governmental programs of health insurance, of hospital care, of medical research and of planned parenthood; for better working conditions; and for more fresh air and sunshine for more people. Such concern is for the humanist not mere evidence of religion, but is of the very essence of religion.

The emotional, the aesthetic, and the intellectual needs of man imply for the humanist concern for psychiatric services, for art in all of its forms, and for the free play of free minds in discussion and in speculative thought.

Only a relatively small portion of the human race has thus far been able to fulfill physical, emotional, and intellectual needs. Society has not been organized for the greatest good of the greatest number, much less for the greatest good of everyone. Humanism must aim at a social order designed to meet all the needs of the whole man and of all men.

5. What I have said leads with ease to a fifth, and for our present purposes, final social implication of Humanism, viz.: That, since the well-being of all men is the objective of the humanist ideal, we must direct our efforts toward a world order embracing all men.

Being a person who lives close to facts, and who has respect for possibilities, the humanist will not, in his pursuance of a world order, become enmeshed in paper systems which any alert mind can grind out by the ton in the isolation of his study. But he will observe as a fact the increasing interrelatedness of the world in economics, in services, and in cultural interests. He will be fully aware that peace is a condition of world well-being. He will take into account the rivalries of people and nations and be diligent in efforts to resolve conflicts. He will view with sympathetic understanding such world devices as the old League of Nations and the present United Nations, always being aware that the possible must take precedence over the ideal.

But the humanist will be too realistic to pin his hopes for the building of a world community on any process short of a long program of fostering a grass roots democratic and humanistic culture growing out of, and rising above, the conflicting cultures of the world. A long look toward the past and a keen awareness of the present will protect us from programs unrelated to actualities.

Here again we are not faced with unrealistic and visionary choices such as attempting to build a world sovereignty by 1952. The program and the machinery of UNESCO are available and offer the beginnings of intercultural processes that are essential in the building of a world community. We should familiarize ourselves with this program and foster its study and understanding.

The social implications of Humanism are of necessity more general than specific. And yet there is something morally and legally specific about our attitude on race; something currently and politically specific about our attitude toward dictatorial forms of society; something intimately and individually specific about personal responsibility for putting purposes into our world; something vitally and pressingly specific about the meeting of the needs of our whole being; and something atomically and dangerously specific about the issue of a world community.

Humanism is a planetary-centered movement, but it offers no Utopia with the dawn of tomorrow. It believes in the method of intelligence, but it is no blueprint to impose upon the fluctuating scenes of the future. It points a direction, and it has confidence that man has the ability so to plan and act that his hopes and his dreams may play a determining part in the movement of the human race to build here on earth a worthy habitation for the whole man and for all men.

CHAPTER 4
Scientific Method and Scientific Knowledge in Humanist Philosophy

As noted in Chapter 1, essays advocating scientific or naturalistic versions of humanism appeared in *TNH* in its first year of publication in 1928. Nonetheless, the 1933 HMI does not use any form of the word "naturalism." But the 1973 HMII refers to naturalistic humanism as encompassing all five of the types of acknowledged modern humanism, including scientific humanism. This change is a manifestation of other changes in the role of naturalism in humanism.

Chapter 1 sets forth how humanist writers in *TNH* and *TH* adhered to the view that humanist philosophy drew on scientific naturalism, even to the point that some viewed it as the same as humanism. More, however, viewed humanism as a distinct philosophy, with a corresponding epistemology. These latter writers focused not so much on the specifics of naturalism, as on whether and how naturalism informs humanist philosophy. They are the focus of this chapter. Due to a combination of space limitations and brevity of treatment in the available essays, not all aspects of scientific naturalism relevant to, or incorporated into, early modern humanist philosophy are covered.

An important factor in the arguments of writers focusing on naturalism's influence is of course the distinction between epistemological (now methodological) and philosophical (now metaphysical) naturalism, summarized in the essay by Horace J. Nickels in this chapter. Given the intertwining of scientific naturalism and the role of science in humanism, their arguments are considered in the context of humanist views of science and its application in technology.

Epistemology of Scientific Naturalism: The Origin of Technology

Roy Wood Sellars observed that the adoption of the scientific method in a positive religion or philosophy represented a paradigm shift (*TH* 13:2). Epistemology based in science ever since has required theists to prove the existence of their deities and associated values. Accordingly, Sellars linked philosophical naturalism with science (*TNH* 6:6). That feature strongly differentiates scientific naturalism from the so-called "literary humanism" briefly discussed by Harold Titus in his essay in Chapter 1 and Corliss Lamont in his essay in Chapter 3.

R. Lester Mondale argued at the time of HMI that the new generation of humanists was more scientific than the previous, which included Sellars (*TNH* 5:4). The origin of Sellars's linkage was the rise of the new version of naturalism referred to as "scientific naturalism." It corresponded to his acceptance in another essay in *TNH* of the philosophy of physical realism, i.e., "things exist and ... we can know a good deal about them quantitatively and qualitatively" (*TNH* 7:2). As opposed to the earlier pragmatic naturalism, scientific naturalism referred to naturalism with scientific epistemology. Sellars described this type of naturalism as a break from the "reductive naturalisms of the past." This then-new aspect of naturalism is of course now referred to as methodological naturalism.

In advancing a nontheistic religious humanism, HMI states in its sixth affirmation that "Religion must formulate its hopes and plans in the light of the scientific spirit and method." Accordingly, humanism in HMI was indeed methodologically naturalistic.

Nickels' attribution of "radical empiricism" (in the footnote) to methodological naturalism is noteworthy. James subsumed scientific naturalism into his pragmatism using that phrase. Of course, the modifier "radical" raises the question of degree. The phrase implies that others at best used empiricism selectively, such as theistic religionists and earlier natualists. Nickels' statement that scientific naturalism is a religion shows how little he departs from James. Without doubt, Nickels was not the only writer in

Humanist Philosophy 1928 – 1973

TNH and *TH* up to 1973 who associated empiricism with naturalism or humanism and asserted comprehensive empiricism is compatible with religion.1 Of course, other writers have argued against scientistic tendencies in humanist philosophy, as discussed in Chapters 7 and 10.

Nickels also summarizes the methodology of naturalistic epistemology. Similarly, Corliss Lamont defined naturalistic humanism in terms of the methods of reason and science (*TH* 8:2). For the scientific method combines the human faculties of reason and observation to arrive at scientific knowledge. Maurice S. Visscher suggested that scientific knowledge is what distinguishes humans from other species (*TH* 10:1). Nonetheless, Oliver L. Reiser lamented in 1936 that science was not sufficiently incorporated into our democratic processes (*TNH* 9:2).

R. Buckminster Fuller's included essay starts with the premise of scientific knowledge. His observation that anything that is possible is also natural is a central truth arising from methodological naturalism. In other words, all technology has a naturalistic origin. That even religionists accept some level of technology again shows that, strictly speaking, all people are naturalists or, Nickels's term, empiricists. The question is to what degree. Nickels, then, was right to add the modifier, "radical," in that humanism makes no exceptions. In humanism, empiricism and its demand for evidence applies to *everything*. Yet, as noted in Chapter 7, humanist philosophy acknowledges that humans have much to learn.

Fuller advocates scientific epistemology for humanism that is comprehensive, corresponding to the radical empiricism of Nickel's methodological naturalism. While Fuller acknowledges, as did Visscher, that humans are capable of scientific knowledge, he reserves to humans alone not the overall capacity to reason, but the capacity to generalize. In fact, he argues that humanism embraces this ability to the extent that humanists must as far as possible adopt a comprehensive view of the world.

Experimentalism as Seeking New Knowledge and Evidence-Based Decisionmaking

Humanism incorporates the contingency of knowledge that science does. In both science and humanism, knowledge is dependent on the current state of scientific evidence and the conclusions that evidence supports. Scientific naturalism provides the methodology, namely, the scientific method, and identifies the source of knowledge for humanists, nature and its laws. Necessary to sourcing new knowledge is a core dimension of the scientific method in humanism that Dewey called "experimentalism." Horace S. Fries outlines in his essay in this chapter how experimentalism differs from theology. Rather than being handed down from the highest religious authorities, new knowledge in experimentalism is discovered by the active effort of trial and error, by experimentation and observation.

Humanism recognizes the nature of scientific conclusions, including human understanding of nature itself, as human constructs.2 Some authors also discussed the need for moral conduct by scientists to protect the integrity of the pursuit from human failings.3

Fries thus points out that experimentalism as philosophy encourages efforts to create new, better knowledge intentionally. That corresponds to humanism's emphasis on action. Seeking knowledge requires adhering to the principles of the scientific method for ensuring solid evidence as a foundation for conclusions constituting knowledge. Fries argues strongly that application of the scientific method is further a conscious choice that each person must implement at each decision in life. The failure to do so can only result in a failure to move forward on the only reasonable basis for knowledge.

As noted above, HMI hails the scientific spirit. Its twelfth affirmation calls for creative pursuit to encourage achievements that improve human life. The 1973 HMII implores the use of critical intelligence to solve human problems. As noted in Chapter 1, humanism calls for action. Clearly, naturalistic humanism is experimentalist.

Humanist Philosophy 1928 – 1973

Metaphysical Naturalism in General

Metaphysical naturalism is the contemporary name for philosophical naturalism. Whether secular or religious, naturalists all view humans as a part of nature, as, for example, Paul Kurtz's essay in Chapter 1 sets forth. Indeed, renowned naturalist William K. Brooks said that nature is all there is.

Nickels goes on to portray aspects of naturalist philosophy that humanism has adopted. For example, he argues that naturalism accepts the same resources as a theist. The difference is that the naturalist finds the source of those resources in nature, rather than the supernatural. While Nickels does not address humanism, humanism certainly accepts those resources that any theist can prove exist.

At the same time, naturalism takes pains to make sure scientific inquiry is properly done and socially controlled. While humanists find certain criticisms of science rooted in ignorance or supernaturalism to be unjustified,4 they nonetheless consider social regulation of the scientific endeavor to be essential. Sidney Ratner argued strongly in *TH* that every decision by a scientist is a moral and ethical one (*TH* 17:1). Harold A. Larrabee's 1943 essay in Chapter 9 gives a solid accounting of all the pressures on scientists in wartime and peace. Not surprisingly, then, Paul Kurtz elsewhere advocated strong social, i.e., democratic, regulation of what scientists do (*TH* 32:6). He argued that normative ethics of scientific research must govern scientists' choices and methods of experimentation. Of course, when he was writing, the field of philosophy of science was newly in the full throes of wrestling with many questions brought on by much new scientific knowledge. Likewise, Erwin W. Fellows's essay in Chapter 3 sets forth some basic principles for governing scientific activity so that it is in the interest of all. Of course, society has been battling about what regulations to impose to this day. Furthermore, it has been struggling with the question about what moral education should be given to scientists, as discussed in Chapter 9. Similarly, social regulation of technologies that have arisen from new scientific knowledge has been equally contentious, and the contributions of humanist writers in *TH* through 1973 are covered in Chapter 8.

Despite the advent of methodological naturalism, some authors to this day suggest that, like humanism, metaphysical naturalism can nonetheless be a religion. But as the discussion of scientific and religious humanisms in Chapter 2 shows, scientific humanists had already begun to argue that humanism was not a religion shortly after the 1933 publication of HMI. Gradually, more writers began to take that view. It may account for the replacement in HMII of "religious humanism" as the umbrella term for modern humanism with "naturalistic humanism." Arguably, naturalists were slower to move away from the religion model than humanists.

Science, Metaphysical Naturalism, and Human Values

Far more controversial is the source of values in metaphysical naturalism. Generally, it has sought human values from nature. George E. Moore's 1903 claim, the so-called "naturalistic fallacy," that naturalism cannot cite a source for values compelled philosophical naturalists to define the sources of values. However, given the focus of writers in *TNH* and *TH* on humanism, few essays posited notions about naturalism.

Algernon D. Black, in his essay in Chapter 11, as well as a couple other humanists in *TH*,5 argued that a limitation of scientific naturalism is that science does not provide values. Black points out that science can be used to destroy as much as to build. He argues that humanism is necessary to tame science for the welfare of all humans. Similar to Moore, he contends that metaphysical naturalism cannot provide values. Kurtz, in his essay in Chapter 1, designates human values as the contribution of humanism over and above naturalism.

Opposing this view, proponents of metaphysical naturalism have proposed several bases for values. They have raised the issue of whether, if those asserted sources are viable, humanism should or does take values from metaphysical naturalism. In addressing this question, naturalistic values must be the starting point.

Nickels in his essay in this chapter sets forth the idea that naturalism focuses on human experience. That corresponds to the idea that even our understanding of nature itself is a human construct. Unlike Black, he says that values in naturalism arise from situations of solving problems, with an eye toward satisfying changing human needs. A few, but certainly not all, writers in *TNH* and *TH* place the source of *humanist* values in human problem solving, as discussed in Chapter 3.

In contrast, Harold Buschman's included essay argues that the values of evolutionary naturalism, similar to Nickels's position, can inform humanist values. Buschman argues thereby that humanism is not a positivism, which would be the case if the humanist values that are simply declared in humanist value statements are not linked to something more.

Of course, the idea that naturalism might provide a source of values for humanism was only one part of the discussion about the origin of humanist values. Certainly, evolutionary theory is generally accepted scientific knowledge valued by humanism. Whether *humanist values* come out of that theory is treated in Chapter 3.

The Function of Science

Even if it does not provide values generally, humanists have found other value in science. Visscher propounded science as the basis for determining what is good for the human race as a whole over the long term. He did not acknowledge it, but this principle is naturalistic. Nickels similarly holds up the theory of evolution as an example of scientific knowledge that has helped humanity understand its place in the universe. In light of it, humans cannot think of themselves at the center of the universe.

More broadly, Adolf Grunbaum argued in *TH* that the scientific method can help humans "select among the visions" for the future of humanity (*TH* 14:4). Unfortunately, he does not clarify how his proposition works in practice. A bit clearer, Alfred G. Smith's essay in Chapter 5 talks of science as harnessing the forces of nature for improving the lives of humans. The essays on ethical systems and moral codes in Chapter 8 provide a few substantial examples. Certainly, humanists at least have a consensus that the usefulness of scientific knowledge is a humanist value taken from metaphysical naturalism.

Pluralism and Relativism in Science and Humanism

A significant difference between science and most theology is that science is relativistic. Fries lays out this distinction succinctly. Science shares the characteristic of being relativistic with humanist philosophy, as discussed in Chapter 1. Nickels' essay in this chapter observes that the universe itself is pluralistic. Science describes the universe, so it is pluralistic, too. Fries does not point it out, but science is relativistic also because the universe is: scientific knowledge about the universe is contingent, in that it is relative to a specific set of conditions. The pluralistic and relative nature of science results in particular knowledge being valuable relative to a particular human purpose. Therefore, reflecting those aspects of science, naturalistic humanism is pluralistic and relativistic.

Conclusion

After some fundamental principles of naturalism in its early days, naturalistic humanism changed more quickly than naturalism. Especially on the issues of religion versus philosophy, theism versus atheism, and acceptance of relativism, humanism was out in front of naturalism. One can speculate whether humanism thus ended up influencing naturalism. Of course, many of the questions remain the subject of controversy today. At the same time, theist attacks on naturalism up to the present day evidence that it has continuing value, even if humanism has eclipsed it.

HUMANIST PHILOSOPHY 1928 – 1973

Notes

1. See Everett, Millard S., "Authoritarianism Is The Issue," *TH* 14:5, p. 221 et seq. (1954), p. 222.
2. See, e.g., Herrick, C. Judson, "What a Naturalist Means by Nature," *TNH* 6:3, p. 1 et seq. (1934).
3. See, e.g., May, Mark A., "The Unwritten Code of Science," *TH* 3:11, p. 103 et seq. (1943).
4. For a critique of ten such criticisms, see McCarthy, Harold E., "Science and Its Critics," *TH* 12:2, p. 49 et seq. (1952).
5. See Haydon, A.E., "Humanism," *TH* 6:2, p. 53 et seq. (1946); Hawton, Hector, "Humanism: The Third Way," *TH* 11:6, p. 263 et seq. (1951).

The Meaning of Salvation for Scientific Naturalism

Horace J. Nickels
The New Humanist, July-August, 1933

It seems clear that religions are born of the impulse to satisfy the varied, restless cravings of human existence. At least this appears to be the manifest conclusion of a comprehensive, inductive study. Every religion proposes some scheme of fulfilment. Historically, these have been designated as techniques of salvation. Today, we are witnessing the rise of a growing company of men who may be called scientific naturalists. The term characterizes their epistemology, their metaphysics, their theories of value, and their practical procedure. It is the object of this paper[1] to explain what for them corresponds to the salvation techniques of the historic religions. But a preliminary survey of the underlying assumptions is required to insure an accurate appreciation.

Scientific naturalism as a religion rests upon a philosophy of the physical and social sciences. The core of this philosophy is an empiricism which takes its initial point of departure in present experience. It chooses this point of vantage because of its proximity to anything which may be considered knowable. With this as its basic frame of reference, passing on to contiguous and communicable experience, it undertakes to examine the foundations of knowledge and to set up its theory of value.

First of all, it scrutinizes every way to knowledge which has been accredited or suggested—whether it be authority, intuition, reason, or experimental verification. Testing these in the light of present experience, it finds them all defective, but the way of experimental verification seems to yield the least degree of inaccuracy. Authorities of supernatural revelation or of traditional norms are mutually contradictory and their flaws are disclosed by available data. Mystic intuitions serve only to reinforce ideas and attitudes which arise quite irrespective of them; apparently, they never open up new vistas into the unknown. Reason, unchecked, produces phantom worlds, wherein may be woven fine-spun webs of logic which dissolve under laboratory analysis.

The type of experimental verification which scientific naturalism finds trustworthy is that which essays to base itself upon sense perceptions and insists upon their primacy in continuous reference. It employs the check of social consensus to establish and validate the relevancy of these sensory impressions. Then utilizing both induction and deduction to set up its hypotheses, it advances by means of an empirical procedure. This is what is commonly referred to as the "scientific" approach. Experimental verification is the only way to knowledge which contains within itself the means of continuous and cumulative self-correction. A belief, which controverts the most complete array of experimental data on any particular point, becomes unlikely in that respect, and doubt is thrown upon all that it entails. The degree to which it diverges from the criterion of present experience and the consensus of experimental observations marks the degree of its improbability.

Thus equipped with a method for ascertaining relative truths, scientific naturalism proceeds to an examination of values. I have sketched very briefly the ways to knowledge which it finds unreliable and is forced to discard, but the implications of this with respect to values is far-reaching. Historically, values have been previsioned and established on the authority of revelations, cultural traditions, outstanding individuals, institutions, intuitions, or logical deductions. For scientific naturalism, values cannot and should not be exactly previsioned. Only working hypotheses, based upon an analysis of the factors involved in problem situations are possible. Values themselves arise from the resolution of particular problem situations. They have no meaning apart from their relation to specific, concrete actualities.

Scientific naturalists differ somewhat among themselves with respect to their working hypotheses. Some are inclined to regard these as so-called "practical absolutes" or "practical ideals," while others do not wish to invest them with even this degree of authority. The tendency of a rigorously scientific method is to shun vague, generalized goals and to avoid, as far as possible, any fixation of the constructive process by idealized objectives. Some naturalists emphasize the emotional attraction of projected destinations and their integrative function, while others are fearful of the dangers involved. All are agreed, however, that previsioned objectives may emerge only from an analysis of actual problem situations in terms of reasonably possible solutions. They have a relatively temporary validity, serving as experimental projects, and must be altered with changing conditions. This should sterilize them from any qualities of absolutism, perfection, or finality, and from undesirable dictation imposed upon the process by imaginary ends. The ultimate appeal is the maximum satisfaction of human needs, which are themselves in continual flux.

The three factors of major importance for scientific naturalism are its method of knowledge, its theory of value, and its practical procedure. However, there is a perennial interest in synthesizing accumulated evidence into a world view. Such syntheses are necessarily transitory. At any stage, scientific naturalists may sum up their empirical observations and attempt to discern the interrelations of these. But every such metaphysical construction will be altered to a greater or less degree by new discoveries and observations.

I shall try to sketch the outstanding features of a contemporary, naturalistic world view, with particular reference to the philosophy of religion. Scientific naturalists are agreed that all cosmic ultimates are now, and probably always will be, entirely beyond human reach of any sort. It is irrelevant, therefore, to discuss causation; one may only point out relationships. And following the apparent relations as far as it is plausible to do so, the scientific naturalist is left with a pluralistic universe. There have been no metaphysical unifications which do not break down too disastrously at some point or other to warrant a tenable philosophy of religion.

So far as we know, the universe is beginningless and endless. Its constellations evolve and pass away; systems are born and die; worlds are thrown into whirling orbits and as suddenly obliterated by a crash of stars. Astronomical observations reveal our particular world as an unimpressive part of a minor solar system. Far from the ancient view which considered the earth as the pivotal center of the universe, contemporary naturalists are forced to the conclusion that, from the standpoint of the universe at large, it seems to have an infinitesimal significance. Its span of existence is apparently bounded at both ends.

In studying the growth of life forms upon the earth, scientific naturalists agree in accepting the major aspects of the theory of evolution. There are admitted gaps in any evolutionary exposition, and the theory is constantly undergoing radical changes from its earlier, naïve forms, but it does relate in the most plausible manner the scattered evidence of observations and experimentation. By means of this evidence, it is possible to chart a reasonable course of human development. The process is one of increasing complexification, emerging from the level of physical activity and leading through the chemical, biological, and psychical to the plane of social interaction. The human organism seems to be wholly a child of the earth. Though imperfectly adapted to its natural environment, it apparently could not have come into existence nor continue to live outside the narrow strip of atmosphere which circles this planet.

Evolutionary data present a vast array of life efforts that were snuffed out because they were inadequately prepared to carry on. Some have failed through an excess of equipment, others on account of an insufficiency. The evolutionary records evince wastefulness and ruthlessness. They bear witness to the existence of evils which crush the innocent and requite trespassers with punishments out of all proportion to their offenses. Different life forms have had to compete in death struggles for survival, and human beings would not occupy their present status except for a greater flexibility in adapting themselves to a wider, variable range of conditions. Their very existence depends upon the exploitation of other forms of life. Consequently, the scientific naturalist finds the evidence unfavorable to the theory of a beneficent, directing purpose presiding over the complex activity of life processes.

It follows that scientific naturalism can no longer regard the human race as the focal point of universal concern. Traditional views, whether emphasizing the transcendental potentiality or the degradation and helplessness of man, put him and his salvation at the center of cosmic interest. Scientific naturalism is primarily concerned with humanity, but not because it supposes this to be a major cosmic intention. It discovers many factors favorable to human life and many adverse. So, from an inclusive standpoint, the universe appears to be indifferent. As long as environmental conditions maintain a sufficient balance of these factors on the side of its survival, the human race seems assured of its earthly sovereignty. But when a radical change occurs, as scientific deductions lead us to anticipate some millions of years hence, man will apparently reach a limit to his powers of adaptation and the course of human life will end.

Moreover, the net result of empirical evidence—what data we have as well as what we lack—inclines the naturalist against a belief in the existence of separable souls. The mind-body relationship is still a moot question, but in general, scientific naturalists consider it highly improbable that thinking and willing could take place apart from a physical organism. Indeed, do such terms as thinking, willing, and the like have any significance except in describing the behavior of a living organism? For the naturalist, they do not; and he is not likely to be interested in debating the contingency of a past or future state of awareness divorced from personal, reflective consciousness. Furthermore, many naturalists discover what a belief in the immortality of the individual is, after penetrating reflection, undesirable. They feel no delight in the prospect of a really endless personal survival, even with life at the best. And what a colorless existence would be one deprived of the faculties and joys necessarily pertaining to life in the physical world! Consequently, it is the opinion of most naturalists that this idea would not be advanced so persistently except for the age-old inheritance of rationalized, primitive notions.

For scientific naturalism, the debate of free-will vs. determinism seems a battle of words. Apparently, the element of choice is an aspect of the functioning of natural processes which have a relatively long overwhelming weight of authority. The analysis of man laid stress upon the psychological factors of his nature. These are distinguishing characteristics of contemporary naturalism. Its world view is not fitted to a rationalistic pattern, ideal, or preconceived goal. It is impatient with the maze of epistemological and metaphysical speculation which to such a great extent has distracted the energies of men from the solution of maladjustments crying for immediate attention.

Scientific naturalism is assured that men possess within themselves the abilities and have at hand the tools to achieve a highly satisfactory life for all the members of a world society. That contention seems to require special emphasis and clarification, since in this regard the position of naturalistic humanism is commonly misrepresented. The naturalist believes that he has at his command all the resources which are actually available to the theist. It is simply that he cannot give these a theological explanation and function. The objective appears possible of attainment by the utilization of solely natural and social forces. At any rate, scientific naturalism is convinced that, unless this is accomplished by men, it will never be realized.

In the second place, naturalists believe that human nature is malleable. From the viewpoint of contemporary naturalism, there are varying degrees of durability in the patterns of cosmic behavior, but nothing in the world is static. Human life, as an integral part of nature, is subject to change and capable of considerable readjustment. If evils are looked upon as obstacles to be overcome, rather than as outworkings of a divine plan or as essential manifestations of an Absolute, more enthusiastic intelligence can be summoned to the task of eradicating them. Scientific naturalism recognizes that human beings are conditioned by their physical and social environment and that the life of a social group, as well as of the individuals within it, may be significantly altered by the manipulation of the physical influences and social organization.

In the third place, naturalism is persuaded that salvation is and will be primarily a matter of social concern. To be sure, it is achieved both through the development of individual personalities and the reconstruction of the social order. These two objectives are inseparable aspects of a single process. But since it is impossible to develop a large enough number of superior individuals or achieve a high enough degree of development under the traditional social-economic systems, scientific naturalism is placing its dominant emphasis on the reformation of social organization. This is in contrast with the time-honored stress on individual salvation. Character development and the stimulation of personal creativity is thwarted over large areas by the exploitations of anti-social control. Individual development on a wide scale will be negated until changes in the social structure arc effected.

Finally, scientific naturalism conceives of salvation in terms of this-worldly, human, social values. It bids men turn from eschatological expectations and *a priori* ideals, from improbable dreams to possible results, from remote hopes to immediate problem solutions. When energies and skills are directed this way, wishes which seem unlikely to be fulfilled dwindle in importance. Values are realized in present situations and in creative action for this world rather than in anticipation of an imaginary world to come. Life activity becomes the progressive answer to human needs and hungerings whose satisfaction lies within the reach of human powers. Scientific naturalism is convinced that, if these social values are made possible for every member of society, it will insure a satisfying life for all men.

Notes

1. "Scientific naturalism" is the philosophy of "naturalistic humanism." Expressed as a religious way of life, it may be classified as "religious humanism." The writer prefers to use the term "scientific naturalism" in the present instance because it is more precise in definition and because it emphasizes the experimental aspect of this approach. He wishes to stress its radical empiricism.

Commitment to Humanity

R. Buckminster Fuller
The Humanist, May-June, 1970

I often hear myself spoken of as a technologist. I chose various strategies in my life in order to be effective, and those strategies did bring me into technology. A great many people therefore think of me as being so vigorously concerned with technology that I lack humanist considerations. But my commitment has always been to humanity.

The recitation of my various undertakings seems to many people to be numerically impressive. But the list would not be even mildly surprising to one who had lived the particular kind of life that I have. Perhaps it would be useful to reflect upon some of the influences in my life and on some of the basic assumptions that emerged in my thought.

I should point out that I deliberately peeled off in 1927 from the patterns I had found to represent what most members of society felt were the bounds of social considerations, And because I deliberately took a new direction, I had a great deal of time at my disposal. In my life there has never been a moment for which I have been more grateful than that one. While it is true that I started in this new direction it 1927, 1 want to make it clear that even before then I was completely committed to humanity.

The Love and Life of a Child

An important influence in my life was the death of our first child. Born just as World War I was ending, our child first caught the flu, followed by infantile paralysis and spinal meningitis. She survived those things and lived until just before her fourth birthday. You can imagine the intense love we had for this wonderful darling who was physically incapacitated. The illnesses did not affect her brain, but she was unable to run around and gratify the drives and curiosities all new life has. She was forced to gain information through other people's motions and to use their senses.

She demonstrated extraordinary compensations of the Emersonian kind. Her sensitivity to what the people around her were thinking became astounding. Many, many times, as one of us had formulated a thought and were just about to speak, she would utter the words first. Frequently, the thought and the words involved would not really be within her ken. This certainly convinced me that a young life is born with a very great potential.

A Second Child

With the birth of our second child, I found myself doing the first really good thinking, thinking on my own, that I had ever done. I became convinced that the responsibility of this new child had to be very great. It was a fantastic responsibility, a new life coming to us. I said if this new child were to be the kind of child I hoped she would be, she would become very unhappy if, as she grew older, she found I devoted myself to trying to bring advantage to her, then found herself in a world where there was great disadvantage for others. But, on the other hand, she would be extremely happy if she discovered as she grew up that I had committed myself, not merely to solving problems for her, but I had committed myself to the attempt to solve humanity's problems.

By that time I had become convinced that the conditioned reflexes of my fellows, both my contemporaries and people older than myself, were so badly aimed, so miscued with regard to what seemed to me to be some of the verities, that I had no feeling I could ever be of any use to humanity by trying to persuade my fellow man to behave in ways different from the ways they were behaving.

I pondered a great deal on what the individual, operating on his own initiative, might be able to do on behalf of his fellow man. I wondered if there might not be ways in which he could be more effective than massive corporations and massive states. I searched for strategies which might be employed to those ends. I decided there were two questions involved, First, how can an individual function? Second, what would be an individual's highest priority? It seemed quite clear that new life has an extraordinarily high potential, and any way in which I could modify the environment so that new life and all the new potentials might prosper would be worthwhile. I was confident that all life is born genius, and simply gets degeniused very rapidly by circumstances.

Modifying the Environment

It then became very clear to me that I should be concerned with reforming the environment and not with reforming human beings. By environment I mean everything that is in me, not just some things and not just static objects, but the behavior of all nature including, particularly, human beings. I decided to rearrange the scenery; and I became interested in ways in which nature permits the scenery to be rearranged.

I became thoroughly convinced that the phenomenon of entropy, in which all local systems lose energy, meant that every local system in giving off its energy gave it off to the environment and therefore ordered the environment. All local systems are continually generating change and have periodicity. Local systems all have patterns that do not correspond with other systems, and they are unique. While each is regular and orderly as it gives off its energies, these do not necessarily mesh, and they seem to be disorderly with regard to the rest of the system.

The Balance of Nature and Generalized Principles

I began to search for what might balance this, because I became convinced that nature does balance everything. Quite clearly the stars are giving off energies in disorderly rays and that's how we are able to see them and their radiation. I thought it possible that our own world and the work of man aboard our particular planet were gathering energies and that energies are arriving here in the form of cosmic radiation and energy from the sun and being impounded. We find vegetables and algae impounding energy. Biological systems are producing by photosynthesis orderly molecules that are clearly anti-entropic. Thus, a form of order develops. But I thought that by far the most powerful order that we know is the ability of the human mind to sort and discover principles.

There has been considerable confusion over the words "generalized principles." In literature, when a man speaks about a generalization, it means the speaker is covering too much territory too thinly to be persuasive. In science, a generalization is the statement of behavior that has been discovered to be operative and that holds true in every special case without exception. The human mind can detect this principle to be operative and holding true in every special case quite independent of the materials, and seemingly in very different circumstances.

I will give a very simple illustration in terms of the principle of leverage: we can review very quickly how someone first discovered leverage. Nobody told him about it. You go through a woods. You find that due to a storm trees have fallen before you. You want to go in as direct a line as you can, so you find yourself climbing over some of the trees. One of the trees you are climbing over suddenly begins to go down slowly. You feel the sinking and retreat from it, and the tree rises again. You discover that this enormous tree is lying across another tree and for that reason lifts easily. That is the beginning of scientific generalization, because not only could it be any tree but it could have been a steel bar or a column of reinforced concrete. The mathematical principle concerns the distance from the fulcrum and the amount of leverage in respect to the distance the log is lifted.

I find that only human minds seem to have this kind of generalizing capability. The brain is always dealing with specialized cases; it is a system of storing and retrieving special information. What is unique about the mind, it seems to me, is the absolutely weightless capability to survey experiences and discover a generalized principle operative. But having discovered a generalized principle, you find that you cannot design a generalized pattern yourself, even though you understand it. You can only design special cases. The physical side is always going to be the special case, and the metaphysical side is always going to be the generalization— complete, abstract, weightless. This seemed to me a very powerful point.

Humanist Philosophy 1928 – 1973

Education for Specialization

While at Harvard, I learned from my friends and all my reading and studying that at all of the universities in the land there was an increasing trend to specialization. Alfred North Whitehead wrote about the specialization at Harvard and other universities. He pointed out that in Europe a graduate scholar could go on with his work and find the authorities and the right books on various subjects that he would like to study. You simply had to find the right man. But Harvard was the first university to inaugurate completely separate graduate schools. Whitehead said it was because Americans liked the idea of specialists and believed that specialists meant champions and a very powerful team, and this would mean that society would prosper. But Whitehead also pointed out that the graduate school with its completely separate buildings and staff was a very expensive undertaking, and it became very much isolated from the rest of the university activity.

The nuances of specialization multiplied very rapidly. Bright individuals were persuaded to go into the graduate schools by examination and sifting. And these bright ones are now arriving at the graduate schools with a much finer specialization, with all energies going into a linear acceleration in that specific direction. So, like rockets, they get very far out. Maybe it would be like stars, but like stars they would be very remote from one another.

Whitehead also pointed out that these specialists did not find any spontaneous way in which they could communicate about their specialization. So they all talked about baseball. Because they were not able to put together their high potential, and society was expecting some harvesting of the potential, it had to be left to others to integrate their capabilities. So, Whitehead said, having deliberately sifted out the bright ones and making them all specialists who couldn't put their work together, you had to leave it to the dull ones to put things together. I call this Whitehead's Dilemma.

The great corporations tended to specialize. Automobile corporations produced an automobile. They recognized that it could not run across an open field. A roadway is part of an automobile, but is too complex a part of an automobile for them to produce. What they did was to manufacture a very attractive automobile and tantalize society, so that they would want roads. But they left it to the politicians, the dropouts who were not capable of specialization, to build the roads. The politicians saw that the people wanted roadways in order to be able to realize the automobile and enjoy it, and so they simply produced fantastic amounts of roadway in order to be elected. In fact the larger and more comprehensive the undertaking, the more it tends to be left to lower and lower echelons to coordinate matters. This also seems be the case in international affairs, where the most talented don't often operate.

Whitehead pointed out that because Harvard specialized, other private and public schools immediately felt that they had to do it also. So, specialization and the graduate school idea became rampant throughout society.

Training of the Comprehensivist

I was astonished to find exactly the opposite was operative at the Naval Academy. They deliberately sorted their students and they deliberately set about to make comprehensivists of the brightest. And they did this for a very fundamental reason—the Navy had to be concerned with the whole world or nothing, for three-fourths of the earth is water. Up to and including World War I, when I was in the Navy, men were being prepared to operate the most powerful tool in the world, the battleship. It incorporated everything that man had learned in chemistry, physics and mathematics about generalized principles, and every general case wherein you could arrange to carry the greatest hitting power for the greatest distance with the greatest accuracy and the least effort. You could float a fantastic amount of technology you couldn't possibly move around on land.

I saw that the individual being prepared to take command of a battleship and operate it with his own common sense was going to have to operate autonomously—there was not going to be any contact with central authority. He had to know how to handle thousands and thousands of men, keeping them in good health, well-disciplined, and trained;

he had to know how to build, and how to anticipate in a very long way because this was very long-distance thinking. He had to understand what the wishes of his society were; he had to understand what the wishes were of those who were running the world; for the battleship, in its day, was the basis of world power and strategy.

I became fascinated with the fact that at the Naval Academy they were training their men to be *comprehensivists* –to understand the world, to understand technology, etc. The Navy was able to take a ton and throw it and hit a ship over the horizon—and on the first throw. This required a high level of organized capability. I was at the Naval Academy at a very extraordinary moment, during the last days of the organized development of the comprehensivist. They were the extraordinary days in which the mastery of the earth was held by the British Navy, the American Navy then being a second-rate Navy which had not yet achieved parity. After World War I, we learned to scramble messages electronically, and at this point authority was centralized. The Navy started specializing after that, and it began to develop the submarine and the naval aviator, etc. I was among the handful of young men at the Naval Academy at the time when those who were running the world were having to educate young men to eventually take this generalized type of capability. If you were really interested and wanted to listen and find out, you realized you were being taught how to run the world. You were learning to look at things in a big way.

I think I had very powerful thoughts while in the Navy. I thought about the kind of responsibilities that I had, particularly when I was the skipper of smaller ships, and the fact that I was trying to understand technology in larger terms— ballistics, theories of ships, navigation, even large patterns of commerce and industry. I was interested here in the impressive harvesting of science that had gone into the extraordinary naval equipment; and I was one of the young human beings trained to understand that equipment and understand the bigger patterns. Yet I thought that something was missing here. What I recognized as wrong was the assumption that enormous resources and capability must be used destructively. Clearly the assumption goes back to statecraft and to Thomas Malthus.

Until Malthus, all the great empires of man—Genghis Khan, Alexander the Great, Julius Caesar—existed when men thought the earth was infinitely extensive. The empire was civilization and outside of the empire you kept some very dangerous people. Beyond the empire there were only dragons. The British Empire was the first empire of man to arise after man realized that he was living on a sphere.

The sphere was a closed system and not an open system. In an open system such as the Roman Empire there were an infinite number of variables. If you didn't like the way things were going, there were an infinite number of possibilities. With the closed system, however, we have Thomas Malthus, the first man to derive the total vital statistics of the closed system. From these statistics Malthus found that people were reproducing themselves much more rapidly than producing goods to support themselves. They were reproducing themselves at a geometrical rate and only producing goods at an arithmetical rate. Therefore, it was suddenly disclosed that man was designed to be a failure. There would never be enough for him. It was an horrendous kind of fact. Thirty-five years after Malthus we have the scientists, the geologists, and the biologists being taken around this closed system by men whom I call the great outlaws, because they lived outside the law. They wrote the law and theirs was the only law there was, and they made it as they went along. Because they realized that scientists could see things they could not, these great outlaws, who were really masters, took their scientists around the world to see what the resources were that could be developed. That's how Darwin made his trip around the world on *The Beagle*.

Darwin could not have developed the theory of evolution in the Roman Empire because he would have had to include dragons to the nth power. But you cannot have any theories with references to dragons under a closed system.

Humanist Philosophy 1928 – 1973

A Specialized Society

I find our society since World War I has specialized more and more. There has been an enormous amount of specialization, and we find our society assuming today that specialization is logical, desirable, and "natural." You learn that there are no alternatives. It is naturally that way—that is the way it is.

But I find life is born comprehensive—prone to be comprehensive. It seems perfectly clear to me that nature is so competent at designing specialists that if she had wanted man to be a specialist, she would have had him born with a microscope at one eye and a telescope at the other. What I find unique about man is not what he does with respect to any of the other living species—that is, physically with his internal organics—that is even mildly impressive. But where he is utterly unique is the way he employs the mind, and his development of the awareness of the extraordinary generalized principles that are operative in the universe, and his employment of them in special cases.

So man is able to discover, as Bernoulli did, the principle of pressure differentials, for example. What is unique, then, is the discovery of the principles, the employment of them, and the ability to exchange tools.

Man and Toolmaking

I did a case study of my hands. I can do things with my hands. I can cup my hands, but I need my hands for something else besides water. I found I needed water, all right, but when I went after berries I got very far away from water, and I kept getting thirsty. So I invented a vessel, and I can close it and I can carry it. This vessel can handle heats my hands cannot handle; it can handle acids my hands cannot handle; and I can make it a thousand times bigger than my hands—I can make it ten thousand times bigger than my hands. It begins to lose its similarity to hands and people lose the realization that this exists in the universe only by virtue of man. It's part of man.

Man has learned, then, how to externalize his own functions and to leave them behind. So that now you can use my hands, and we can go on from generation to generation of our hands, interchangeable hands. There are no tools that man has developed that are not extensions of the original integral functions, though the functions become, like the special cases in generalization, not too visible. They are always that way.

I don't find anything that has been done by man, that we call mechanics, that isn't part of his internal organism. He was apparently designed with this capability to externalize his internal metabolic regenerating organisms. And he is developing external metabolic regenerating organisms to take care of more and more human beings and extend the capability to all men so that all men can enjoy total resources no matter where they are.

There is something very big going on, and there is something that evolution is confronting man with that he doesn't understand too well. I find very unsympathetic and short-sighted statements being made about technology and thinking-as-mechanics as something very independent of man. It is not so. There are many living species that develop external equipment—for instance, the bird's nest and the spider's web.

All creatures, as with any system including inanimate systems, give off their energies and therefore alter the environment by doing so. Living creatures alter the environment a little more as they give off more energies; they alter it much more than the inanimates. The altered environment requires alteration of the patterning of the living creatures. There is the "epigenetic landscape," the interplay of living creatures altering an environment and of an environment altering the creatures. This goes on and on and it is what we mean by evolution. It is inexorable and irreversible. Many creatures alter the environment in non-discrete ways. Other creatures alter it in discrete and preferred patterns; as, for instance, the bird's nest.

Toolmaking is the externalization in discrete ways aiding the evolutionary process and the regeneration of the species.

Man is not unique as a toolmaker at all, but he is unique in the degree to which this capacity is extended by virtue of his mind and his ability to understand those generalized principles. And he is the only one to really alter those tools, change those tools, and try to get better tools.

The Phenomenon of Technology

I am very eager to have humanists participate with me in my feelings about the phenomenon of technology—a word that is bandied about constantly and often thought of as the cause of our troubles and pain. I do not see technology as something that is foreign to man. I hear the word "natural" and I hear the word "artificial" and I am convinced that those words are words of ignorance.

I am convinced that whatever nature permits is natural, and that which nature does not permit, you cannot do. And if nature has this as a generalized principle, it has in it the option that man can employ to alter the environment to the advantage of his fellow man. There are ways in which you can alter an environment to decrease the freedoms of your fellow man. But you can also go very far in increasing his degrees of freedom and accelerating the rate at which he can comprehend, communicate, and be effective. That is what we are doing.

Craft and Industrial Tools

I have divided all the tools produced by men into two main categories, and they have helped me a great deal in differentiating out factors and problems. I call one craft tools and the other industrial tools. By craft tools I refer to all the tools that can be produced by one man starting nakedly in the wilderness without any information or aid from anybody else. So the stone becomes a tool; the stick becomes a tool. Then man makes a spear and it is even more effective—and he keeps modifying. These things the individual can develop out of his own personal experience, and he is prone to do so out of his own personal experience.

By industrial tools I mean all the tools that cannot be produced by one man. And I discovered a very important thing—that is, that the first industrial tool was the spoken word. So I think the spoken word was the beginning of industrialization, the beginning of the ability to relay one's experience to another man, to the next generation, when man began to compound his advantage. With craft tools, you have a very limited man, limited to where his own feet will take him, limited by his unevenly distributed resources. He's very limited in total experience and in time and capability. The industrial is quite the other way; it represents the integrated information of all men and all time. It's a very extraordinary power.

The Leonardo-type Man

There have been men in our history who have become well-known to us by virtue of their tool-inventing and tool-using capabilities, and their conceptualizing of tasks they could do—tasks they have done on behalf of their fellow men. I will simply call this kind of man the Leonardo-type. He was a very comprehensive toolmaker, tool-conceiver, tool-user and a large problem addresser and solver.

In going back to our earliest known history of man, we find that life was formidably difficult. Man knew so little. He had inbuilt hunger and thirst so that he would be sure to have the drive to get food, so that he would regenerate and reproduce himself. Man had little knowledge about what would support life. He didn't know what berries were poisonous, etc. The people who were relatively the strongest were able to overpower the animals. Men were beset with diseases. There was a great deal of fighting and struggling, and human beings died very young. By and large men could not rationalize the experience that life was meant to be an end in itself. Men, therefore, thought about the afterlife.

In ancient Egypt it was the afterlife of the Pharaoh that absorbed so much energy. We find that Leonardo-types began to emerge. You can see him in Egypt building pyramids for the afterlife of the Pharaoh, his patron. Here the "scaffolding principle" developed; i.e., the tools invented and used in one period were retained for use by later builders. In ancient Rome great effort was made to take care of the afterlives of the nobles, later of the middle class, until finally the idea emerged during the Christian era that toolmaking should be used to take care of the afterlife of everybody.

In time the tool capability increased even more. They might not only take care of everybody, but take care of the living life of the King. This is really where the divine right of kings comes in—the new patronage of the Leonardo-type. This proliferated and in Magna Carta days people said, "We'll take care of the living life of all the nobles, too." Then this was extended to the middle class. This brings us right up to our present century and the point where the proliferation of tools is so great that the thinking man might be able to take care of the living needs of all men. Until our time the artist was making end products for the patron. It is only in our era that the process has changed, and that we produce not only for the patron but for all mankind.

In the middle of the 21st century Henry Ford may be identified as the great Leonardo-type, even though he would be absolutely astonished. He thought of his work as utterly prosaic, but he might then be thought of as having had Leonardo-type conceptualization. And the idea was that from this point on the artist makes tools and the tools make the end product, and this is mass production. That's where we've come to in our age. Since 1900 we've gone from less than one per cent of humanity to more than 40 per cent of humanity enjoying a higher standard of living than was known to any human beings—or dreamt of by any human beings— before the turn of the century. From less than one per cent to more than 40 per cent, and every bit of that has come indirectly as a fallout from technology.

The Building World and Performance Per Pound

I had been learning in the Navy as a comprehensivist what I found my fellow man did not seem to be aware of as a specialist. But I could see very readily as a comprehensivist in contradistinction to the land the world of building.

On the land we find men identifying security with heavier, wider, and higher walls. The psychology of man on the land is: the bigger, the more secure. On the sea, however, I found a completely different story. In building a ship you had to do things in terms of its floatability. And there is basic displacement, and you can only have a ship, whatever size of the ship and whatever that volume is, that's all the weight you can have in your ship and your cargo.

The great secret of the Navy through all the ages was never published. Nothing has been more classified than the information of what your ship did for the same amount of weight, for the same amount of time, same amount of energy, and same amount of muscle: How you could up your advantage. *They were continually doing more with less.* And now in the air, even more with less. And the more with less in the air in the last 60 years has been fantastic.

Now everything at sea was done in terms of performance per pound, or energy, or time. When I went into the building world, I found something that was extraordinary. I've been asked to speak to the architectural societies in almost every country of the world, and, every time I meet with architects, I will always ask: "Will you please tell me what the building we are in weighs? Could you tell me roughly within 100,000 tons? Tell me within a million tons?" I will say this to architects and get no responses. Quite clearly, if you don't know what a building weighs, you have certainly never been thinking about performance-per-pound.

I found, here on the land, man was thinking and operating out of fear and producing greatness and massiveness. The epitome of this was the Maginot Line, and the Maginot Line was suddenly and absolutely finished—whoever had the hardware, that was all. Fortresses have no meaning any more, but society is still thinking fortress, still thinking bigness. Performance-per-pound came from the sea technology and not from the land.

But if we are going to take care of everybody in the world with our extraordinary production capabilities, we are going to have to know something about our performance designs, and we are going to have to do more with less. I find that society not only has no book about this but that there is no chapter, there is no paragraph, there is not a sentence in any book in economics about doing more with less because it's the most highly classified idea that man has ever had.

Humanist Philosophy 1928 – 1973

This began to hit me very hard in my early days and by 1927 I said it could be that this concept of the Navy is a specialized case of a generalized principle of how to solve problems, which, if properly employed, might prove wrong Malthus's negative idea of man multiplying faster than his resources.

I'm perfectly confident that there is an ability to do more with less that makes it possible to do so much with so little, that we could take in everybody with a higher standard than anybody has ever known. There are aspects about technology that I feel are very, very important for humanists to understand. I think the universe has in it, waiting, the capability for man to become a success instead of, as Malthus assumed, a failure. One reason everybody loves babies is that when they are born they are so clearly designed to be successes. And everybody feels that they would like to have that chance at success again before they get all messed up. And we have that chance now. But it is going to be a design revolution, not a political revolution.

It seems perfectly clear to me that all of our society is operating in really great ignorance, and lacking understanding. I make a distinction between two classes of goods: what I call weaponry and livingry. By livingry, I mean that we use this great capability to actually make life a success. Yet we keep saying in great ignorance, we can't afford to do it. We don't care about the things that need to be done and we develop our technology only on the edges of war.

So part of the doing more with less would be to really produce the most extraordinary kind of matter control. I have done this with the geodesic dome, which is really an experiment of how you can do more with less. There are almost 10,000 of these domes in more than 50 countries m the world, many of them delivered by air. They are designed for full Arctic hurricanes and full Arctic snowloads and earthquakes. They have been standard-tested for any of those stresses, and they are good for all of them. And they weigh an average of less than three per cent of the weight per closed cubic foot of any known alternative engineering. They are getting even lighter too. Our whole building world, as we know it, is really dying. Our building world is the house—the shell costs more and more and is getting smaller and smaller, and it gets more expensive—expensive to the point where it is fantastic.

Concluding Remarks

I feel that evolution is intent to try to make man a success. And I find man in very great ignorance and not really understanding what is happening to him. Evolution is apparently intent, and the universe has made it possible for us to increase our performance-per-pound of the design revolution. To make it possible to enjoy the whole earth without interfering with another man or profiting at another's expense.

I'm quite confident now that we are going to have to be really on our own. I would be very worried about the whole thing if it were not for biology and anthropology and the fact that all human tribes and all biological species become extinct through over-specialization. Specialization is inbred at the expense of general adaptability. When you've lost adaptability, then you are extinct. Man was becoming more and more specialized and developing enormous capability to produce energy, with nobody to coordinate him.

We were becoming so specialized that we were about to lose, when suddenly one of our civilization tools, the computer, which is an extension of our brain and can operate faster than our brain, came into being. I'm quite confident that the great antibody to our specialization is the computer. The computer and what we call automation is about to take over the specialization and force man back to his innate comprehensivist role—to be really the humanist.

The Theology that Obstructs Science

Horace S. Fries
The Humanist, Spring, 1944

The terrific power over natural processes which science has released in the past three hundred years — our growing technological controls, our machines and gadgets — have not only made democracy a relevant and enticing political ideal. This power has also made economic plenty for all a real possibility. For the first time in the history of men, famine and poverty are outmoded occurrences. So-called industrial democracy has become a respectable and realistic ideal.

But the age of scientific power has not as yet brought to a close the subsidiary ages of political and economic revolutions. On the contrary, the scientific power we have, now enables us to pursue our wars and revolutions with unimaginable destructive might. Navies of the air, under the sea, and explosive mines under the ground have transformed the idea of political revolution from an ideal of hope into a deadly threat, from an instrument of progress into one of destruction. Leaders on the frontiers of thinking today seem to agree on all hands that to unsnarl the modern Gordian knot of social conflicts, and to secure progress and democracy, we must resort to a different method. However, this general agreement on the need for a new method goes no farther. For we find at once, within this attempt to secure a peaceful and successful method of social control and guidance, a basic conflict between experimental science on the one hand and, on the other, theological rationalism. This conflict is far from academic. "Liberals" who belittle its significance—sometimes because they confuse tolerance with apathy, and intelligent discrimination with dogmatism—would recognize it for what it is should the Church once receive the full support of big business.

In education the appeal to theological rationalism is disarmingly represented by President Robert M. Hutchins. Here is an excerpt from an address he delivered last October on the occasion of the federation of the four theological schools of the University of Chicago:

> In this view, the closer the connection between the theological school and the university the better it will be for the theological school.
> And the better it will be for the university. ... Theology is not merely the queen of the sciences because it induces a certain humility in all the others by reminding them of what they cannot know, and attempting often vainly, to redeem them from the sin of pride. Theology and the theological school are at the apex of the university and its studies because they seek to supply the answers to the ultimate questions about the most fundamental matters with which the university is concerned. ...
> Metaphysics and natural theology deal with these questions, too. But intellectual history reveals nothing so clearly as their inadequacy for the task. The existence and nature of God, the character and destiny of the human soul, and the salvation of man are problems which remain obscure in the light of natural reason. Theology, which adds faith to reason, illuminates them.[1]

In philosophy the appeal to theological rationalism is represented, though by no means exclusively, by neo-thomism. This is, so to speak, the "official" philosophy of the Catholic Church. Just as Tom Paine and the men of the enlightenment fought the good fight against theology and reaction under the banner of "rationalism," so today we must fight the good humanist fight for the method of science against the explicit appeal to thirteenth-century theology and philosophy. For the representatives of this theological-rational approach are quite frank and outspoken in their claim that experimental social science has definite limits, and that any attempt to overstep the bounds is an error.

Not all Catholics accept entirely the "official" philosophy of the Church and some non-Churchmen have a similar philosophy. But until the fundamental issues between these two approaches—experimentalism and theological rationalism—are sharpened and clarified, many liberals both within and outside the Church will line up in some of their activities with social forces which they would reject outright, could they clearly identify them.

If and as social conditions become more confusing and discouraging, the trans-rational and irrational theologies which are beginning to flourish again will become more important competitors with theological rationalism. But the human effect will be practically the same. For the "intellectual" content of both, relative to a technological and scientific age, is purely symbolic. In either case effective social decisions will be made by some human being or group which is accepted as The Authority. Since neither of these approaches affords a basis for the intelligent choice of authorities or for the actual guiding of human decisions, the effective basis will be the confused *status quo* which term, we are informed, is Latin for "the mess we're in." This means that the most powerful existing institution will in effect make the social decisions for these philosophies. That institution is big business. This does not mean, however, that these decisions will be successful even for the institution from which they flow. For "power" which is not the power of knowledge and understanding can wield a big stick to its heart's content. But as fascism demonstrates, it cannot steer the course of human events. Only a growing experimental and ethically concerned knowledge of social institutions and human traits can furnish us with the power which is wisdom.

The first question that may come to a critical mind might run something like this: How can one who assigns the development of science as a cause of the chaos of contemporary times line up on the side of experimentalism against theological rationalism? For is not this a self-contradiction?

The Cartesian Revolution (the revolution, that is, of the coming of science) was a severe jolt to existing social and moral guiding principles. These had been in process of slow formation in the Occident for the preceding fifteen hundred years—from the intermingling of the ancient Hebraic tradition with the Platonic tradition in early Christianity on through the thirteenth century of Thomas Aquinas. According to this great tradition, moral and religious principles are eternal and abiding. In one way or another, for about two thousand years, they have been taken together as constituting the very essence of The Rock of Ages. They were the unchanging substance of The Everlasting Arms. But as the opponents of experimentalism have emphasized, and as its advocates recognize, the method of science is relative. Experimental science discovers no Everlasting Arms. For a logic which takes experimentalism as its norm there can be no absolutes, no unchanging truths. Even change and time themselves are relative and changing matters. The "laws" and principles of science are genuine realities, to be sure, and very important ones. But they are also abstract intellectual tools; they are instruments for securing control of natural processes and for their own continual improvement and refinement. Like concrete tools and instruments their truth and relevance depend upon the difficulties and problems which call for labor. But in this case it is intellectual labor.

This fact of scientific relativity was driven home by the theory of organic evolution. According to it, the mind of man is an instrument of mutual adjustment between the organism and its environment. It is a tool for living life—like seeing, hearing, breathing, and smelling. Not only may the "laws" of nature themselves change or evolve (as a distinguished non-experimentalist, Alfred North Whitehead, claims) but the basic "rational" principles we employ for discovering these laws are themselves subject to change.

To date, for most of us, and certainly for our social order, this scientific, evolutionary relativity has come to spell chaos and confusion. In education it has often meant the want of adequate guidance, the lack of satisfactory aims.

In morality, the confusion is quite as evident. It has become a commonplace, though a false, inference that since moral principles are relative, therefore, whatever I believe to be right for me is really right – for me; though perhaps wrong for my neighboring family or nation. Thus why should anybody be bothered with moral questionings, for isn't everybody the final judge?

Humanist Philosophy 1928 – 1973

I need hardly mention the chaos in religion—its ceaseless splitting into sects. The mutual conflicts and theological battles that came with science and the reformation are familiar facts. During the last three hundred years age-old religious principles have undergone a gradual decadence into empty symbols, without intellectual content and without the power to guide men in a novel technological age. The efforts and failure of modern philosophers (Spinoza, Leibnitz, Kant, Hegel, Spencer, etc.) to supply a new content—these are also familiar facts. The sociology of religion has revealed clearly enough that there is no absolute religion. Theological rationalism, accordingly, rejects sociology. But from this scientific fact we too often mistakenly infer, on our part, that religious questions, like morals, are *merely* personal matters. Thus we commit ourselves in practice to an *unconcern* with the improvement of the tools with which to formulate life's aims and ideals more adequately.

In summary, then, our first answer is this: We have yet to become truly scientific, that is, experimental, in our thinking about moral, religious, and educational problems. The weight of the great Hebraic-Greek tradition of Christianity was too great to enable the modern world to accommodate itself successfully to science within a brief three hundred years.

It is for this reason that we might choose the birthday of John Dewey as the symbol of a new age—which we may all hope and strive for, even though none of us may live to see it flourish.2 For he is distinguished by the devotion and success of his efforts to clarify the meanings of experimentalism as applied outside the laboratory in the world of practical political, economic, and educational activities. Not only has evolution yet to catch up with some of his ideas, but so has every rational creature in the evolutionary process — including Mr. Dewey himself. I am convinced that once we are clear on some of the basic aspects of the experimental approach, a new hope and a new ideal will take hold of us and move us to feats as revolutionary, as daring, and as noble as those which characterized many of the creative agents of the Age of Reason and the Romantic Movement. And judging from the success of the scientific method within *those fields in which it has been applied*, we may legitimately hold to even a greater faith than theirs in the ultimate success of our efforts.

Interestingly enough the confusion of prescientific and scientific ways of thinking even pervades our traditional ideas of science. It helps to perpetuate the costly and groundless assumption that science cannot be employed as a method of ethical inquiry and practice. But consideration of this confusion leads to the second answer to the question—why experimentalism?

It is not the scientific *method* as the way of experimental thinking which is the cause of our destructive misuse of the power which science affords us. It is rather our failure to be experimental in our use of scientific power in our daily lives and in the organization of our social institutions. The real scapegoat of our contemporary ills is the fact that we have applied science *non-experimentally*. As experimental humanism has emphasized, we are still looking backward over our shoulder to the thirteenth century, and earlier, for guiding principles instead of trying to induce new principles by an experimental and ethical approach to our own current problems.

The enemies of science charge that this appeal to experimentalism involves a rejection of history. This charge is false. For the only guiding principles we have to work with are those which history affords us. But we must choose one way or another among incompatible historical principles. Furthermore, we must choose between taking *certain* historical principles as final authorities, on the one hand, and, on the other, the use of historical materials in an attempt to formulate *new* principles and institutions experimentally on the authority of the *method* of science.

This choice is now being made. We are entering a radically new period of human history—of that there can be little doubt. This new period may flower the marriage of human aspiration with the method of science. But it may be a new dark age; a darkness not "velvet and cool," but crude and rough, made powerful and mighty with all the powers that science has released.

This choice is now being made, and all of us are helping to make it. It is being made in local, community and personal decisions even more, perhaps, than in Washington, Moscow, and London; even more, I believe, than in our planetary battle fronts, important as these are. It is being made in decisions about our local schools and state universities; about the selection and salaries of our teachers, about what they will be encouraged to say or discouraged and even prohibited from discussing with their pupils; about the recently renewed and somewhat successful efforts to inject religion into the public schools of this country and to bring the Church and state into interdependent union again. The choice is being made in our everyday decisions about our local libraries: what books to order, how to encourage the purchase and use of liberating materials, how to prevent certain prohibitions that operate here as in the schools, what magazines to subscribe for, how to encourage the intelligent use of our libraries by our children and community.

This list of current practical applications of the basic issue of our time could be considerably extended—to fields of art, labor, management, politics, and even the rationing of food and fuel. I shall call attention in conclusion to only one other application which is as pervasive, serious, and as difficult in our country as any of these I have mentioned. This is the problem of race prejudice and race discrimination. It has been brought to almost every door by the war. And it, like the others, is being decided by us every time we run across a case of race discrimination or an attitude of prejudice.

Our attempts to solve even this problem are helping to decide the underlying issue between what I have called experimentalism and theological rationalism. For as we bump into cases of this kind we can express one of three attitudes: We can join the quiet chorus (not so quiet recently in certain vicinities) of voices approving our own race and disapproving the others. We can join the louder but much smaller chorus which hurls moral invectives against the persecuting race. Or in the third place, we can try as calmly as possible to look at each case of conflict as it arises in an effort imaginatively and experimentally to resolve the conflict in a way which will bring greater enlightenment and understanding to those involved on both sides.

In so far as we choose the last method and try to generalize it in our practice to all cases of human conflict, social, political, economic, and intellectual, we are practicing and living the philosophy of the new age, the age of the marriage of science and human aspiration, which we all hope lies just before us.

Notes

1. *The Maroon*, October 29, 1943.
2. Cf. Otto, M.C., "John Dewey, Philosopher of a New Age," *The Social Frontier*, May, June, 1937. Note the interesting coincidence between the date of Dewey's birth and the publication of "The Origin of the Species."

Humanism and Positivism

Harold Buschman
The New Humanist, March, 1929

The critics of Humanism are fond of pointing out that Humanism, i.e., Neo-Humanism is a reappearance of positivism. The recent contribution of the Rev. Edwin Wilson in the January number of the New Humanist was a rebuttal of this criticism, or if not a rebuttal, at least an effort at clarification by pointing out four distinct differences between Humanism and Positivism. Humanism is a product of the twentieth century whereas the Positivism of Comte was a nineteenth century philosophy. Humanism as a twentieth century religious movement is quite different as Mr. Wilson points out, from Comte's Positivism. Mr. Wilson does not, however, silence the critics of Humanism.

There are two ways in which the critics of Humanism can attack Mr. Wilson. First they can show that the differences which Mr. Wilson suggested are merely the accidents of time and that over against opposing religious movements, Humanism today stands just as Positivism did in its days, that is, it occupies relatively the same position. A second and more cogent argument is that if Humanism is compared historically with Comte's philosophy the differences which Mr. Wilson advances are indeed evident, but if Humanism as a movement is compared with Positivism as a movement these differences become not less real but certainly less fundamental. As a movement Positivism, as Mr. Wilson well knows, despite his lack of mention of it and the comparatively lengthy treatment of the personal background of Comte's philosophy, was not altogether identical with the system of Comte. And so, when critics of Humanism compare Humanism with Positivism they do so in many cases without having read Comte's biography, much less his works. They do so on the basis which the philosophers have directly or indirectly taught them. From the philosophers they learn that the essence of Positivism is its denial of the right of existence of any metaphysics. The real question for Humanists to answer is: Is Humanism at one with Positivism in denying the right of existence of metaphysics?

Having answered that question the distinctions made by Mr. Wilson become important. If the answer confirms the suspicions of many that Humanism does make such a denial then the man with a metaphysical bent can justly classify Humanism and Positivism together and attack or partially support both from the same premise. If the right of existence is not denied to metaphysics then the question arises: what are the criteria of Humanism, and do these criteria necessarily link it up with a definite metaphysics?

We do in fact see Humanism allying itself with evolutionary Naturalism, not with the system of any one man, to be sure, any more than Positivism identified itself solely with Comte. Is this alliance with Naturalism implicit or explicit? Is Humanism positivistic or metaphysically naturalistic. If Humanism crystalizes sufficiently to become naturalistic, the critics can shift their attack and will undoubtedly stop equating humanism and Positivism.

Humanism, if I may venture a positive statement, is not Positivism, not only in the sense that Mr. Wilson has suggested but also in a philosophical sense. It cannot become dogmatic in its denial of the right of existence of metaphysics. It may neglect it, though this attitude will be challenged. It can, nay must insist, in any case, that any metaphysics shall be critically grounded, and most stringently so! Humanism will have to guard itself not only against being identified with Comteism Positivism but also with epistemological Positivism. Only in that wise can it successfully meet especially on the popular level the many pseudo-philosophical, pseudo-theological works that for the most part obscure the problems confronting earnest minded people by combining Humanism and Positivism, or Humanism and Christianity with obvious apologetic intent.

If Humanism can keep the lamp of criticism burning it will be doing a fundamental and most important work. To do so, however, Humanism itself must be in all its aspects thoroughly self critical. The problem then arises: Can Humanism as a critical movement maintain itself and still retain any prophetic vigor? The answer would depend upon what one means by prophetic, what one hopes to do. If the Utopian attitude stands firm in the background and replaces sound metaphysical speculation Humanism is doomed to the same failure that overtook the Utopian aspects of religious Positivism. If Humanism contents itself with being genuinely critical, which also means sanely speculative, it cannot be dislodged. In philosophy not Comte but Kant is the ruling spirit today, and there seems but little danger of his being replaced. The lines that lead out from Kant are many in number. Some of these lines have deserted the genuinely critical attitude but the center holds firm.

The great experiment of the nineteenth century and the early twentieth century was the search for a religious attitude which was not dogmatic. The goal of that practical experiment has been virtually achieved. The experiment, long since begun but just emerging into full view in our days, is the building of a life attitude which is at once genuinely critical and genuinely religious. If Humanism furthers this experiment it may or may not maintain itself either as a fellowship or a movement, but in any case its work will then never have to be undone.

CHAPTER 5

Humanism Explores the Unknown and Defines the Uncertain

Fear and Loathing (Not) in Mid-Century Humanist Philosophy

Exploration of the Unknown, Not Fear of It

Essays in the last chapter described how humanism's scientific orientation encourages the seeking of knowledge about some aspect of human existence. In that light, the "unknown" is simply something not yet understood. Nonetheless, despite rejecting supernaturalism, humanism of course acknowledges the reactions that humans often naturally have to the unknown. People with these reactions have used terms such as "mystery" and "mystical" to label the unknown element of the experience that triggered a particular reaction.

Humanist writers in *TH* up to 1973 have discussed these reactions in two different ways. Kenneth L. Patton in Chapter 7 discusses what he calls "natural mystics." But clearly these natural mystics are not like other mystics, in that they accept that there is a bodily element to their reactions to the unknown. Rupert Holloway argued in *TNH* already in 1933 that this bodily element invokes emotion (*TNH* 6:3). By inference, Patton's feeling of emotion, such as awe, is the bodily part of the natural mystic's experience of the unknown. Accordingly, Patton's version is examined in the context of humanism's understanding of emotion and spirituality in Chapter 7.

In contrast, Gerald Barnes argues in this chapter that mysticism is the mythologization of human experiences that lack a scientific explanation. He focuses in part on "mystics" who rely on secular dogma to explain some part of reality. He describes how these dogmas may be ideological, nationalist, and/or pseudoscientific. He argues that these dogmas, like religions, arise from the unknowns and the psychological need for faith in a "larger life." He suggests that instead of mysticism, humanists should view the unknowns as mysteries. As Barnes alludes, his approach aligns with agnosticism, in that where the lack of evidence suggests the nonexistence of the mysterious, it does not prove its nonexistence. It simply accepts the unknown as unknown. Accordingly, some humanists have extended Barnes's analysis of mysticism to a visceral rejection of alleged paranormal experiences.1 Those views presaged the organized effort in the secular movement to actively debunk supernatural explanations for the unknown.

The edgier part of mystery verges on the frightful and the terrifying. Karel Cuypers discussed in *TH* ways in which theists promulgated fear of unknowns to gain adherents (*TH* 22:5). He noted that humanism rejects terrifying accounts of the unknown along with the more benign mystical one. Humanism views both the terrifying and the mystical accounts as harmful to proper understanding of reality. They cloud perception and undermine the certainty that comes from knowledge. When fully exploited, they hinder the pursuit of scientific explanation for the unknown.

Isolating Uncertainty to Define It

Uncertainty is intrinsic to human experience of reality. By its search for new knowledge, science, a human construct, undertakes the task of explaining uncertainty. The contingent certainty of knowledge gained from scientific evidence that humanist philosophy incorporates lasts until new evidence compels a new understanding.

Accepting that reality, humanism equally confronts the uncertainty that technological advances can introduce to human interaction. After all, humanism is experimentalist, in that it advocates pursuit of new scientific evidence and the technology that it can bring.

New technologies arising from scientific advances can compel the development of new human values in the face of uncertainty that the technologies create. In this chapter, Linus Pauling makes poignant the necessity for societal change due to the development of nuclear weapons technology. Van Meter Ames's essay included in Chapter 3 addresses the assertion that another source of uncertainty in humanism is the fact that science does not put forth value propositions. He acknowledges that science cannot tell us good from bad. But as discussed in that chapter, science can provide ways of assessing different value choices. Those methods help reduce uncertainty and confusion, but do not generate or rank values. Thus, the need for new values arising from new technology is not within the realm of incomplete *knowledge* about reality giving rise to uncertainty.

A philosophy based on science, such as humanism, relies on the best available scientific evidence. But our knowledge is incomplete. Of course, incomplete knowledge leaves openings for theists to fill with deities. The first half of Alfred G. Smith's essay in this chapter discusses the old example that theists have no other explanation than deities for the vagaries of the universe. Philipp Frank wrote in *TH* about how theists, seeking certainty, try to reconcile theistic beliefs with scientific knowledge. He methodically deconstructed various religionist arguments on how the theory of relativity and quantum physics are compatible with the existence of deities (*TH* 59:1). Appropriately, Alfred E. Kuenzli noted that psychologists had begun to scientifically determine the effects of uncertainty upon human development when deities are removed from the equation (*TH* 20:3).

Humanists have their own concerns about science, which bear on the reliability of its answers to uncertainty. Rudolf Dreikurs (*TH* 26:1) noted that interpretations of scientific evidence can easily bear the political and social bias of the analyst. To counter bias, interpretation of scientific evidence requires strict adherence to the principles of logic, in order for true knowledge to result. Yet Dreikurs pointed out that even the principles of logic have to be modified to allow for more than two (usually opposite) values. In any event, humanism's unwavering comprehensive application of the best available logic is another place where humanism breaks with theology.

More generally, Dreikurs warned against misuse of the scientific method as dogma. He argued against the incessant demand of certainty from science. He noted that statistics, in particular, are commonly improperly circumscribed, misinterpreted, or misapplied. Due to the complexity of human interactions, the social sciences are especially prone to those problems. He emphasized the need for careful attention to the observers in social science studies in designing studies that will meet the requirement of verification through reproducibility.

The focus on statistics raises another aspect of humanism's approach to uncertainty. As Ted Brameld's 1930 essay in this chapter incisively perceives, given that much of scientific knowledge is not absolutely conclusive, it is probabilistic. Accordingly, Maurice S. Visscher noted that scientists use degrees of probability to differentiate certainties from uncertainties (*TH* 10:1). They ascribe scientifically estimated percentages of possible outcomes to known causes, with the rest left to indeterminate probability due to other known causes or uncertain causes. In addition, Dreikurs clarified that probabilities of these sorts pertain to aggregates of interactions of matter and energy, but not to attempts to establish cause and effect at the atomic level. Kuenzli discussed probability in terms of the differing approaches to uncertainty embodied in religion and humanism.

Brameld notes further that the humanist response is to always seek new evidence, whether it confirms or disproves existing conclusions. Humanism embraces probabilism because it helps achieve a more nuanced understanding. By clearly separating the certain from the uncertain, it isolates the extent of uncertainty in a particular conclusion. He observes that as complexity increases, so does, generally, uncertainty. As Dreikurs put it, truth is statistical.

Brameld criticizes probabilism in humanism for not capturing the quality of reality and human experience. He was writing in 1930, and scientists have since learned more about qualitative aspects of human nature and experience. But despite initial advances, such as in quantum chromodynamics, vast areas of the qualitative nature even of physical reality remain for future generations to explore and explain.

Millard S. Everett argued that humanism provides individuals with a framework for understanding the nature of reality (*TH* 62:4). It embraces the uncertain and the probabilistic nature of human existence. Everett lauded the value of education in comprehending probabilities and in their advantageous use. That framework gives individuals the best possible working knowledge of how to weigh, and be comfortable with, the risks of daily life while living in accordance with their values.

Smith goes a step further. He shows how humanism accepts chance and luck by embracing the probabilities. Humanism "harness[es]" them to work to advance human wellbeing. In effect, he points to the influence that human action can have on which outcomes are possible and on the probability of particular possible outcomes. Achieving that influence on behalf of humanist values is one reason humanism values action, as discussed in Chapter 3.

Notes

1. See, e.g., Muller, Herman J., "Modernized Magic: A Protest," TH 20:4, p. 227 et seq. (1960).

Mysticism or Mystery

Gerald Barnes
The Humanist March-April, 1962

This world is a mystery compounded of mysteries. The universe embracing universes, the stars and planets, the behavior of the atom, gravity, electricity, protoplasm, heredity, personality, life, death all contain miracles beyond our grasp. Our prehistoric ancestors struggled with an inscrutable world. So do we, and so, if we survive, will our distant offspring. There will always be unsolvable riddles around us, among us, within us. Such are the facts of life.

How do people react to this innate mystery of existence?

Some art frightened or angry and try to intimidate or appease the unknown forces. Others are filled with delight and wonder at the privilege of beholding and participating in such marvels. Still others are consumed with curiosity and a thirst for understanding. Most of us, sooner or later, experience all of these feelings; but there are two contrasting ways of dealing with mystery that concern us here.

The first is the way of the authoritarian mystic.*

He is not content to live on friendly terms with mystery, to explain it little by little through experience and patient experiment. Uncertainty about man's origin, significance and final fate he finds intolerable. So he constructs a theory in which the facts, as he sees them, might logically be related. So far, so good. His behavior is intelligent, even scientific. Rational man has a deep urge to structure his experience. But usually the mystic goes on to build this theory nearer and nearer to his wishes—which may be naïve—paying less and less attention to any evidence that might modify or disprove it. More and more it becomes a "self-sealing" system, setting forth and explaining The Truth. Eventually he may become the worshipper of his own creation and the harsh critic of those who do not accept it. As an individual, this kind of mystic is comparatively harmless, but when he and his disciples solidify their creed into an aggressive institution, the personal and social disadvantages become obvious.

It will be objected that "authoritarian mystic" is a contradiction in terms; that the mystic abandons dogma to search for a deeper, more genuine religious experience. The latter part of the statement is true. He does repudiate the conventional dogma but, typically, he proceeds to structure a new dogma of his own and to insist that this is The Truth. Christian mystics rejected pagan dogma; Protestant mystics rejected Catholic dogma; but most of them settled back into some form of authoritarianism. There are important exceptions which we will consider later, but a realistic study of the behavior of mystics will, I believe, show most of those of the West to have been authoritarian.

At first the mystic's theology is likely to be over-logical, over-intellectualized, as when Calvin concluded that unbaptized infants must burn in Hell. But almost inevitably the emphasis swings from reason to faith. "It is the heart not the reason that feels God" says Pascal; and Chesterton, after arguing for Roman Catholicism by a series of persuasive appeals to reason, insists that reason is untrustworthy and that faith is the only path to eternal truth.

Most religious mystics eschew pragmatism even while recommending it in one of its most naïve forms. They exhort us to have faith, to believe, since by acting out our faith we will later get understanding. But "understanding" thus acquired may be misunderstanding. Common sense and logic suggest that belief should follow knowledge and understanding rather than precede them. For centuries our ancestors believed that witches caused physical and mental disease, and this belief "worked so well" that the persecution of witches was almost institutionalized. Says Radhakrishnan, "If we believe absurdities we shall commit atrocities." Other illustrations will occur to the reader: the certainty that the earth is the center of the universe, the belief that man is a special organic creation, the conviction that suffering must be the result of sin. All these orthodoxies "worked" for the people that accepted them. All have been tragically difficult to unlearn. "Tradition," says Ruth Benedict, "can be as neurotic as any patient." The therapy is long, expensive and not always successful.

Humanist Philosophy 1928 – 1973

Perhaps a perverse parody of religious mysticism may be enlightening.

The Authoritarian Cynic

Can anyone doubt, asks the authoritarian cynic, that the Almighty is an evil genius with a sadistic sense of humor. Then let him open his eyes and look around him. Consider first the unscrupulous, cut-throat struggle for existence, the brutal truth that life can be preserved and enhanced only by the utterly wasteful and wholesale destruction of life. This vicious conflict, vividly documented in such films as *The Sea Around Us* and Walt Disney's nature movies, is typical of all life from micro-organisms and plants to warriors, gangsters, capitalists, politicians, diplomats and fanatics, religious and secular. Anthropology and history abundantly prove that man is "a predator, a hunter, a meat-eater and a killer." By arranging a fantastically high birth rate, the Almighty has ensured that the death rate by violence, by famine, by loathsome disease, by natural holocaust and war, will also be fantastically high; and that killers, from polio and cancer to Genghis Kahn and Hitler, will have plenty of fresh meat. And yet we are solemnly told that life is sacred, that a sparrow does not fall to the ground, etc.; an ironical bedtime story, if they could but understand it, to the millions of beasts in our slaughterhouses, and the thousands of dogs and cats stretched on the vivisectionist's rack.

Moreover, the All Powerful, after slyly giving man a sense of justice, evidently delights in frustrating it by widespread injustice: the sins of the fathers visited upon innocent children, the brave and the generous rotting in concentration camps, the prisoner persuaded to betray his friends by the torture of his children before his eyes. And to cap it all He makes this evil, sin and injustice the necessary price of freedom, without which life is not worth living. Could alternatives be more cruel and immoral? Could rules of the game be more stupidly unfair?

Add to this the evil probabilities in human personality: the cunning injection of unconscious hate into sexual and parental love; the perverse psychological mechanism by which insecurity and fear lead to intolerance and blind rage, particularly among races whose difference in skin color neatly singles them out for discrimination and persecution. A wily trick indeed! Remember, too, the diabolical alchemy which turns love of in-group into hatred of out-groups and transmutes national loyalty into disloyalty to mankind (as shown in the bomb tests). Finally consider the fact that man's technical intelligence is cunningly designed to outdistance his social intelligence, thus making certain that he will run amok again and again until he has destroyed himself.

All this seems evident and true to me, concludes the cynical mystic, but if you find it hard to believe just accept it on faith and live as though it were true. Believe that the Almighty is infinitely and incomprehensibly evil. Live selfishly, brutally, cruelly. Trust no one. Expect meanness, ingratitude, disloyalty, malevolence on every side. Remind yourself daily that Satan's in his Hell and all's wrong with the world. Thus your faith will lead you to a true understanding of ultimate reality—which, believe me, is anything but pretty.

The Many Mystics

What nonsense, you exclaim. This mystical structure is full of special pleading and unscientific conclusions. The principle of compensation, which finds some good in all evil and some evil in all good, has been shamefully exploited to find everything fundamentally evil. Talk about wishful thinking!

Of course you are right. But, given his assumptions, the cynic's logic and evidence are not easily dismissed. And the religious mystic, performing somewhat along these lines—in reverse—also produces solemn nonsense. He assembles the jigsaw fragments of "reality" into a whole which satisfies and convinces him. The cynic arranges other fragments into a quite different over-all design. The problem of good is as stubborn a riddle to the cynic as is the problem of evil to the theologian. Each calls the other naïve, presumptuous, close-minded, arrogant, blind and, probably, wicked. Fortunately we do not have to choose between them.

Then there are the secular mystics, all idealists in their way. There is the fanatical nationalist who fits the "facts" of history and world politics together in such a way that his nation is (a) the favorite of God, (b) the nucleus of the world, (c) always right and (d) victim rather than aggressor. Like the mystics above he "thinks" by rearranging his prejudices, and arrogantly assumes that those who disagree with him are stupid, unpatriotic and, probably, wicked.

There is the communist who mystically insists that there is no God, but that Marx is the infallible prophet of a Godless world moving inevitably toward a Utopian destiny. The communist thoroughly "understands" history and predicts the future with the naïve confidence so typical of the fanatic. Because he is unquestionably "right" he has a brutal way with dissenters. Despite or because of his idealism, he is one of the most bigoted mystics of all time.

The ideological structure of the fascist is opportunist rather than idealistic. As a result his mysticism is unusually barbarous and destructive.

The socialist, the capitalist, the segregationist, the followers of any rigidly doctrinaire ideology are kin to the authoritarian mystics insofar as their thinking and behavior approach fanaticism. "The True Believer," says Eric Hoffer, "is without wonder or hesitation."

Institutionalized mystics, sacred and profane, are of course highly competitive. Though they weld their in-groups into enthusiastic co-operation, they often tear the larger community to pieces. As Charles H. Cooley has remarked, the one true God of one group may be a devil to another and vice versa. Witness the religious wars of the 16th century, the more recent race eruptions, and the totalitarian conflicts of modern neurotic nationalism. Doubtless mysticism has its values and a case might be made for it. It has made unquestionable contributions to idealism, religion, philosophy and art. Nevertheless its historical record is hardly attractive.

Are there mystics among the scientists? If we define the term broadly, the answer seems to be yes. "What is the nature of life?" asks Ashley Montagu dramatically, and answers, "In one word, co-operation . . . another word for the same thing is love." "Evil, the immediately or ultimately painful," says Ralph S. Lillie, "is inherently unstable." Certain psychologists have insisted that love is inborn but hate is learned. Are not these scientists approaching the mystical? If there is adequate and convincing evidence for such dogmatic statements, I have not seen it in their books or elsewhere. On the contrary, there seems to be considerable evidence that the struggle for existence is deeply competitive, and that the word "love" cannot explain all that goes on in this contradictory old world. Mr. Lillie has a right to his opinion of evil, but anthropologists and historians may well wonder at the inexhaustible vitality and astonishing longevity of the "inherently unstable." As for love and hate, is it not fairly obvious that the predispositions for both are inborn, and that both are learned, i.e., culturally determined, as to their specific expression? Perhaps these men are seeing truth above the facts rather than through the facts. This does not necessarily mean that they are wrong, but that their attitude is mystical rather than scientific.

Incurable Idealists

Although they may exist, no peoples or cultures have been found without some sort of religious belief involving the supernatural. This does not prove the existence of supernatural personalities (until comparatively recently everybody believed in a flat world), but it does suggest that most people have a psychological need for some kind of faith in a larger life. Despite his faults and limitations, man seems to be incurably idealistic. R. L. Stevenson gives eloquent expression to this conviction in *Pulvis et Umbra*.1

> Poor soul, here for so little, cast among so many hardships, filled with desires so incommensurate and so inconsistent, savagely surrounded, savagely descended, irremediably condemned to prey upon his fellow lives: who should have blamed him had he been of a piece with his destiny and a being merely barbarous? And we look and behold him instead filled with imperfect virtues: infinitely childish, often

admirably valiant, often touchingly kind; sitting down amidst his momentary life, to debate of right and wrong and the attributes of the deity; rising up to do battle for an egg or die for an idea; singling out his friends and his mate with cordial affection; bringing forth in pain, rearing with long-suffering solicitude, his young. To touch the heart of his mystery, we find in him one thought, strange to the point of lunacy: the thought of duty; the thought of something owing to himself, to his neighbor, to his God: an ideal of decency, to which he would rise if it were possible; a limit of shame, below which, if it be possible, he will not stoop.

Because man is an idealist and sees so much around him that offends his sense of justice and decency, he must figure out some reconciliation between things as they apparently are (and ought not to be) and things as they must be if life is to be significant and worth living. The alternative is a cynical pessimism repulsive to a healthy organism. This reconciliation is his religion, broadly defined. Psychologists call it a wish projection (the terms may be used inter-changeably). Its objective truth is partial or doubtful, but because it more or less successfully meets a human need, it "works." Karl Marx and Mary Baker Eddy had their respective reconciliations or wish projections. Marx, as Max Eastman has observed, persuaded himself that the world was inevitably moving in the direction of his ideals; that capitalism, the root of all evil, was certain to be destroyed and a just, classless society was certain to evolve. He was nearer to the religious mystics than the scientists, among whom he so confidently claimed to belong. Mrs. Eddy's reconciliation was more simple and perfect. The evils in life which seriously offended her moral sense or contradicted her religious principles simply had no deep reality. There were only the "errors" and illusions of the spiritually immature. Similarly the orthodox Christian depreciates the wrongs of this life by setting them in the perspective of the perfect life eternal; and is convinced that Christ's vicarious sacrifice can deliver him from sin and death. These and many other wish projections have comforted and strengthened countless millions of men and women. In other words they have "worked" as far as the true believers are concerned.

Reconciliations of what unfortunately is with what idealistically must be are not, of course, original with each believer. Rather they are developed by religious seers and passed down the centuries. Since they are all wish projections, there is much truth in the saying that man makes God in his own image. Later generations who "inherit" such a God remodel him in line with their wishes and ideals. This is obvious in comparing the cruel and jealous Jehovah of the Old Testament with the Loving Father of the New. We are frequently assured that religion ennobles the believer and improves his character and conduct. Not necessarily. Those who create a barbarous, intolerant God in their own image, and then worship this wish projection, are debased rather than ennobled. Furthermore they pass on this mystical concept to future generations as "the One True God." Something like this caused the religious wars, the inquisition and, in a sense, the late Russian purges. Marx, the mortal, is almost worshipped by the Bolsheviks. Incidentally his image has undergone some lively reconstructions to coincide with the wish projections of a Lenin, a Stalin, a Malenkov, a Khrushchev. If Marx could see his present projection in Moscow, he would neither recognize nor approve it.

Idealism with Humility

Most of us are looking for a flashing insight that will give life a more or less reassuring significance. Our wish projections, reconciliations, hypotheses, differ according to our cultures and individual personalities; and these differences are often fundamental.

If religious reconciliations and wish projections meet a deep human need; if they are a comfort and inspiration to all cultures and nearly all individuals; what, then, is so objectionable about mysticism? There is a double answer: first wish projections differ vastly one from another; and second, the attitudes of believers toward their wish projections vary significantly.

Humanist Philosophy 1928 – 1973

There are, of course, undogmatic mystics like Ramakrishna; and there are groups like the Quakers and the Unitarians who calmly repudiate authoritarianism in their theology and their human relations. They are not fanatics or what Eric Hoffer calls "true believers." But they are hardly typical.

The trouble with the typical mystic is his arrogance (though apart from his religion he may be a retiring fellow). He is likely to be aggressive and open to the charge of "cosmic impiety." He knows the unknowable. He knows that the fragments of reality fit into a sublime total design; and he knows how they fit.

In contrast is the idealist who takes his wish projection seriously but not with uncritical solemnity. He knows that it has faults and is ever striving to mature and perfect it. His reconciliation, like a scientist's hypothesis, is a growing, dynamic concept, not a static creed; a working principle to be tested by study and experience, not a finished portrait of The Truth to be humbly accepted and never questioned. Far from believing in order to understand, he moves toward understanding by doubt as often as by conviction. He is agnostic in that he accepts mystery as unknown —though not necessarily unknowable in the future.

This attitude inevitably determines the character and quality of his reconciliation. It will hardly be scientifically naïve nor philosophically presumptuous. It is likely to be tough-minded, realistic and adaptable in a way that the doctrinaire mystic can neither understand nor forgive. Finally, the agnostic will be tolerant toward other sincere reconciliations; more eager to study them sympathetically than to condemn them offhand. He will be inclined to say to the authoritarian mystic, "Bet your life on your totalitarian universe if you like, but refrain from forcing it upon simpler and, perhaps, wiser people."

Albert Einstein was a deeply religious man. He spoke naturally of God, and spent the later years of his life in a devoted search for the "unified theory." This he hoped would give scientific evidence for his religious belief. Yet he never pontificated; never boasted that he was refuting the "uncertainty principle"; never claimed to know what he had not proved; never doubted that reason was an indispensable tool in seeking any kind of truth. A great man and a great scientist, he was modest, relaxed, and curious in the presence of mystery. "The most beautiful thing we can experience," he said, "is the mysterious. It is the source of all art and science."

He found it "hard to believe that God would play dice with the universe," yet he never claimed to have evidence or revealed knowledge to the contrary. I feel sure he would not have contradicted Alfred Noyes:

> It might be
> The final test of man, the narrow way
> That he should face this darkness and this death
> Worthily and renounce all easy hope
> All consolation, all but the wintry smile
> Upon the face of truth.

Regarding the "structure of reality," Einstein wrote, "I believe that at the present time nobody knows anything reliable about it." And again, "only a significant progress in mathematical methods can help us here." And again, "Here is the logically simplest relativistic field that is possible, but this does not mean that nature may not obey a more complex field theory." Note the tough-minded alertness against believing something because it is plausible, ingenious, flattering or comforting.

Must We Be Sure?

If we distrust the mystical approach to life, what is the alternative?

Must we reduce all life to certainty? Can we not refrain from reading the mind of God or from constructing a grandiose Purpose for a Godless world, or from dogmatic pronouncements about personal immortality or lack of it? Must we persuade ourselves that we understand more than we do? Can we not learn to say, "I don't know" and mean it? If this attitude involves regrettable insecurity, perhaps such insecurity is our lot. Maybe we can learn to live dangerously and even to enjoy it. The theory, so well put by Rebecca West, that "the greatness of God stretches under human destiny like the net below trapeze artists" is one that we have been taught to need, but, with William James, we may well question whether it is really the essence of morality or of mature intelligence. In the words of H. J. Muller, "The felt need of a personal God—not to mention a personal immortality—is a product of our tradition, not a requirement of human nature or the religious spirit itself."

Mystery itself is awesome and inspiring. Perhaps we can learn to feel something of the same wonder and humility towards it that we have been enjoined to feel toward God. John Muir, a sturdy agnostic, used to climb a tall Yosemite spruce during terrific thunderstorms, and commune with mystery by swaying wildly between earth and sky.

"Any definite idea of God," to quote Cooley again, "must be trivial or fatuous. There is no way to know Him but by knowing life, and we do that by living as largely, faithfully and thoughtfully as we can." Such wisdom would seem to appeal to the scientist, the philosopher, the artist, the humanist or the liberal student of religion.

Norman Cousins doubts if anybody knows enough to be an atheist. Can we not broaden the statement to include all authoritarian mystics? What do we really know about all these "certainties"? No God? Dozens or hundreds of gods? God and Devil? One God? One God? One God? Strange that totalitarianism, which has such a bad record in the field, should be so confidently and universally recommended for The Home Office. Why not a Committee of Gods co-operating in democratic administration for the universe? Preposterous? But is there any overwhelming evidence for the all-embracing unity so essential to the mystic's peace of mind? James talks rather reasonably and persuasively of a multiverse. Surely there is no proof that all the bits of reality fit into an imposing and significant design. A possibility, yes, and perhaps not beyond the pale of human discovery; but at present a mystery. Why pretend to the contrary?

Many religions state or imply that the universe, or at least the earth, has been designed for the use and glory of man. To many natural scientists this assumption seems a choice bit of wishful thinking. They see little evidence that this earth was made for man or that he will be here indefinitely. Apparently he was hardly noticed when he arrived and will scarcely be missed if he goes. We are assured there must be a God behind a creation so marvelous. But is God less marvelous than his creation? Then what marvelous cause has created God? This simple and ancient question is still unanswered. Whichever way we turn we are eventually confronted with mystery.

Most religions seem eager to prove that God is infinite in goodness and power. We need not embrace the cynic's mystical creed to find such a God implausible. James has remarked that God is apparently no gentleman. We might add that he seems frequently insensitive, mischievous, irresponsible, or at least badly overworked.

In *Conversation at Midnight*,2 one of Millay's characters addresses the orthodox mystic thus:

It is you, Anselmo, who are stiff-necked and arrogant, not I;
It is you who refuse to submit your will.
You cannot conceive that there might be that of which you cannot conceive; you are arrogant;
You endow all things with human attributes; you do not hesitate
To call the inconceivable "Father."
In vain do you strike your breast; in vain do you say
In a humble voice, "Domine, non sum dingus";
Whose arrogance knows no bounds; who have presumed to name
A mystery "God," and give it a bride and a child.

In contrast, one of Aldous Huxley's characters in *The Genius and the Goddess*3 gives the creedless creed of the skeptic. "Reality never makes sense ... In the raw, existence is always one damned thing after another, and each of the damned things is simultaneously Thurber and Michelangelo, simultaneously Micky Spillane and Maxwell and Thomas à Kempis. The criterion of reality is its intrinsic irrelevance."

Humanist Philosophy 1928 – 1973

Living with Mystery

Which shall we choose? Again, we do not have to choose. Is it not better and wiser to live with mystery in an uneasy and exciting marriage—some call it living in sin—than to accept any substitute for the whole truth as we see it? If we eagerly and open-mindedly examine all evidence as it comes in, reservation of opinion in such matters seems the part of intelligence and maturity.

It is the least mystical elements of religion that are most credible, profound and enduring, and which are—not incidentally—the common core of all the great faiths: the law of kindness and love, especially toward the rejected and unfortunate; the respect for personality, particularly as regards children; and above all that most intelligent and practical of all precepts, the Golden Rule. While competing mysticisms wax and wane and often strive to destroy each other, these comparatively simple attitudes and conduct patterns have met the supreme pragmatic test—have "worked" for a million years or more, and have grown stronger, it seems, in their struggle for survival. They are older than man and may well outlive him. We find them in stone-age peoples and even among animals. They have brought significance, or at least islands of significance, into the confusion and strife of an amoral world. They are part of the mystery of life which, in a measure, we have learned to understand and appreciate. Our faith in the idealism which they exemplify can be an intelligent faith, based on the sort of evidence a scientist might respect. Why may we not devote our minds and hearts to such ideals without the more or less immature trappings of some more or less naïve mysticism?

Let us admit, however, that some of these incredible beliefs of the mystic might just happen to be true; that things may be radically different from what they seem, even to our most learned scientists. For instance there just might be another spiritual dimension which could reconcile some of the contradictions we have been considering. Suppose we are looking at a log's end in two dimensions. We will take it for a flat disk and can have no notion that it might be the trunk of a tree or the gable of a house.

Thus our two-dimensional wisdom could turn out to be three-dimensional foolishness. It follows that, while at present justified in doubting the mystics, we should be ever alert and ready to doubt our own doubts, as new evidence reveals their fallacies. The dogmatic doubter is akin to the mystics whom he ridicules.

Let us admit, too, that mystics, even authoritarian mystics, have often seen life in wider and deeper perspective that have most of our philosophers, artists or scientists; that they have had pure and fresh insights about social responsibility and the brotherhood of man, backed by the courage to fight for their convictions against the deadening institutional conformity of their times. Some of them have been radicals in the best sense of the word, even though their dogmatism has made their teachings easy to pervert for selfish and illiberal ends.

We cannot be sure whether or not their visions were worth the appalling price they cost us in bigotry, intolerance and hate, but we can hope that the great mystics of the future, inspired by the wider horizons of the modern world, may avoid over-structuring their intuitive interpretations of the unknown and may refrain from belittling and condemning the convictions of sincere people who happen to disagree with them.

But is not this a bleak and lonely faith to live by?

It is, if unexplained mystery terrifies us; if we are primarily interested in security; if we must eventually have a happy ending; if the battle is not worthwhile unless we are certain *now* that our side will eventually win. But there is still much to live for. We have a chance of answering, partially at least, some of the great questions of religion; and the answers may be inspiring. Meanwhile we have the privilege of exploring mystery; using our emotions, our imagination, our reason, our experience, each to supplement and correct the others. We do not know that the structure of reality is a beautiful, morally satisfying whole, but we do know that billions of men and women have had visions of beauty, goodness and truth, and have often approached these visions in their personal lives, their human relations and their community organization. And we do know that we, like them, may live after death in our children and in the memories and achievements of those who have known us. Why should the idealist require more immortality than this?

Perhaps life as a whole has no significant meaning. We do not know. But there is much evidence that we can *give* it meaning, here and there, as men and women have done in the past. Those who have honestly tried to live by the golden rule and think by the scientific method have found that life is a challenge, and sometimes a delight, to the vigorous body, the lively mind and the generous heart. At least it is an interesting and valiant quest. There are many good companions along the way, and the weather and scenery are often glorious!

"Man should live nobly," writes David Cecil, "though he does not see any practical reason for it, simply because in the mysterious inexplicable mixture of beauty and ugliness, virtue and baseness in which he finds himself, he must want to be on the side of the beautiful and the virtuous . . . must want to make his character as like as possible to the things in his experience which call out his admiration and sense of glory."

Here, like the mystic, we come back to faith as an absolute essential of the good life. This faith is neither flattering nor comfortable nor certain nor authoritarian. It does not place man confidently at the center of the universe nor assure ultimate victory of his ideals. But it has this merit: it is determined to "see life steadily and see it whole"; it is willing to live with mystery where knowledge leaves off.

Gerald Barnes is Emeritus Professor of Sociology in Boston University. Among his published articles are: "Education for 1950," A.A.U.P. Bulletin, *April 1945, "Democracy and the Birth Rate,"* Antioch Review, *Summer 1950, and "The Population Explosion and Business,"* Boston University Business Review, *Fall, 1961. The present article was first published in the* British Faith and Freedom, *Spring, 1960.*

References

* For the purposes of this essay, the mystic is one whose beliefs about the eternal verities are unsupported (or disproved) by scientific evidence. Such beliefs may be more, or less, original with the believer. The authoritarian mystic is convinced that others should believe as he does; and he acts accordingly. Obviously, there are all degrees of authoritarianism.

1. In *Across the Plains*, by R. L. Stevenson, Charles Scribner's Sons, New York.
2. *Conversation at Midnight*, by Edna St. Vincent Millary, Harper & Bros., New York, 1937.
3. *The Genius and the Goddess*, by Aldous Huxley, Harper & Bros., New York, 1955.

Humanism and Peace

Dr. Linus Pauling
The Humanist, March-April, 1961

What have we as human beings, to hope for? We suffer from attacks by the vectors of disease, from accidents, striking with the blind malevolence of chance from the ills accompanying the deterioration of age; and also, in a sense the most viciously, from man's inhumanity to man, especially as expressed in the evil institution of war.

I believe that we can have hope, and that we can win a great victory not only over the plague of man's natural condition, the physical ills that beset us, but also over the terrible plague of man's oppression by man, over the evil of war.

The world has been changing rapidly during recent decades. This change has involved especially a greater understanding by man of the causes of human suffering. We now know that certain combinations of genes, which in some cases can be predicted to occur with high probability, lead to gross physical or mental defects which cause great suffering for the person who is so afflicted and for his parents and others. We know now that the pool of human germ plasm is continually being changed by gene mutation, and that the natural process of removing deleterious genes from it, in order to preserve its integrity involves much human suffering.

We are faced with an ethical problem, characteristic of the many that have to face as our knowledge of the nature of human beings and of the world increases. Shall the deleterious genes that exist in the pool of human germ plasm, and that would otherwise continue to increase, be removed by the suffering and death of millions of children, or by a procedure that attempts to recognize them and to prevent the conception of these defective children?

This question is one of ethics, of philosophy in the sense expressed by Corliss Lamont, that philosophy involves the analysis and clarification of human actions and aims, problems and ideals. Many admirable statements have been made about these matters in the past by great philosophers and teachers.

I believe that there is great value in the philosophy of humanism—that the chief end of human life is to work for the happiness of man upon this earth (and we might soon have to add the moon and then Venus and other planets).

Humanism, as I understand it, is a rational philosophy. It rejects the mysticism and supernaturalism of the revealed religions, it rejects life after death and the idea that suffering in this world may, for the righteous, be compensated for by the bliss of an after-life. Included in this rejection of the supernatural is the rejection of a belief in an omniscient, omnipotent, and omnipresent god who watches over and cares for human beings, interfering sometimes in response to prayer, with the ordered regularity of events as determined by natural laws.

Humanism is a philosophy of service for the good of all humanity, of application of new ideas, of scientific progress, for the benefit of all men—those now living and those still to be born.

Dr. Albert Schweitzer believes that not only man but also other forms of life should be included in the field of our concern. He has expressed this belief in his principle of Reverence for Life. I would like to go further: I advocate the principle of Reverence for the World.

This is a wonderful world in which we live. Yet some of its wonders are being annihilated, destroyed, so that our children's children will never be able to experience them. I do not like to think of the beautiful minerals, beautiful crystals, that are being removed from the ground and destroyed in order to make more copper wire or uranium rods, especially for the useless activities of preparation for war. There will never be a second crop of minerals.

Instead of the principle of maximizing human happiness, I prefer the principle of minimizing the suffering in the world. The difference between maximizing happiness and minimizing suffering requires weighting of the factors involved. On a scale of income, we may select a certain value as standard—one that is just enough for a satisfactory life, different, of course, according to duties and circumstances.

An increase of 80 percent in income would give some added happiness—but the suffering caused by a decrease of 80 percent surely deserves a far greater weight, perhaps 10 or 100 times greater.

THE EVOLUTION OF HUMANKIND

Man has reached his present state through the process of evolution. The great step in evolution was the mutational process that doubled the use of our brain 700,000 years ago; this led to the origin of man. It is this that permits the inheritance of acquired characteristics of a certain sort of learning through communication from one human being to another. Thus abilities that have not yet been incorporated into the germ plasm are not lost until their rediscovery by members of following generations, but instead are handed on from person to person, from generation to generation. Man's great powers of thinking, remembering and communicating are responsible for the evolution of civilization.

Yet a man or woman is not truly an organism, in the sense that a rabbit is or a lion or a whale. Instead, he is a part of a greater organism, the whole of mankind, into which he is bound by the means of communication—speaking, writing, telephoning, traveling over long distances, in the way that the cells of a rabbit are interconnected by nerve fibers and hormonal molecular messengers.

This great organism, humankind, is now master of the earth, but not yet master of itself; it is immature, irrational; it does not act for its own good, but instead often for its own harm.

We must now achieve the mutation that will bring sanity to this great organism that is mankind. Must this be a mutation of some of the genes in the the pool of human germ plasm? Perhaps such a genetic mutation, providing for example, extrasensory perception and instantaneous communication among all human beings, would do the job; but I fear that we do not have time for this mutational process to be effective. The human race may cease to exist in a decade.

We must accordingly hope that the mutation can instead be in the |nature of the giant organism, humankind, itself—a mutation in the means of communication, in the nerve fibers of the organization, that will transfer to this whole great organism some of the desirable and admirable attributes that are possessed by the units of which it is composed, the individual human beings. The attributes that must be transferred from the units, human beings to the great organism, humankind, are sanity (reason), and morality (ethical principles).

I believe that this change will occur. I believe that we are now forced to this change by the development of weapons that could destroy the world, and that will do so unless the nature of the great human organism changes in time.

One hundred sixty-nine years ago Benjamin Franklin said, in discussing the progress of science, "It is impossible to imagine the heights to which may be carried, in a thousand years, the power of man over matter. O that moral Science were in as fair a way of improvement, that men would cease to be wolves to one another, and that human beings would at length learn what they now improperly call *humanity*."

THE IMMINENT PERIL

The power of man over matter has increased so greatly during the last two decades that for the first time it has become possible for mankind to be wiped out by man.

I estimate that the United States now has material enough for 125,000 nuclear weapons, and the U.S.S.R. enough for 60,000. I can provide reasonable substantiation of the first number, but the second is not much more than a guess. Of these weapons, some tens of thousands are probably in the megaton class: each one with explosive energy about equal to or even several times greater than that of all of the explosives used in the whole of the Second World War. One 20-megaton bomb, such as the Bikini bomb exploded by the United States on 1 March, 1954, and the similar bombs exploded by the U.S.S.R. and Great Britain, could destroy completely any city on earth.

If the weapons now existing in the stockpiles of the great nuclear powers were to be used in a thoroughly efficient manner they might suffice to kill everybody on earth. Even if used inefficiently, as they probably would be in a nuclear war fought during the next few years, hundreds of millions of people, most of them in the highly developed nations of the world, would be killed, and there is grave doubt that civilization would survive.

Moreover, the military scientists who devote themselves to the "games theory" of nuclear war engage in a serious discussion of nuclear devices, "doomsday machines,"" the function of which would be to destroy all human life, to leave not one single human being alive on earth. Mr. Herman Kahn, without discussing such devices in detail, conjectures that if the building of one such machine were started today and the project were sufficiently well supported, the machine could be built by 1970 at a cost of 10 to 100 billion dollars. He discusses the possible military threat that a nation with such a device could exert upon the rest of the world in order, through blackmail, to impose its national will upon the world.

I have made an analysis of a method of killing everyone on earth first proposed in 1950 by Dr. Leo Szilard. This method involves the use of hydrogen bombs with the addition of the element cobalt, so as to produce radioactive cobalt, cobalt 60, in large amounts. I have calculated that for six billion dollars—one twentieth of the amount spent on armaments each year by the nations of the world—enough cobalt bombs could be built to assure the death of every person on earth, with a great factor of safety (or of unsafety).; the The radioactive cobalt uniformly spread over the surface of the earth would for several years provide more than enough radiation every few hours to cause any person exposed to it to die of acute radiation sickness. No matter what sort of protection were to be devised, it is highly unlikely that any human being could remain alive.

Nuclear weapons are cheap. A 20-megaton bomb that could destroy New York or London or Moscow and kill six to ten million people contains only $85,000 worth of explosive materials. Plutonium costs $14 per gram, $4,000 for the ten pounds needed for the trigger of the bomb. The 200 pounds of lithium deuteride that constitute the second stage costs about $4,000; the expensive material, deuterium, can be separated from ordinary water by the hydrogen sulfide-water countercurrent method at a cost of $68 per pound. The material for the third stage, 1000 pounds of ordinary uranium metal, cost $17,000.

We are faced with a choice among three alternatives: (1) to continue the arms race without restriction; (2) to change war, by abolishing megaton weapons, in such a way as to make it "credible" or "rational"; (3) to abolish war, work steadily toward the goal of total and universal disarmament, and replace the use of military might in the conduct of world affairs by international agreements and international law, in such a way that disputes between nations are settled in accordance with the principles of justice and morality.

I believe that we shall be successful in moving forward rapidly toward the goal of peace and disarmament.

PROGRESS TOWARD DISARMAMENT

To work toward the goal of total and universal disarmament is the policy of the great nations of the world. On October 28, 1960, Ambassador James J. Wadsworth of the United States told the United Nations that total world disarmament could be achieved within five or six years with faith and "a real sense of urgency" on both sides.

Ambassador Wadsworth said "we want – earnestly, deeply and sincerely—general and complete disarmament under effective international control. We are not backing off from that one inch. ... We want to begin progress toward our goal now, to take those measures that can be taken now while at the same time we are trying, concurrently, to solve the problems that lie ahead in reaching the goal of general and complete disarmament."

Prime Minister Macmillan of Great Britain has said that complete and general disarmament must be the avowed goal of all nations. Chairman Khrushchev of the U.S.S.R. strongly advocates total and universal disarmament and has pledged that the U.S.S.R. will permit complete inspection and international controls within the U.S.S.R. when total and universal disarmament has been achieved.

Humanist Philosophy 1928 – 1973

During recent years there has been significant, although slow, progress toward this goal. For over two years, since October 31, 1958, the representatives of the governments of the three great nuclear powers have been negotiating at Geneva toward the formulation of an international agreement to stop the testing of all nuclear weapons. Most of the clauses of the agreement have been written and accepted by the negotiators.

The completion of this agreement and its acceptance by all nations will be a great and significant step toward world disarmament and peace. It is proper that the negotiators should move ahead with care; they must not make a serious mistake. On the other hand, the length of time required for the negotiation seems to be excessive.

For example, one of the problems that has long awaited solution is that of the number of veto-free on-the-site inspection trips, to determine, as can be done, whether or not a set of seismic disturbances that had been recorded on the inspection instruments was an earthquake or was the result of the surreptitious underground test of a nuclear weapon (all tests in the atmosphere can be detected). About 100 earthquakes with an energy equal to or greater than that of a small atomic bomb, of the Hiroshima-Nagasaki type (in kilotons), occur each year in the Soviet Union. About 30 of them can be definitely identified as earthquakes from the seismological records, leaving 70 that might be investigated. In February, 1959, Prime Minister Macmillan suggest that the U.S.S.R., the United States, and Great Britain should establish a fixed yearly quota of veto-free inspections which could be carried out without hindrance on the territory of each of the nuclear powers concerned. Only July 26, 1960 the Soviet delegation to the Geneva Conference, with authorization of the Soviet government, stated that three veto-free inspection trips could be made each year within the territories of the Soviet Union. The United States had asked that twenty be allowed.

It seemed to me at the time that negotiation of the number could and should proceed rapidly: that the United States could suggest 19, the U.S.S.R. 4, the United States 18, and so on, until agreement was reached at either the arithmetic mean or the geometric mean of the two values originally proposed. Instead, month after month went by with no indication of progress, until on March 3, 1961, the Atomic Energy correspondent of *The New York Times*, John W. Finney, reported from Washington that the United States was preparing to make a concession on a crucial issue. He wrote that according to high State Department officials the United States was preparing to reduce its demand to about 17 inspections a year in the Soviet Union, and, moreover, that Soviet diplomats had been dropping hints that Moscow would raise its proposal from 3 to perhaps about a dozen per year. We may accordingly hope that when the negotiations are resumed (on March 21, 1961), there will not be a deadlock at about 17, on the one hand, and perhaps a dozen on the other, but instead that a reasonable compromise, of the sort that could be suggested by anyone, will immediately be found and accepted.

FURTHER FUTURE STEPS

There is another issue that may cause trouble in the bomb test negotiations. Last summer the United States proposed that a committee of nations be set up to decide whether a State or authority that desires to sign the agreement not to test nuclear weapons and to permit international inspection of its territory would or would not be allowed to do so. The U.S.S.R. made strong objection, stating that the treaty should be open for accession by all States on an equal footing, without any discrimination, that the doors should be thrown wide open for all States to become parties to the treaty, that all countries should accede to the treaty in order that peace be established firmly and that any State that wishes to assume the obligation devolving from the treaty should be given the possibility of doing so. In the discussion, on August 4, 1960, Ambassador Wadsworth and Ambassador Tsarapkin brought out that the problem was essentially whether the Chinese People's Republic or the Chinese Nationalist government would be allowed to sign for Mainland China and for Taiwan. There is accordingly the possibility that civilization will come to an end because of a minor political disagreement centering about Taiwan.

Humanist Philosophy 1928 – 1973

I hope, however, that the bomb-test agreement will be completed without delay, ratified by the Senate, and in the period of a few years signed by all of the nations in the world. I hope that this step will be followed by the formulation and acceptance of other agreements, including effective agreements to stop the manufacture of more nuclear weapons, to stop the manufacture of short range and long range missiles and of great bombers, to dismantle more and more of the existing nuclear weapons and the machines by means of which they might be delivered, to stop research on other weapons, especially bacteriological and chemical, and ultimately to stop all military activities, always with the best possible system of controls and inspection.

At every stage the steps to be taken must be such as to increase the safety of the United States, of the U.S.S.R., and of other nations and the safety of all people in the world. It is not difficult to take action that increases our safety, because we are far from safe now—we are, in fact, in greater danger than ever before in the history of the world. Nevertheless, all of the international agreements must be made with great care, so that they are fair—that they deal fairly with the different nations involved. This will, of course, mean that to us the agreements will seem to favor the Russians and to the Russians they will seem to favor us. We must recognize that because of the bias given to us by our point of view and given to the Russians by their point of view, a fair agreement will have this aspect to each of us.

In the meantime, we must be careful not to take actions that increase the difficulty of achieving the goal of total and universal disarmament through international agreements and international law.

It is evident that the spread of nuclear weapons to more nations or groups of nations would increase the difficulty of achieving disarmament. NATO Commander General Norstad has proposed that they turn over stockpiles of nuclear weapons to that NATO group of nations. Secretary Herter also proposed that five Polaris submarines with their compliment of 80 missiles with megaton nuclear warheads be turned over to NATO and that an additional 100 Polaris rockets with megaton nuclear warheads be sold to NATO, at one million dollars for each. To carry out these actions would be a tragedy. The only hope for the world lies in achieving control of the methods of waging war and ultimately to reach the goal of total and universal disarmament. Every step that we take should be carefully considered with respect to whether or not it increases or decreases the difficulty of reaching this goal. The transfer of nuclear weapons to NATO would be a calamitous step toward world destruction.

THREE POSITIVE PROPOSALS

Positive action must be taken also to achieve the incorporation of China to the world community of nations. The Chinese People's Republic is probably well on the way toward development of its own nuclear weapons. Instead of encouraging this activity, we should be making a strong effort to include the Chinese People's Republic in the negotiations for world disarmament.

A positive proposal that needs to be revived is that of the formation of a buffer region in Europe—the Rapacki Plan. Such an action, the disarmament of 95,000 square miles of Western Europe (West Germany) and 212,000 square miles of Eastern Europe (East Germany, Czechoslovakia, Poland) would be a valuable contribution to the cause of peace. When this plan was proposed in 1958 it was harshly rejected by the Western powers. Edouard Ghait, in his book *No Carte Blanche to Capricorn: the Folly of Nuclear War Strategy* says "Up to a few years ago the intellectuals in Western countries very sincerely felt that it was the U.S.S.R. that must bear the major responsibility for the armaments race and the state of tension throughout the world. The harsh rejection of the Rapacki Plan, the frightening paucity of the arguments used in this connection, dealt a terrible blow to the faith the intellectuals still had in the 'free world' and its struggle for peace, democracy, and a better future. Up to that time everything had been simple. Everything could be blamed on the Russians. And then the name of Rapacki was heard, and it echoed like a reproach to which there can be no answer."

Humanist Philosophy 1928 – 1973

In October 1959 *The New York Times* reported that United States armaments manufacturers had begun to pour massive and technical experience into the reviving West German Arms industry.

In 1960 the United States Senate spent 55 minutes in deciding to pass a $41 billion dollar appropriation for arms. There are about 40 million families in the United States. Accordingly in this short time of 55 minutes the Senate approved an expenditure for the year of $1000 per American family for armaments. Then the Senate debated for five and one half hours a bill for disarmament studies—studies of ways in which the economic dislocation that might follow disarmament agreements and a decrease in military budget could be minimized—and after the long debate the bill was voted down as "extravagant."

Per United States family this is one cent for disarmament studies—debated for five and one half hours and then rejected as extravagant!

We can no longer afford to evade our responsibilities. The time has come now when morality must win out in the world. The survival of the whole human organism now depends upon whether or not we can work together for the common good.

I believe that we can have hope. I believe that we can win the final victory over the immorality of war, that the nations of the world will give up war, will become moral; that the fine ethical principles that are now accepted by the units of humankind will be taken over also by that whole great organism itself; and that we, all the people of the world, who together constitute this greatest of all organisms, the whole of humanity, the culmination of the great process of evolution, will move forward together into the world of the future, a world of peace and morality and ever-increasing happiness.

Address to the American Humanist Association at Cleveland, Ohio, on March 17, 1961, responding to election as Humanist of the Year for 1961. Dr. Pauling is Professor of Chemistry at the California Institute of Technology in Pasadena and received the Nobel Award in 1954.

The Vanity of Wisdom

Alfred G. Smith
The Humanist, July-August, 1955

About twenty-two hundred years ago, Hannibal and his elephants were hurrying to demolish Rome, and the Romans were demanding that Carthage be demolished. Other empires sided with Rome, and sometimes against it, and sometimes against one another. It was an age of war, an age of empires that could not coexist. These wars were more than contests between military forces; they were crusades of ideologies and cultures. In Palestine the contest was between Hellenism and Judaism.

In that age of conflict, victory and defeat often lay in the balance, indeterminate, but either outcome bore the same harvest for all the empires and cultures. It bore a harvest of ruins. The cost and destruction of war wiped out the middle classes, which consisted largely of farmers. Bankrupt, these farmers left their country homes to swell the big cities where they helped spawn an uprooted cosmopolitanism and a freelance skepticism. They became dejected cynics who could only be cajoled by bread and circuses. It was an age of transition which abandoned old furrows and orbits. Like other transitions, it drifted into vague consequences, and as this age drifted, men became derelicts in vagary, losing their vision of purpose and design in the world. Life became a meaningless cycle of incidents.

I

In this age of transition lived the man who wrote the last book of the Old Testament. He also lived in an area of transition, for he lived in Palestine at the cross-roads of East and West. This man was a preacher and he preached the intimations of his times. "Vanity of vanities, saith the Preacher, vanity of vanities; all is vanity ... I have seen all the works that are done under the sun; and, behold, all is vanity and vexation of spirit."

The Preacher, Ecclesiastes, was a cosmopolitan and a worldly man. He had seen all the works that are done under the sun and that demolished all his illusions about this world. And he no longer deferred to any other world. In his short discourse he speaks thirty times of the "things under the sun" but he never refers to the Jehovah of Israel once. When he spoke of God he only referred to an indefinite Creator. Ecclesiastes preached a thoroughly secular sermon. His wisdom is a thoroughly secular wisdom. He does not speculate about salvation, heavenly cities, or kingdom come. His only concern is with the strategy of secular living. And his secular wisdom is that "a man hath no better thing under the sun, than to eat, and to drink, and to be merry." There is nothing better than bread and circuses for everything is vanity and vexation of spirit anyway.

Living in the midst of transition, Ecclesiastes could discern no pattern or purpose in the flux of events. He believed that even if there were some sense in things, men could never know what it was. "As thou knowest not what is the way of the spirit, nor how the bones do grow in the womb of her that is with child: even so thou knowest not the works of God who maketh all." The ways of the world are impenetrable to human reason or understanding. Therefore Ecclesiastes saw himself as a helpless victim of inscrutable events. He saw himself as a martyr of fate.

Fate is the flux of events as seen by their martyr, and as Ecclesiastes sees it: "To everything there is a season, and a time to every purpose under heaven; a time to be born, and a time to die; a time to plant, and a time to pluck up that which is planted; a time to kill, and a time to heal; a time to break down, and a time to build up." There is a time to every purpose, but men can never know what time it is. Men cannot know the way of the spirit or of the world. Yesterday is past and tomorrow will come, but nobody knows when or why. Even if men could know, their knowledge could not change a thing. For fate alone sanctions things to happen in their time. In a world of fate men can neither shift nor dodge a single prospect.

Indeed, the world was first set spinning by a cause that is unknown to men, and it has spun ever since in an aimless whirl that is the ruin of men. This whirl takes us around and around in a circle to nowhere. "One generation passeth away, and another generation cometh: but the earth abideth for ever. The sun also ariseth, and the sun goeth down, and hasteth to his place where he arose. ... The thing that hath been, it is that which shall be; and that which is done is that which shall be done: and there is no new thing under the sun." This is fate in a closed universe.

The world of Ecclesiastes is a world of unknown inevitables. But it is more than a world of fate; it is a world of chance. Fate determines whether things are in season or out of season, but chance determines nothing. While fate is relentless, chance is haphazard. In the world of chance everything is an unpredictable accident, without order or design. Hence foresight and planning are utterly impossible. Whirl remains king and men are its playthings, whisked aimlessly around.

Chance is the flux of events as seen by their plaything, and as Ecclesiastes sees it: "I returned, and saw under the sun, that the race is not to the swift, nor the battle to the strong, neither bread to the wise, nor yet riches to men of understanding, nor yet favour to men of skill; but time and chance happeneth to them all." The plaything finds no justice in the rewards of life; only chance and double dealing.

The martyr and the plaything are like the crisp and multicolored leaves of the transition between autumn and winter. Then these leaves sweep along the ground in a wild and willy nilly dance. They tumble over themselves and over each other. Their animation is a mere vanity, for they are dead things blown by the wind. Each leaf is the martyr of his season and the plaything of a gust of chance.

Men are equally inane, dancing jigs unseen in a blind universe. For men are effects, not causes, and whatever they may do makes no difference. The world of fate and the world of chance are indifferent to human hopes and ventures. This cosmic indifference deflates all human exploits to mere conceits. Yet men are vain, and for them indifference can never be neutral. For them indifference is rejection. Thus, because they are rejected, life becomes worthless. It does not matter if happiness is outweighed by misery, or pains are more painful than pleasures are pleasurable. Life is worthless because man simply does not matter. "Therefore I hated life, because the work that is wrought under the sun is grievous unto me; for all is vanity and vexation of spirit."

There is a vanity in trivial conceits and there is a vanity in cosmic exploits, but all of life is vanity because the world is not interested. Fate and chance are in the saddle and man is of no account. He only bays at the moon. Thus wisdom is of no account either. In a world of inevitable fate, a wise man can change nothing; and in a world of irrational chance, a wise man can know nothing. Wisdom is vanity. It earns no rewards, for the race is not to the swift. Wisdom merely heightens our awareness of a disinterested universe and confirms the judgment that our lives are simply spent in serving time. "I gave my heart to know wisdom, and to know madness and folly: I perceived that this also is vexation of spirit. For in much wisdom is much grief: and he that increaseth knowledge increaseth sorrow."

II

We cannot dispute a man's disposition or reject his feelings of rejection. His reflexes are what they are. But we can explore how he justifies his feelings. We can test what he takes for granted, and we can examine his argument. This only brings to light some superficial reasons for his outlook, but even these can let us hail or spurn his philosophy for ourselves.

Ecclesiastes feels ensnared in a web of fate and causality, and he feels helpless. The tyranny of this indifferent web strangles any power he can have of his own. He may even feel that he is helpless when other things are powerful, that only when all other things are helpless, he can be powerful himself. Ecclesiastes takes for granted that the power of fate and the power of his own determination are each autonomous and independent of one another. But such a separation of powers is an absurd assumption.

As I put the bread in the toaster this morning I was dependent on gravity which dropped the bread into place. I was dependent on electricity and heat which toasted the bread for me. I could not make toast by my own powers alone. It is startlingly obvious that if I were not caught in a web of causality I could not even make toast.

Unaided by the powers of a causal world we are helpless. We can meet our desires and gain ground on our visions only in a world of fate: but we must turn that world to account. We must harness it. Gravity, electricity, and heat are of no account by themselves. They cannot make toast either. If they are to satisfy any purpose or desire, we must set them to work. Man, therefore, is not the martyr of fate. He is its employer. The seasons come to him and go, but it is he who sows and harvests the seasons.

Even in this world of fate, however, man is still not free. He remains a victim and a plaything. One man is born deformed and another dies before his prime. Men remain surrounded by undeserved misery, unjustifiable wretchedness, and unfair afflictions. Life continues to distribute its rewards haphazardly. This is chance.

But we can reduce the margin of chance in life, as we have reduced the chance of death from disease, of starvation from poverty, and of anguish in the heart. As we harness the forces of nature, we subdue the winds of chance that have us at their mercy. Through medicine, science, and inquiry, we tame the capricious universe and make it serve the human cause.

The flux of events may be blind, void of any purpose or design, but we can mold and harness it to whatever destiny we prescribe. We can fix our destiny and demolish the world with atoms, or we can call for only bread and circuses, and disown our need for further satisfactions. But whatever we prescribe, our destiny, our goal and values can be molded to our own design.

Ecclesiastes may believe that any values we design are whimsical conceits, a vanity of vanities all without substance. And yet our values cannot be denied. They give our lives whatever meaning they can have, and put in order the world of flux. We cannot blandly license the vanity of all our values; we must rather cultivate the values of our values and keep them under constant scrutiny. Out of this pursuit we must form the wisdom that we desperately need. For Ecclesiastes said himself, or one of his early editors did, "that wisdom giveth life to them that have it."

HUMANIST PHILOSOPHY 1928 – 1973

Alfred G. Smith is assistant professor of anthropology at Antioch College. This summer he is an exchange professor at University of Oregon. A man of wide interests, Dr. Smith repairs flutes as a hobby.

Probabalism: A Hardy Foe of the Absolute

Ted Brameld
The New Humanist, January, 1930

And now appears Professor A. E. Murphy at the University of Chicago with a philosophy called, for the time being, Probabalism. In full armour this enthusiastic warrior charges such defenders of the righteous as Eddington, and relentlessly turns them inside out. At last, some of the tough-minded will say, we have a man who shows with iron-bound logic, and a knowledge of recent scientific developments, just why so many pious fellows have failed to prove the existence of God and Goodness by means of electrons and equations.

Herein, so far as it has been understood from a lengthy series of lectures, we shall attempt to state what this new theory stands for. And following this, perhaps it will be possible — even with disregard for the prostrate Eddingtons — to find a flaw in Probabalism itself. The theory begins with an epistemological assumption: there are some facts which we have reason to believe, and our judgments about these may be accepted as true. The simplest of them are, of course, common-sense beliefs; but even our complex and abstruse judgments of science are subject to the same assumption, the acceptance of which is necessary to all knowledge. The resultant beliefs are, moreover, only probable, because they are possibly wrong; that is, they are always relative to the evidence at hand, — to their operational verification, as Bridgman (one of Professor Murphy's sources of authority) puts it in his "Logic of Modern Physics." There is always an element of contingency which may cause us to reject in the future a belief held now.

And how do our scientific beliefs thus arise? They are, essentially, merely those features of any event which are found to be relevant to the problem at hand; they become universals, therefore, just insofar as they may discard features which are irrelevant. Thus, such qualitative facts as color may prove to be unnecessary to a physical operation; but color, as well as biological and psychological facts of many kinds, are subject to abstract formulation in other ways. And even values, although not capable of the same sort of measurable generalization as, for instance, the electron, are also nevertheless intrinsically subject to scientific formulation.

Many of these facts, then, must be set down additively: instead of trying to bring all of them under increasingly general and static principles, we see nature now as irreducibly complex. The features of every event are constantly relative to their context, to the problem at hand, whether they be limited to single common-sense operations, or to wide physical application. They are meaningless otherwise, and mental characteristics may thus be regarded as significant for one operation while physical characteristics may for another. Why, therefore, the mental should be explained in terms of the physical, or vice versa, becomes a superfluous problem. Where we are concerned with a world of human purposes or values, mind becomes relevant; but where we are merely to discover, in the pre-human world, physical antecedents of events, then to explain them in terms other than the physical becomes irrelevant and meaningless. It is no longer necessary merely to ignore the pre-human, as Professor Dewey has done; for to fear entanglement in an absolute, or in a series of judgments leading thereto, is now erroneous. Our judgment, although relatively independent and abstract, is not therefore false. It does not pretend to prejudge the future or to do more, for instance, than treat these physical antecedents as relevant to physics' own problems but irrelevant to human problems.

Nor can the idealistic logician argue that since this judgment is a partial one we must posit a great series of interconnected judgments to take up what single ones omit — a series ultimately enmeshed in one final, infinite Whole. For so long as you make a judgment at all, it is always about what you have reason to believe. To demand a reason for this reason, therefore, calls for a reason different from a reason, i.e., unreason. Probabalism thus would build up resistance against our absolutistic inclinations by pointing out that logically no absolute is possible.

The whole difficulty has arisen from mechanism. This theory of philosophy, in attempting to nail reality down to static, physical concepts, has provided an opening wedge for all the various brands of anti-mechanistic metaphysics. It has failed in its own attempt, because all-embracing unrelative concepts of the sort it defends are always seen to contain less than reality itself; e.g., the quantitative measurements of physics completely exclude the qualitative aspects of experience. And then the new physics of Einstein and his collaborators has further destroyed the mechanist's position by showing that even the latter's precious measurements are relative to arbitrary frames of reference. The absolutist then comes along and posits a mind-stuff or a deity to account for what is otherwise left out. These are precisely the tactics of the sainted Eddington.

Yet, while many will find Probabalism a refreshing exposé of unhealthy philosophy, many, too, may find it unsatisfactory just because it is so exasperatingly logical. There is a need, these latter will say, for the illogical — for the types of "thinking" which are dumped into that convenient receptacle for undefined left-overs, mysticism. Nor, it seems to me, would such a criticism be wholly wrong, provided they nailed down mysticism to a meaning like that found, for instance, in Eugene O'Neill's "Lazarus Laughed."

You will remember that Lazurus in the play returns from the dead with the secret of reality in his heart. A tremendous joy courses through him, a joy so pure and so overwhelming that it bubbles over into exhilarating laughter. "Death is dead," he keeps repeating. "There is only life." O'Neill describes his laughter as a "great birdsong triumphant in the depths of the sky, proud, powerful, infectious with love."" Lazarus cries to his followers, "As Man, Petty Tyrant of Earth, you are a bubble pricked by death into a void and mocking silence! But as dust, you are eternal change, everlasting growth, and a high note of laughter soaring through chaos from the deep heart of God! ... Once, as squirming specks we crept from the tides of the sea. Now we return to the sea! Once as quivering flecks of rhythm we beat down from the sun. Now we re-enter the sun! ...We will to die! We will to change! ... We are the Giver and the Gift laughing, we will our own annihilation!"

Humanist Philosophy 1928 – 1973

If we remember that laughter, in prosaic psychological terms, is the release of nervous feeling following a restraint or an abruptly new situation, we can perhaps understand even without resorting to the delightful impossibility of a Lazarus how an overwhelming experience might suddenly reveal the pettiness of finitude, and how such a discovery would fill one with a mysteriously, mirthfully joyous grasp of the magnitude of that universe of which one is a part. He who senses in O'Neill's play an attempt to grasp reality as a total essence will, then, be likely to understand how a philosophy like Probabalism, with its rigid insistence upon fact, is inadequate.

Probabalists would not, of course, necessarily deny this charge: "We are not concerned," they would merely say, "with what the mystic wants to think." But if they admit even as much as this, do they not themselves provide an "opening wedge" for an absolutism of some sort? Nor do I mean necessarily an absolutism of the extreme sort depicted in the soul of Lazarus. I mean, for instance, the consequences which might follow from pursuing the "brute datum" constituting the fact about which I have reason to believe, itself not within knowledge because not a judgment, and therefore perhaps not ultimately different from the *ding-an-sich* of Kant out of which eventuates his whole absolutism. I mean, too, the "assumptions" which science has so far found necessary to its search (for instance, the "simplicity of nature"), which are condemned by the probabalist because they are non-operational, and yet which are not replaced by another technique to assure the scientist that he is getting toward a more satisfying knowledge. I mean the vague, confused "yet-unknowns" of nature which lie just outside our grasp, and too the merely potential means by which Probabalism insists we shall eventually be able to subject all facts to scientific method—matters which we have no reason to believe, which certainly are not operational, and yet must have some meaning since we at least talk about them and are forever seeking them. And I mean, finally, any kind of philosophy which tries to find a satisfaction for its curiosity about that which lies beyond the already determined—a satisfaction sought in symbolic drama perhaps, or again in metaphysics.

We must say, therefore, that to the extent that probabalism demands assumptions and unknowns it reaches beyond its legitimate sphere of activity. It becomes an empiricism colored with rationalism. It bursts the chains of its premises because it wants to grow. It yields to the urge to embrace—as Lazarus mystically embraced infinity—all dangling judgments, all electrons and values, into one concrete Whole.

Ted Brameld was a Fellow in the Philosophy Department, University of Chicago.

CHAPTER 6
Religious Humanism as Nontheistic, Naturalistic, and Instrumental

The Legacy of Modern Humanism's Origins

The HMI was primarily a statement of religious humanism. Not every HMI principle advanced a religious humanism, but its preamble clearly calls forth a new nontheistic religion of humanism.

The term "religious humanism" has been variously defined. Some writers equate the term with the concept of humanism as a religion. Indeed, John Dewey's definition of "religious" is so broad as to bring one writer in *TH* to complain that it "would include anything one believes deeply in."[1] Jerome Nathanson's included essay defines it as "a way of life."

Others talk about a religious humanism more in the sense of a secular humanism that accepts religious, i.e., "spiritual," experience. Linguistically, the phrase, "religious humanism," encompasses even that kind of hue. Thus, Paul Kurtz's essay in Chapter 1 says "[r]eligion for the humanist refers primarily to a quality in human experience."

The question is of course salient today. In 2013, Ronald Dworkin in his last book spoke of "religious atheism."[2] Under the first sense of "religious humanism," Dworkin's phrase is a classic oxymoron. Under the second, it would fall at the far end of Dewey's continuum of what may plausibly be called "religious." A little closer to the middle of that continuum is the phrase, "religious secularists," that an author in *TH* used in reference to nontheistic religious humanists.[3]

The notion of religious humanism as the religion is the subject of this chapter. Arguments that humanism should not be viewed as a religion are mentioned in Chapter 2.

The notion that the "religious" in humanism is secularly "spiritual" is covered in Chapter 7.

Nontheistic

In 1929, Alfred W. Hobart wrote that humanism should be considered agnostic (*TNH* 2:9). Contemporaneously, Roy W. Sellars described religious humanism as "religion adjusted to an intelligent naturalism" (*TNH* 6:3) and "a novel and revolutionary type of religion" (*TNH* 6:6). Horace S. Fries' contemporaneous essay argued for a godless naturalistic religion (*TNH* 7:1). In 1959, newly chosen AHA President George E. Axtelle called humanism "a religion, an intellectual and moral outlook shaped by the more sensitive and sympathetic souls of our time" (*TH* 19:2). A few years later, Julian Huxley described his evolutionary humanism as a new religion (*TH* 22:1). Yet all agreed religious humanism was nontheistic.

Nathanson discusses humanism as a religion in comparison to the Ethical Culture religion. Nathanson notes that both are nontheistic.

Naturalistic

That religious humanism is naturalistic fits hand in glove with its nontheism. Methodological naturalism's requirement of evidence leads to the conclusion that there are no deities. Similarly, Nathanson is consistent with HMI in stating that religious humanism is not supernatural, is rooted in human nature, and sees no evidence that nature is evil. It is decidedly naturalistic. Nathanson contrasts it with Ethical Culture, which, at least when he was writing, was not strictly naturalistic.

Fries pointed out that naturalism brings religion back to reality. Science inherently excludes supernaturalism, but confronting nihilism—the idea that values cannot be compared—takes more. Its lack of deities forces religious humanism to seek values elsewhere. For the slow pace of social progress, even naturalism has no easy solutions. In the face of that gap, Fries assumed that humanism offers hope of a better future, even a utopian one. That view would be controversial even today.4 He countered objections to naturalistic religion that it does not offer certainty of an improved future with the fact that theism does no better. Furthermore, Fries went beyond the notion that nothing prevents the future from being improvable to assert that naturalism has a better chance of resulting in a better future than does theism.

Fries observed that naturalistic religion leaves the notion of retribution in some theist religions behind. That of course is important to ending tribalism. More importantly, he broadens the view to the effects of all our actions. Rather than dwell on intent, naturalistic religion looks at the effects of our actions, because they limit all that follows. For Fries, naturalism compels one to look not backward with guilt and remorse, but forward with an eye toward creating what we want and, one might add, correcting the undesired effects of our experiments and misjudgments. Of course, doing so optimally requires the scientific approach to understanding all of reality that scientific naturalism provides.

Instrumentalist

Making religion hone to reality plays into John Dewey's instrumentalism at the core of Harold Scott's included essay. Scott argues that religion must be an instrument or tool advantageous to human wants and needs. That element consists of openness to refining values, rather than ossifying them. His religious humanism is thus pragmatic, experimental, and instrumentalist. For the refining of values, individual experience is data. Therefore, religious instrumentalism is naturalistic, not supernatural. On these bases, he sees religious instrumentalism also as a basis for hope.

Accordingly, religious instrumentalism is not mystical or transcendental. Scott's religious humanism replaces deities with the universe. His religious humanism is thus similar to deism, the religion replacing deities with nature. But rather than take human values as given by that universe, as does deism, Scott sees values in humanism as chosen by each individual human.

A New Kind of Religion?

Thus, as A. Eustace Haydon's included brief essay points out, humanism as a religion is very different from traditional theist, supernaturalist religions. He acknowledges that the definition of religion as the pursuit of the good life is rather broad. Not surprisingly, he downplays the question of *whether* humanism is a religion.

Taking a contrary position, Sellars's essay in this chapter expounds upon his view that humanism is a religion. He argues that humanism is so suited to religion that religion will over time become more humanist and humanism more religious. Of note, reading the essay closely, however, one sees that by "religion" he refers only to Christianity. In this context, he foresees a synthesis of humanism and this religion. For him, humanism in 1941 is too "aristocratic."

Sellars does not elucidate the ways humanism can become increasingly religious. On the one hand, it won't start accepting deities, supernatural theories, or nonnaturalistic epistemology. On the other hand, it has been creating canons of humanist values and rituals for marking life events. Another way humanism might become more like religions is by further accepting naturalistic understanding and valuing of spiritual and emotional experience. Writers on these issues in *TNH* and *TH* are discussed in Chapter 7.

Given recent global trends showing people leaving theistic religions, only time will tell whether Sellars was right. However, the contrast between HMI and the 1973 HMII suggests that humanism was already becoming less religious. HMII names religious humanism as only one of five types of naturalistic humanism.

Humanist Philosophy 1928 – 1973

Notes

1. Geiger, George R., "The Centennial of John Dewey," *TH* 19:5, p. 259 et seq. (1959), p. 259.
2. Dworkin, Ronald, *Religion Without God* (Harvard U. Press: 2013), p. 5.
3. Schneider, Herbert W., "The New Humanism," *TH* 13:1, p. 31 et seq. (1953), p. 32.
4. See, e.g., Rifkin, Lawrence, "What About Hope?" *TH* 72:1, p. 40 et seq. (2012).

Humanism as Religious Instrumentalism

Harold Scott
The New Humanist, September-October, 1935

The philosophical world is familiar with the term, "instrumentalism" as applied to that part of current thinking that sets forth practicality as the road of human progress. Observation of the practice of religion suggests a widely held view, however inarticulate it may be, that can properly be called religious instrumentalism.

Religious instrumentalism rests on the belief that religion is that quality that resides in activities and attitudes that gives them, in human terms, value and meaning. In this view religion becomes an instrument employed by man for his satisfaction and advantage. It does not assert that man is the most important thing in the universe, nor that the universe exists for man alone. It does not attempt to answer the question of the total meaning of man or of the universe. Perhaps to itself the most important thing in the universe is the ant. If so the ant is not to be reproached for ignorance. Possibly the ant is right. It does not say that the most important thing in the universe is man, but only to man the most important thing in the universe appears to be man. To achieve the greatest values he should regard religion as a tool, an instrument, and a technique. He should regard religion as in a large measure susceptible of being appropriated and modified for his own good. Too often religion has been considered the end and man the instrument. Religious instrumentalism addresses itself to the question as to how man may best exploit religion for his satisfaction. It does not attempt to reduce religion to a quantity, or dilute its quality, to fit man's needs, but limits itself to whatever may be appropriated and employed by man, without denying that this does not exhaust all areas of religion. This conception makes its chief claims for acceptance on the grounds of practibility. It does not deny or discard any of the generally approved methods of arriving at truth but places main reliance on pragmatism. Its norms are set up or discarded, not primarily by pure logic, but in accordance with the results of experimental living, observed, checked, and calculated, on the theory that one of the functions of religion is to promote man's satisfaction.

Religious instrumentalism is tentative, creative, experimental and, at some points, opportunistic. It does not attempt to be to be a logical system to explain all. It is not a system but an attitude an interpretation that seeks to capture and assimilate whatever values and meanings can be discovered. The supreme desires of man appear to be achieved in terms of value, meaning, and appreciation.

The practice of religion is the process of assigning value and meaning to all of experience. Thus the conclusions of all intellectual fields may be a part of its data.

In respect to the question of reality, religious instrumentalism interrogates the physicists. They say it consists of units of energy. There is no substance in the sense of anything being static. Man lives in a dynamic universe. There are not many ultimate reducible energies, but one energy. In respect to reality religious instrumentalism is dynamic monism. If science changes its opinion in respect to reality that changed opinion will become the opinion of religious instrumentalism.

Whatever may be the ultimate, reducible, reality, the universe appears to be composed of, or filled with, entities that are separate, discrete, and unique. The principle by which energy is grouped or arranged into patterns or configurations may be called "God." God may be defined as that principle of configuration whereby the universe results in value, meaning, and appreciation in human terms.

Religious instrumentalism does not deny cosmic meaning, purpose, ends, or value. It does say man cannot deal with them, and they are not a part of his data. Being man, he cannot experience them. There is no such thing as unconscious experience. Man may assess the value and meaning of every part of his experience. The experience of man is expanding. If, at any time in the past, man's experience had exhausted his existential medium obviously his experience could not have continued to expand. On the strength of such evidence as is available religious instrumentalism maintains the hypothesis of energy in flux, of change, evolution, growth, disintegration, and configuration. It draws a picture of creative activity, of limitless combinations, mutations, and permutations. The resident actuating cause of all this may be called "God." It urges the acceptance of incompleteness and expectancy as the only philosophic outlook appropriate to man.

Religious instrumentalism rejects supernaturalism because it applies the term "natural" to all human experience. It says that likely experience is what the psychologists say it is, the reception of data from stimuli. In theological terms it is participation in the activity of the existential medium. Supernaturalism assumes there are phenomena beyond human experience. If there were man could not know it. As soon as man becomes conscious of phenomena they become a part of his experience which by definition is natural. There is no point in calling any part of man's experience supernatural. To do so is to introduce the notion of disorderliness. The work of the exact and nearly exact sciences show an orderly universe. Those who believe there is disorder in the universe have the burden of proving it. The world of science says "No." Religious instrumentalism sees the intellectual undergirding of religion, called theology, as a derivative and summative discipline, always subject to modification by the data of other fields. Science does not sustain the alleged supernaturalism of historic religion. Religious instrumentalism believes it modest and wise to defer to science in the field of science.

Religious instrumentalism deplores the use of the term, "mystical" as descriptive of any part of its position. It says that human experience exhausts the field of human activity and states. There may be unexplained experiences but no inexplicable experiences. Mysticism has never explained itself in sensory terms. Again it is modest and wise to refer such questions to experts in that field. Psychologists say they know of no non-sensory experiences. Mysticism has insisted on knowledge coming to an individual in a way that was unusual, immediate, indescribable, and ineffable. It has made it a way of obtaining knowledge of supernatural entities. Usually it has hinted at the activity of a power outside of man's experience and understanding. As a summative discipline, religious instrumentalism must refuse to allow the mystic to try his case in other than the court of psychology.

Religious instrumentalism rejects the transcendence of God as being a poetic speculation that has been useful at some cultural levels, but for which no evidence is available. Such a conception no longer has utility in man's efforts to manipulate his existential medium in his favor, or comfort in his efforts at reconciliation with its non-manipulative aspects. The transcendence of God is too romantic a way to explain what is already implied in the inductions of science. Religious instrumentalism abandons all positions that newer learning shows to have lost explanatory value.

So far as religious instrumentalism utilizes the idea of deity at all, it embraces a conception that may be called "absolute immanence," that is an immanence that is devoid of any notion of transcendence. It is the quality of being intimately, vitally, or structurally, identified with the inner nature of the cosmic process. It operates from within. It is completely intrinsic.

Religious instrumentalism rejects pantheism which says that reality is seen as one, and that one, in its totality, as in its parts, is God. In popular language pantheism says, "All is God." Religious instrumentalism says, "God is in all."

Religious instrumentalism says that the terms good and bad are always relative and have reference to man's attempt to achieve satisfaction. It does not deny that there may be good and bad beyond his experience: but he is confined to his experience, thus it is necessary for him to interpret the universe in terms of what it means to him. In other words he has to look at the universe as an intensely personal matter, and call the several parts of his experience "good" or "bad" according to whether or not they advance his satisfaction. It ought to be admitted that this is experimental and pragmatic.

Is the problem of evil soluble? Religious instrumentalism cannot answer, "Yes." The concept of eternity is nearly imponderable. How completely man may search out the secrets of the universe is highly speculative. On the basis of the present bulk of the unknown in man's existential medium, and his comparatively microscopic presence in that medium, it seems almost presumptuous to assume that he will ever expand his experience to the extent that he can understand what he now calls the problem of evil.

Religious instrumentalism has the advantage of presenting a world view that, without demanding extravagant faith, gives assurance, hope, and a basis for struggle. It is already implicit in a large part of the current practice of religion. It may easily become explicit as an interpretation of religion.

Humanism and Ethical Culture

Jerome Nathanson
The Humanist, March-April, 1951

Jerome Nathanson is a Leader of the New York Ethical Culture Society and the author of Forerunners of Freedom. *Here he responds to our invitation to present what he feels are differences and similarities between the philosophies of Humanism and Ethical Culture.*

This is not a day of religious reaction, although the dominant media of communication give the impression that it is. It is rather a day in which the voices of reaction have become more strident and the church militant, knowing a main chance when it sees one, deploys its forces with great tactical skill. Its task is made easier by the fragmentized liberalism which, because of its disunity and confusion, can offer it only sporadic opposition instead of sustained confrontation. And thus, while we are not yet living through a religious reaction, we may be witnessing the prelude to it.

I take it that this is the crisis of our age—for without re-examining the tedious questions of whether and how and why ideas affect institutions or institutions shape ideas, we should be able to take it for granted that religious reaction, if it comes, will be part and parcel of a wider social and political reaction. Any concern with the freedom of the human spirit which is to be more than a pious sentimentalism, accordingly, has to be concerned with achieving coordinated efforts among religious liberals.

Since there are Humanists, as there are Ethical Culturists, who bridle at such words as "religion" and "religious," let us make clear how we are using them. "Religion" is here defined as a way of life. "Religious reaction" designates dogmatic insistence on a way of life organized around the idea of the supremacy of a personal God and the fate of human beings in a postulated hereafter. "Religious liberalism" means a way of life organized around the idea that nothing is more important for people than what happens to people here and now.

With these propositions in mind, let us briefly examine the relations of Humanism and Ethical Culture, as one step in the necessary coordination of liberal efforts.

From a broad point of view, both Humanism and Ethical Culture are humanistic. They are man-centered religions. This is not to say that they are addicted to that corrosive ethical relativism which, using the dictum that "man is the measure of all things" as a springboard, plunges into that morass in which ethical judgment is reduced to matters of taste or biography or history. It is to say that their faith in human good, present and future, is rooted in the possibilities of human nature.

It follows, therefore, that they both reject the proposition that man is essentially evil, whether in its orthodox Christian or orthodox Freudian version, with the corollary that redemption is necessarily dependent upon the ancient rite of holy communion or the modern ritual of psychoanalysis. Nor do they, in this rejection, fall into the trap of affirming that man is essentially good. Instead, they accept human nature as indefinitely flexible, with vast possibilities for good and evil, believing that the ways in which life is lived, individually and collectively, determine whether the potentials for evil or those for good are to be actualized.

What, then, is to be man's reliance in the endeavor to actualize the possibilities for good? Not the acceptance of a rigid creed, the observance of a fixed ritual, nor prayers for the intervention of God's grace. Man is to rely on his own efforts, on his intelligence and good will. These may be frail reeds, as the poignancy of human experience amply testifies. Such as they are, however, both for Humanism and Ethical Culture, they are all we have—and what they have enabled human beings to achieve over the centuries should not seem wholly negligible to an unjaundiced eye.

In view of the fact that both Humanism and Ethical Culture are both thus broadly humanistic, why are they organized as separate movements? This is a question which has troubled increasing numbers of members in both movements, as it has confused many others who, sympathetic with each, have held aloof from both. It is because there are important differences between the two movements that they are separate. These differences need not stand in the way of a growing coordination of effort, but they can be glossed over only at the expense of the organized integrity of the movements. To understand this clearly requires consideration of their distinctive positions.

Humanism, as we use the term, is a world apart from the humanism of Erasmus or that of Paul Elmer More. For us, rather, it is one phase of the movement of scientific naturalism. Naturalism is the belief that whatever is is natural, as opposed to supernatural or extra-natural. Put differently, it defines nature as whatever happens. This sounds simple enough, until we ask ourselves: What does happen?, and, How do we know what happens? For human purposes, the latter is the key question, for although a great many things may happen to us that we do not know or certainly do not understand, the only things manageable by human beings are those we do know and can understand. This is where the "scientific" part of "scientific naturalism" comes in. For it affirms that, while we may get hunches about what happens in a great many different ways, those hunches are converted into knowledge only as we use intelligence or, more accurately, as we use intelligence organized along lines of controlled experimentation, which is science.

Such scientific naturalism becomes humanistic when it is animated by a concern with increasing communication and community among people, with raising the level of human relations. Communication and community may have a "mystical" quality about them, depending upon the labels one prefers for certain experiences, if not upon one's capacities for certain kinds of experience. However that may be, Humanism is the religious torchbearer of scientific naturalism. This is its distinctive mission.

Now Ethical Culture, while it has within its ranks many thorough-going Humanists, as a movement is no more committed to any one knowledge-process than it is to any one metaphysics. Its founder, Felix Adler, was a neo-Kantian transcendentalist. And in its membership, as among its Leaders, are many who might technically be labelled intuitionists rather than scientific naturalists. It would be beside the point at the moment to go into the practical implications of these positions, just as it would be to discuss their relative warrant. The present point is that, while Humanism is pluralistic as it looks at nature from the inside, Ethical Culture is pluralistic as it looks at nature itself, in its approach to the universe.

This latter pluralism is not an evasion, a refusal to take a stand on a matter of paramount importance. It is rather a pluralism of conviction, just because the matter is one of paramount importance. It is a conviction, based on the experience of the race, that creedal quarrels are as footless as they are often bloody, and that they have the tragic consequence of hopelessly dividing those who should be united in their common humanity. It is a conviction that mankind never will see the universe in any one way, and that there is no good reason why it should. It is a conviction that there are endless paths to the endless truths the universe unfolds, endless ways of building new truths on old ones, and that a wide-open welcome to each and all that forward man's ethical quest is both prudent and wise.

It may sound like an invidious comparison to put these distinctions in a nutshell by saying that while all Humanists could be Ethical Culturists, not all Ethical Culturists could be Humanists. It is not intended as such. It is meant simply to underscore their different approaches, as movements, to the nature of nature and to the relations of experience and nature.

But when all is said and done, despite their differences, the two movements are joined in a common concern. That concern is with contributing whatever we can to the increasing community of mankind. To find ever better ways, together, of making that contribution would mean to draw others, and still others, into an ever-widening circle of common effort. And who knows but what, this way, the gathering clouds which now seem to portend reaction might sometime fertilize the soil for a greater growth of human freedom than the world has ever seen.

Humanist Philosophy 1928 – 1973

Humanism Has Its World View, Techniques and Ideals

A. Eustace Haydon
The Humanist, Autumn, 1942

Whether or not we recognize in humanism a modern embodiment of man's religious quest will depend upon our understanding of the nature of religion. If we are dominated by the Christian tradition with its emphasis upon belief and its separation of the religious and the secular, it will seem like a falsification of humanism to call it religion. On the other hand, if we survey the great Oriental cultures, where religion is a way of life with the emphasis upon what a man does rather than upon what he believes, we may feel that humanism fits this religious pattern fairly well. Humanism is not merely a philosophy of life; it is certainly not a new sectarianism; it cannot be confined within the limitations of a church. It is a new orientation of culture pointing toward the realization of the good life for all men. And it is precisely this social quest for the good life that modern research has defined as the essential, historic nature of religions.

When modern scholars began the scientific study of religions they were shackled by their Christian heritage. They defined religion as belief in the supernatural. The search for the origin of religion became a search for the origin of the god idea. It took fully fifty years to escape this bias and to see the world-wide, age-long history of religions in more complete perspective. This is not the place to picture that tortured battlefield on which definitions of religion challenged each other for two generations. (At the turn of the century John Morley said there were already ten thousand definitions of religion.) Gradually other phases of the religious complex in addition to theology claimed a place in the sun. The values which men were trying to win came to the focus of attention and the practical and ceremonial techniques for achieving these values were included in the picture. It was generally conceded that religion was social. The result was a definition of religion which included the values of the ideal, the techniques and the technology. It was clear that the values were central, the techniques and the gods only means of guaranteeing their realization. Only one step more was necessary to see that the desires of men reaching out for fulfilment underlay the changing forms of every religion. The values might change, the techniques become endlessly diverse with altered conditions, the gods die or grow into new forms—the one thing that remained was the unwavering drive of desires for satisfaction. While at any time, in any culture the religious complex consists of worldview, techniques and ideal, these are always the creations of the life process of the group and may vary or change continuously. Religions ever create their own embodiments in terms of geography and social conditions, knowledge of the world and human powers of mastery. It seems best to define this universal process as man's social quest for the values of the good life. Humanism is this process in action today.

As a product of the new age, humanism is certainly very different in form from traditional religions. Yet it is necessary to remember that they are very old and that they took their historic forms to overcome the conditions of periods of frustration. In the early ages, religion was the unifying bond of cultures and was interested in the winning of a good life on the earth. Only when disaster repeatedly overtook man's best efforts at culture building did he turn to compensatory other worlds or project his ideal into the future. Only when human powers proved futile in the wrestle with social maladjustments did man fall back for the ultimate guarantee of his hopes upon the gods. Moreover the old religions are responding to the modern climate. Modernism is a popular mode. Hesitantly, still clinging for security to fundamentals with frequent, frightened flights back to the haven of faith, religious leaders are coming to terms with modern knowledge, experimenting with social idealism and accepting responsibility for the making of a good world. In the process of revitalizing their systems to meet the changed conditions of a new age, the old religions are acquiring a humanistic tone.

Humanism can be vital and forthright because it is not hampered by the necessity rationalizing a heritage of ideas and institutions. It does not try to put new wine into old bottles. Like all religions humanism has its world view, techniques and ideal. The world view is based on our modern knowledge. The sciences provide the techniques for actualizing values. Masters of the scientific method in all areas of culture may furnish the analysis of problems and create the programs for the progressive realization of a good society in which the values of the good life may be available to all the sons of earth. The ideal is a good world in which the so-called "spiritual values"—justice, love, brotherhood, cooperation and peace—may find embodiment in behavior. Analyses of myriad, tangled situations will yield the ideals and the programs to implement them as man moves toward the desired harmonious synthesis of culture.

Humanism differs most sharply from religions, both past and present, in its worldview. All the religions of the world, theistic and atheistic, spiritualistic and materialistic, this-worldly and other-worldly have agreed in assuming that the universe, in its true nature, is the source, support and guarantor of the values of the ideal. The humanist has surrendered this comforting faith. Accepting the tentative findings of modern science, he is contented to live dangerously without cosmic guarantee and the walled security of eternal truth. Neither the Orient's faith in eternal, timeless perfection, nor the Jewish-Christian faith in a divine purpose threading the events of time seems justified by historic facts. For good or ill man must accept responsibility for putting purpose into human history. The good life he failed to achieve with the help of the gods, he must now try to win by his own ability, intelligence and goodwill. That human power and intelligence can transform the world has been demonstrated by the happy and tragic experiences of the last century. The humanist dares to believe that goodwill, backed by modern techniques, wisdom and resources, can make the old religious dream take on the forms of actuality.

Whether or not humanism is called a religion is of no great importance. The historian of religions may recognize it as a vital, modem manifestation of the religious quest, but after all, humanism needs no borrowed halo. It is the tide of the future, overflowing all boundaries of occupation, sect, race, nation and culture. It is a new cultural climate luring the multitudes to new hope in all lands. If it fulfils its promise and provides an intellectual and practical synthesis of world cultures it will command a deeper loyalty than any religion can claim.

Humanism as a Religion

Roy Wood Sellars
The Humanist, Spring, 1941

Undeniably there is something imaginative and daring in bringing together in one phrase two such profoundly symbolic words as humanism and religion. An intimate union is foreshadowed in which religion will be become humanistic and humanism religious. And I believe that such a synthesis is imperative if humanity is ever to achieve a firm and adequate understanding of itself and its cosmic situation.

But there is need for definition and clarification. How should these terms be taken? What kind of synthesis does the religious humanist have in mind? What directives and directions does he set before himself?

*****

Of these two linked terms humanism is the less ambiguous. There have been, of course, different emphases in the modern world from the period of the rebirth, or Renaissance, of the fifteenth century to our own troubled and congested time. There was first, the moment of taking stock, of assimilating the culture of the past in the humanities, a somewhat fevered and hasty assimilation, if you will, and yet genuine and laying the foundation for modern art and literature. Without it Michelangelo, Shakespeare and Goethe could not have appeared. The renewed stimulus of the antique world counted for much in the growth of the modern, in which Western man was again trying to find, under what promised to be more favorable circumstances, release and self-expression. To literary humanism was added the scientific motive and method, from the beginning lustier and more practical than ever before. More quietly and with less acclaim philosophy set to work to reanalyze and reconstruct basic ideas.

Such, in a broad way, is the context of humanism. It is a term which symbolizes man's discovery of himself and, therein, of his possibilities. It signifies human endeavor, human achievements, the sweetness and bright promise of life. Yet I make haste to warn the reader that humanism has never been sentimental and unaware of the forces of evil and of obscurantism. It always fought an uphill fight, always encountered resistance, always knew itself to be little more than ferment in a huge society given over to struggles for power and mere existence. But who can deny that, in the various directions and emphases of humanism, there was the promise and potency of human maturity?

Nevertheless, humanism was, almost perforce, isolated and aristocratic. It was for the educated, for the classes, for those who could come under the sway of its ideas and values. And it suffered continually from this isolation in perspective and power.

*****

Let us turn now to religion, that intenser, vaguer, more diffuse, more daemonic, more ambiguous of our two terms. I shall not attempt here to give a formal definition, even if I considered such an attempt feasible. It will suffice to call attention to religion as it manifested itself in that redoubtable, religious movement called Christianity, an historical blend of noble ethics, superstition, theism, otherworldliness, fanaticism, sacerdotalism, salvationism and super-naturalism. We all know how many different blendings of these ingredients there are and have been. To this extent each church has had its own variety of Christianity and even its own *acknowledged* varieties; nay more, its *unacknowledged* varieties.

To attain sharpness of focus let us look broadly at Christianity, first, in the Ancient World of its origins and then in those forms of it most adjusted to the scientific and philosophic ideas of the present, namely, in those phases of modernism which fluctuate between deism and theism and vaguely trust the larger hope.

Scholars quite generally agree that Christianity arose more among the masses than the classes. Its ethical atmosphere was concrete and personal and stressed charity and comradeship rather than duty and public service. There is even reason to believe that, in the early days, this normal note led the small Christian community to approach the condition of a "love-communism" in which brothers and sisters in Christ would have something approaching a common purse. The beliefs entertained with conviction were also concrete: the resurrection of the body, literally, the rising up of corpses; salvation through the supernatural power of the Lord; the reversal of worldly values. It must be remembered, first of all, that it was a period of political decline and increasing loneliness and pessimism. The gulf between rulers and the ruled, the rich and the poor, had become a chasm. The philosophies of life upon which the educated had come to rely, Stoicism, Epicureanism and Neo-Platonism, and which taught them some measure of self-sufficiency and resignation, were unknown to the masses of the city-proletariat and the slaves. Such a concrete religion with its faith and symbols was the sole escape from despair and unintelligibility. And politically and economically things went on from bad to worse. Christianity had inherited from the Jews a firmly vouched-for story about divine things and had added a personal saviour, personal immortality and a Heavenly City. It is scarcely to be wondered at that this community expanded and finally was adopted by the Roman State. When the total picture is explored by scholars a sense of inevitability arises. But into that question we cannot at present enter.

As Christianity felt the need of explicit doctrine clothed in the terminology of the learned, philosophy was at its service. And orthodoxies were formulated in opposition to heresies, Gnostic and Christian. The two great theistic systems used through the centuries by Christian theologians were the Platonic and the Aristotelian with Stoicism furnishing at times a pantheistic note. The result was an abstract and rarified cosmic framework within which the very concrete and human drama of faith and hope, of fear and despair, of miracles and prayer, of personal immortality and wish-fulfillment could unfold.

*****

But what have we now? The world of super-Copernican science, of astrophysics, of evolution, of man's increasing self-knowledge and cosmic knowledge. As education penetrates to the people, even in societies dedicated to the transmission of inherited ideas, doubt enters with regard to the marvelous Christian epic of long ago. We have been moving into another epoch, an epoch of social activity, of the breaking down of class barriers, of the extension of scientific ideas. The atmosphere has become increasingly alien to certain of the ingredients in that complex blend called Christianity. The anthropomorphism has become evident, the miraculous, childish and repugnant. Sacerdotalism is not liked because so often authoritarian and reactionary. In fact, the whole perspective which had meaning in the passing epoch has less vital meaning to this. Even the ethics of Christianity is seen to be too little social in its emphasis though there are noble Christians who are seeking to remedy this falling and give a social application to the ethics of brotherly love. All honor to them!

The impact of the ideas and demands of the new epoch in which we live has long been evident in those forms of Christianity called modernism. Liberals in religion have sought to make adjustments in their beliefs and hopes while keeping as much of the framework as they could conscientiously retain. In this period of tension and ferment profoundly religious men do it, that is, men who demand a definite and intelligible account of human life, its actual situation, its significant values and its destiny in the universe so that they may not drift about in merely inherited unrealities but pilot the ship of their lives with some assurance of what ports to aim at and what cargoes of goods to take on;—such men, I say, are searching for a more empirically founded and reasoned account of the verifiable directives, aims, and circumference of human living.

To the thoughtful of our day, humanism is being offered as this kind of a religion, a religion akin to science and philosophy and yet not a mere abstract of these specialized endeavors. It is a call to an imaginative interpretation of human living after mythology and superstition have been quietly and firmly put to one side as no longer a thoroughfare for an adult humanity. Religious humanism rests upon the bedrock of a decision that it is, in the long run, saner and wiser to face facts than to live in a world of fable which even the institutionally cultivated will-to-believe of the churches can in these days scarcely clothe with a sense of reality. But such a decision, important as it is, is not enough. Humanism faces the task—a cooperative one—of determining what is possible, significant and desirable in human living. As one who has meditated long years on such a theme I have my suggestions some of which were embodied in the *Humanist Manifesto*. Into the details I cannot here enter. It must suffice to say that an integral and humanistic naturalism has in it possibilities of direction for human living which promise much for this distraught and bewildered epoch.

CHAPTER 7

The Roles of Emotion and Spirituality in Humanism

Two Taboos in Humanism?

The Dialectic Between Reason and Emotion in Humanism

With its focus on the scientific method, humanist philosophy emphasizes the importance of reason. The role of emotion has been more ambiguous. Early modern writers in *TNH* and *TH* barely addressed it. Not until the advent of the humanistic psychologists and feminists did the question begin to get serious attention.

Barbara J. Bates's 1960 essay in this chapter raises core issues that remain relevant today. She argues that humanism is too theoretical to address "the emotional challenge of life." Humanism must acknowledge the stress and emotional element of human life. Only then can it find ways to offer the solace that religion has given for so long.

Roy P. Fairfield's citation of Abraham Maslow as 1967 Humanist of the Year credited Maslow and other humanistic psychologists with bringing the study of emotion into naturalism and humanism (*TH* 27:3). He suggested that doing so saved humanism from "extreme rationalism." Although he did not say so, the historical association of humanism with rationalism is the source of humanist philosophy's problem. Reason, i.e., rationality, is central to both.

Harry Elmer Barnes gave an historical overview of Classical rationality (*TH* 21:3). In that view, emotion is quite simply irrational. Rationalism arose alongside the invention of the scientific method, which excludes emotional considerations. H. J. Eysenck's included essay refers to the reputation of humanism as essentially equivalent to rationalism. The nature of rationality also echoes in the criticisms of humanism in the other essays in this chapter. Thus, rationalism's notion that emotion is to be minimized may be one source of humanist philosophy's inadequate incorporation of it.

Eysenck argues that humanism's association with rationalism has also partly arisen from the emphasis of humanist critique of religion. Certainly, rationalism verged on atheistic challenges to religious claims. Like that of rationalism, humanism's critique is based on science. Thus, rationalism's rejection of emotion has been imported into humanism through that channel as well.

To counter the neglect of emotion, some writers in *TH* have advocated particular ways of accepting and embracing emotion in humanism. Eysenck argues that humanism must emphasize the emotion of compassion. He suggests that compassion should be a basis for humanist ideals, i.e., values, which science cannot provide. He ends with a plea for compassion in humanism, in order to balance the power of reason. Reason, he says, provides the means; compassion, the ends. Other writers advocated emotions like love[1] and joy,[2] among others.

Bates argues that humanism must even embrace difficult emotions that can arise from life's experiences that go contrary to desires and hopes. These emotions, when internalized, can keep an individual from self-actualization. Of course, humanist philosophy promotes values that allow people to be and act freely so long as they do not cause harm to others. But where a person has internalized negative emotions about himself or herself, reason can help release them in a way that makes the person freer to more fully embrace who he or she is.

Thus, Bates acknowledges the tenet of humanism, like rationalism, that reason must properly limit emotion. But clearly, humanists have advocated recognition of the important contributions that emotion makes to life and philosophy. Some writers have suggested elements of a dialectic, but even today, much work remains to be done in that regard.

The Best of *The Humanist*

Spirituality in Humanism

"Spirituality" is a loaded word, fraught with religiosity. Many humanists shun its use respecting anything humanist. Some, like Harald H. Titus in his essay in Chapter 1, and Lloyd Morain and Oliver Reiser in their essay in Chapter 2, generally equate the spiritual with the religious. Humanists who view humanism as a religion have the least quarrel with that easy kind of equivalence. For example, Albert Schweitzer, who came to value humanism as a religion, stated late in life that humanism is "the only true spirituality" (see Sabiston, *TH* 22:4). But even Patton, the natural mystic, rules out the existence of a separate "spirit" from the mind.

More compelling is the thesis that spirituality can be completely natural, that is, not religious. Proponents of this view argue that spirituality is essentially normal human reaction to overwhelming experiences. Henry Strong Huntington argued that civilization will not have a stable basis until the "spiritual hunger" that he says most people feel is met on a daily basis (*TH* 10:1). While acknowledging the devices religions have used to try to meet that hunger, he asserts that humanism has not come up with its own natural solution to the problem. Algernon G. Black's essay in Chapter 11 goes much further, including all sorts of basic needs and longings in the scope of his definition of "spiritual."

Other writers have addressed the issue. Carl J. Friedrich in 1944 called for a humanism that not only champions reason, but also reflects the more spiritual values of Eastern cultures. Friedrich's call came out of his analysis of Lewis Mumford's critique of fascism, capitalism, culture, and religion in *The Condition of Man*. That analysis led Friedrich to discern something lacking in Western culture and humanism up to that time (*TH* 4:4).

Closely in line with Friedrich's assessment is Maslow's included statement as Humanist of the Year in Chapter 3. He mentions "the spiritual life" as one of the elements of intrinsic values. He places life "in the world of nature," and later states that the "value life" includes the "spiritual."

Humanist Philosophy 1928 – 1973

He goes on to say that "the spiritual life is instinctoid" while being capable of "education."

Black's essay explores natural explanations for spirituality. He implicitly affirms that not all humans have "spiritual" feelings; however, those who do gain much from them. He offers that humanism presents a way of life with dignity that affirms the value of each individual and all life. Thus, his most poignant observation about the meaning of "spiritual" in humanism may be the following: "that his life has meaning not only for himself and his fellows and the generations to come, but also in the larger context of the universe."

Kenneth L. Patton's essay in this chapter proffers a hint of how that happens. The essay does not mention humanism and is only vaguely agnostic, but it propounds a natural mysticism that is generally compatible with naturalism. The essay is included in this chapter, instead of Chapter 5 on the unknown, because of the *way* he talks about natural mysticism. Spirituality often includes wonder, as does Patton's version of nontheistic mysticism. His mysticism is sensual, within the natural human senses, in that it results from "acute awareness." Patton ascribes a physical dimension to that mysticism, consisting of a natural reaction to the awareness of nature. But it is Patton's discussion of mystical feelings when in the presence of another human, still a part of nature, that is most interesting.

Unlike even some humanists, Patton is obviously one of those people who has a lot of spiritual feelings. He describes human interactions, even fleeting ones on a crowded street, as mystical adventure. He suggests that while these kinds of perceptions have in the past been called religious, they have little to do with religion. His key insight, however, is that, "All added together, things heard, seen, felt, things seen as a whole, in large impression, things felt rather than known in detail, things known by feeling rather than by thought or reason, give us the mystical experience of being with another person." That he cites artists, musicians, poets, and the like suggests the origin of connection between humanism and the humanities. At the very least, he rebuts those theists who claim that humanists, freethinkers, atheists, and other secular people have no basis for experiencing awe and wonder at the universe in toto or in detail. Morain and Reiser's essay also rebuts that canard.

For some humanists, the question of spirituality in humanism is semantic. For them, the "spiritual" is simply human feelings in reaction to events or natural beauty or whatever other context is cited. Others will insist that their feelings have a stronger basis, whether rooted in a reminder of the frailness of human civilization or even existence, or of the simple awareness of how fortunate we humans are to exist and be aware of the universe around us, given the massive scale of change over vast periods of time. Viewed in that way, the essays in this section on spirituality capture a disconnect between those two camps in the humanist community that persists to this day.

Notes

1. Friedrich, Carl J., "Organic Humanism," *TH* 4:4, p. 145 et seq. (1944), pp. 150, 151.
2. See, e.g., Kurtz, Paul, "Joyful Humanism," *TH* 27:2, p. 39 et seq. (1967).

Emotional and Intellectual Humanism

Barbara J. Bates
The Humanist, November-December, 1960

At least once in the lifetime of every human being there is a need for complete self-examination. This is usually precipitated by some great personal crisis, accompanied by emotional and mental upheaval. The stresses to which we are all subject lead us to an intersection where we must make a choice, perhaps even detour the whole course of our lives. Without this moment or perhaps many such moments, we would be vegetables, living that unexamined life which Socrates said is not worth living.

Such an experience is exemplary in the old-fashioned revival meeting, in the group therapy of Alcoholics Anonymous, and in the emotional catharsis of psychiatry. I believe the need is just as important in the life of a Humanist with one difference: that he can approach his self-criticism logically, without the hysteria of the convert or the hangover of the contrite alcoholic.

Humanism can be a "soul-saving" movement for those many of us who do not believe in the immortal soul. It can be a humanitarian effort without the clash of a tambourine. The Humanist has come to humanism intellectually, knowing that religion is not the solution to mankind's ailments. What he must then do is to examine his own motives and theories within an emotional as well as intellectual framework. The appeal of religion and other "salvation" movements is one of emotional dynamics; this explains the power some movements are able to accumulate.

It is all very well and very necessary for us to hold our Humanist meetings and express our theories about the rights of mankind. But there are men, and children, flesh and blood human beings, all around us who need humanism as a straw to grasp before the stresses of their lives pull them under. How many personal tragedies or family breakdowns can be prevented by a real grass-roots humanism by each member of our intellectual Humanist groups. Religion provides solace for millions of people for one reason: Humanism is still too theoretical. Humanism as a great working force in the world is going to have to meet the emotional challenge of life—the life of people in trouble.

It is the duty of the individual Humanist to examine his own humanism squarely and without recourse to procrastination and guilt. An emotional Humanist feels compassion for men in trouble; an intellectual Humanist deplores the social causes of mankind's trouble. One reaches out his hand; the other sends a committee.

Mrs. Charles R. Bates, Secretary-Treasurer of the new Sacramento chapter of the AHA, is a graduate of the University of Nevada, the wife of an architectural designer, and the mother of two small children.

Definitions of Humanism: Reason with Compassion

H. J. Eysenck
The Humanist, March-April, 1971

It is unlikely that all humanists would agree on a definition of the term "humanism"; what I shall do is simply to suggest what to me are the essentials of humanism, without thereby trying to imply that others would necessarily agree. Indeed, I feel sure that old-fashioned humanists, with the smell of bloody battles against religion still in their nostrils, will feel shocked at the cavalier disregard I may show for furthering such battles. I am strengthened, however, by my belief that at the bottom of humanist attitudes lies belief in the power and importance of *reason*. Indeed, the terms "humanist" and "rationalist" used to be almost interchangeable. Opposition to religious beliefs was originally inspired by the fact that where humanists put their faith in reason, religious people put their faith in faith. Thus, the first part of my definition of humanism would involve a stress on the use of *reason* in dealing with inanimate nature and with other human beings. This inevitably involves the rejection of revealed religion, and in that sense I am at one with old-fashioned humanists.

I think that important differences arise when one attempts to extend the range of this definition beyond religion. All humanists are agreed that religion is not based on reason, but not all humanists would follow me in declaring that there are many other beliefs that are equally lacking in any rational basis. One such belief, for instance, is nationalism — that is, the belief that one's own nation is in some sense supremely endowed with all the good qualities of humankind, that one's nation has never waged an unjust war, and that it must be supported through thick and thin. Political beliefs are also firmly held and may share with nationalism the doubtful honor of having replaced religion as the main stronghold of fervent but unreasoned support and faith. Socialism and capitalism both find their blind adherents even among people who ought to know better; these kinds of people are incapable of subordinating the fervor of their political beliefs to the searching scrutiny of empirical research and factual investigation. Racism is another candidate for this modern rogues' gallery; many people hold very firm but inadequately based beliefs in the inferiority or superiority of one race with respect to other races. Finally, there are modern pseudoreligious belief systems (for example, Communism, psychoanalysis) which are advertised as being "scientific," but are no more so than the Church of Christ, Scientist. I believe that from the point of view of humanism (or rationalism) these modern heresies are much more dangerous than religion. I believe that humanists should be far more concerned with introducing the rule of reason into these fields than with fighting the old, long-won battles against religion all over again.

To young people nowadays, humanism, like religion, wears a long Victorian beard and seems quite dated and irrelevant to modern problems. It seems to me that humanism ought to update itself and turn to more urgent tasks than those which confronted it when religion was still strong and vicious. We might even find that modern religion is in many ways an ally rather than a foe. Ministers of many religions, for instance, have denounced South African doctrines of apartheid more strongly and loudly than humanists have done, and the same is true of segregation in the Southern states of the U.S. Religion today in many respects is little but an ethical guide. Many officials of the various Churches would find difficulties in adhering to the 39 Articles or in passing even minimum tests of religious orthodoxy. There are still relics of the old Adam to be found, but on the whole it would seem to me that humanists should look for worthier foes.

To me, the word "reason" in this respect implies science. Science is the embodiment of the rational attempt to solve problems posed by nature or by human beings in their variegated absurdity. Few people would deny that this is so with respect to physics, chemistry, or astronomy; many would be surprised to hear it asserted with respect to psychology. Most of our problems nowadays, however, are psychological in origin — war, strikes, and overpopulation are all caused by human beings, and failure to control the impulses that lead to these disastrous consequences is largely due to lack of scientific knowledge in the field of psychology. Yet we already possess a good deal of knowledge, laboriously acquired through laboratory investigations and the statistical analysis of empirically observed phenomena in everyday life. It should be the task of humanists to make themselves familiar with such knowledge as exists already and to press for its use in the solution of human problems. Furthermore, humanists should be in the forefront of those asking for the support of further research into these complex and difficult problems. It is not reasonable that we should waste a billion pounds on developing a plane that can transport an infinitesimally small number of people from London to New York in a slightly briefer period of time than has previously been required, but spend less than one quarter of 1 per cent of this sum annually on research in all the social sciences!

To my definition of humanism I would add one further term: compassion. To me, humanism is *the use of reason in human affairs, applied in the service of compassion.* Reason by itself does not set our aims, but provides merely the means through which our aims can be reached. It may be possible to develop a scientific ethic, that is, to prescribe our aims along purely rational lines. This has certainly been attempted by many well-known persons. I am doubtful, however, whether such an attempt will succeed; certainly at this writing there is no general agreement on any such system. Consequently I think that the addition of a qualifying clause such as that suggested above is needed. Reason can tell you that there is no scientific evidence to show that the Negroes transported as slaves to the U.S. were in any sense biologically inferior to their masters; reason by itself cannot tell you that whether these slaves were inferior, equal, or superior to their captors, the very notion of slavery is obnoxious and must be eradicated. Any argument that purports to accomplish this conclusion along purely rational grounds will be found to be based on premises that themselves are taken as axiomatic and that prejudge the issue. I may be mistaken in this, but to me it seems that, at the present time at any rate, the addition of compassion to reason is needed if we want to make humanism something other than a cold, selfish pursuit of a person's immediate self-interest through entirely rational means. A given slave owner might argue — with reason! — that his own self-interest was best served by keeping his slaves working all day for him, by breeding genetically superior slaves from them through the application of genetic principles, and by selling the resulting children at a good profit. Can reason disprove him? Reason to me marks out the method to be used on all occasions by humanists; compassion marks out the ideal in the service of which reason is employed.

The revulsion many people nowadays feel against science illustrates well why to me reason alone cannot suffice as a definition of humanism. Science, being the embodiment of reason, is equally capable of being employed in devising new medical methods of saving life and in devising new military methods of destroying life. Religion today is more clearly committed to compassion than are science and reason. Hence, I find it difficult to quarrel against religion (as an ethical rule) with the enthusiasm I would have felt 300 years ago when it arrogated to itself a position in which supernatural revelation was considered infinitely superior to reason. In rejecting religion altogether, humanism may be throwing out the ethical baby with the supernatural bathwater. My definition of humanism would try to reconcile these two fundamental contributions—reason and compassion — without both of which life on this planet is unlikely to continue, and would be intolerable even if it did.

H. J. Eysenck is Professor of Psychology at the London University Institute of Psychiatry. Among his books are Sense and Nonsense in Psychology *and* The Biological Basis of Personality; *he is also chief editor of* Behavior Research and Therapy. *Professor Eysenck is a Board member of the British Humanist Association.*

Natural Mysticism

Kenneth L. Patton
The Humanist, Autumn, 1943

The University of Chicago has many churches sprinkled among its buildings. With gothic arches and jewelled windows, organs and carved wood, berobed preachers, choirs and symbolic sculpture, there is no lack of trappings intended to induce in one the religious mood. Nor would anyone deny that there is something thrilling and awesome in the tall stateliness and colored gloom of such buildings. But I do not believe that you and I can really appreciate them, any more than we can really appreciate another man's father and mother, wife and children, for what they mean to him. These buildings were borrowed from a people who found in the creation of such architecture the expression of their sense of mystery and devotion. They are not our creations, nor are they genetically derived from life as we live it, so we can be little more than sympathetic spectators, even though our generation saw fit to recreate these buildings in our midst. We are visitors in another man's house, strangers among another man's idols.

Around noon most days Dr. Haydon has a tryst with some friends of his — pigeons and squirrels. They know him so well that they are all about him as soon as he appears, if they are not there waiting for him and their peanuts and corn. About the windows of his room on the top floor of Swift Hall there is always a gathering of pigeons. It has always been my opinion that there is more real religion in the scene of this ruddy faced, white headed gentleman with the birds about his head and the squirrels at his feet than in all the fine churches on the campus. Here is nothing strange and archaic and medieval; here is direct and personal communion of a man with the earth which is his mother and the creatures which are his brothers and sisters.

To those who are used to religion as something set aside in their lives, something other than participation in nature, other than exhilaration of body and vigor of mind, it may seem that at best this is only a very naïve and pagan sort of communion. Well, perhaps the pagan with his immediacy and vitality of participation in his world had something better than we have. Perhaps the man with an eagle feather in his hair, the girl with a rose in her ear and a boy beside her, are closer to the mystery of life and the wonder of the world than those who with chants, candles, robes and bendings, thumb through the worn out pageantry age after age.

Which brings us to ask the question, "Is the man of today a mystical animal, and if so, where and how does he find his mystic experiences?" I can remember when I expected to be spoken to, to be called, to be assured. If I could only see and hear, then I would know, but never the strange voice spoke. This may mean that I am deaf and blind where others can hear and see; so I am often assured.

But with the surety of all who believe that they have tasted religion in person and at its source, I am convinced that I see and hear where others are deaf and blind. To me, those who practice orthodox ritual resemble a crowd of people watching a mystery play in the cathedral square of some medieval town. They are entranced with the familiar antics on the stage, forgetful that these are the doings of actors playing from a script. The play becomes the real world; the artificial and unnatural becomes the natural. The sun and the hum of insects, the dust and the heat and the press of the crowd are forgotten. The mass, the rosary, the idol, the mystic state induced by fasting and vigil seem to them the real world and the final reality.

It is interesting that the makers of the medieval cathedrals could never quite escape the rich natural world around them. The gargoyles grinning from the cornices of Notre Dame are as pagan as any images in the world. The stone pillars, the doors and walls, are adorned with animals, ferns and leaves of the forest, vines, flowers and fruits of the field. The abundance of nature finds full expression in the lavish sculpture of the artisan, himself scarcely touched by the blight of formal religion, and the churches grew in that part out of the teeming world in which he lived. Our own churches could stand some such vital connection.

The man who enters the mystery of life and his universe through the gate of natural mysticism has a different expectation from his mystical experience than the one who regards it as the voice of a divine being. The experience is important in a different context and for different reasons. The natural mystic does not accept his experience as authority in matters where science, logic and history can serve him better. He looks upon the mystic experience as something akin to a hunch, something he must follow for want of better evidence. He scours the dope-sheets of science for all the confirmation he can get before he places his bet, but there is a great realm where science is still unsure and fumbling. Science still has no way to predict without fail which horse will win the race, or what man will fall in love with what woman, or the why and wherefore of beauty. Many of our experiences are still below the level of expression and language. The musician suggests them in wordless sound. The poet puts words together strangely to elicit new overtones. Words failing, the lover must turn to the pressure of hands and a kiss. Sometimes the wonder of the world is so much that all one can do is stand, fill the lungs with air, laugh for an unknown joy, and just be. Then we know that the body has an older and deeper wisdom than the mind has learned to handle. It is an alogical, sensual, instinctive exuberance. The body enjoys sheer existence, action for its own sake, energy for the sake of energy. Then a man feels somewhat as a tree or a horse must feel, creatures who are undisturbed by philosophy and meanings and reasons why; just to be, that is enough.

It has been claimed that the mystical experience is above the range of sensual experience, thereby derogating the senses and elevating the mind or the soul into a higher realm of awareness. But studies would indicate that there is no division between the mind and the body, the soul and the flesh. If we had no senses we would have no spirit; we should be unfeeling and unknowing lumps. The impact of existence comes to us primarily through the ears, eyes, nose, mouth and tactile sense. The greatest artists and poets have been people of acute and perceptive senses. The mystic state is a sensual state; in its highest form it is a state of acute awareness. It is feeling when the whole being is fused and concentrated on feeling. The man who fasts his way into it is greatly aided by the disturbance of his digestive organs and the increase of blood in the brain.

The natural mystic acknowledges the earthy nature of his reactions. He is not afraid of his body and its feelings, revelling in the sights, sounds, colors, tastes, smells, textures of the world. They are all grist of his mystic mill. The objects which the city man has about him are those least likely to open communication between himself and nature. They are largely his own artifacts. They speak to him not of nature but of what man has done to nature. The mossy stone, rusted and pitted by wind and rain, lying in its native grass, says something that the coldly cut stone of our buildings does not say. The tree alive in its soil says something that polished and stained wood fails to communicate. Admitting other values are accrued in the transfer, the fleece and fur on the backs of animals has something it does not have on the back of a woman. There is more to be found in working the earth in a garden than in opening a can of peas. If one is to find the mysticism of natural experience he must avail himself of nature. We are all children of earth, and there is a depth in us that is enriched and impregnated only through the soil. The life of the mind needs the life of nature and the mystical, sensual awareness of the living forces moving through and around man.

There is another source of natural mysticism with which the city dweller is in constant contact; that is human nature. Men are also natural beings, and the intercourse between men is nature speaking to nature. We are the earth speaking to the earth. Here again the sensual nature of mysticism impresses itself. Through the ear and eye we gather impressions of our fellows, which somehow have more meaning than what seems to be in just what we have seen and heard. These sensations suggest mysteries and associations which we have experienced within ourselves and with other men. All added together, things heard, seen, felt, things seen as a whole, in large impression, things felt rather than known in detail, things known by feeling rather than by thought or reason, give us the mystical experience of being with another person.

Humanist Philosophy 1928 – 1973

To walk down a street, with men and women streaming by, each face an insight into a life, a burning impression, the set and swing of their bodies, the liveness of their hair, the knowingness of their eyes, hints of joy and grief, the energy of young people burning like a quick fire, the calm of age like glowing coals, the magic of movement and muscle harmony, the flowing balance of walking or running, the smile lighting the whole person, the happiness to meet a friend, and beneath the thin mask each of us wears, the ever-present sense of mystery and loneliness and wonder. Every human association is an adventure in natural mysticism; to be with people is to handle mystery; it is to live in wonder and glory. I remember that once I looked up from reading a book in a library and saw the head of my neighbor in space, round, heavy, the atmosphere flowing about it, breathing, pulsing, warm and pink with life. It startled and stung me. Mostly we walk unseeing and unfeeling, the sounds and sights flowing unheeded over and around us. We need to be jabbed awake to the richness of our own living surroundings and our own burning selves.

There can be no separation between natural and religious mysticism. The experience of nature and human nature is religious experience. I have never heard the strange voice of a divine being, but I have heard the authentic voice speaking to me. It is speaking constantly; we need only to turn from our business and see and hear. The one who has lived fully within the spirit of natural mysticism can never honestly be petty or unsympathetic toward his fellow men. We see that our comparisons and revilings are too often for things of small concern. There is enough mystery in even the village idiot to give the greatest of men pause and convince him of miracle. No life is a mean thing. A wise and patient sympathy, a broad and natural humor, pervade the criticism of the natural mystic. Here breed forgiveness and understanding.

CHAPTER 8
Working Out Humanist Morals and Ethics

Humanism's Struggle With Remaking Morals and Ethics

William R. McKenzie wrote in *TH* that humans are neither good nor bad by nature. Regardless of their learning, their moral quality can always be improved (*TH* 23:3). For humanism to effectuate that view, it must put forth morals and ethics. Chapter 3 discusses values that humanists advance. Those values certainly must inform humanist morals and ethics. Although writing about particular ethics and morals could fill volumes, curiously few essays in *TNH* and *TH* through 1973 address them.

Horace S. Fries suggests in his essay in Chapter 4 that science can be used in ethical and practical inquiry. Specifically, he calls for making decisions about moral, religious, and educational problems on a scientific basis. He advocates the idea, disdained by so many theists and conservatives, that knowledge can be used proactively on a social basis. In response to the disdain, Fries acknowledges the difficulty of this proactive approach. Indeed, while his cursory example concerning racial prejudice and discrimination remains relevant to US public policy discourse, he does not set forth a methodology for doing it. That task is left to others.

Personal Ethical System

Rollo Handy, in his essay in this chapter, asserts that naturalistic ethics focus on how to fulfill human needs or satisfy human desires, which echoes one basis for naturalistic humanist values. He views the construction of ethics as necessarily emphasizing human behavior and its consequences. Science, Handy says, can elucidate which human behavior can satisfy a particular need or desire. Unfortunately, he does not contribute how that is to be done.

Gerald A. Ehrenreich set forth the modern view that humans learn moral values as children and then as adults choose their moral values (*TH* 16:5). For Ehrenreich, each individual has his or her own ethical system. He identified the value of ethical systems that include self-esteem. But as a psychanalyst, Ehrenreich was generally not interested in labeling particular behavior immoral. That reluctance corresponds to the relativistic nature of the scientific method.

A key aspect of Ehrenreich's discussion is that he is talking about an ethical system, but using terms like "moral value." He is asserting a relationship between ethics and values. That assessment comports with his discussion of ethics and morals in the context of an individual's choices of behavior. Likewise, Albert Ellis in his included essay presents a number of ideas for what he almost interchangeably calls both an "ethical code" and a "moral code."

Another important element in Ehrenreich's essay was his discussion of "good" and "bad." From his vantage point as a psychoanalyst, he viewed these terms as generally harmful. For they tended to elicit feelings in the subject of righteousness or guilt, respectively. Indeed, humanism as relative thinking takes the view, hinted at in the last section of his essay, that the effort should be to find what is "better." The ancient Greek Protagoras said that the wise person is the one who can persuade us that a *better* course of action exists. As Ehrenreich suggested, reason and emotion play into that determination.

Moral Code

On the nature of morals, Handy says that naturalistic humanism views morals as a social phenomenon, in contrast with one's private values.1 He briefly acknowledges the role of culture in the formation and enforcement of morals. However, few writers attempted to describe even partial aspects of a humanist moral code in *TH* through 1973.

As noted in the preceding part, moral codes are another subject of Ellis's essay. He starts from the premise of plurality of values, which is essential to humanism. His discussion of the choices, limitations, and application of moral codes is particularly valuable. He acknowledges, for example, that they must be relative and contingent. But in the end, rather than follow that discussion with a general statement of a humanist moral code, he applies his standards to the single topic of human sexuality. (He was writing in the US in the 1960s.) Ellis concludes by relating his moral code to humanist values, as the source material.

Helen Mayer Hacker's essay in this chapter provides a good contrast to those of Ellis. The latter writes about sexuality from a man's perspective. Hacker calls out broader double standards in the way US culture and society view women differently from men, to the detriment of women. In that way, her essay echoes recent problems in the secular movement arising from sexism and harassment that highlight a distinction between mere secularism and humanism. In the larger picture, of course, the double standard against women is only one among many double standards on various bases that range from race to disability to sexual orientation and beyond. The lesson from Hacker's essay is that humanist moral codes, not to mention ethical systems, must incorporate the perspective of all those to whom they apply.

Even more broadly, the notion of moral double standards directs our attention, as Handy does, to the frequent conflict between individuals' behaviors and courses of action. While human law may resolve conflicts, human laws may themselves be judged from a moral standpoint.

Kirkendall's essay in this chapter acknowledges the natural occurrence of moral conflicts. It then delineates the proper characteristics of morals that mitigate the effects of the conflict and facilitate their resolution. Kirkendall focuses on morality from a particular value. He expresses the value in his statement of the proper foundation for morality, namely, "[c]oncern for the quality of interpersonal relationships." Ellis describes this as a "major concern" for humanistic ethics and morals. Echoing Handy's consequentialism,

Priscilla Robertson wrote that relationships are to be judged by their consequences (*TH* 16:5). Humanism values quality interpersonal relationships, which follows from its embrace of the social nature of humans and democracy, a system dependent on highly functional personal relationships. From this value, Kirkendall goes on to draw important conclusions about the characteristics of a moral code with a broad pro-social basis appropriate to humanism and society.

The Ongoing Challenge

Paul Kurtz posited in *TH* that scientific advances call forth not only new values, but new ethics and morals. He advocated normative ethics, i.e., developing ethical and moral principles. However, he eschewed systems and codes, advocating situational ethics, solving ethical questions based on specific facts. Certainly, situations differ, but that approach capitulates to the complexity that Handy and others acknowledge in envisioning their systems and codes. Of course, the limited progress on systems and codes made to the present day suggests that more have taken Kurtz's route than Handy's.

More atemporally, Kurtz said that humanist normative ethics must strive to "advise, recommend, evaluate, and prescribe policy and practice" (*TH* 32:5). Accordingly, writers in *TH* have published narrowly drawn essays on a smattering of policy issues, from birth control and control of one's body,[2] to modification of human genetics.[3] Essays of that kind published in *TH* up through 1973 alone could easily fill a separate volume. Nonetheless, many, many gaps remain. Thus, while much work is needed on explicit humanist personal ethical systems and moral codes addressing values previously addressed by theology, humanists must also continually address new and developing moral and ethical issues that arise from technological developments.

Notes

1. Some writers often use "moral" and "ethic" interchangeably. Somewhat like Handy, I prefer "moral" as a reference to the standards applied to others, and "ethic" as a personal choice of applied value. See, e.g., Murn, Charles, "On Deriving Humanist Morals and Ethics: Death and Dying," *The Human Prospect,* 5:1, p. 59 et seq. (2015).
2. See Thomas Szasz, "The Ethics of Birth Control, Or: Who Controls Your Body?" *TH* 20:6, p. 332 et seq. (1960).
3. See Verle E. Headings, "Optimizing the Performance of Human Genes," *TH* 32:5, p. 9 et seq. (1972).

Ethics, Human Needs, And Individual Responsibility

Rollo Handy
The Humanist, January-February, 1967

I. WHAT IS HUMANISM?

"Humanism" is a label that obviously has been used for a great many purposes. In this paper, the humanism which is opposed to supernaturalism is emphasized. A humanist, in the present sense, may believe there is sufficient evidence to indicate the nonexistence of a supernatural realm, or he may prefer to remain technically agnostic on that point and hold instead that there is no need to use supernaturalistic categories, entities, and processes to describe and explain what goes on in this world. In either case, the kind of humanism I am discussing tries to describe and explain all that goes on (including the objects of inquiry in the physical, biological, and behavioral sciences) in terms of so-called natural processes. Human behavior is understood as including thinking, feeling, believing, etc., as well as more overt behavior.

Such a view is still extremely broad and can encompass many different approaches. For example, it is compatible with both highly optimistic and highly pessimistic views of the potential of human beings and is compatible with many views about the appropriate emphasis to be placed on the human part of the cosmos as contrasted to the rest of the cosmos. Such differences can be illustrated by quotations from Corliss Lamont and the early Bertrand Russell.

Lamont says:

> To define twentieth-century Humanism in the briefest possible manner, I would say that it is a philosophy of joyous service for the greater good of all humanity in this natural world and according to the methods of reason and democracy.[1]

Russell says:

> Brief and powerless is Man's life; on him and all his race the slow, sure doom falls pitiless and dark. Blind to good and evil, reckless of destruction, omnipotent matter rolls on its relentless way.2

Although I take a more optimistic view of the potentialities of humanity than many people do, I also believe that humanists too often become overly sentimental about man and that they sometimes project many of the traditional attributes of a supernatural God upon humanity in general.

The kind of humanism I espouse rejects both supernaturalism and idealism (to use traditional labels) in favor of a thorough-going naturalism. At the same time, it is a more hardheaded attitude than that held by some humanists; and it avoids any tendency to deify man and thus reinstate some of the supernaturalistic tendencies supposedly eliminated at the outset.

II. WHAT IS HUMANISTIC ETHICS?

Within the broad type of humanism just sketched, there is room for many kinds of ethical theory. This is not an appropriate place to list and to analyze critically the major types of humanistic ethical theory. What I shall do instead is discuss some of the general ideas that would be acceptable to many, but not all, humanists and then move on to those aspects of my view which would not be widely accepted by other humanists.

In general, naturalistic humanists think that all human values are grounded in this-worldly events, relationships, experiences, etc. Such an approach opposes the view of many writers that value terms designate "non-natural" properties or that the uses of value terms cannot be elucidated in terms of "natural" events. Obviously, supernatural properties are likewise not appealed to by naturalistic humanists. Putting the matter another way, whatever goods are to be achieved by humans are this-worldly goods. Naturalistic ethics, in this sense, is likely to emphasize categories such as the satisfaction of interests, of needs, of desires, etc.

The kind of humanistic ethics now being discussed is likely to put considerable emphasis on the consequences of human behavior. This is not, of course, to say that human motives and intentions are unimportant in ethical theory, but obviously the impact of one's actions on others and on one's own future is highly important. To be done an injustice through the good intentions of another may be more acceptable than being done the same kind of injustice through the bad intentions of another, but presumably our main interest is in eliminating the injustice.

Naturalistic humanism is likely to emphasize morality as a social phenomenon, rather than as a purely, or primarily, private or individualistic matter. Both the good and the bad things we do and suffer are almost inextricably bound up with other people, with the social system in which we live, and with culturally determined patterns of behavior and response. The task, as many humanists see it, is not somehow to reform the spirit, but rather to socialize human drives.

Moral systems, then, are seen as forms of human behavior to be inquired into using scientific methods. The sanction for any particular moral rule is to be found in the natural world (not in some supernatural or non-natural area); and the matrix of morality is social.

A More Specific Approach

Although I have no way of assessing the degree of sympathy that would be found among humanists for what I have to say in this section, certainly many humanists will disagree with my view.

In the history of ethics, there have been many disputes about how selfish man is and the extent to which selfishness is socially and culturally conditioned. Many writers have urged that the most fundamental drive is self-preservation; hence, any adequate ethical theory must be based on selfishness. Other writers have emphasized, with a considerable show of evidence, the malleability of human nature and have maintained that what seems so fundamental about selfishness is true only in certain types of social organization. Obviously, this kind of issue is not easily settled. For one thing, the terms central in such discussions — selfishness, egoism, egotism, etc. — are given many diverse interpretations, and much confusion ensues.

However, if we adopt a relatively broad notion of self-preservation and bypass the issue of trying to specify precisely how strong the drive for self-preservation is compared to other drives, it seems plausible to say that the individual's drive for self-preservation is extremely strong, and an ethical theory ought to give considerable weight to it. In my opinion, the aim is not to attempt to make people less interested than they now are in their own self-preservation, but rather to try to structure our social organizations so that one's own betterment is dependent upon the betterment of others. In other words, we should try to organize human institutions so that rather than one person's success being dependent on the failure of others, everyone's success should be dependent upon the success of others. This obviously is no easy matter, and in many cases the resources to be allocated are in fact fixed and one must divide them unequally. But there are other instances in which resources are expansible, and to give someone a large portion does not necessarily mean that others go hungry.

All of this becomes extremely complex, especially when we deal with rewards such as prestige and reputation. In one sense, of course, prestige becomes meaningless as a reward unless it is distributed unequally. But prestige may be allocated by the group either to those who are most successful in "doing in" their fellows, or to those who are most successful in helping their fellows. Naturally, the latter alternative is the one I advocate.

Value Terms and Human Needs

What I have said so far may seem hopelessly naïve in some respects, so let me emphasize that I do not believe that my wishes, or anyone else's, are easily made fact. How economic rewards, prestige rewards, or self-satisfaction rewards are allocated is obviously dependent on a multitude of factors, including the basic mode of socio-economic organization under which people live. But cultural anthropologists have amassed enough evidence to show how amazingly variable so-called human nature is. The question is not whether humans biologically are flexible enough so that the drive for self-preservation can be channeled in socially desirable ways, but rather whether we can arrange our social institutions so that rewards are allocated in a way satisfactory to a humanistic ethics.

Before we can answer this question, we must understand more precisely how value terms can be used within a humanistic framework. My suggestion is that value terms be directly linked to human needs. "Value" is specified as follows. "X is a value" = "X satisfies a human need." Obviously then, a major point is how needs are construed. Here we must rely on the results of the sciences bearing on human behavior. Quite probably the most adequate present specification of "need," whatever it may be, will change in the future, as more scientific evidence becomes available. In the same way, the lists of needs that scientific inquiry may disclose will also change as inquiry proceeds. But, for just these reasons, ethical theory and ethical practice would then be closely connected to the best available information about human behavior. This, in my opinion, is the major virtue of the theory.

Let us consider a few consequences. The need theory would make the determination of values objective rather than subjective, in the sense that something's being a value would be a fact, even if the people involved did not realize it. What satisfies a need would be a value even if it were not so recognized. The need theory thus rejects the emotivist contention that ethical language only or primarily expresses or evinces attitudes. Since needs are regarded in a scientific way, intuitionist or supernaturalistic approaches are also rejected.

Although this view makes ethical judgments objective, in the sense that whether or not something satisfies a need is not dependent on an individual's opinion, the theory is in one sense relativistic, since human needs have presumably changed in the course of evolution and presumably will continue to change. Also, differing social contexts will generate differing needs. In short, there is no assumption here that there is any one set of absolute needs that will apply to all humans, past, present, or future, under all circumstances.

An obvious question concerns what needs humans in fact have, and how the term "need" is specified. In the present proposal both questions are regarded as scientific questions. "Need" is taken here to be, roughly, "an event or condition that aids the human to function adequately." What constitutes adequate functioning is, of course, an important question. To repeat, the suggestion of this paper is that those scientists who have investigated human behavior in its many ramifications are best equipped both to say what needs humans have and to specify what adequate functioning is.

One can hardly overemphasize the importance, for the present view, of rejecting any approach searching for the meaning of "good," "value," etc. If the best available specifications of "need" should turn out to have undesirable consequences for a humanistic ethical theory, then the whole project of specifying value in terms of need would be rejected. An experimental attitude is what is advocated here; I believe using needs as the key to an ethical system presently looks promising, but in no respect would I urge that the approach be followed if scientific inquiry should indicate that the hopes I have for the need theory are unwarranted.

Under the present proposal, "satisfies a human need" refers to any need for any human. If a qualified physician finds that Mr. Y needs morphine, then morphine is good for Mr. Y in that situation. At any given time, needs may exist for some person, or persons, or everyone, which are not recognized, and anything satisfying those needs would be a value (even though we are not aware of it). And something not recognized as being able to satisfy a need, but actually capable of so doing, would also be a value. In regard to objects, then, a fuller way of expressing the present proposal is: "X is good for Y in situation Z" = "X satisfies Y's need in situation Z." In regard to human actions, an action that results in the satisfaction of a need is valuable, and a contemplated but unperformed deed could be judged valuable if it would satisfy a need when performed. Finally, it is not intended that temporary states of satiety for X would result in X's ceasing to be valuable. Food is valuable, even if a given man at a given time is not hungry.

Those familiar with recent meta-ethical discussion will realize not only how controversial, but how sketchy the above proposal is. The aim here is not to work out a detailed and relatively complete theory, but only to indicate the main thrust of the proposal within the context of humanism.3 However, one of the obvious objections to the present proposal should be discussed.

The critic will probably ask how the present approach would handle "bad" needs, and how a conflict among needs would be resolved. The first point has been discussed indirectly. If scientific inquiry shows that there are genuine needs which a humanistic ethics regards as in some sense bad, there are several possibilities. If the incompatibility between the results of the inquiry and humanistic ethics is great enough, the only thing to do, as mentioned earlier, may be to reject the need theory. If the incompatibility is judged as a minor one and the theory otherwise seems to be more useful than alternative theories, then the judgment that the need is "bad" might give way. However, a basic assumption of this paper is that the adequate functioning of humans is a desideratum which is basic to a humanistic approach, and hence the incompatibility referred to above is not likely to arise.

Conflicts among needs are almost certain to arise, and a complete ethical theory needs to have some way of resolving such conflicts. Probably this can be handled by adopting a rule that on the level of individuals the greatest possible satisfaction of needs should govern, and that on the level of groups the greatest possible satisfaction of needs for the group should govern. In the case of conflict among groups, the greatest possible satisfaction of needs for all mankind should govern. Obviously, various elitist views would reject those rules, but some such rules seem implied by a humanistic approach to ethics.

To conclude this section, then, the intent has been to link ethics closely to scientific inquiry into human behaviour through the device of specifying "value" in terms of "needs." The proposal is a tentative one and subject to future modification or rejection as scientific inquiry proceeds. No attempt has been made to develop a complete theory.

III. INDIVIDUAL RESPONSIBILITY

Many interesting and significant issues could be raised here. For example, the important issue of individual responsibility from the point of view of a social group — under what circumstances is it sensible for the group to hold the individual responsible for his behavior?[4] Because space permits only a few matters to be discussed, the focus, rather, will be on individual responsibility from the point of view of the person who finds himself in disagreement with the views of some larger group. We all have to learn how to live with people who are wrong or whom we believe to be wrong.

What follows is linked to the earlier sections of this paper, but not in a tight fashion. One could hold something like the theory sketched earlier and reject the view of responsibility developed here, or vice versa.

Those who support unpopular or unconventional views frequently find themselves in difficult situations in the groups within which they function. To cite only one example: a college teacher may strongly oppose the admissions policy of his college, or the degree to which student life is controlled, or the promotion policy of the college, or the curricular emphasis of his department. The kind of situation I have in mind encompasses issues of many degrees of importance and groups of all types—social, economic, civic, political, academic, etc. I am thinking not only of such cases as the integrationist in the deep South, but also the professor who objects to the playing of Christmas carols on campus. What is such a nonconformist to do?

On the one extreme, he may take a purist approach, seizing every opportunity to denounce existing practices with which he disagrees, avoiding compromise, and fighting the good fight. On occasion, such reformers achieve notable success, but they often become functionally isolated from the larger group and thus have no effect on decisions, and sometimes they are fired. If they are separated from the group, either in the sense of being ousted or in the sense of being isolated, they have lost the opportunity for reforming, from within the group, the practices to which they object.

On the other extreme, we have those who are so worried about influencing decisions that they almost always hide their views, go along with the majority, and think of themselves as consolidating their position within the group so that one fine day they can strike a blow for what they hold dear. The difficulty is that the fine day never arrives, for the person never sees himself as having enough strength to do what he wants.

The purist and the opportunist described here are, or course, caricatures; however, examples approximating both types of behavior are not difficult to find. From the point of view of the reformer who wants to make changes, neither extreme works. How then does the responsible individual behave so that there can be progress, desirable change, and humanization of deplorable conditions?

In my view, there is no simple answer, no maxim or group of maxims providing a magic key. In order to support this view, I want to look more closely at the situation within which the dissenter must operate.

In this connection, I think a great disservice is done by those who romantically pose the problem in terms of the individual totally opposed to the group. We are all so molded by our culture and by our relations to others that the starting point must be man as a bio-social organism, not the individual somehow separated or abstracted from his social connections. Almost everything we want to do is in many ways dependent on others. The most deviant among us still accept a great many socio-cultural norms, and their very deviation is expressed in terms of what is culturally available. Protesting youth, for example, choose clothing, hair styles, etc. that are culturally regarded as appropriate to the opposite sex. Or if neatness is a dominant socio-cultural norm, sloppiness may become a symbol of dissent. To take more significant examples, reformers and radicals of all shades of opinion primarily oppose neither the whole culture nor the whole of a smaller group to which they belong, but only segments of the larger organizations.

Many humans in many walks of life are convinced that it is relatively easy for man to control various aspects of his civilization. Those who hold optimistic views on such matters should read "Man's Control Over Civilization: An Anthropocentric Illusion," by the anthropologist Leslie A. White.5 He says:

> During the last century we have witnessed attempts to control tiny and relatively insignificant segments of our culture, such as spelling, the calendar, the system of weights and measures, to name but a few. There have been repeated and heroic attempts to simplify spelling and make it more rational, to devise a more rational calendar, and to adopt an ordered system of weights and measures instead of the cumbersome, illogical agglomeration of folk measurements we now use. But what successes can we point to? Reform in spelling has been negligible. We have succeeded to a considerable extent but not wholly in eliminating the u from such words as honor. But to do away with silent letters, such as the b in lamb, is too big a mountain for us to move. And such spellings-and-pronunciations as rough, cough, dough, and through are much too strong to yield to our puny efforts. It usually takes a great political and social upheaval to effect a significant change in spelling or a calendrical system as the French and Bolshevik revolutions have made clear. And as for the metric system, it has found a place among the little band of esoterics in science, but yards, ounces, rods, pints, and furlongs still serve — awkwardly and inefficiently — the layman.
>
> We begin to wonder. If we are not able to perform such tiny and insignificant feats as eliminating the b from lamb, or modifying our calendar system, how can we hope to construct a new social order on a worldwide scale?

White does not hold that human effort lacks efficacy. He denies that "it is futile to try because what one does counts for nought," but goes on to say:

... what one does, how he does it, and the end and purpose for which it is done is culturally determined ... More than that, what a person or group desires is determined or at least defined by the culture, not by them. What constitutes the "good life" for any people is always culturally defined.

In short, in my opinion, the situation is not Promethean man against the group, but rather the dissenter who on the basis of his identification with and support for some aspects of his socio-cultural milieu opposes others aspects of that milieu. A person who truly rejected all of his culture literally could not live.

So far, what has been said may possibly be interpreted as a glorification of the larger group and support for always conforming. This is not so. After all, the martyr or the purist may succeed in making changes. But, more important, the same kind of problem I have been discussing occurs within dissenting groups. For example, the person rejecting some entrenched cultural belief, such as that of a supernatural god, has to resolve problems generated in working with others who share his rejection of that belief. If he is to further his cause, he must work with others and almost certainly will be involved in differences of opinion. How militant an approach is justified at a given time? On what occasions may it be best to affect a compromise of some kind? How hard, at a given time and place, should one push for the elimination of school prayers?

In short, to get anything done, some cooperation is necessary. Whenever several people try to cooperate there will almost certainly be differences of opinion — about principles, priorities, strategy, and tactics. The typical situation, then, is striking a balance between having things exactly as one wishes and compromising enough to get support from others.

What then is advocated, and how is this related to the earlier sections of this paper? As emphasized previously, there is no magic key. But, in general, the more fundamental the human needs involved, the more careful one must be that the compromise does not lead either to doing nothing or to "selling out." For example, within one small community there may exist both public financial support for religious displays at Christmas time and gross economic exploitation of some ethnic group. One can't fight all battles at the same time, and it would seem unreasonable not to focus most attention on the economic exploitation. However, if the evidence indicated that it would be literally impossible to change the system of exploitation significantly, at a given time, and the evidence also indicated that there was a good chance of furthering the separation of church and state, temporarily most reformist energies might appropriately flow into the latter effort. One danger, of course, is that it is always tempting to say that the difficult is impossible; the dangers of rationalization in such matters are grave. One of the easiest ways of being irresponsible is to hold that no matter what efforts are brought to bear in a given situation, that situation cannot be changed. On the other hand, there are times when it is clear that desired change must be extremely slow or it cannot occur at all. On many occasions in world history, no matter how intelligently and effectively men of good will worked, there was no genuine possibility of eliminating chattel slavery. Those who insist on all or nothing can be irresponsible, since the result may not only be "nothing," but there may also be a genuine setback for the principles involved.

Such general situations can be difficult to judge, for there are other occasions when a compromise may be worse than "nothing," in the sense that the compromise may blunt matters enough so that no further improvement occurs for a long time. What I am suggesting, then, is that one important type of irresponsibility is the failure to weigh evidence carefully and intelligently in an attempt to maximize the satisfaction of human needs to the greatest extent possible in a given situation.

In short, discussions too often revolve around an abstract consideration of high principle, with no attention paid to the problem of how much change is possible given a specific setting. Social science findings can be especially helpful here. If the logical weight of the evidence were the only or the main factor leading to change, many present atrocities would have long since ceased to exist. In addition to great attention to the logical weight of the evidence, then, we also need to pay close attention to the whole question of how certain social phenomena become so entrenched, how they might be changed, etc. For example, we need to learn about the needs which traditional supernaturalism helps to satisfy, even if we believe we have adequate evidence that those same needs could be better satisfied in some other way. We should also learn what socio-economic circumstances bolster traditional supernaturalism and how to effectively produce changes in that area. We need to realize, more clearly than reformers often do, that anti-human social structures which serve powerful vested interests will not disappear simply when their anti-human characteristics are clearly described and understood.

In my view the responsible individual cannot be content merely to enunciate his principles, avoid temptation, and trust to his purity. He must make difficult but important judgments as to how those principles can be put into effect, how to persuade others to accept them, and how to generate a socio-cultural milieu in which the principles can be successfully applied.

Rollo Handy is professor and chairman of the department of philosophy, State University of New York at Buffalo. He is interested primarily in value theory and philosophy of social sciences.

NOTES AND REFERENCES

1. Corliss Lamont, *The Philosophy of Humanism* (New York, Philosophical Library, 1957).
2. Bertrand Russell, "A Free Man's Worship," reprinted in Robert E. Egner and Lester E. Denonn, eds., *The Basic Writings of Bertrand Russell* (New York, Simon and Schuster, 1961).
3. Those concerned about a fuller and more technical treatment may be interested in R. Handy, "A Need Definition of 'Value,'" *The Philosophical Quarterly*, Vol. X, 1960.
4. I have discussed this issue in "Determinism, Responsibility, and the Social Setting," *Philosophy and Phenomenological Research*, Vol XX, 1960.
5. This essay is Ch. XII of his *The Science of Culture* (New York, Grove Press, 1949).

Rationality in Sexual Morality

Albert Ellis
The Humanist, September-October, 1969

I

What constitutes a rational approach to sexual morality? "Rational," according to the dictionary, means based on or derived from reasoning. More specifically, an argument is rational when it takes into account the facts of reality, is based on empirical evidence, is not merely rooted in fantasy and wishful-thinking, and is logically consistent with its own basic premises. Applied to human affairs, rational does not mean rationalistic: for rationalism is the doctrine of accepting reason as the *only* or *absolute* authority in determining one's opinions or course of action, and it is the belief that reason *rather than* the senses is the true source of knowledge. Rationalism, because of its dogmatism and absolutism, can actually be—as it is, for example, in the philosophy of Ayn Rand—an irrational, religious creed. Rationality, on the other hand, includes reasonableness, practicality, moderation, open-mindedness, provision for change, no allegiance to supernaturalism, and lack of condemnation of individuals who have opposing views.

The main thesis of this article is that if sexual morality is to be rational, it would better be a consistent subheading under the main heading of general morality. Sexual behavior is only an aspect of human behavior; and although it is an important aspect, it is not unique, special, and all-important. Indeed, it usually cannot be divorced from socializing, relating, communicating, and various other forms of human contact and collaboration. Consequently, a sex act is immoral, unethical, or irrational not merely because it is sexual, but because it is also in some respect non-sexually wrong, mistaken, or inefficient. Even rape, which by practically any code is almost always immoral, is not wrong because it involves intercourse, but because it consists of forceful, freedom-depriving, injurious intercourse; and it is its breach of human consent rather than its sexuality which constitutes its wrongness.

What are the main principles of humanistic ethics, from which principles of sexual ethics can be logically derived? No one seems to know for sure, since invariant and absolutistic ethical ideals do not seem to be achievable; nor are they particularly *human*. Utopias, as recent sociological thinkers have been pointing out, are unrealistic and unattainable, because one of the main characteristics of men and their societies is that they change over the years. Nonetheless, I shall attempt to establish some general ethical postulates which I believe are rational—meaning reasonable—and humanistic today, and which are even likely to have some relevance for the near, and perhaps even more distant, future.

In stating these rational moral postulates I shall try to abide by a principle which seems to me to be based upon empirical evidence and logical reasoning: namely, the principle of duality or plurality. Man tends to think in monolithic, one-sided ways; to look for absolute rules, for certainty. But practically every idea or answer seems to have at least a two sided, and often a many-faceted, aspect. Thus, human behavior is adequately explained by both heredity and environment; personality includes cognition and emotion; sexual happiness stems from stable and varietist relationships; people would better be concerned with here and now experience and future pains and pleasures. To understand what makes individuals tick without examining and taking into account the variegated influences upon them is to arrive at a narrow and unrealistic view of what they are and could be.

It is my thesis that a dualistic or many-sided point of view can be applied to the ticklish and still highly unresolved problem of human morality. It is also my thesis that although moral codes generally emphasize an individual's harming others, they usually ignore the equally important question of his defeating his own best interests; and they often forget that he may be just as unethical in the latter as in the former case. In the following attempt at stating moral principles, I shall, therefore, include propositions that concern themselves with self-defeatism as well as social sabotage, and I shall consider a pluralistic approach to "right" and "wrong." Using this framework, I hypothesize that an ethical code that includes the following rational ideas would hardly be perfect, but it would be more practical than various other codes that have been dogmatically iterated over the centuries.

II

(1) An individual would better strive primarily for his own welfare (usually, for continued existence and for maximum satisfaction and minimum pain); but since he almost invariably lives in a social group and his satisfactions and annoyances are importantly bound up with group living, he had better also refrain from unduly interfering with the welfare of others.

(2) A person would better try to live in the here and now and to enthusiastically enjoy many immediate or short-range pursuits; but he had also better keep an eye on tomorrow and give up some immediate gains for longer-range, future satisfactions.

(3) A moral code would better be constructed on the basis of as much empirical evidence about human beings and their functioning as it is possible for the morals-makers to obtain; but they had better realize that morality is also based on a value system or set of assumptions: such as the assumptions that pleasure is "good" and pain is "bad."

(4) There probably cannot ever be any absolutely correct or proper rules of morality, since people and conditions change over the years and what is "right" today may be "wrong" tomorrow. Sane ethics are relativistic and situational. However, the nature of human beings and their environment is, and is likely to continue to be for some time to come, so ordered that a few moral rules will probably remain fairly stable for most groups under most circumstances. For example, "do not kill, lest you be killed," "love begets love," and "work hard to change the obnoxious conditions that you can change but gracefully lump those that are inevitable," are likely to retain some degree of truth for a long time to come.

(5) It is generally better for one to follow the customs and laws of his social group, the flaunting of which will bring real and noxious penalties. But to some degree one would better determine in his own mind the customs he thinks are insane and the laws he considers unjust and try to change or avoid them, even at the risk of some penalty.

(6) No person, group, or thing is holy, sacred, all-important, or godly; nor is any person, group, or thing totally villainous, demoniacal, worthless, or hellish. But many things are more valuable for certain purposes than others. Thus, freedom and justice are not necessitous; and slavery and injustice are not completely horrible. But for most of the people most of the time freedom and justice are important, desirable conditions.

(7) Moral codes would better be democratically applied to all individuals and groups within a given community; but discriminative morality, which is differentially enforced on elite and non-elite groups, may have advantages as well as disadvantages and need not be entirely bad.

(8) In a well-ordered and reasonably fair society, the citizens would better resort to verbal protest, the ballot box, and peaceful demonstrations in order to try to effect desired changes in social processes; but in an unfair or ill-ordered society, resort to force, violence, or mob rule may sometimes help effectuate progressive change.

(9) Man would better base his morality on humanistic precepts: on the nature of man and his desires (rather than the assumed nature of supernatural gods and their supposed desires), and on the fulfilling of these desires in the present, near-future, and more distant future. But man also has the power to significantly change some of his "nature," "desires" and "humanity." It is "natural" and "human," for example, for man to be hostile, destructive, and warlike; and a rational ethical code may therefore include, as one of its purposes, the goal of trying to teach him to be less "natural" and "human" in these respects, and more "natural" and "human" in other more collaborative respects.

(10) Humanistic ethics include the primacy of human over sub-human goals, desires, and satisfactions. Cattle, for example, can ethically be raised and slaughtered for

human food. But man would also better be duly humane and uncruel to animals because in being needlessly brutal to them, he also tends to become callous to human suffering and slaughter.

(11) Rational ethics include provision for slight and serious modification of virtually all moral codes, especially as environmental conditions change and perhaps the biological nature of man changes too. But the alteration of ethical postulates would better be carefully approached, with considerable concomitant fact-finding and discussion, since more harm than good may easily be wrought in the process.

(12) Immorality would better not be defined in terms of an individual's harming or acting unfairly toward another, but in terms of his *needlessly* or *gratuitously* injuring other. For in the normal course of social living and consequent competition for jobs, sporting victories, sweethearts, or status, it is impossible for a person not to harm another— unless, of course, he is always a loser. However, in determining whether A necessarily and therefore justifiably harmed B (as, for example, when he ran off with the most desirable girl at a party when B very much wanted this girl for himself) or whether A needlessly and unjustifiably harmed B (as when he ran off with B's girlfriend, even though he already had one of his own), it is frequently difficult to decide exactly what is and is not necessary to A's happiness. A could contend that he "needed" the girl B wanted in both these instances; and if he were actually madly in love with B's girl even when he already had a perfectly "satisfactory" girl of his own, many objective observers would uphold his "need." Although it is easy to say that one individual is immoral when he "needlessly" and "gratuitously" and "unfairly" injures or deprives another, it is difficult to give exact and invariant meanings to these modifying terms; so that "true" immorality is often most difficult to determine or measure.

(13) A major concern of humanistic ethics would better be the facilitation of interpersonal relationships. As Lester Kirkendall and Curtis Avery have noted, "Whenever thought and choice regarding behavior and conduct are possible, those acts are morally good which create trust, and

confidence, and a capacity among people to work together cooperatively." But man does not live by interpersonal relationships alone. His intra-communications are an integral part of his intercommunications; and he can enjoyably relate to and become absorbed in nonhuman organisms and things. Ethics includes his whole range of activity and not only his relationships with others. *I-Thou* relationships, as Martin Buber has pointed out, are highly desirable and uniquely human; but they arise out of and are experienced in the context of *I-It* relations. As Buber states: "In all the seriousness of truth, hear this: without *It* man cannot live . . . The communal life of man can no more than man himself dispense with the world of *It*, over which the presence of the *Thou* moves like the spirit upon the face of the waters."

(14) Man is to some degree individually responsible for his actions. Theoretically, he has a measure of so-called free will and can, at least if he works very hard at thinking and acting, choose to perform or not to perform certain intrapersonal and interpersonal acts. But he is also powerfully influenced by his inherited biological tendencies and his social environment; consequently, although he is partly responsible for, or causes, his own behavior, he is never entirely accountable for it.

(15) When an individual commits a wrong, mistaken, inefficient, self-defeating, or antisocial act, he may justifiably be termed a wrongdoer or—more accurately—a person who has performed this or that incorrect deed. As a fallible human, it is an unscientific overgeneralization to say that he is an evil or bad person. This statement implies that he was born to be more immoral than the vast majority of other people, will inevitably continue to be wrong, deserves to be severely punished or damned as a total human being for being mistaken, and if there were some kind of life after death, should be eternally consigned to the tortures of hell for having committed misdeeds. These statements cannot be empirically validated; and there is some factual evidence that some of them are often false.

III

Assuming that the foregoing general rules of ethics have some degree of validity, what are their correlates in terms of more specific rules of sexual morality? As far as I can see, they are along the following lines:

(1) An individual would better strive primarily for his own sex-love satisfaction; but since he lives in a social community and is going to be importantly affected by the sexual pleasures and annoyances of others, he had better also refrain from unduly interfering with the sex-love welfare of these others. This means, negatively speaking, that he had better not be dishonest with his potential or actual sex partners; that he had better not take advantage of minors or incompetents merely for his own satisfaction; that he is immoral if he coerces unwilling individuals to have relations with him; and that it is generally wise for him to follow the sex laws of his community if these are actually enforced with harsh penalties. On the more positive side, it would be better if he fully and freely expressed his feelings to his sex-love partners; genuinely was interested in their satisfactions as well as his own; sincerely tried to help them with their general and sexual problems, including their puritanism, sex phobias, compulsiveness, and inability to relate; and tried in some ways to help create the kind of a world in which other people were sexually alive, unblocked, and ethical.

This does *not* mean that the moral individual would necessarily go along with and bolster the prolongation of others' sex love guilt, shame, and self-deprecation as many puritans urge him to do. He might not, for example, "respect" a female's virginity, or her tendency to feel terribly hurt if he loved and then left her, or her horror of his using "dirty" words. He might either decide to stay away from her and look for less disturbed partners; or he might decide, keeping in mind her own good as well as his possible satisfactions with her, to help de-propagandize her, induce her to surrender her sex-love hang-ups, and enable her to widen her potentialities for living. In these "seduction" attempts, he would take the same attitude as he would take in trying to influence or "seduce" another individual to change his or her conservative political, economic, or religious views and to become more liberal.

(2) A person would better try to have sex-love relations in the here and now and to enthusiastically enjoy many immediate or short-range sexual pursuits; but he had also better keep an eye on tomorrow and give up some immediate sex-love gains for longer-range, future satisfactions. This means that the individual is often wiser if he gives up present erotic pleasures for future ones. Thus, he may refrain from having intercourse with a minimum of foreplay in order to enjoy longer-lasting and deeper gratifications by employing more foreplay; forego some amount of sex today because prolonged participation (and lack of sleep) may sexually knock him out for several days to come; resist going to bed with an easily available girl because he might enjoy himself much more thoroughly with one not so easily bedded; and forbear having mere sex relations for sex that is combined with companionship, love, or other values.

The individual is often a saner, long-range hedonist if he gives up present sex-love pleasures for future nonsexual gains. Thus, he may leave his girlfriend relatively early in the evening because he has an important test to take or conference to attend the next morning; choose to live with X rather than Y because, although she is not as good a sex partner as Y, she is much easier to get along with domestically; or decide that love relationships with women take up too much time in his very busy life and therefore refrain entirely from having affairs or honestly enter only casual sex relationships with females.

(3) A code of sexual morality would better be constructed on the basis of as much empirical evidence about human beings and their functioning as it is possible to obtain. Historical, anthropological, and psychological studies tend to indicate that human beings are quite varietist or non-monogamic in their sex desires. They are easily attracted to each other sexually on very short notice, but their vital interest significantly wanes after prolonged sexual contact and shared domesticity, at least in many instances. Although they may like intense sexual attraction, passionate romantic love between two people rarely outlasts a few years of living together. People who lust after each other sexually

may detest each other in many nonsexual ways. Those who have notable nonsexual compatibility may lust for one another minimally. Moreover, large numbers of people can sexually desire and even be intensely amatively attached to two or more members of the other sex simultaneously. If these are common sex-love realities, then certain ethical codes—as lifetime devotion and sexual fidelity to a single member of the other sex—are, although advantageous in some respects, almost impossible for the average individual to achieve; and they would better be significantly altered or made preferential rather than mandatory.

When all is said and done, sexual morality still has to be related to some underlying value system that is not completely determined by empirical findings. Some typical values that a humanist assumes in his sex codes are that human life and its survival are good, that pleasure is better than pain, self-acceptance better than self-deprecation, tolerance better than bigotry, societal change better than inflexibility and stasis; and that human beings are more important than lower animals, than external objects, and then assumed gods. Given these assumptions, and the known and probable facts about people and their social relations, a fairly consistent and "rational" code of sex ethics can be constructed. But if other assumptions are made—such as the premise that people will be rewarded in some kind of afterlife if they meekly bear pain and deprecate themselves during their earthly existence—a quite different sexual code might logically follow.

(4) There probably cannot ever be any absolutely correct or proper rules of sex morality, since people and conditions change over the years. When man lived in an agrarian-pastoral society, where contraception was virtually unknown, young people married in their early teens, there were no good medical methods for combatting venereal diseases, and it may well have been wise to interdict premarital intercourse and adultery. Today it may be equally idiotic to ban these forms of sex.

At the same time, considering what the nature of human beings is and is likely to continue to be for a considerable time to come, it is unlikely that rape, sexual murder, or an adult's taking advantage of a young child will be considered a perfectly justifiable and ethical act. Nor is it likely that, from the standpoint of ethical self-interest, extreme sexual dissipation or the individual's neurotically and rigidly sticking to a single limited form of sex activity will be considered a desirable or good mode of sexual comportment. Although the act of sex can practically never be deemed bad or immoral, the manner in which the individual performs this act may well be self-defeating or antisocial, and hence immoral.

(5) Normally, it is better for an individual to follow the sex customs and laws of his social group whose flaunting will bring real and noxious penalties. Thus, if he is highly likely to be socially ostracized, fired from his job, or jailed for engaging in non-marital sex relations or homosexuality he had better give serious consideration to refraining from such activities—no matter how silly or unjust he may consider the laws of his community to be. He would be wise, of course, to work very hard, through speaking, writing, and political activity, to change the laws of his society; but while they still exist and are being enforced, he may well have to obey them. If, on the other hand, the individual is vigorously opposed to the sex rules and laws of his land and objectively perceives he can fairly easily get away without fully heeding them, he may often be wise in discreetly or secretly flaunting them. Thus, although adultery and non-coital sex relations leading to orgasm (legally termed "unnatural sex practices" or "sodomy") have been banned in many of our states for the past century, there are virtually no indictments or convictions under such laws; and though technically illegal, it is generally quite safe, to unobtrusively ignore them. Again, although it has long been considered "wrong" or "illicit" for young people in our culture to have premarital intercourse, most males and many females actually achieve reputation and status by having them. Disobeying the sex rules of one's community is often sane and moral, especially when one is convinced that these rules themselves are essentially insane and immoral.

(6) No sex act is holy, sacred, all-important, or god-impelled, except by arbitrary definition. Sexual intercourse is hardly holy, since abstinence, masturbation, and non-

coital sex relations are legitimate practices that have distinct value to many people. Marriage is not a sacrament, unless a couple think it is; and when it is viewed in this manner it has enormous limitations, problems, and anxieties attached to it. Even love between the sexes is never all-important, as many individuals live happy existences with minimal or no experience of it. Whenever, in fact, a sex, love, or marital act is deemed to be sanctified, it tends to become more important than the human individuals partaking in it; and from a humanistic standpoint, immorality, or the needless sabotaging of human satisfaction, then tends to occur.

On the other hand, many sex acts are more valuable for certain purposes than are other activities. Thus, sex with companionship or love may, at least in the long run, be more enjoyable than sex without affection (and an hour in bed with a new partner may be more exciting than an hour with one's usual partner). A rational individual will try to maximize, without unduly attempting to deify, his sexual enjoyments; and he will similarly try to help his partner achieve the more important, rather than the all-important, satisfactions. Similarly, the rational individual will try to minimize sexual constraints and annoyances, without ridiculously amplifying them or damning those who are instrumental in sexually frustrating him.

(7) Sex codes would better be applied undiscriminatingly to all competent adults in a given community, and applied under a single standard that pertains to both males and females. Women, for example, would not, under a rational code, be criticized and penalized more severely than men for unconventional sex behavior or for illegitimacy. Nor would teenagers and younger children be arbitrarily and unduly held in check sexually, except for special reasons (such as their diminished ability to take proper contraceptive precautions). Sexual discrimination, however, may never be completely eradicable and may even have some advantages. Thus, in almost any conceivable society in the present and near future females are more likely to select as sex partners males who are handsome, strong, sexually competent, bright, and self-accepting. A total

sexual democracy, where there is equal justice for all, therefore is probably not going to exist.

(8) In a well-ordered and reasonably fair society, the citizens would better resort to verbal protest, the ballot box, and peaceful demonstrations in order to try to effect desired sexual changes. Thus, feminist movements have helped win a good many rights for women during the last fifty years that they had previously not had; and some powerful organizations are presently still working for greater equality of the sexes and are doing so in peaceful ways, using due processes of law. But it is conceivable that if sexual tyranny reigned – if males, for example, began physically subjugating and violating women or if people taken in fornication or adultery were literally killed (as the Old Testament recommended in the case of females caught in adulterous acts)—then violent revolt against the oppressors might possibly at times be in ethical order.

(9) Man would better base his sex morality on humanistic precepts rather than the assumed nature of supernatural gods and their supposed sexual rules, and on the fulfilling of human desires in the present and future. The fact that the lower animals have certain sexual proclivities and the supposition that Jehovah and Jesus had certain hard and fast sex rules have nothing to do with humanistic sex ethics. Our sexual morality would better be based on human biology and social learning. If men and women frequently enjoy oral-genital relations, they can hardly be deemed to be immoral on the grounds that such relations are "bestial" or "ungodly."

But man also has the power to significantly change some of his sexual "nature." He can train himself to be sexually constant in spite of his natural varietism. He can employ modern technology (such as electric vibrators, electronic music, and strobe lights) to affect his sexuality. He can use drugs, hormones, and other substances to make himself more or less sexual. There seems to be no good reason why he should not experiment in various ways to modify his sexual desires and potentialities, as long as he can increase his satisfactions in this manner without unduly surrendering or minimizing other advantages and benefits.

(10) Humanistic ethics include the primacy of human over subhuman sex goals, desires, and satisfactions. If lower animals are employed, for example, for purposes of bestiality, for the obtaining of sex hormones or stimulants, or for other purposes, this is normally an ethical pursuit of man. But humans would better be duly humane and uncruel to animals in any sexual use they make of them, because otherwise intra-human values tend to suffer.

(11) Rational ethics include provision for slight and serious modification of virtually all sex codes, especially as environmental conditions change and perhaps the biological nature of man changes too. If we discover, for example, an entirely harmless, perfect method of birth control, codes which now make it unethical or illegal for fourteen-year-olds to have sex relations with each other or for adults to have intercourse with young teenagers might well be liberalized; while if new forms of venereal disease break out and are rampant, more stringent rules regarding non-marital relations might be in order. But the alteration of sex customs and laws would better be carefully and intelligently approached.

(12) Sexual immorality would better be defined not in terms of an individual's acting unfairly toward or harming another but in terms of his *needlessly* or *gratuitously* doing so. A boy may harm a girl if he accidentally gets her pregnant; but he may not be unethical unless he has adequate contraceptive means available and he gratuitously and foolishly decides not to employ them. However, since it is easy to interpret the terms "needlessly," "gratuitously," and "unfairly" sloppily, and since a sex-love partner can be exploited with little trouble, people would often do best to lean over backwards not to injure or to take advantage of each other sexually, even when at first blush it appears that they are legitimately and needfully doing so.

(13) It is preferable for partners, in their sex-love affairs, to concentrate on their interpersonal relations and to have *I-Thou* relationships in some instances; but insistence on maintaining deep interpersonal *I-Thou* relationships in all or most instances is unrealistic, impinges on the freedom of choice of the partner, and is likely to cause immense amounts of anxiety and rigid constraint. Sex or sex-love

relations of an "exploitative" or *I-It* nature are perfectly ethical as long as they are entered honestly, with the full consent of the "exploited" mate.

(14) Man is to some degree individually responsible for his sex actions and therefore would better accept the penalties of performing them. But he is also powerfully influenced by his inherited biological drives and the social environment in which he is reared; consequently, although he is partly responsible for, or causes, his own sex-love mistakes and misdeeds, he is never entirely accountable for them. With considerable hard work and thinking, he can control many, but never all, of his sex ideas, desires, and acts.

(15) When an individual commits a wrong, mistaken, inefficient, self-defeating, or antisocial sex deed, he may justifiably be termed a wrongdoer or a person who has acted irresponsibly. But because he is a fallible human, it is an unscientific overgeneralization to say that he is an evil or bad person, a rotter or a louse. He is only a mistake-maker who will tend to make more sexual errors in the future if he is savagely condemned and cruelly punished. It would be far better if he were fully accepted as an imperfect creature, were not totally devaluated or damned, and were encouraged to become more problem-centered rather than self-centered, so that he could work at being a little less error-prone in the future.

IV

Sexual morality, then, when seen in terms of rationality, essentially consists of the individual's following certain sane, sensible, and non-defeating values. He normally wants to live a good life, including a good sex-love life; he also wants to live it, almost always, within the context of some social group. Cunningly, he follows rational rules that will prevent him from foolishly harming himself, and will stop him from senselessly and needlessly harming others, and thereby in the short or long run damaging himself. Sexual morality is merely a subheading under general, humanistic morality.

The fact seems to be, though we often deny it, that human beings are both biologically and sociologically prone to think, emote, and act in self-defeating and immoral ways—in their general and in their more specific sexual behavior. They believe, usually with great vigor and bigotry, several major irrational ideas. For example, they very frequently insanely hold that they positively must be loved and approved by others; that they are no damned good as human beings when they perform imperfectly; that other people absolutely should and must act fairly and nicely toward them (and if they do not are complete blackguards who should be utterly damned for all time); and that they should live in a world of supreme certainty instead of the real world of probability and chance.

As a result of these highly irrational ideas, people in our own and other cultures tend to think crookedly about themselves, about others, and about the world. They spend considerable time and energy condemning themselves and others —instead of observing that although a person's deeds or performances may indeed be wrong or inefficient, he as an ongoing process, and as a living human, cannot be legitimately given a report card and thereby deified or damned. And they keep railing at the universe for not being easier to live in than it is—instead of actively working to diagnose its ills and evils and to change them. Consequently, they make themselves inordinately anxious, guilty, depressed, hostile, self-pitying, defensive, and avoidant.

Sexually, people tend to be, if possible, even more irrational than they are non-sexually. They not only condemn themselves and each other for various wrongdoings, but they frequently inaccurately define what is wrong. Thus, if we were to apply the standards of sexual morality listed above to our everyday behavior, we would probably discover that most of the sex acts that have been historically deemed to be sinful in our society—such as masturbation, premarital intercourse, non-coital sex relations leading to orgasm, and occasional homosexuality—are not really unethical, since they do not needlessly harm their participants nor anyone else. But many of the conventional and highly legal sex activities in our culture—such as a husband's insisting that his wife satisfy him without his taking any real pains to satisfy her or a wife's refusing to divorce a husband for whom she has little desire or liking—are actually quite immoral.

A genuinely humanistic view of ethics would indicate that people are only wrong or immoral when they gratuitously harm themselves and/or injure others; and that this is true for sexual and nonsexual actions. A humanistic outlook would perhaps even more importantly hold that even when he is indubitably wrong, no person is to be damned or condemned for anything he thinks, says, or does. His deeds may very well be foolish or immoral, but he is never a louse for performing them. If he works very hard against his biologically based and socially inculcated tendencies to be an arrant, overgeneralizing, bigoted, religious-minded blamer of himself and other humans, he can enable himself to lead a much more satisfying sex, love, marital, and general existence.

Albert Ellis is a psychologist and prolific writer on the subject of sex in contemporary life. Among his many books are Folklore of Sex, Sex Without Guilt, *and* The Intelligent Woman's Guide to Manhunting. *He is also director of the Institute for Rational Living. The above article is one of a series of articles dealing with humanism and sexuality which is being edited by Lester Kirkendall.*

Why Can't A Woman ... ?

Helen Mayer Hacker
The Humanist, January-February, 1971

The Double Standard Defined

The double standard appears to be on the decline in contemporary America. Even the term is omitted from the index of many recent marriage and family textbooks; when it is found, the page references are sparse and compact. Laymen no longer seem to know what the double standard is, for informal questioning indicated few persons could even offer a definition. A professional writer thought it referred to the difference between what we practiced and what we preached; a young secretary said it referred to the conflicting standards in sexual morality now facing youth; a specialist in medieval history talked of the contrast between morals of the past and the present. No one seemed aware that traditionally the double standard has meant differing sex rules for men and women — rules that are more stringent for women than for men.

Biblical Origins

So far as Western civilization is concerned, the double standard originated with the Hebrews. It has been said that the first five books of the Old Testament were five lashes upon the back of woman. We find in Leviticus that a man was permitted sexual pleasure with any woman who was not the sexual property of another man. He could also defend his own female sexual properties against the encroachment of other males — often to the point of death for either the woman involved or both of the guilty pair. A woman was expected to be a virgin at marriage. If not, she could be stoned to death at the door of her father's house. Not only was no such requirement made for her husband, but if he falsely accused his bride of lack of virginity, his only punishment was the payment of a fine to her father. A wife suspected by her husband of infidelity might be made to drink some "bitter water" by a priest who then observed certain physical consequences of the potion as confirmation or refutation of her guilt. No similar tests of male virtue, however, are to be found in the Bible, nor was a man restricted to one wife. (It may be noted, parenthetically, that the very word "virtue" testifies to the double standard. It is usually applied only to women and has acquired a narrow, sexual connotation. If used for men at all, it refers to physical and moral strength in areas that have nothing to do with sex.)

The New Testament on women:

Wives, submit yourselves unto your own husbands, as unto the Lord. For the husband is the head of the wife, even as Christ is the head of the church: and he is the saviour of the body. Therefore as the church is subject unto Christ, so let the wives be subject to their own husbands in everything.

St. Paul: Ephesians, 6

Let your women keep silence in the churches: for it is not permitted unto them to speak; but they are commanded to be under obedience, as also saith the law. And if they will learn any thing, let them ask their husbands at home: for it is a shame for women to speak in the church.

St. Paul: 1 Corinthians, 15

This historical example of the double standard in operation suggests a further specification in defining it; namely, what some writers have called a "double" double standard. If women are required to be chaste, but men are not, a question arises concerning the source of sexual partners for unchaste men. Obviously, the double standard implies two categories of females: one category to whom the standard applies and another to whom it does not. For the Hebrews this second category consisted of female slaves and prostitutes. The term "fallen woman" may have passed out of modern vocabularies, but there remains some tendency for men to seek non-marital contacts with women whom they define as being outside the pool of eligibles for marriage, that is, women of a lower class or caste, different religion or ethnic group, or considerably older women — essentially, women who are in some sense foreigners or outsiders.

Double Standard Still Exists

There is much evidence that the double standard is still strong today. Kinsey found that one-fourth of the men in his sample, as compared to three-quarters of the women, were willing to marry a non-virgin. This difference in attitude, however, may reflect only the reality of the social scene: Simply in terms of availability, women who wish to marry must often marry a sexually experienced male. Also to be mentioned is Kinsey's finding that men permit themselves more adultery and take a more lenient attitude toward themselves in this regard than toward their wives. So far as popular attitudes go, if a husband strays, the wife is supposed to ask herself how she failed him; such onus is seldom placed on the husband. Only recently has the Catholic wedding ritual been changed to require a vow of fidelity from the husband as well as from the wife.

This persistence of the double standard is seen also in the relative absence of male prostitutes for women, implying either that women do not have the same sexual needs as men or that they should not satisfy them anonymously. Indeed, unmarried women may not make open claim to a "sex life," although in some enlightened circles being engaged or in love may permit them a full sexual relationship. An extension of the primary sexual double standard, moreover, is evidenced in the greater social opprobrium visited upon women in such matters as lying, swearing, drinking, smoking on the street, immodesty, and so forth. It is also more difficult for unmarried women than for unmarried men to obtain contraceptive devices. Yet the most striking example of all is the stigma attached to unmarried motherhood, as opposed to unmarried fatherhood. Of smaller social significance, but not to be overlooked, is the police harassment of prostitutes while sparing their clients.

Yet while the double standard continues to hold sway, most of the historical circumstances, both material and cultural, that sustained the double standard have lost their force. The Industrial Revolution provided the impetus for the emancipation of women — economically, legally, socially, and sexually. Concentrations of population in urban centers and quickened social and geographic mobility loosened the hold of familism. Arranged marriages fell into abeyance as young people sought their own mates. New ideologies of equalitarianism spread to women, and existing mythologies concerning the natural order of things, including the nature of women and the proper relationship between men and women, were examined in the light of a rationality borrowed from capitalistic production. Cross-cultural studies, increased social contacts brought about partly by world wars, sex research and theorizing — all contributed to the attrition of Victorian sex mores. With the present ability to separate sexual recreation from procreation and to eliminate venereal disease, one might suppose that the last underpinning of the double standard had been removed.

Apologists Still Exist

Apologists for the double standard, however, are not lacking in the modern world. Though it may no longer be deemed essential to protect the great mass of upper-class and middle-class women from situations in which the father of a child conceived out of wedlock can easily abdicate responsibility, other excuses are found for maintaining the double standard. Justifications are made most frequently on the individual level — that is, they are couched in terms of putative differences in the physical and psychological needs of men and women — although more sophisticated arguments still defend it as functional for the whole society.

One argument, for instance, continues to reiterate that the sex drive is more imperious in men than in women and that it demands more variety of sexual objects, while women are naturally passive and monogamous. It further stipulates that young males especially experience greater physiological pressures than young females and that female sexual maturity proceeds more slowly. Any such appeal to biology always runs up against the difficulty of disentangling the purely biological from the social development of human beings. The interplay between biological and social factors is complex and subtle. Until that probably impossible time when boys and girls are raised in exactly the same way, when there is no difference in cultural expectations for the two sexes, we shall not be able to give an answer of any scientific validity to the question of whether men's sexual needs by nature are greater or more various than those of women.

It is interesting to note, however, that in some societies the opposite assumption is made about the relative strength of male and female sexuality. In *Sex and Temperament in Three Primitive Societies*, for instance, Margaret Mead reports that the Tchambuli of New Guinea do not expect a young widow to abstain from sexual relations until her next marriage has been arranged. Rather they say: "Are women passive, sexless creatures who can be expected to wait upon the dilly-dallying of formal considerations of bride-price? Men, not so urgently sexed, may be expected to submit themselves to the discipline of a due order and precedence." Here we have an example of the reverse double standard!

Actually even in Western societies women have often been regarded as inherently more sexual than men. According to early Christian thought, asceticism was a virtue reserved for men; sexual license was projected onto women, who were regarded as seductive temptresses. The familiar utterance of Tertullian sums it up: "The sentence of God on this sex of yours lives in this age. You are the devil's gateway. You destroy God's image, Man." Presumably if it were not for the lust-inspiring machinations of women, men would not be swerved from their high and noble purposes. Some modern writers also believe that without social repression women's sexual interests might exceed those of men, because women are not subject to the same biological restrictions. Robert R. Bell, for example, fears that "in the future, the number of marital sexual problems involving a lack of satisfaction for the woman will possibly increase" with far more serious results than those produced by our current attitudes. (The double standard is implicit in Bell's concern with the adverse psychological effects on men rather than with the frustrations suffered by women.) In this context the double standard is buttressed by the differential sexual socialization of boys and girls and acts as an "intervening variable" in maintaining a sexual inequality of man and woman that keeps them relatively satisfied with each other. Again, one might instead point to the alternative of a reverse double standard in which polyandry, rather than polygyny, might be the norm!

Another and related line of defense of the double standard is the assertion that women's sexual gratification is of a different order from men's. The most fervid exposition of this argument is found in *Modern Woman: The Lost Sex* by Ferdinand Lundberg and Marynia F. Farnham. They believe that unless a woman "deeply and wholly" embraces the idea of becoming a mother, "she fails to attain full sensual pleasure from the sexual act." Since as a "sexual free-lance she does not obtain sufficient confidence-inspiring emotional support" (that is, she lacks confidence that the man "will stand by and assume the role of father to a possible child"), it follows that women from motives of pure self-interest will agree to confining their sexual relations to marriage. On the other hand, since anticipations of paternity do not affect the sexual gratification of the male, he has no reason to impose a similar restriction upon himself. If there is merit to this position, then, in view of the fact that current efforts at population control may doom women to lives of sexual frustration, perhaps psychoanalysis rather than economics should be called the "dismal science." Fortunately, there is no evidence that women who use contraceptives experience less sexual pleasure than those who do not.

A third argument for the double standard points to differences in male and female roles in sexual intercourse. According to this argument, men need sexual experimentation in order to perfect their role as the active partner, whereas women need no practice to make them perfect. As Lundberg and Farnham say, the sex act for women is easier than rolling off a log — all they have to do is be the log. Assigning such a passive role to women belies the findings of much contemporary sex research, particularly that of Masters and Johnson. Rather than multiply words in this connection, one might note that the first husband of Colette, the famous French writer, sent her to a brothel to learn those techniques that he hoped would make her a more pleasing wife. Nevertheless, even if we were to grant that a sexually experienced groom is desirable, it does not follow that his wife should be a virgin. In fact, as Bernard Shaw remarked, "Virgins are for ploughboys." And if by some chance the groom were a virgin, his bride's ability to initiate him adequately might indeed be preferable to his gaining experience with a prostitute or casual contact.

A corollary to this proficiency argument is that relationships with understanding and skillful women are necessary for men to build up confidence in their sexual prowess. Here again, however, it is illogical to say that what is important for men should be barred to women. For that matter, women also may feel shy and inept and have grave doubts concerning their desirability in an intimate relationship.

Furthermore, the kind of experience that men acquire in body-centered rather than person-centered relationships will militate against their developing the full potentialities implicit in an interaction characterized by mutual caring and affection.

Other Justifications

The preceding defenses of the double standard have been geared to assumed biological, psychological, or otherwise universal and inevitable differences between men and women. Other justifications are admittedly relative to certain times, places, and social groups, and focus on the advantages for women who abide by the double standard. The double standard is said, for example, to protect "respectable" women from male sexual demands before marriage and from husbandly expectations of activity in sex play after marriage. In other words, as in other areas of life, the level of aspiration for women is lowered and they are relieved of the burden of freedom. Not completely, however, since men have never believed that all virgins outside of marriage were unavailable as sexual partners. The crucial question here is not so much whether sex and marriage go together but the relationship between sex and love. Only to the extent that men are willing to separate sexual expression from love will they "spare" their love object and find sexual gratification with more casual partners.

As suggested earlier, a rationale of the double standard is also often based on its contribution to social order. In the past, female departures from the sexual code were subject to greater social censure because they carried the potentiality of disrupting the family-system. Malinowski, for example, stressed the importance of the principle of legitimacy, according to which a male social sponsor must be provided for every child to guarantee it a place in the social structure. The need for such a male social sponsor was predicated on a type of social organization in which men directed the economy and women were confined to particularistic, rather than universalistic, roles. Since unmarried fatherhood was socially less visible than unmarried motherhood, the onus for preventing illegitimate births fell upon women. They became the guardians of morality, and their whole socialization was directed to this end. In recent times, however, the women's liberation movement has protested such discrepancies in social stigma as not befitting equalitarian social sex roles. The emancipation of women has lessened the importance of men's pursuing sexual favors as a test of their masculinity as well as the necessity for women to complete a non-marital pregnancy or be condemned for having it terminated.

While few would overtly uphold the double standard in terms of traditional masculine and feminine roles, the basic idea has reappeared in a more subtle guise; namely, it is said to lend stability to heterosexual unions. Proponents of this view say that if women were as free as men in their sexual conduct, they would flit from man to man. The transitory nature of many male homosexual relationships is adduced as proof. Women are the ones who seek and enforce long-lasting commitment. But while it must be granted that lesbian relationships tend to greater longevity than their male counterparts, these too are probably more transient than heterosexual affairs. Of course, all homosexual relationships lack the social support that is available even for heterosexual affairs. Still, there are no good studies of the durability of heterosexual liaisons; so it is difficult to know whether it is the withholding attitude of women or the institutionalization of marriage that stabilizes man-woman relationships. If modern marriage changes its basic function from child production and child care to providing an oasis of intimacy and communication in a world of confusion, alienation, and anonymity, then men may be expected to value it as much as women.

Logically, this argument need not designate which sex should be the one to play "hard to get." Men, rather than women, might be the ones to trade sexual favors for security and affection, as indeed they did, the Vaertings suggest, in the woman-dominated states of ancient Egypt and Libya. In recent history, however, men have been the sexually-indulged sex: To make the mountain go to Mahomet would seem too great a feat for social engineering. Again, a cross-cultural glance may prove instructive. According to Margaret Mead, the Arapesh of New Guinea maintained stable conjugal partnerships without benefit of the double standard, as did many other non-literate peoples. Of course one cannot tear isolated traits out of their cultural context, but even examination of the total fabric of contemporary American social life would reveal the double standard as a corroded bulwark against marital dissolution. Protection from superficial and ephemeral erotic intrigues must be found elsewhere, if at all.

The Need for Experimentation

The outlook of a pluralistic, libertarian society might well be to recognize the fact that some individuals will find contentment in enduring monogamous unions—perhaps only after a painful period of trial and error — while others will prefer to continue in a state of what Bernard Farber has called "permanent availability."

The dyadic pair — or even the nuclear family — does not exhaust the possibilities of an emotional haven in a depersonalized, mobile, industrial society. The hippies, establishing their little islands of holiness and peace, represent an alternative to what Barrington Moore has termed the barbaristic survival of obligations based on blood rather than free choice. The hippie movement has provided a home away from home, a surrogate family for young people who outgrow their parental families but are not yet ready or willing to fit into mass society. Further, the hippie movement symbolizes the theme of sexual equality and plays down cultural differences between the sexes — as witness their insistence that men may be gentle and women aggressive and their merging of sexually related symbols of adornment, such as long hair, beads, bells, colorful clothes, and so on. Sexual exclusivity is not valued, and to some extent the hippie commune may be seen as one big, happy, incestuous family. While the hippie "tribal society" may not be the wave of the future — after all, this country has witnessed the failure of a whole succession of utopian communities from Brook Farm to the Perfectionists of Oneida — it does suggest that present concepts of sex morality, including romantic love as the basis of marriage, the family as the optimum child-rearing agency, the present definition of the complementarity of the sexes, and other shibboleths, be subject to re-examination and possibly discarded. It also suggests the possibility of social experimentation with new avenues of group belongingness and personal identification.

The Double Standard is Obsolete

From any point of view, it would seem that the double standard, whether orthodox or "permissive with affection," is on the way to becoming culturally obsolete. Among the reasons for this are the following:

1. It conflicts with current social efforts toward equality of the sexes in other aspects of life. Women are pressing for equal opportunities in jobs, education, politics, and other fields. Why should they experience discrimination

in affectional and/or sexual matters? The double standard violates the sense of fair play and justice.

2. It is increasingly less needed for the protection of women or for the ego and libidinal gratification of men. Modern women can earn their own living, exercise free choice in regard to maternity, and rid themselves of venereal disease. As their social position improves, they can exonerate men from guilt and responsibility. Similarly, men, no longer needing recourse to a group of "bad" women, have shifted to more subtle ways of validating masculinity than sexual conquest and are more frequently looking to women for companionship.

3. It no longer fits the cultural and structural basis of society. Family and lineage have lost importance; free mating has replaced kin control; occupational inheritance has been broken; bequeathing property is less significant; emphasis on blood ties has weakened; individual autonomy as a cultural ideal is growing; divorce and remarriage are more frequent; rationality and hedonism are gaining popularity; responsibility for the maintenance of children is being shifted to extra-familial agencies; etc.

The Humanization of Sex

If the double standard is abrogated, the question naturally arises, What single standard will take its place? Will it be the old male standard, the Christian single standard of abstinence outside marriage, the compromise of permissiveness with affection, or "free love"? Sophisticated moderns, bereft of absolute ethical precepts, seek to examine their motives rather than their actions. If sexual intimacies are justified only by love, then many practice a form of self-hypnosis to lift the burden of guilt. And when love disappears, it is less painful to blame self or other for superficiality and shallowness or inability to communicate than to accept the fact that love is mutable. Perhaps the humanist morality will adopt Nelson Foote's concept of sex as play, and men and women will collaborate as equal partners in evolving mutually satisfying rules for the great games of love, sex, and marriage. The double standard as a relic of the era of "Man for the field, woman for the hearth" will yield to the equalitarian concept of male and female roles in the family and outside.

Tentatively, it may be suggested that the new sexual ethic will center on respect for the personhood of those involved. Potential sex partners will feel the responsibility of ascertaining to the best of their ability that their action will have the same meaning to both of them or, if there are discrepancies, that these are clearly understood and mutually acceptable. They may also ask themselves to what extent they are acting freely and in accordance with the image that they would like to have of themselves. In contrast to the double standard, which denies the equal humanity of women, new sexual rules should foster a humanistic sexuality in which all are subjects.

Helen Mayer Hacker is Associate professor of Sociology at Adelphi University, where she has been "drafted by students to conduct a course in women's liberation." She has investigated social sex roles and family patterns in the United States, Italy, and India and is author of articles in professional and popular journals. Her book Women: Wives and Workers *will be published by St. Martin's Press.*

Searching for the Roots of Moral Decisions

Lester A. Kirkendall
The Humanist, January-February, 1967

Everyone working in the field of human relations, including teachers, religious workers, youth workers, counselors, and social workers, is keenly aware of the average person's concern for deciding what is "right" or "wrong." Persons in other occupations — politicians, editors, businessmen, laborers, manufacturers, bus drivers — are likely to regard moral considerations as the special concern of those who are deeply and obviously immersed in human relations situations. Actually, all of us, regardless of occupation, are involved in thinking about and resolving moral issues. Because any talk about morality is suspect, some people have suggested that I entitle this article "A Viewpoint of Ethics." I have decided against their advice for these reasons: Morality has about it a sense of deep-seated concern with behavior and the treatment human beings accord each other. That is the concern of this paper. Furthermore, because many people have construed morality as a theological concept involving professional religionists, they feel that ideas of morality have little bearing on daily living. In this they are wrong. Morality, because it is a problem of human interaction, is a problem for all of us at all times.

The essence of morality lies in the quality of interpersonal relationships which can be established among people. Moral conduct is that kind of behavior which enables people to experience in their relationships a greater sense of trust and appreciation for others, increases the capacity of people to work together, reduces social distance, and continually furthers one's humane outreach to other persons and groups. Such behavior increases one's sense of self-respect and produces increasingly a sense of personal harmony.

Immoral behavior is just the converse. It dehumanizes. It creates distrust, destroys appreciation for others, decreases the capacity for cooperation, lessens one's concern for others, causes persons or groups to shut themselves off or be shut off from others, and decreases an individual's sense of self-respect.

Of course, this formulation is nothing new. It has been implicit in religion for centuries. It is the basic issue in the injunction "Love thy neighbor as thyself," and the question, "Am I my brother's keeper?" The concept is central to both our personal and corporate lives, and we need to study it, pursue its ramifications, and put it into practice.

The most important task in the world today is the building of relationships that will enable people to communicate fully and effectively enough to understand one another. Until we can build understanding, until we can communicate, until we can feel a sense of unity and brotherhood, we will not have peace, either internationally, among our friends, or in our families. The important moral issue is not whether some act has or has not occurred, but how can sound relationships be built.

Concern for the quality of interpersonal relationships seems a sound and essential foundation for morality because it is in harmony with the nature of man. True, "the nature of man," is not unalterably established. I am making an assumption. To me, the evidence is conclusive enough that man by nature seeks sociality and cooperative relationships. One of his deep needs, if not his deepest, is to be associated happily, acceptably, and harmoniously with his kind. His sense of self-respect and worth comes from the feeling that he has contributed to the welfare and well-being of those who have accepted him.

The evidence that man's desire for acceptance by his group is more imperious that any of his other urges is impressive. Some may think that self-preservation takes precedence. Yet we see parents who sacrifice everything, even life, for their children. The annals of human behavior relate many incidents, whether in peace or war, of men and women who have given their lives for others. Human beings will risk their own lives to rescue others, and they need not even be acquaintances.

The more we know about the universe and the principles that govern it, the more we are impelled to widen our horizons and to acknowledge that all men are kin. Those who try to justify barriers between racial or ethnic groups get no comfort from science. Most of the barriers we erect between groups are based upon irrelevant differences and erroneous assumptions. Regardless of the color of their skin, men fall prey to the same diseases, they respond to love, recoil from or fight against hatred, and feel anger, jealousy, and pride. Racial and sex differences, places of residence or citizenship do not alter the basic nature of the human being. The desire and need for acceptance remain, and we have no reason for believing this will change. To my way of thinking, moral judgments and practices should be based on an unchanging factor common to all men, not on social customs or authoritative statements concerning what specific acts are right or wrong.

Modern methods of communication and transportation bring people into closer and closer contact with one another. That this close association is so marred by war indicates that we still live by a very primitive concept of human relations; and does not necessarily prove that man is by nature hostile and warlike. The distrust that exists between the scientist and the military security officer can be traced to this distinction. Knowledge and understanding developed according to scientific principles disposes the scientist to further his outreach and sweep aside artificial barriers. He recognizes that only as man exchanges experiences, knows and understands others, can he grow. To the military mind, however, boundaries and lines of demarkation are more significant. The maintenance of such barriers spells safety, and even though he may recognize there is a tremendous gamble involved in this approach, he sees it as the only way to insure survival. Because their assumptions are based upon diametrically different philosophies, I believe there can be no true reconciliation between these two groups.

Let us consider what an interpersonal relationships approach to morality requires:

1. *All of our behavior must be scrutinized to determine its moral significance.* When a person is called immoral, we usually think that he has indulged in sexual misbehavior. The popular conception of immorality is largely related to sex. Stealing, lying, or degrading another person are not usually referred to as immoralities. But moral standards must apply to all behavior, rather than having a restricted meaning which associates them with only one type of behavior.

Sarcasm, for example, is an immorality because it usually creates feelings of distrust and suspicion and builds a barrier between those who use it and those against whom it is used. Obviously, corruption in government is immoral. When we believe that our public officials are dishonest, we feel we cannot depend on them. Being unable to trust our leaders, we can no longer communicate with each other or work together effectively with our government. Corruption destroys the fabric of cooperation.

The grading system in our schools, as it commonly operates, also produces immoral consequences. Grades, as they are commonly handled, build a feeling of competition among students which impairs relationships. One student may refuse to help another because if he did and if the student he helped improved his standing, then his own standing might be endangered or lowered.

The use of words in a deceptive, ambiguous way is also immoral. It makes communication difficult or impossible and hampers or defeats people in their efforts to work together. We have seen much of this in international relations. A predatory nation will invade a country and shield its aggressive designs by bandying words like "liberation" and "freedom." Lewis Mumford, in *Faith for Living*, says, "Man's greatest triumph in producing order out of chaos, greater than law, greater than science, was language. To keep the channels of human communication clean is a duty as primal — as holy — as guarding the sacred fire was for primitive man. He who debases the word ... breeds darkness and confusion and all manner of foulness."

2. *Our moral judgments must stem from a consideration of how acts affect relationships rather than from a determination of whether or not an act has occurred.* When immoral conduct is mentioned we usually expect to hear a description of an action. This may satisfy curiosity, but the significant question is "How did this action affect the quality of human interaction?" An illustration of the confused thinking which results from concentrating on the act rather than the quality of the relationship is the common question parents ask, "Is it right or wrong to spank a child?" I have led many parent discussion groups,

and as a leader I used to be disturbed when the question arose because I had not been able to come to a conclusion myself. My uncertainty was caused by the sense of guilt I felt over having spanked my own children.

A simple experience one day provided a new insight. My two children and I were playing on the living room floor. Eventually, when I had had enough and was leaving the room, my six-year-old son ran up and shoved me over backwards. I jumped up and continuing in the spirit of fun chased him around the room, caught him, turned him over my knee, and spanked him. It seemed great sport, and he tried to push me over again, actually challenging me to repeat what I had done. Afterwards, I realized that in the play situation I had probably spanked him harder than I had ever spanked him as a disciplinary measure. In the play situation he had laughed about it and courted more, but when spanked in a disciplinary sense, he had acted terribly upset. I realized then that it was not the physical force of spanking which made the difference. What was it?

Concerning disciplinary spanking, many people at this point will say that a child knows when he has done something wrong. But I know of numerous instances when this awareness was not so upsetting. For example, the time I caught my son raiding the jelly jar, I could not keep from smiling at the expression on his face as he looked up and saw me standing beside him. His expression was proof that he knew he was wrong, but upon observing my smile he broke out in a broad one of his own.

A child's upset from a disciplinary spanking may come from two things. First, the child may feel outraged and demeaned that someone he loves and trusts would treat him with such indignity. Second, to the child the spanking may seem to destroy the relationship between himself and the parent. It seems a rejection and the child can do nothing about it. The injury is to his feelings and his sense of belonging. He is disturbed at his inability to repair the relationship since he is unable to communicate his feelings to his parents.

While I believe that the net effect of most spankings is to damage relationships and therefore that spankings are wrong, I also realize that one can say something to a child without ever touching him physically and damage the relationship more severely than if physical punishment had been used.

3. *We all become parties to the morality or immorality which characterizes a particular situation.* Cheating in school is an example. The prevalent attitude is that cheating is bad and is indulged in by students who are lazy and lacking purpose. They are students who "just don't want to get anything out of school." It is they who are at fault, who are wrong, or immoral. But to place the responsibility solely with the student is a vast over-simplification. Cheating results essentially from a breakdown in relationships and from the incapacity of pupils and teachers to communicate with each other. Students do not cheat on something which they believe is important to them and their well-being. Nor do people try to outsmart leaders who they are convinced are working sincerely for their welfare. Cheating is highly unlikely to occur where relationships are good, communication is possible, and motivation is high.

I believe I could take almost any group of students and regardless of how strongly they may feel about honesty in their school work, teach them in such a way that by the end of the course they would be cheating. How would I do it? I would put as much arbitrary pressure on them as possible. I would schedule unexpected tests. I would include references for class recitation that the students had little or no opportunity to read. I would give little chance for any exchange of feelings or opinion between myself and the students. I would show my distrust for them by telling them I did not trust them: "Don't try to put anything over on me; you'll be sorry if you do." I would make the course appear as purposeless as possible, that the students were studying things because I required it rather than for any worthwhile objective. I would rely on my authority as a teacher to support my statements and actions. Out of this breakdown in relationships and failure in communication would come cheating in class. If I taught this way, I would begin believing that all students are undependable and dishonest. Yet I myself would have created the kind of relationship that caused their dishonesty.

We usually get from people the kind of behavior we expect because we are so guided by our expectations that we tend to set up relationships which produce them. A young man may say, "you can't trust any woman," or a young woman may complain that "you can't depend on any man." Such reactions tell more about the person speaking than they do about men or women in general. What the young woman, for example, is revealing is that she probably conducts herself towards members of the other sex so as to produce suspicion and distrust.

4. *This approach to morality helps makes moral living a pleasant joyous experience.* It is so in harmony with the nature of man and so potentially fulfilling of the need for acceptance that moral conduct becomes much more satisfying and rewarding than immoral conduct. The feeling of satisfaction that can come with moral living has been experienced by most people and is identified by many different names — spirit, morale, brotherhood, etc.

Moral living is often depicted as a glum, dour, and joyless existence. As one of my students put it, "I should think if a person lived a moral life always, it would be a dull life." Of course, he was thinking of morality in an entirely different sense. Some of the common religious terminology, less prevalent today than a generation or two ago, expresses this point of view that to do evil is very easy and attractive, to do right is very difficult and unpleasant: for example, "the straight and narrow path" to heaven and the "primrose path" to hell.

One of the more frequent criticisms of the approach to morality I am advocating is that religion has been left out. Naturally, this depends on how religion is defined. If it can be defined as a respect for and a belief in people, and a concern for true brotherhood among men, then this concept would seem genuinely religious. It is true, however, that morality has been discussed here without reference to supernaturalism or a supernatural deity.

Some people would say that there must be something bigger than oneself, something outside of oneself for which to work; with this I wholeheartedly agree. Surely the idea of working for the improvement of interpersonal relationships and toward a brotherhood of all humans is a concept bigger than the individual. It has power and motivating force; in fact, it is the concept that religions have always advocated, though in different words and through other approaches.

I have confidence in the desire and capacity of men to love their fellow humans. It is the universal in all of us. Those seeking something to base their trust in who feel that this is too feeble a reed on which to lean are only saying that they have never really been close to their fellow men. We cannot experience brotherhood if we must always be pretending, refusing to reveal ourselves, and putting up a false front.

Someone once said to me, referring to the counseling work I do with people experiencing marital and sexual difficulties, "You hear so many stories of human misconduct and mistakes, you must lose all faith in people. I can't see how you can listen to some of the things you must hear and still believe in human nature and human beings."

The counseling situations which this person thought should have cost me my confidence in people are actually what have built it. I have never worked with anyone, no matter what kind of person he seemed to be, who did not want to be accepted and appreciated by others and to work in harmony with people. It sometimes takes a long time before these desires are revealed, but they are always there. In other words, everyone wants to be moral.

This concept of morality does not eliminate conflict in choice, or even conflict in relationships. Immediate desires and long range objectives are not always in harmony. Nor is a relationship always a good one just because it exists. It may be a close relationship, but a smothering, inhibiting, defeating one. Morally, parents must try to free their children for a mature ongoing life as independent adults. Young adults are sometimes in agony because they are forced to choose between what their parents call "loyalty" and freedom and a life in their own right. Such parents will attempt to tighten the bonds with charges of ingratitude and selfish behavior. As a moral issue the matter is clear cut. The child must choose the path which frees him as an individual and leads him to broader and broader relationships featured by trust and understanding.

A relationship which creates solidarity and unity in one group by making its members hateful, fearful, and distrustful of other groups is not a moral relationship. A school, for example, will sometimes try to achieve school unity and morale by creating a rivalry with another school, a rivalry which leads to distrust, suspicion, and hard feelings. This is the same evil of excessive nationalism and war itself. A tremendous feeling of national unity, a sense of closeness, good will, and harmony may result from fearing another nation, or from the effort to defeat or destroy another nation. Such unity, as we have learned to our sorrow, is immoral.

Our code of moral conduct must be centered on the concern for the improvement of all human interpersonal relationships. This is a concept which can be understood and accepted by all men, by the theist and the nontheist, the educated and the uneducated, the old and the young. It provides us with a universal common ground, and enables us to forget the old debate about whether or not there is an absolute.

It becomes clear that, rather than an intellectual acceptance of verbal injunctions, moral behavior is a living process in which one is satisfactorily related to others. Our entire society relies far too much upon exhortation to secure our so-called moral behavior and pays scant attention to conditions which make trust, understanding, and love possible. Yet it is precisely trust, understanding, and love that engender genuine moral behavior. Indeed, they are the very foundation of morality.

Lester A. Kirkendall, Professor of Family Life at Oregon State university, is a director of the American Humanist Association and the Sex Information and Education Council of the U.S. He is the author of Premarital Intercourse and Interpersonal Relations *(1961), which has just been released in a new paperback edition.*

CHAPTER 9
Humanistic Psychology and Freedom

Humanistic Psychologists to the Rescue

The Introduction mentions the advent of psychologists in *TH* following several decades in which philosophers dominated its pages. The development of humanistic psychology in the 1950s added a new dimension to humanist philosophy's challenge. This chapter includes highlights of essays by humanistic psychologists and others on these developments through 1973.

Priscilla Robertson's essay in this chapter is a good starting point to discuss humanist views of psychology. She posits a tendency for moral behavior genetically built in the human brain. She sees evidence of this in Kurt Goldstein's assessment that humans naturally seek "self-actualization." That seeking is the source of creativity. Robertson sees self-actualization as a moral process involving values.

Abraham Maslow's essay in this chapter elaborates on the notion of self-actualization. When it was published in 1970, humanistic psychology had fully engaged this concept. Maslow makes the critical point that the valueless view of the physical sciences does not apply to life sciences, including human psychology. Maslow points to the unconscious as the source of an individual's values and disvalues. Robertson notes that in psychoanalysis, people may voluntarily change from more authoritarian values to more humane values, but not the reverse. A change in an authoritarian direction generally constitutes a reaction to a negative experience.

Maslow calls for a "cognition of being," defined as the technology of happiness. Certainly, his discussion of "peak experiences" exemplifies just that. H. J. Eysenck's 1971 essay in Chapter 7 argues that the scientific aspects of the field of psychology need to be enhanced. He particularly calls for more research into individual and group psychology as the basis for destructive human behavior, such as war, violent protest, and overpopulation. Maslow elsewhere in *TH* acknowledges the need for "a humanistic and transpersonal psychology of evil" (*TH* 29:6). Eysenck urges humanists to use knowledge gained from study of individuals' inclinations, in order to prevent destructive behavior.

In this chapter, Carl Rogers juxtaposes the nature of being with a good life. He, too, speaks in terms of cognition. Early in the essay, he expresses surprise that "the good life" is no one thing for his psychoanalysis patients. Rather, achieving the good life consistently requires a process of living. This process primarily consists of cognition that freely moves in directions chosen only by the individual. Essential to that freedom are self-awareness and openness to experiences. For Rogers, this is the path by which creativity is achieved.

Meaning and Freedom

Complementing Rogers's stipulation that individuals must choose a direction, Lloyd Morain and Oliver Reiser argue in Chapter 2 that humanism considers meaning to exist only inside the individual. Meaning does not exist in the world waiting to be found. Rather, each individual creates his or her own meaning in the course of living life. Thus, this notion of meaning provides the psychological basis for values pluralism in humanism. The effect was like adding a foundation to the structure of humanist philosophy that had previously sat on squishy ground. It was a huge step forward.

Corliss Lamont demonstrates in this chapter how the contingency of the universe, as discussed in Chapter 1, explains aspects of human existence. The innate power to choose among possible courses of action reflects a contingency in human thought that is commonly referred to as freedom of choice. Rogers, in his address as Humanist of the Year (*TH* 24:2), concurred with that view. In this way, human psychology reflects that same contingent nature of reality, of the universe itself. While reality limits the possibilities, we choose among them. Our choices are part of the causes of our experiences. At the same time, Lamont points out that causes beyond our control that we encounter along the paths we choose are a matter of luck.

Not all writers in *TH* accept this view of human choice. Rogers' essay referenced in the previous paragraph set forth the paradox that physical science suggests humans are machines without choice, while asserting the power to choose. Echoing quantum physics, he suggests that freedom exists on "a different dimension." Diametrically opposing Lamont's view, Gardner Williams argued that human free will is determined by an individual's predetermined "free will, free choice, and free preference" (*TH* 20:5).

Freedom and Education

In any event, individuals in some sense consciously make their own personal choices. The emphasis in humanism on science has led some writers in *TH* to focus on choices by scientists. Harold A. Larrabee's included essay examines outside influences on scientists. They can isolate scientists morally from public debates about values that should inform their research methods and topics. They can also isolate scientists psychologically, sometimes in the form of a scientist's self-protective coping mechanism. Larrabee notes the intensified pressure on scientists during wartime, an observation in 1943 that still rings true in the conflict-ridden twenty-first century. He ends, though, with a call for scientists to not isolate themselves from the public debate about public policy concerning technology and science, as much for the benefit of society as for themselves.

Larrabbee's analysis hints at the need for moral education for scientists, in order to increase the likelihood that scientists will make socially acceptable choices and choices that reflect humanist values. Contrary to Socrates, humanistic psychology considers virtue to be a trait that can be taught. By extension, so does humanist philosophy.

Paul Kurtz agreed, arguing broadly for moral education of all, not just scientists (*TH* 32:6). That position recognizes secular moral education as necessary to the proper exercise of the freedom that humanism advocates. Maslow, though, views arts education as most important. He argues that it imparts a greater degree of personal development that comes through struggling with problems and choices, and with oneself. That suggestion leads directly into the next chapter's discussion of humanism and the arts and humanities.

On Getting Values Out of Science

Priscilla Robertson
The Humanist, July-August, 1956

There is a widely current view in our society that you cannot get a value system, or a set of ethical ideals, out of science—the objective study of what is. People who believe this can back up their views with the opinions of many learned men, including (unfortunately) some scientists. Their story goes that science is ethically neutral, that it can tell you how to get what you want but is completely blind when it comes to telling you what you ought to want. One version of the myth states that there are "two roads to truth"—the method of reason and experiment, and the method of intuition or faith. Only in the latter realm, supposedly, do values lie. Because religion is intuitive, built on faith, people say it is warmer and "more human," more satisfying than science, which is supposed to be cold and manipulative.

If this view was, for a long time, fashionable even in scientific circles, it is probably because physics was for a long time the queen of the sciences, and physics deals with material that has no value system. For a century or more, other scientists have wished that their disciplines could become more like physics; thus biologists who dissected out separate muscles and psychologists who conditioned reflexes could claim they were copying the objectivity of physics. George Wald, the Harvard biologist, says that when he began to work in laboratories, in the twenties, most of the workers around him did not really *like* organisms. Since then a change has taken place as researchers have begun to study each organism as a whole, with the result that the new biology and psychology can answer questions the older methods could not even ask. Oddly enough, it was those who followed the separate, analytic approach to organisms who felt the need for some extra force, some outside purpose, to keep the isolated pieces running.

The new biology considers that life itself *is* purpose. In biology, states Kurt Goldstein, every fact has a qualitative significance. Indeed, he goes on, the only importance of biological facts lies in their significance for whatever organism you are studying—and this is true whether it be an amoeba or a man. Insofar as the "values" inhere in the "facts," just so far does the theory that you can't get values out of facts break down. A certain number of scientists within the last ten years have repudiated the ethical neutrality of science and have laid barefaced claim to be arbiters of values both for individuals and for whole cultures; at the same time, many more tactful students use their sciences to form judgments without stating an outright philosophy of their right to do so. This article deals with three of the barefaced ones.

Having mentioned Kurt Goldstein, let us pursue his views for a moment. His own work has been largely with brain-injured patients; his book, *Human Nature in the Light of Psychopathology* (1947), deals with what his researches have taught him about healthy human beings. What Goldstein's patients had lost was the "abstract ability," the quality which makes the rest of us human. The sick subjects could copy a picture of "a window," but could not draw, or even copy "a square," because it is an abstract thing. They can see that a beer can opener "goes with" a beer can provided the can is unopened, but they cannot relate it to an already opened can. They cannot figure out new combinations; they cannot choose between possible courses of action. Their reactions are determined by the stimulus in front of them. It is true that this is just what certain determinists say about all of us—but by showing the difference between a healthy brain and an injured one, Goldstein shows that there are at least degrees of freedom, and goes far toward defining what kind of freedom he believes that we, as men, enjoy. Freedom is a prime moral point. Although not every religion, historically, has held that men are free moral agents, nevertheless a good part of the dislike of science today stems from the view that it would take away our freedom by putting every piece of behavior under regular laws. Instead of that, a man like Goldstein restores our confidence in freedom.

To Goldstein the only drive in human nature is the drive toward what he terms self-actualization. The beginnings of this drive may go back to the amoeba as the center of

Humanist Philosophy 1928 – 1973

its own tiny value system, that of seeking and mastering a "good" environment for itself. Much higher in evolution, Goldstein finds that rats actually solve problems in ways that indicate that they enjoy using their mental and physical powers over and above the effort needed to get food in the most economical way. In man, self-actualization becomes creativity. If a man is healthy, his action comes from joy in coming to terms with the world; and only sick organisms stress "self-preservation." Goldstein feels that Freud, trained in mechanistic science, misunderstood the creative trend of human nature and, in his reliance on pleasure-pain, denied the possibility of happiness. Of course the environment may be too hard for human nature, and in this case sickness or neurosis results, revealing much the same pattern (of a loss of capacity to handle abstract conceptions) which Goldstein found in patients who suffered from physical brain injury. Similarly, customs and traditions can interfere with our proper freedom; though by means of abstract attitudes, again, those customs which we actually follow are integrated with our personalities.

To Goldstein the biological individual is primary, and a society which has to ask for general self-sacrifice has something the matter with it. And knowing what he does about the nature of our brains and nerves, he believes that intellectual restriction or emotional frustration are as crippling to the total organism as the wounding of our bodies in war.

A healthy organism is, however, able to restrict itself voluntarily— something the brain-injured could never do. Goldstein says that freedom manifests itself in two ways: first, in our ability both to restrict ourselves and to encroach on others in the interest both of our own and others' self-actualization; and second, in the courage to fight against whatever opposes human nature both within and outside the organism. The point here is that a strict consideration of the biological aspects of the human brain turns out to involve what have always (from another point of view) been termed "moral values." A certain amount of free choice and creativity is built into our brain structure, and it becomes our moral responsibility to respect it.

A scientist who offers a still more insistent assertion that science has the right to judge moral values in absolute terms (and the word "absolute" is his own) is the British psychologist, Money-Kyrle. The introduction to his brilliant little book, *Psychoanalysis and Politics* (1950) tells of the course of its author's beliefs, from the absolute moral values of the late Victorian period when he grew up, through the twenties when relativistic anthropology seemed to make these untenable (the period when it seemed that each culture was self-contained and could not be rated as superior to any other), down to the time when this comfortable amorality fell to pieces as it was forced to contemplate Fascism. As the horror of Hitler's Germany became apparent, no decent person could believe it was "just as good" as other cultures in western Europe. After the war Money-Kyrle was sent to the British occupation zone to sort out "good" Germans from bad. There he came to believe that, even if the judgments of anthropology were relativistic, he could find a yardstick in psychoanalysis which promised an absolute standard for measuring both individuals and societies.

The single quality which Money-Kyrle came to feel was decisive in assessing his individual Germans was the nature of their consciences, which was reflected in the way they felt guilt. He found he could grade consciences along a continuum from "authoritarian" to "humane." Roughly speaking, the authoritarians felt guilty if they had been disobedient, the humanitarians if they had injured another person. Money-Kyrle then states two scientific reasons for judging the humane as the better type. For one thing, accuracy of perception of the outside world is something which is susceptible of objective checking (within recognizable limits and with certain safeguards which are important but which do not invalidate the argument). An authoritarian mind always suffers from a certain amount of distortion of perception, whereas the humane person is invariably more realistic. Since truth can be defined as the accuracy with which what is inside the mind reflects what is outside, and since truth is the one unchallengeable scientific value, the humane conscience is the one that meets this criterion better. The second reason for preferring this type of conscience is that under psychoanalysis patients always move toward the humane end of the spectrum, never in the opposite direction. Money-Kyrle believes psychoanalysis is a process in which people become freer to choose what they really want to be like inside; a complete, or unimpaired, or healed human brain is by nature humane, and realistic.

A perfectly healthy mind is as unattainable in practice as the perfect love of God, or any other of the moral ideals of the past; but the degree to which a person has reached it is, by Money-Kyrle's standards, more measurable. Such a mind would have nothing permanently excluded from its consciousness. Like Goldstein's healthy organism, it would be able to be free. The way Money-Kyrle puts it is that a normal man can be creative because of his reparative type of conscience. Furthermore, he declares it a psychological law that an increase in the capacity for freedom leads to a decrease in the desire for power. "We can now be certain that the character of the non-humanist opponent is an elaborate defense against unconscious and ultimately irrational anxieties within himself."* If these become conscious, his character will change. Leon J. Saul has put the same idea in different words. He says we now have "a scientific basis for morality—it reveals the evil in man as the persisting traumatic infantile, the result of impaired emotional development; and it shows that the true good is not submissiveness to a code but rather an expression of the strength of maturity."

Money-Kyrle believes his system of thinking is applicable to cultures as well as to individuals. Here his argument runs this way: all political desires are means to more elementary ends, which he envisages in the Freudian concept of avoidance of pain and seeking of pleasure (in this definition being less sophisticated than Goldstein). Desires are influenced by opinions, and opinions may be either true or false. If those desires may be termed rational whose influencing opinions are true, then those governments are "good" whose influencing desires are rational. Many obvious difficulties, of course, beset the way of using this yardstick, the most serious of which is that the unconscious fantasies of groups influence beliefs exactly like direct perceptions. As an example of this, Money-Kyrle gives us a description of an authoritarian people who have been granted external freedom but still feel uncomfortable and "guilty" and crave more authority to relieve their guilt. Nevertheless, in the fact that such processes can be recognized Money-Kyrle sees eventual hope for objective criteria.

No one is more aware than Money-Kyrle of how hard and dangerous it may prove to apply his standard of values. Still, his courageous remark at the end of his book—"What is important is not that we claim to have judged rightly but that we claim to be able to judge at all"— certainly sets a new tone in scientific writing.

If we turn from psychology to anthropology, we find that not all anthropologists agree with Money-Kyrle that their science deals in relative values only. Weston LaBarre, for one excellent example, finds "a basis for ethical and political decision" in man's evolutionary past. His book *The Human Animal* (1954) shows that human society is just as firmly rooted in biology as ant society. The very possibility of family life came about when primates added a non-seasonal sexuality to the ancient mammalian concern of a mother for her young—in other words when a female could be interested in a husband and children at the same time. Only in a permanent group like this could children be taken care of through a longer infancy; only where this was true was it possible for language to be developed. With language came the possibility for larger groupings, for a real society. Thus for LaBarre morality, a social product, goes right back in a clear chain to biological satisfactions— expanded by man's brain power and symbol systems into cultural satisfactions, it is true, but so deeply founded in "pleasure in other people's bodies" that this author says the only two *unqualifiedly* good things in human life are connubial and parental love.

Along with this firm basis for sound morality, however, the reasons for "man's disastrously wrong analyses of reality and himself" are also rooted in his organic nature. Long infancy can teach people to love dependency and infantilism. Guilt or indifference to "sound organic functioning" can be taught by guilty or indifferent mothers. And finally, our symbol systems are so attractive and so elaborate that they may run off at a tangent, away from mature biological functioning, instead of serving to deepen and enrich our connections between mind and body.

Any living thing has purposes, says LaBarre (thus echoing Goldstein); and it has to assert these purposes against an indifferent environment. Evolution brings more complicated purposes, and in man these can be elaborated by culture and language to be as deep or high as we wish. As social and symbol-using animals, that's our business, but we must never lose touch with the meanings created for us by our carnal nature.

It is obvious that the findings of this kind of science are at variance not only with the great Christian tradition which has considered love an alien grace-gift from somewhere outside human nature, but also with Freud, who felt that civilization is a product of the frustrating of the sound organic functioning praised by LaBarre. All three of the scientists here discussed have come to believe that humanity has moral goodness built into it as insistently and as biologically as hunger. Goldstein believes the soundly functioning human brain is creative and courageous in itself (not just when it has to outwit the id); Money-Kyrle shows that soundly functioning perceptions lead to reparative consciences, and thus to kindness as well as creativity. And LaBarre finds in family love a steady and sweet support for all the rest of human society.

Aristotle it was, with his customary good sense, who first remarked that the important thing about ethics was to find out what the "nature" of man is, and then to act in accordance with that nature. Only today, however, are our learned men beginning to find out through incredibly refined scientific methods what the most hidden springs of that nature are, and they prove more profound and more subtle than anyone suspected even as late as thirty years ago.

* Note: Money-Kyrle is not referring to "non-Humanist" opponents, but readers of this magazine will have no difficulty about the pertinence of his remarks even when written with a capital H.

THE BEST OF *THE HUMANIST*

Priscilla Robertson, newly appointed editor of The Humanist, is author of Revolutions of 1848: A Social History. *This article is the first of a series on the relation of science and values.*

Peak Experiences in Education and Art

A. H. Maslow
The Humanist, September-October, 1970

The Humanist *wishes to pay special tribute to Abraham H. Maslow. The following article, received before his untimely death, is a revised version of an article that will appear in the book,* Humanistic Frontiers in American Education, *edited by Roy P. Fairfield. Publication is expected early in 1971. Dr. Maslow, an outstanding psychologist, was a member of the publication committee of* The Humanist *and recipient of the Humanist of the Year Award in 1967.*

Something big is happening. It's happening to everything that concerns human beings. Everything the human being generates is involved, and certainly education is involved. A new *Weltanschauung* is in the process of being developed, a new *Zeitgeist*, a new set of values and a new way of finding them, and certainly a new image of man. There is a new kind of psychology — presently called the humanistic, existential, third-force psychology — that at this transitional moment is certainly different in many important ways from the Freudian and behavioristic psychologies, which have been the two great comprehensive, dominating psychologies.

There are new conceptions of interpersonal relationships. There is a new image of society. There is a new conception of the goals of society, of all the social institutions, and of all the social sciences. There is a new economics, a new conception of politics, and revolutions in religion, in science, in work. There is a newer conception of education, and this forms the background for my ideas of music and creativity.

First of all, most psychologies of learning are beside the point; that is, beside the "humanistic" point. Most teachers and books present learning as the acquisition of associations, of skills, and of capacities that are external and not intrinsic to the human character, to the human personality, to the person himself. Picking up coins or keys or possessions or something of the sort is like picking up reinforcements and conditioned reflexes that are in a certain very profound sense expendable. It does not really matter if one has a conditioned reflex: If I salivate to the sound of a buzzer and then this extinguishes, nothing has happened to me; I have lost nothing of any consequence whatever. We might almost say that those extensive books on the psychology of learning are of no consequence — at least to the human center, to the human soul, to the human essence.

Generated by the new humanistic philosophy is a new conception of learning, teaching, and education. Such a conception holds that the goal of education — the human goal, the humanistic goal — is ultimately the "self-actualization" of a person, the development of the fullest height that the human species or a particular individual can come to. In a less technical way, it is helping the person to become the best that he is able to become. Such a goal involves very serious shifts in learning strategies.

Associative learning is certainly useful: for learning things that are of no real consequence, or for learning techniques that are interchangeable. And many of the things we must learn are like that. If one needed to memorize the vocabulary of another language, he would learn it by sheer rote memory. Here the laws of association can be a help. Whereas if one wants to learn automatic habits in driving, like responding to a red signal light or something of the sort, then conditioning is of consequence. It is important and useful, especially in a technological society.

In terms of becoming a better person, of self-development, self-fulfillment, or "becoming fully human," the greatest learning experiences are very different. In my life, such experiences have been far more important than listening, memorizing, and organizing data for formal courses.

More important for me have been such experiences as having a child. Our first baby changed me as a psychologist. It made the behaviorism I had been so enthusiastic about look so foolish that I could not stomach it any more. It was impossible. Having a second baby, and learning how profoundly different people are even before birth, made it impossible for me to think in terms of the kind of learning psychology in which one can teach anybody anything. I could no longer think in terms of the John B.

Humanist Philosophy 1928 – 1973

Watson theory, "Give me two babies and I will make one into this and one into the other." It is as if he never had any children. We know only too well that a parent cannot make his children into anything. Children make themselves into something. The best we can do, and frequently the most effect we can have, is to serve as something to react against if the child presses too hard.

Another profound learning experience that I value far more highly than any particular course or any degree is my personal psychoanalysis: discovering my own identity, my own self. Yet another basic experience — far more important — was getting married; that was certainly more instructive than my Ph.D.

Thus if one thinks in terms of developing the kinds of wisdom, understanding, and life skills that he would want, he must think of what I call *intrinsic* education, *intrinsic* learning; that is, first, learning to be a human being in general, and second, learning to be *this* particular human being. Once you start thinking in terms of becoming a good human being, and then ask about your high school courses — "How did trigonometry help me to become a better human being?" — an echo answers, "By gosh, they didn't work!" In a certain sense, trigonometry was for me a waste of time. My early music education was also unsuccessful because it taught a child who had a profound feeling for music and a great love for the piano *not* to learn it. My piano teacher taught me in effect that music is something to stay away from. And I had to relearn music as an adult.

I am talking about ends: This is a revolutionary repudiation of 19th-century science and contemporary professional philosophy, which is essentially a technology and not a philosophy of ends. I reject thereby, as theories of human nature, positivism, behaviorism, and objectivism. I reject thereby the whole model of science, and all its works derived from the historical accident that science began with the study of non-personal, nonhuman things that in fact had no ends. The development of physics, astronomy, mechanics, and chemistry was impossible until they had become value-free, value-neutral, so that pure descriptiveness was possible. The great mistake that we are now learning about is that this model, developed from the study of objects and of things, has been illegitimately used for the study of human beings. It is a terrible technique. It has not worked.

Most of the psychology on this positivistic, objectivistic, associationistic, value-free, value-neutral model of science, as it piles up like a coral reef of small facts about this and that, is certainly not false, but merely trivial. I do not want to sell my own science short; we know a great deal about things that do matter to the human being. But I would maintain that what has mattered most has been learned mainly by non-physicalistic techniques, by the humanistic science of which we have become more conscious.

In the social sciences many are discovering that the physicalistic, mechanistic model was a mistake, leading us ... to where? To atom bombs. To a beautiful technology of killing, as in the concentration camps. To Eichmann. An Eichmann cannot be refuted with a positivistic philosophy or science. He just cannot. He didn't know what was wrong. As far as he was concerned, nothing was wrong; he had done a good job. He *did* do a good job, if you forget about ends and values. I have pointed out that professional science and professional philosophy are dedicated to the proposition of forgetting about values, excluding them. This, therefore, must lead to Eichmanns, to atom bombs, and to who knows what! The tendency to separate good style or talent from content and ends can lead to this kind of danger.

We can now add to the great discoveries Freud made. His one big mistake, which we are correcting now, is that he thought of the unconscious merely as undesirable evil. But unconsciousness also carries in it the roots of creativeness, of joy, of happiness, of goodness, of its own ethics and values. There is a healthy unconscious as well as an unhealthy one. And the new psychologies are studying this at full tilt. The existential psychiatrists and psychotherapists are putting it into practice. New kinds of therapies are being practiced. We have a good conscious and a bad conscious, a good unconscious and a bad unconscious. Furthermore, the good is real in a non-Freudian sense. Freud was committed by his own positivism.

Humanist Philosophy 1928 – 1973

He was a neurologist. And a sworn oath called for a project to develop a psychology that could be reduced to physical and chemical statements. This is what he dedicated himself to, though he himself disproved his point!

And how do we explain this higher nature that I claim we have discovered? The Freudian explanation has been reductive. Explain it away. If I am a kind man, this is a reaction formation against my rage to kill. Somehow, the killing is more basic than the kindness. And the kindness is a way of trying to cover up, repress, and defend myself against realizing the fact that I am truly a murderer. If I am generous, this is a reaction formation against stinginess. I am really stingy inside. This is a very peculiar thing. Somehow there is a begging of the question that is now so obvious. Why did he not say, for instance, that maybe killing people was a reaction formation against loving them? It is just as legitimate a conclusion and, as a matter of fact, more true for many people.

But, to return to this exciting new development in science, I have a very strong sense of being in the middle of a historical wave. One hundred and fifty years from now, what will the historians say about this age? What was really important? What was going on? What was finished? My belief is that much of what makes the headlines is finished, and the growing tip of mankind is what is now developing and will flourish in 100 or 200 years if we manage to endure. Historians will be talking about this movement as the sweep of history; they will say that as Whitehead pointed out, when you get a new model, a new paradigm, a new way of perceiving, new definitions of the old words, suddenly you have an insight. You see things in a different way.

One consequence generated by what I have been talking about is a flat denial, an *empirical* denial (not pious, or arbitrary, or a priori, or wishful) of the Freudian contention of a necessary, intrinsic, constant opposition between the needs of the individual and the needs of society and civilization. It just is not so. We now know something about how to set up the conditions in which the needs of the individual become synergistic with, not opposed to, the needs of society and in which they both work to the same ends.

Another empirical statement can be made about what we call "peak experiences." We have made studies of peak experiences by asking groups of people and individuals such questions as, "What was the most ecstatic moment of your life?" or "Have you experienced transcendent ecstasy?" One might think that in a general population, such questions might get only blank stares. But there were many answers. Apparently the transcendent ecstasies had been kept private because there are few if any ways of speaking about then in public. They are sort of embarrassing, shameful, not "scientific" — which many believe is the ultimate sin.

But we found many trippers to set them off. Almost everybody seems to have peak experiences or ecstasies. The question might be asked in terms of the single most joyous, happiest, most blissful moment of your whole life. You might ask questions of the kind I asked: "How did you feel different about yourself at that time?" "How did the work look different?" "What did you feel like?" "What were your impulses?" "How did you change if you did?" I want to report that the two easiest ways of getting peak experiences (in terms of simple statistics in empirical reports) are through music and through sex. I will push aside sex education, as such discussions are premature — although I am certain that one day we will not giggle over it, but will take it quite seriously and teach children that like music, like love, like insight, like a beautiful meadow, like a cute baby or whatever, there are many paths to heaven. And sex is one of them. And music is one of them. These happen to be the easiest ones to understand.

For purposes of identifying and studying peak experiences, a list of triggers can be made. The list gets so long, however, that it becomes necessary to make generalizations. It looks as if any experience of real excellence, of real perfection, of any moving toward perfect justice or toward perfect values, tends to produce a peak experience. Not always. But it's a generalization I would make for the many kinds of things that we can concentrate on. Remember, I am talking here as a scientist.

Humanist Philosophy 1928 – 1973

This doesn't sound like scientific talk, but this is a new kind of science.

We know that from this new humanistic science has come one of the real childbearing improvements since Adam and Eve; that is, natural childbirth, a potent source of peak experiences. We know just how to encourage peak experiences; how women can have children in such a fashion as to have a great and mystical experience, a religious experience if you wish— an illumination, a revelation, an insight. That is what women say in interviews. They become a different kind of person because there ensues what I have called "the cognition of being."

We must make a new vocabulary for all these untilled, unworked problems. "Cognition of being" really means the cognition that Plato and Socrates were talking about; almost, you could say, a technology of happiness, of pure excellence, pure truth, pure goodness, and so on. Well, why not a technology of joy, of happiness?

Let's proceed to music in this relation. So far, peak experiences are reported only from what we might call "classical music." I have not found a peak experience from John Cage (or from an Andy Warhol movie, from abstract expressionist painting, etc.). I just haven't. The peak experiences that have been reported as great joy, ecstasy, visions of another world or another level of living, have come from the great classics. On the other hand, music also melts over and fuses into dancing and rhythm. So far as this realm of research is concerned, there really isn't much difference; they melt into each other. Music as a path to peak experiences includes dancing. It also includes the rhythmic experience, even very simple rhythmic experience — the good dancing of a rumba, or the kinds of things that the kids can do with drums. (I don't know whether to call the latter music, dancing, rhythm, athletics, or something else.)

Love, awareness, and reverence of the body are clearly good paths to peak experiences. These in turn are good paths (not guaranteed, but statistically likely) to the "cognition of being," to the perceiving of the Platonic essences, intrinsic values, the ultimate of being. And these paths are a therapeutic-like help toward both the curing-of-sicknesses kind of therapy and toward the growth of full-humanness. In other words, peak experiences often have consequences, very important consequences.

Music and art can have the same kinds of consequences; there is a certain overlap. They can do the same thing as psychotherapy if one keeps his goals right, knows just what he is about, and is conscious of what he is going forward. We can talk of the breaking up of symptoms like the breaking up of clichés, anxieties, and the like; *or* we can talk about the development of spontaneity, courage, Olympian or godlike humor, sensory awareness, body awareness, and the like. Music and art and rhythm and dancing are excellent ways of moving toward that second means of discovering identity.

Such triggers tend to do all kinds of things to our autonomic nervous systems, endocrine glands, feelings, and emotions. They just do. We do not know enough about physiology to understand why they do. But they do, and these are unmistakable experiences. They are a little like pain, which is also an unmistakable experience. For experientially empty people, including a tragically large proportion of the population, for people who do not know what is going on inside themselves and who live by clocks, schedules, rules, laws, hints from the neighbors (i.e., other-directed people), to kind of trigger provides a way of discovering what the self is like. There are signals from inside; there are voices that yell out, "By gosh this is good, don't ever doubt it!" We use these signals as a path to teach the discovery of the self and self-actualization. The discovery of identity comes via the impulse voices, via the ability to listen to your own guts and what is going on inside of you.

This discovery is also an experimental kind of education that may eventually lead us into a parallel educational establishment, into another *kind* of school, where mathematics can be just as beautiful, just as peak-producing, as music. Of course there are mathematics teachers who have devoted themselves to preventing this. I had no glimpse of mathematics as a study in aesthetics until I was 30 years old, when I read some books about it. And one can find the same kind of experience with history or anthropology (in the sense of learning another culture), social anthropology, palaeontology, or the study of science.

Here again I want to talk data. If one works with great creators, great scientists, the creative scientists, that is the way they talk. The picture of the scientist — his image as one who never smiles, who bleeds embalming fluid rather than blood — must change. Such conceptions must yield to an understanding of the creative scientist who lives by peak experiences, who lives for the moments of glory when a problem is solved and when suddenly through a microscope he gets a new perception, a moment of revelation, of illumination, insight, understanding, ecstasy. These are vital for him. Scientists are very shy and embarrassed about this. They refuse to talk about it in public. It takes a delicate kind of midwifery to extract it; but it is there, and I have got it out. If one manages to convince a creative scientist that he is not going to be laughed at for these things, then he will blushingly admit the fact of having a high emotional experience at the moment in which the crucial correlation turns out right. They just don't talk about it. As for the usual textbook on how you do science, it is total nonsense.

My point is that if we are conscious enough of what we are doing and are philosophically insightful in doing it, we may be able to use those experiences that most easily produce ecstasies and revelations, peaks and illumination, bliss and rapture. We may be able to use them as models by which to re-evaluate all kinds of teaching.

The final impression that I want to try to work out is that effective education in music, art, dancing, and rhythm is intrinsically far closer to the kind of education I think necessary than is the usual "core curriculum"; that is, it is closer to the goal of learning one's identity as an essential part of his education. And if education doesn't do that, it is useless. Education is learning to grow, learning what to grow toward, learning what is good and bad, learning what is desirable and undesirable, learning what to choose and what not to choose. In this realm of intrinsic learning, intrinsic teaching, and intrinsic education, I think that the arts are so close to our psychological and biological core, so close to this identity, this biological identity, that rather than think of these courses as a sort of whipped cream or luxury, we must let them become basic experiences in our education. They could very well serve as a model; the glimpse into the infinite that they provide might well serve as the means by which we might rescue the rest of the school curriculum from the value-free, value-neutral, goal-lacking meaninglessness into which it has fallen.

A Therapist's View of the Good Life

Carl R. Rogers
The Humanist, September-October, 1957

My views regarding the meaning of the good life are largely based upon my experience in working with people in the very close and intimate relationship which is called psychotherapy. These views thus have an empirical or experiential foundation, as contrasted perhaps with a scholarly or philosophical foundation. I have learned what the good life seems to be by observing and participating in the struggle of disturbed and troubled people to achieve that life.

I should make it clear from the outset that this experience I have gained comes from the vantage point of a particular orientation to psychotherapy which has developed over the years. Quite possibly all psychotherapy is basically similar, but since I am less sure of that than I once was, I wish to make it clear that my therapeutic experience has been along the lines that seem to me most effective, the type of therapy termed "client-centered."

Let me attempt to give a very brief description of what this therapy would be like if it were in every respect optimal, since I feel I have learned most about the good life from therapeutic experiences in which a great deal of movement occurred. If the therapy were optimal, intensive as well as extensive, then it would mean that the therapist has been able to enter into an intensely personal and subjective relationship with the client—relating not as a scientist to an object of study, not as a physician expecting to diagnose and cure, but as a person to a person. It would mean that the therapist feels this client to be a person of unconditional self-worth: of value no matter what his condition, his behavior, or his feelings. It would mean that the therapist is genuine, hiding behind no defensive facade, but meeting the client with the feelings which organically he is experiencing. It would mean that the therapist is able to let himself go in understanding this client; that no inner barriers keep him from sensing what it feels like to be the client at each moment of the relationship; and that he can convey something of his empathic understanding to the client. It means that the therapist has been comfortable in entering this relationship fully, without knowing cognitively where it will lead, satisfied with providing a climate which will provide the client with the utmost freedom to become himself.

For the client, this optimal therapy would mean an exploration of increasingly strange and unknown and dangerous feelings in himself; the exploration proving possible only because he is gradually realizing that he is accepted unconditionally. Thus he becomes acquainted with elements of his experience which have in the past been denied to awareness as too threatening, too damaging to the structure of the self. He finds himself experiencing these feelings fully, completely, in the relationship, so that for the moment he is his fear, or his anger, or his tenderness, or his strength. And as he lives these widely varied feelings, in all their degrees of intensity, he discovers that he has experienced *himself*, that he is all these feelings. He finds his behavior changing in constructive fashion in accordance with his newly experienced self. He approaches the realization that he no longer needs to fear what experience may hold, but can welcome it freely as a part of his changing and developing self.

This is a thumbnail sketch of what client-centered therapy comes close to, when it is at its optimum. I give it here simply as a brief picture of the context in which I have formed my views of the good life.

A Negative Observation

As I have tried to live understandingly in the experiences of my clients, I have gradually come to one negative conclusion about the good life. It seems to me that the good life is not any fixed state. It is not, in my estimation, a state of virtue, or contentment, or nirvana, or happiness. It is not a condition in which the individual is adjusted, or fulfilled, or actualized. To use psychological terms, it is not a state of drive-reduction, or tension-reduction, or homeostasis.

HUMANIST PHILOSOPHY 1928 – 1973

I believe that all of these terms have been used in ways which imply that if one or several of these states is achieved, then the goal of life has been achieved. Certainly, for many people happiness, or adjustment, are seen as states of being which are synonymous with the good life. And social scientists have frequently spoken of the reduction of tension, or the achievement of homeostasis or equilibrium as if these states constituted the goal of the process of living.

So it is with a certain amount of surprise and concern that I realize that my experience supports none of these definitions. If I focus on the experience of those individuals who seem to have evidenced the greatest degree of movement during the therapeutic relationship, and who, in the years following this relationship, appear to have made and to be making real progress toward the good life, then it seems to me that they are not adequately described at all by any of these terms which refer to fixed states of being. I believe they would consider themselves insulted if they were described as "adjusted," and they would regard it as false if they were described as "happy" or "contented," or even "actualized." As I have known them I would regard it as most inaccurate to say that all their drive tensions have been reduced, or that they are in a state of homeostasis. So I am forced to ask myself whether there is any way in which I can generalize about their situation, any definition which I can give of the good life which would seem to fit the facts as I have observed them. I find this not at all easy, and what follows is stated very tentatively.

A Positive Observation

If I attempt to capture in a few words what seems to me to be true of these people, I believe it will come out something like this:

The good life is a *process*, not a state of being.

It is a direction, not a destination.

The direction which constitutes the good life is that which is selected by the total organism, when there is psychological freedom to move in any direction.

This organismically selected direction seems to have certain discernible general qualities which appear to be the same in a wide variety of unique individuals.

So I can integrate these statements into a definition which can at least serve as a basis for consideration and discussion. The good life, from the point of view of my experience, is the process of movement in a direction which the human organism selects when it is inwardly free to move in any direction, and the general qualities of this selected direction appear to have a certain universality.

The Characteristics of the Process

Let me now try to specify what appear to be the characteristic qualities of this process of movement, as they crop up in person after person in therapy.

An Increasing Openness to Experience

In the first place, the process seems to involve an increasing openness to experience. This phrase has come to have more and more meaning for me. It is the polar opposite of defensiveness. Defensiveness I have described in the past as being the organism's response to experiences which are perceived or anticipated as threatening, as incongruent with the individual's existing picture of himself, or of himself in relationship to the world. These threatening experiences are temporarily rendered harmless by being distorted in awareness, or being denied to awareness. I quite literally cannot see, with accuracy, those experiences, feelings, reactions in myself which are significantly at variance with the picture of myself which I already possess. A large part of the process of therapy is the continuing discovery by the client that he is experiencing feelings and attitudes which heretofore he has not been able to be aware of, which he has not been able to "own" as being a part of himself.

If a person could be fully open to his experience, however, every stimulus—whether originating within the organism or in the environment—would be freely relayed through the nervous system without being distorted by any defensive mechanism. There would be no need of the mechanism of "subception" whereby the organism is forewarned of any experience threatening to the self. On the contrary, whether the stimulus was the impact of a configuration of form, color, or sound in the environment on the sensory nerves, or a memory trace from the past, or a visceral sensation of fear or pleasure or disgust, the person would be "living" it, would have it completely available to awareness.

Thus, one aspect of this process which I am naming "the good life" appears to be a movement away from the pole of defensiveness toward the pole of openness to experience. The individual is becoming more able to listen to himself, to experience what is going on within himself. He is more open to his feelings of fear and discouragement and pain. He is also more open to his feelings of courage, and tenderness, and awe. He is free to live his feelings subjectively, as they exist in him, and also free to be aware of these feelings. He is more able fully to live the experiences of his organism rather than shutting them out of awareness.

Increasingly Existential Living

A second characteristic of the process which for me is the good life, is that it involves an increasing tendency to live fully in each moment. This is a thought which can easily be misunderstood, and which is perhaps somewhat vague in my own thinking. Let me try to explain what I mean.

I believe it would be evident that for the person who was fully open to his experience, completely without defensiveness, each moment would be new. The complex configuration of inner and outer stimuli which exists in this moment has never existed before in just this fashion. Consequently such a person would realize that "What I will be in the next moment, and what I will do, grows out of that moment, and cannot be predicted in advance either by me or by others." Not infrequently we find clients expressing this sort of feeling. Thus one, at the end of therapy, says in rather puzzled fashion, "I haven't finished the job of integrating and reorganizing myself, but that's only confusing, not discouraging, now that I realize this is a continuing process. ... It is exciting, sometimes upsetting, but deeply encouraging to feel yourself in action and apparently knowing where you are going even though you don't always consciously know where that is."

One way of expressing the fluidity which is present in such existential living is to say that the self and personality emerge from experience, rather than experience being translated or twisted to fit a preconceived self-structure. It means that one becomes a participant in and an observer of the ongoing process of organismic experience, rather than being in control of it.

Such living in the moment means an absence of rigidity, of tight organization, of the imposition of structure on experience. It means instead a maximum of adaptability, a discovery of structure in experience, a flowing, changing organization of self and personality.

It is this tendency toward existential living which appears to me very evident in people who are involved in the process of the good life. One might almost say that it is the most essential quality of it. It involves discovering the structure of experience in the process of living the experience. Most of us, on the other hand, bring a pre-formed structure and evaluation to our experience and never relinquish it, but cram and twist the experience to fit our preconceptions, annoyed at the fluid qualities which make it so unruly in fitting our carefully constructed pigeon holes. To open one's spirit to what is going on *now*, and to discover in that present process whatever structure it appears to have—this to me is one of the qualities of the good life, the mature life, as I see clients approach it.

An Increasing Trust in His Organism

Still another characteristic of the person who is living the process of the good life appears to be an increasing trust in his organism as a means of arriving at the most satisfying behavior in each existential situation. Again let me try to explain what I mean.

In choosing what course of action to take in any situation, many people rely upon guiding principles, upon a code of action laid down by some group or institution, upon the judgment of others (from wife and friends to Emily Post), or upon the way they have behaved in some similar past situation. Yet as I observe the clients whose experiences in living have taught me so much, I find that increasingly such individuals are able to trust their total organismic reaction to a new situation because they discover to an ever-increasing degree that if they are open to their experience, doing what "feels right" proves to be a competent and trustworthy guide to behavior which is truly satisfying.

As I try to understand the reason for this, I find myself following this line of thought. The person who is fully open to his experience would have access to all of the available data in the situation, on which to base his behavior; the social demands, his own complex and possibly conflicting needs, his memories of similar situations, his perception of the uniqueness of this situation, etc., etc. The data would be very complex indeed. But he could permit his total organism, his consciousness participating, to consider each stimulus, need, and demand, its relative intensity and importance, and out of this complex weighing and balancing, discover that course of action which would come closest to satisfying all his needs in the situation. An analogy which might come close to a description would be to compare this person to a giant electronic computing machine. Since he is open to his experience, all of the data from his sense impressions, from his memory, from previous learning, from his visceral and internal states, is fed into the machine. The machine takes all of these multitudinous pulls and forces which are fed in as data, and quickly computes the course of action which would be the most economical vector of need satisfaction in this existential situation. This is the behavior of our hypothetical person.

The defects which in most of us make this process untrustworthy are the inclusion of information which does not belong to this present situation, or the exclusion of information which does. It is when memories and previous learnings are fed into the computations as if they were this reality, and not memories and learnings, that erroneous behavioral answers arise. Or when certain threatening experiences are inhibited from awareness, and hence are withheld from the computation or fed into it in distorted form, this too produces error. But our hypothetical person would find his organism thoroughly trustworthy, because all of the available data would be used, and it would be present in accurate rather than distorted form. Hence his behavior would come as close as possible to satisfying all his needs—for enhancement, for affiliation with others, and the like.

In this weighing, balancing, and computation, his organism would not by any means be infallible. It would always give the best possible answer for the available data, but sometimes data would be missing. Because of the element of openness to experience, however, any errors, any following of behavior which was not satisfying, would be quickly corrected. The computations, as it were, would always be in process of being corrected, because they would be continually checked in behavior.

Perhaps you will not like my analogy of an electronic computing machine. Let me return to the clients I know. As they become more open to all of their experiences, they find it increasingly possible to trust their reactions. If they "feel like" expressing anger they do so and find that this comes out satisfactorily, because they are equally alive to all of their other desires for affection, affiliation, and relationship. They are surprised at their own intuitive skill in finding behavioral solutions to complex and troubling human relationships. It is only afterward that they realize how surprisingly trustworthy their inner reactions have been in bringing about satisfactory behavior.

The Process of Functioning More Fully

I should like to draw together these three threads describing the process of the good life into a more coherent picture. It appears that the person who is psychologically free moves in the direction of becoming a more fully functioning person. He is more able to live fully in and with each and all of his feelings and reactions. He makes increasing use of all his organic equipment to sense, as accurately as possible, the existential situation within and without. He makes use of all of the information his nervous system can thus supply, using it in awareness, but recognizing that his total organism may be, and often is, wiser than his awareness. He is more able to permit his total organism to function freely in all its complexity in selecting, from the multitude of possibilities, that behavior which in this moment of time will be most generally and genuinely satisfying. He is able to put more trust in his organism in this functioning, not because it is infallible, but because he can be fully open to the consequences of each of his actions and correct them if they prove to be less than satisfying.

He is more able to experience all of his feelings, and is less afraid of any of his feelings; he is his own sifter of evidence, and is more open to evidence from all sources; he is completely engaged in the process of being and becoming himself, and thus discovers that he is soundly and realistically social; he lives more completely in this moment, but learns that this is the soundest living for all time. He is becoming a more fully functioning organism, and because of the awareness of himself which flows freely in and through his experience, he is becoming a more fully functioning person.

Some Implications

Any view of what constitutes the good life carries with it many implications, and the view I have presented is no exception. I hope that these implications may be food for thought. There are two or three of these about which I would like to comment.

Creativity as an Element of the Good Life

I believe it will be clear that a person who is involved in the directional process which I have termed "the good life" is a creative person. With his sensitive openness to his world, his trust of his own ability to form new relationships with his environment, he would be the type of person from whom creative products and creative living emerge. He would not necessarily be "adjusted" to his culture, and he would almost certainly not be a conformist. But at any time and in any culture he would live constructively, in as much harmony with his culture as a balanced satisfaction of needs demanded. In some cultural situations he might in some ways be very unhappy, but he would continue to move toward becoming himself, and to behave in such a way as to provide the maximum satisfaction of his deepest needs.

Such a person would, I believe, be recognized by the student of evolution as the type most likely to adapt and survive under changing environmental conditions. He would be able creatively to make sound adjustments to new as well as old conditions. He would be a fit vanguard of human evolution.

Basic Trustworthiness of Human Nature

It will be evident that another implication of the view I have been presenting is that the basic nature of the human being, when functioning freely, is constructive and trustworthy. For me this is an inescapable conclusion from a quarter-century of experience in psychotherapy. When we are able to free the individual from defensiveness, so that he is open to the wide range of his own needs, as well as the wide range of environmental and social demands, his reactions may be trusted to be positive, forward-moving, constructive. We do not need to ask who will socialize him, for one of his own deepest needs is for affiliation and communication with others. As he becomes more fully himself, he will become more realistically socialized. We do not need to ask who will control his aggressive impulses; for as he becomes more open to all of his impulses, his need to be liked by others and his tendency to give affection will be as strong as his impulses to strike out or to seize for himself. He will be aggressive in situations in which aggression is realistically appropriate, but there will be no run away need for aggression. His total behavior, in these and other areas, as he moves toward being open to all his experience, will be more balanced and realistic, behavior which is appropriate to the survival and enhancement of a highly social animal.

I have little sympathy with the rather prevalent concept that man is basically irrational, and that his impulses, if not controlled, will lead to destruction of others and self.

Humanist Philosophy 1928 – 1973

Man's behavior is exquisitely rational, moving with subtle and ordered complexity toward the goals his organism is endeavoring to achieve. The tragedy for most of us is that our defenses keep us from being aware of this rationality, so that consciously we are moving in one direction, while organismically we are moving in another. But in our person who is living the process of the good life, there would be a decreasing number of such barriers, and he would be increasingly a participant in the rationality of his organism. The only control of impulses which would exist, or which would prove necessary, is the natural and internal balancing of one need against another, and the discovery of behaviors which follow the vector most closely approximating the satisfaction of all needs. The experience of extreme satisfaction of one need (for aggression, or sex, etc.) in such a way as to do violence to the satisfaction of other needs (for companionship, tender relationships, etc.)—an experience very common in the defensively organized person—would be greatly decreased. He would participate in the vastly complex self-regulatory activities of his organism—the psychological as well as physiological thermostatic controls—in such a fashion as to live in increasing harmony with himself and with others.

The Greater Richness of Life

One last implication I should like to mention is that this process of living in the good life involves a wider range, a greater richness, than the constricted living in which most of us find ourselves. To be a part of this process means that one is involved in the frequently frightening and frequently satisfying experience of a more sensitive living, with greater range, greater variety, greater richness. It seems to me that clients who have moved significantly in therapy live more intimately with their feelings of pain, but also more vividly with their feelings of ecstasy; that anger is more clearly felt, but so also is love; that fear is an experience they know more deeply, but so is courage. And the reason they can thus live fully in a wider range is that they have this underlying confidence in themselves as trustworthy instruments for encountering life.

I believe it will have become evident why, for me, adjectives such as happy, contented, blissful, enjoyable, do not seem quite appropriate to any general description of this process I have called the good life, even though the person in this process would experience each one of these feelings at appropriate times. But the adjectives which seem more generally fitting are adjectives such as enriching, exciting, rewarding, challenging, meaningful. This process of the good life is not, I am convinced, a life for the faint-hearted. It involves the stretching and growing of becoming more and more of one's potentialities. It involves the courage to be. It means launching oneself fully into the stream of life. Yet the deeply exciting thing about human beings is that when the individual is inwardly free, he chooses as the good life this process of becoming.

Carl R. Rogers, for some years leader of the Counseling Center at the University of Chicago, is now Professor of Psychology and Psychiatry at the University of Wisconsin.

Freedom of Choice

Corliss Lamont
The Humanist, March-April, 1965

When the fatalistic Mohammedan fighters in the motion picture *Lawrence of Arabia* wanted to persuade Colonel Lawrence of the impossibility of one of his proposed military ventures, they said "It is written." To which Lawrence's spirited answer was always "Nothing is written." And the film in each case proceeds to show how he carried out the venture against immense odds.

Actually, Lawrence was not right, nor were the Arabs. The truth is that in human life there is a great deal that is inexorably determined ("written,") and a great deal that springs from man's free choice ("free will" in traditional terminology). Both Lawrence and the Arabs made the mistake of considering these concepts, freedom of choice and determinism, to be mutually exclusive, as if there must be universal determinism *or* absolute freedom. Philosophers, too, have sometimes made the same error.

In modern times man has gained enormous control over Nature by discovering a multitude of scientific laws and then using them to his own advantage. Those laws represent determinism and are always the expression of if-then relations or sequences. *If* the temperature drops to 32 degrees Fahrenheit, *then* water freezes into ice. Fortunately, many human functions, such as breathing and the circulation of the blood, are automatic and deterministic. At the same time an individual functioning on the level of intellectual deliberation can exercise true freedom of choice in deciding between two or more genuine alternatives.

When a man wishes to go somewhere in his car, he relies on its built-in determinisms of self-starter, accelerator, steering wheel and brakes. But it is he, not the automobile, that makes the decision as to precisely what road he will take or what his destination is to be. This is an everyday example of how freedom utilizes determinism. In fact, successful human living is built upon this basic principle, which reaches its apex in a machine civilization like that of the United States. There is, then, in human existence a constant, interlocking pattern of *both* freedom and determinism.

Human freedom of choice always operates, of course, within definite limits. It is conditioned by natural law, by the past, by the present environment, by economic circumstance and other factors. All men are governed by the law of gravity and yet have very wide liberty of movement. To cite another familiar example, persons who play chess abide ordinarily by its established rules, which represent determinism; but within that broad framework a tremendous variety of moves are possible, and they represent freedom. The same principle holds true for all competitive games and sports.

The *if* of every if-then law points to the fact that chance or contingency is involved in the occurence of any *if*. When such occurrence is initiated, by a human being or by a nonhuman force, certain specific consequences will necessarily follow. But Nature does not decree when and how any particular causal law will come into effect. As Professor Sterling P. Lamprecht states in his brilliant book *Nature and History*: "Necessity and contingency, so far from being unconnected ideas to be taken, one wholesale and the other retail, are supplementary ideas which belong together in the analysis of every separate event."

Contingency occurs when two independently initiated event-streams, with no common cause behind them, meet at a definite point in space and time. We must say that the more than 400 persons killed by lightning annually in the United States are victims of chance in the form of very bad luck. To analyze an instance of contingency in more detail, let us look at the collision in mid-air over Chesapeake Bay on November 23, 1962, between a United Airlines Viscount and two whistling swans weighing some eight pounds each. When the bodies of the birds penetrated the tail mechanism of the plane, the pilot lost control and the Viscount plunged to earth. All seventeen aboard were killed.

It is my claim that no matter how far back into the past we are able to trace the event-stream represented by the Viscount and the event-stream represented by the swans, we shall find no relevant common cause that started both causal series on their respective ways so that they inevitably intersected on that November day. This was the first airplane accident involving whistling swans in the records of the Federal Aviation Agency.

If contingency really does exist as an ultimate and pervasive trait of the universe, then the thesis of universal necessity cannot be logically upheld and the hard-core determinist is proved wrong. His position is that the great cosmic juggernaut rolls on inexorably and that each event and thing of the present down to its last detail, including his own argument and my answer, has been predetermined since the beginning of time. The existence of contingency undermines that position and opens the door for freedom of choice, without guaranteeing that it will come into being.

For only thinking creatures such as men have freedom of choice. They possess this capacity because they usually do not need to react immediately to a challenge or problem in a speedy stimulus-response manner. They are able instead to stand away temporarily from the flux of events and to delay a decision while they reason concerning the advantages or disadvantages of the different alternatives that may be followed. It is well to remember that the word "intelligence" originates in the Latin *inter* (between) and *legere* (to choose)."Choosing" means making up one's mind.

In the intellectual process that leads to a decision the individual ordinarily employs general concepts or "universals," as they are called in philosophy. As Professor Charles Hartshorne puts it, "our very power to form general conceptions in a sense in which these are beyond the reach of other animals is the same as our not being determined by irresistible impulse, habit or antecedent character, to be one mode of acting in a given case ... Freedom in the indeterministic sense is thus inherent in rational understanding as such, understanding through universals."

Suppose that you are living in a fairly large city and that you want to go with your wife on a Saturday night to a good motion picture. Going to movies is, then, your general idea; and under it can be subsumed the various possibilities, the particular instances, listed in the leading newspaper or some magazine like New York's *Cue*. You talk the plan over carefully with your wife and finally select pictures that you both agree would be worth seeing.

Then you check on the time when each movie begins and how long it will take to get to each theater. Finally, you make your choice and take a bus to the theatre in question.

I insist that a complex thought process such as I have just described is not mere play-acting for setting up an evening's entertainment that was predetermined prior even to one's general desire to see a movie. On the contrary, such a weighing of pros and cons is a serious exercise in deliberation that in itself all but implies freedom of choice. The determinist argument that even human thinking and its results are all decided in advance turns thought into an incomprehensible and superfluous appendage of Homo sapiens.

That argument also robs the concept of potentiality of its fundamental meaning. For "potentiality" means the presence of *plural* possibilities in Nature and in the lives of human beings. If universal and absolute determinism rules the world, then there is always and everywhere only one potentiality, namely, the potentiality of that which actually occurs.

This doctrine runs counter to logic, common sense, and human experience.

A potent reason for the widespread acceptance of the determinist thesis is a rather common misunderstanding of the operation of cause and effect. Many individuals look upon the present as merely the effect of preceding causes and forget that the present in its multitudinous forms is itself an active cause. It is the spearhead of all activity, the great forward thrust of universal being. In truth, the past, which is dead and gone, does not create the present; it is the present which creates the past. For the present alone exists, and the past has efficacy only as embodied in the substance or structure of some present went or object. As the dynamic present forges ahead it leaves its past behind it, making a trail as it were, as a skier gliding downhill through the mow, or a boat producing a foamy wake.

Human beings, functioning as causes themselves, constitute the surging crest of an ongoing and unending wave of the present. And now we return to the theme of contingency. When man-as-cause acts upon some subject matter external to himself, there occurs, unless a regular pattern has been previously established, a conjunction between two separately initiated event-streams. This is why freedom of choice is inextricably linked with contingency. When I decide one evening to drive to the movies in my car, I am the immediate cause-stimulus for the event-stream represented by my automobile.

In that situation true freedom of choice is possible for me owing to the open world of contingency as compared with the closed world of omnipotent determinism. So it is that a free choice becomes a free cause. The human individual, a thinking, initiating, choosing agent, can be and frequently is the free cause of his actions. This knowledge, I believe, helps to build up the morale of a man and stimulates him to greater creativity. It also gives deeper meaning to human ethics, for awareness of freedom of choice brings home to every individual that he must take full responsibility for his actions.

Now at the end of my analysis I raise an issue that is usually mentioned at the start of discussions on freedom of choice: the very strong intuition native to most men that they are not slaves of fate, but are free to make the choices they do. This feeling is not to be considered conclusive, but only as a hint or hypothesis. It must be checked and double-checked against the available evidence. When this is done, I am convinced that the intuition of free choice emerges as an important truth buttressed by reason.

To summarize, we find eight main points in support of the case for freedom of choice. First, the central issue is not that of freedom versus determinism, since human beings constantly utilize the if-then, deterministic laws of Nature. Second, there is no absolute free choice, since it always functions within limits. Third, the existence of chance or contingency as an ultimate trait of Nature negates the thesis of universal determinism or necessity. Fourth, human thinking continually goes on in terms of general conceptions or universals under which many different particulars or potentialities may be considered; and the reality of these potentialities shows that no one line of action has been foreordained. Fifth, to take seriously the meaning of *potentiality* as signifying plural possibilities in itself controverts the determinist position. Sixth, the fact that only the present exists and that it creates the past makes impossible the determining of present and future by the past. Seventh, freedom of choice encourages ethical behavior. And, eighth, most human beings possess a powerful intuition of free choice.

The Relationship of Science and Morality

Harold A. Larrabee
The Humanist, Summer, 1943

I shall assume that the reader is not particularly interested in setting up two gigantic abstractions, one labelled "Science" and the other "Morality," in order to stage a pyrotechnical display of dialectical virtuosity (if that were possible) or a verbal juggling act in which the writer would attempt to keep both concepts in the air, that is, off the ground, throughout. Let us be semantically sophisticated enough to recognize that both "Science" and "Morality" cover enormous tracts of meaning; and that the best way to talk useful sense about them is to assume, as a first approximation, that science *is* what scientists *do* (and try to do); and that morality *is* what moral people *do* (and try to do). That is to say that for our present purposes it is more important to talk about certain kinds of people and what they are doing (or say that they are doing), than it is to explore the nuances of two extremely broad concepts in verbal juxtaposition. It assumes that the main practical problem of science-in-society is centered in the scientist; and of morality, in the moral individual; and of the relationship of the two, in the scientist as moral (or a-moral, or un-moral, or immoral) individual, and in the moral individual as scientifically-minded person—all of them, of course, in their social settings.

What then, in time of peace, is the scientist *about*? What, as scientist, is he trying to do? Most of them will tell you, I think that in some particular specialty they are trying to find out "what is there"— to satisfy an inner craving for understanding, either as an end in itself or as means to some end, such as human welfare, "progress," or personal rewards in money or fame. What they want to understand is some freely-chosen aspect of the world before them; and the peculiar insight they are seeking consists in perceiving, in what they observe, the exemplification of an abstract theory or law or pattern which they have imagined, and which may be exhibited as "reliable knowledge" to all other competent scientists. Science is also, of course, the organized body of systematized and verifiable knowledge which has resulted from many centuries of such efforts. But living science, as Professor Whitehead has pointed out, "is in the minds of men."

At its peak, it becomes "pure research," a relatively disinterested persistent tracking-down of abstruse and often apparently useless generalizations through myriads of minutely-examined details or cleverly-contrived experiments. And on the plane of genius, where the ideals of science are chiefly shaped, we find men who seem to be necessarily isolated from the common affairs of their fellows, and from the immediate demands of the social environment. Even though he is obliged to live in their midst, the top-rung scientist appears to be striving for an absolute independence of mind which cuts him off from his fellow-mortals. Of our greatest theoretical scientist, Willard Gibbs, it was said that he "worked alone . . . without need of personal conversation on the subject, or of criticism from others." As Emerson said of Archimedes and Newton, Nature "guarded them by a certain aridity. If they had been good fellows, fond of dancing, port, and clubs, we should have had no *Theory of the Sphere*, and no *Principia*. They had that necessity of isolation which genius feels."

But surely, you may object, not all scientists are geniuses, much less recluses endowed with any such degree of mental self-sufficiency While "great science" may be the work of taciturn egotists afflicted with that perpetual over-concentration of attention known as absent-mindedness, there are thousands of lesser workers in the scientific vineyards who are gregarious conformists to the point of being "good fellows." The mass production of scientists in this country, amounting to nearly 15,000 doctorates in the last seven years (4,644 of them in chemistry alone) has greatly diminished their reputation for personal eccentricity. Most of them have developed the protective coloration of the business man, asking chiefly to be let alone to pursue their specialties in peace.

Yet it remains true that the traditional ideals of science, the criteria by which scientific eminence continues to be judged, place a premium on single-mindedness, and promote what I shall call "moral isolationism", in at least three respects. It is notorious, to begin with, that the ability to make use of scientific method in some one specialty is no guarantee whatever of its application to other departments of inquiry. Listen to a chemist, Professor M. G. Mellon of Purdue University, as he describes some of his *confrères*: "It is not common to find scientists who can be generally trusted for scientific soundness of judgment on non-scientific subjects. Winning a famous scientific prize or holding an important position give no assurance that the individual's opinions on economic, political, religious or social questions have any considered factual basis. This abandonment of the scientific method by many scientists when they close the doors of their laboratories, reminds one of the pseudo-religionist who goes to church on Sunday and then grabs all he can on Monday." To these examples of the complete failure of the educational theory of transfer of training, Professor Mellon gives the name of "partially scientific scientists." To their number should surely be added those sincere and well-meaning supernaturalists who are tentative in the laboratory, but dogmatic and obscurantist in their dicta concerning morals and religion. They find no great difficulty isolating scientific sense from fundamentalist nonsense in two separate compartments of their minds; and it is to them, alas, that the unlightened public often looks in vain for light and leading, on the strength of the scientific reputations which have been earned by the scientific segments of their brains.

A second form of moral isolationism that is traditional among scientists consists of the attitude which ignores as irrelevant any consideration of the ways in which scientific work is made physically and socially possible. Scientific research being no longer restricted to "the proper occupation for the leisure of an English gentleman," it must somehow be financed on a long-run basis, since only in the rarest cases is it immediately profitable. The four commonest sources are: private industry, chiefly large-scale industry; government; colleges and universities; and endowed foundations. To the extent that the last two are dependent upon private industry for their endowments, the actual alternatives narrow down to "large-scale industry or the State." Yet one looks in vain through scientific periodicals, until very recently, for any realistic discussions of the matter. As Professor P. W. Bridgman well says: "It seems to me that scientists are curiously obtuse as to the social conditions which make possible their existence as a class."

Some of the historical reasons for this obtuseness, however, are not far to seek. The scientist, we know, prides himself on his ability to eliminate the personal equation. "Results are results," if they can be verified by others, no matter where or by whom or under what circumstances they were originally obtained. The trouble is that the truism that the mundane circumstances of the scientist *are* often irrelevant to the scientific validity of his results, has been expanded into the falsehood that, as long as a scientist can do his work, it does not make any difference to anyone what kind of a society supports him, or on what terms. This is the view which maintains that, as long as a scientist is free "to do his own work in his own way," he ought not to inquire too closely into the morals of the institution or the social order which grants him the privilege. His only object, as scientist, being to advance human knowledge by getting on with his research, he should try to strike the best bargain that he can, making whatever compromises are necessary to insure his being left as undisturbed as possible. You recognize, of course, the common human failing of moral isolationism, of which *all* of us are guilty in some degree—a lack of imagination behind the responsible demand for freedom in our own particular bailiwick without paying the price for its maintenance. When it fails, as it always does fail, there comes the attempt to buy one's way out as cheaply as possible. The scientist wants his kind of freedom; and the price he is usually tempted to pay for it is unquestioning social conformity. The latter is even accounted a scientific virtue; to know nothing and care less about social problems proves his complete and absolute devotion to science. As long as the security of his all-important work is not threatened, this second type of "partially scientific scientist" is therefore likely to be a stout defender of the status quo, and one of the "most docile and amenable of citizens."

The third type of moral isolationism to which scientists are especially prone has been far more frequently a subject of public discussion than the two already mentioned. I refer to the alleged lack of social responsibility on the part of scientists for the consequences of their achievements. Does scientific advancement of knowledge carry with it any responsibility for its subsequent use or misuse? Or does scientific objectivity and detachment call for complete indifference to what others may do with one's discoveries? Both the common man's asking of this question, and a common answer, are contained in a recent play by J. B. Priestley, in which Gridley, a ship's engineer, says to Fletherington, a research chemist, "You're all wrong. You're a nuisance. You're a menace." Fletherington replies: "I'm not, I'm simply a chemist, a scientist." Says Gridley: "I know, I know, and today you're trying to blow us up and tomorrow you'll be trying to dose us with poison gas. What do you want to go and make the foul stuff for? Before you're finished, you fellows 'ull do the lot of us in." Fletherington answers: "I'm very distressed to hear you talking like this, Mr. Gridley. I've never willingly hurt anybody in my life. All I do is research." Gridley replies: "Yes, and look at the result. Blowing us up, burning us alive, poisoning us. Just stop your damned research!"

But before we jump to the conclusion that all scientists are immoral if they continue to commit indiscriminate acts of research without giving a thought to the probable consequences and trying to control them, we had better consider some of the difficulties. As Professor Bridgman has recently pointed out, to restrict science only to those discoveries "which could not wilfully be perverted to harmful uses," would be tantamount to its abolition. "Furthermore," he argues, "responsibility does not exist when there is no mechanism by which it can be determined ... and it is impossible for a physicist or anyone else limited by human fallibility to foresee all the consequences of a discovery, much less, to balance all the good against the bad." At this very moment, the Germans are using a new high-muzzle-velocity V-shaped gun which is said to have stemmed directly from a paper read by Dr. Bridgman to physicists in New York City before the war, although he had taken the step of closing his high-pressure laboratory at Harvard to scientists the Axis countries.

Only society as a whole, he argues further, can control the use of a discovery once it is freely imparted to it. But the question persists whether scientists as a profession (or a group of professions) have not a large responsibility for society's exercise of its control of their discoveries, largely through the patent phases of our economic system. Meanwhile scientific and engineering journals are dotted with impassioned protests against any tampering with our antiquated patent system, which as everyone knows, has lent itself admirably to the formation of gigantic patent pools in cartels and monopolies. As long as scientific societies as well as individual scientists consistently oppose anything but the maximum of *laissez-faire* and private individual enterprise for corporation profits, it is hard to see how they can, at the same time, disclaim all responsibility for the results on the ground of the helplessness of the individual scientist or inventor.

If we venture to think in terms of the post-war world, grave dangers beset us on every hand; but none, it seems to me, is ultimately graver than the possible rise of an American generation of clever, but socially irresponsible technicians "with the physiques of gods and the minds of mechanics," highly trained in the use of means, but without social conscience enough to envisage humane and enlightened ends, or patience enough to pursue them. In other words, a generation of moral isolationists with the old theme-song of "Please Go Way and Let Me Sleep," or of imperialists to the new tune of *"Amerika Uber Alles."* That the imperialism would presumably be a moral one, backed by overwhelming force, would hardly make it more palatable than any other kind.

I have turned the spotlight on some of the complexities of scientists' relationship to morality, not to indict them as a class or to make them feel uncomfortable, and certainly not for the purpose of indulging in any pharisaical professions of philosophical virtue. I have said nothing of the ethics of the scientist within his own profession, which have contributed greatly to ethics in general; and I have not pointed out that a large part of his isolationism is explicable as sheer division of labor and consequent super-specialization. My concern for the social morality of scientists and engineers is based upon my belief that the education of the coming generation in America has virtually been entrusted to their hands, and with it the fearful responsibility of preventing any such catastrophe as I have mentioned.

What I would point out to them in conclusion, is that all three of the peace-time occupational tendencies of scientists toward moral isolationism may well be aggravated rather than diminished by present war-trends. In the first place, the war speed-up may well tend to restrict still further the scientist's use of his sceptical method of thinking to his own particular war-time specialty. Secondly, he may well fall a victim to the illusion that the problem of his economic and social security has been completely solved by the flattering (but temporary) war-time demand for his services. And thirdly, like all good soldiers in the ranks, he will find himself under orders as to ends, and completely released from all responsibility for the uses to which his scientific achievements may be put. I submit that all of these possible developments will be anything but good preparation for the assumption of his share of social responsibility for the post-war work of education and reconstruction.

For better or for worse, the time of serene indifference to politics and economics on the part of scientists (and many others) is past. We are all now being punished severely for our various kinds of irresponsibility and isolationism, our varying degrees of apathetic lack of concern about the way the rest of the world is run. Humanists have lived too much in Ivory Towers; and scientists have lived too much in Towers of Steel and Glass; neither paying enough attention to the foundations of their freedoms, which they have taken for granted.

Human destiny is too valuable a thing to be left permanently in the hands of fanatics, or military men, or the lesser varieties of professional politicians. Henceforth, whatever thoughtful men put first, they must put morality in politics no lower than second. If that means sacrificing a precious bit of scientific specialization, then let us make the sacrifice. Our chemists may lack a final bit of polish on their technique, but they will have some considered ideas about the kind of society their technique is to serve.

The moral losses of ground in every war are tremendous. When this one ends, a vast constructive force will have to be mobilized from a morally dispirited, disillusioned world. Good will without scientific intelligence will fail as it has time and time and again. Scientific intellect without a sense of moral responsibility may never make the attempt. It will take all our scientific morality and all our morally enlightened science to give us a fighting chance.

A portion of this address was given at the Conference on the Scientific Spirit and Democratic Faith, New York, May 29-30, 1943.

CHAPTER 10
Humanism, Science, and the Arts and Humanities

Not Just a Shotgun Marriage

For humanists up on the major issues of the past forty years, prior chapters reveal a surprising fact. The so-called "literary humanism," which is briefly discussed in Harold H. Titus's essay in Chapter 1 and Corliss Lamont's essay in Chapter 3, and which both embraced the arts and humanities and shunned science, has not survived. Since its demise, naturalistic humanism has been attacked for being too scientific, not adequately integrating the emotional side that strongly informs the arts and humanities. In the period covered by the essays in this volume, naturalistic humanism is viewed as having swung too far toward science.

The debate whether humanism is too scientific has paralleled another similar debate. The second debate is about a split between science and the arts and humanities. While similar, the two debates differ in key ways.

Humanism and the Arts and Humanities

E. Burdette Backus wrote early in *TH* that humanism sees value outside of scientific knowledge, such as in the arts and humanities (*TH* 6:3). Corliss Lamont argued further that humanism is a product of the humanities (*TH* 8:2). Accordingly, the idea that humanism and the arts and humanities could be perpetually at odds raises concern. Fortunately, some humanists worked on balancing science and the arts and humanities in humanism.

Frank Lloyd Wright's essay provides constructive criticism, even though he does not use the word "humanism." Certainly, Wright's is a period piece, reflecting the development of modernist architecture, abstract art, and so on. But his stand against machine-like modernism in the arts and humanities pertains equally to humanism. He argues for style oriented toward the individual, not the collective banal masses: the individual not as selfish, self-centered automaton, but the individual as a feeling, living individual. He argues for art and architecture that celebrates democracy while retaining its pioneering spirit, rather than pursuing a style of sterile scientific reason alone. In that way, Wright mirrors some of the writers discussed in Chapter 7, who insist that spirit, emotion, and meaning are integral to humanism's wielding of reason on our commonwealth.

John M. Morris's 1961 essay observes that humanism was a breakout toward new heights of humanness in the field of philosophy, part of the humanities. But he then asserts that despite its impact on philosophy, the advent of humanist thought was not accompanied by concomitant growth in the arts and other humanities disciplines. His source material notably focuses not only on humanism, but society at large. Nonetheless, his references to "humanism" are akin to its usages by arts and humanities specialists and the secular scientists from whom they have allegedly grown apart. His short essay ends with a call for humanists to unite science and the arts and humanities.

Barry Schwartz argued in 1973 for considering various visual artists at the height of their careers in the 1960s to be in one of several humanist categories, including metaphysical, existentialist, or absurdist (*TH* 33:4). Like Schwartz, other writers in *TNH* and *TH* have examined literary luminaries for signs of atheism or humanism. For example, they identified atheism in Shelley;[1] humanism in Faulkner,[2] Camus,[3] and Hemingway;[4] and heterodoxy in Lawrence and Blake, among others.[5] Interestingly, Schwartz cites an artist as saying that "I feel that the artist's hand and heart must be exposed in a work of art." The similarity of that statement and Wright's view is unmistakable.

These analyses arguing that there is atheism, humanism, or the like in the work of artists and writers who have not openly discussed or embraced humanism is anecdotal evidence that at the least, humanist values may be reasonably represented in humanities and the arts. Of course, the analyses reflect a progression over time, so that a reasonable conclusion is that the arts and humanities may have swung back in a humanistic direction. Accordingly, with respect to science, humanism is now more in the same boat as the arts and humanities.

Science and the Arts and Humanities

In keeping with this perspective, Lucile W. Green accepts the notion of the chasm between science and the humanities, going so far as to call it a "cold war." She describes at length a polarization of the "two camps." She pointedly calls for the scientist camp to adopt more "heart." The argument that scientists need more understanding of humanities is discussed further in Chapter 4.

Regarding the humanities, Green argues for increased science education. She proposes science education reforms that she sees as essential to educating humanities specialists about science. Her emphasis is integrating the two more closely.

Green of course squarely places philosophy in the humanities. But this choice inspires the thought that part of the problem is that humanist philosophy—particularly epistemology—has failed to provide the means for other humanities disciplines to sufficiently incorporate scientific knowledge into their knowledge base.

An early essay by Rupert Holloway illustrates one way how. As discussed in Chapters 6 and 8, humanists may have an emotional reaction to something that feels mystical or spiritual. Holloway claimed knowledge of "the unity of the world as a harmony of love and truth and beauty" (*TNH* 6:3). Naturalistic humanism values love and truth and beauty. In contrast, the monism of his "unity" and "harmony" is not part of a humanist understanding of the universe, as noted in Chapter 1. Holloway's is the kind of mistake that any artist or humanities specialist could make if he or she has not internalized the pluralism of the humanist view. It reminds us how deeply the monist religious language, iconography, and thought concerning even the universe are embedded into our minds. Eradicating those images and conceptions takes extended conscious effort by the individual humanist. Green's education is the starting point. But given that humanist philosophy engages directly in discourse that can help specialists in the arts and other humanities to correlate the implications of scientific knowledge to their personal emotional and creative experiences and expression, humanist philosophers must move discussion of those implications into the mainstream.

Isaac Asimov argues in his included essay that true science fiction uniquely advances scientific knowledge and its implications. As a literary genre, it favors realistic portrayal of new and potential upcoming technological applications as well as imaginative technologies, cultures, and life forms. It still shares literature's incentive for portrayals of new *cultural* constructs in their works. He acknowledges science fiction's use not only of plausible social constructs, but also fantastical or satirical content.

Asimov's discussion of technology in literary social satire and fantasy as well as in science fiction suggests a distinction useful for addressing the question of science. On the one hand, educating scientists about humanist values will help inform decisions by scientists about what to research. Of course, funding for scientific research is often political. On the other hand, science is indeed value neutral, and most scientific knowledge inherently has multiple uses, some constructive and some destructive. Those uses are constituted as technology. Even more so than with funding for scientific research, decisions about whether to use technology are not made by research scientists at nonpartisan universities. Rather, they are made by scientists employed at for-profit corporations or by government lawmakers and regulators. Thus, ongoing concern about bringing together science and the arts and humanities is in truth raising a political economic issue, which, in the context of corporate economic power in the US, explains the slow progress that humanism has made in reducing destructive use of scientific knowledge.

Humanist Philosophy 1928 – 1973

Notes

1. French, Roberts W., "Shelley's Vision," *TH* 37:4, p. 132 et seq. (1967).
2. Gold, Joseph, "The Humanism of Faulkner," *TH* 30:2, p. 113 et seq. (1960).
3. Carlson, Eric. W., "The Humanism of Camus," *TH* 30:5, p. 298 et seq. (1960).
4. Grebstein, Sheldon Norman, "Sex, Hemmingway, and the Critics," *TH* 31:4, p. 212 et seq. (1961).
5. Widmer, Kingsley, "The Sacred Sun in Modern Literature," *TH* 19:6, p. 368 et seq. (1959).

Of Thee I Sing

Frank Lloyd Wright
The New Humanist, May-June, 1932

I find myself standing now against the "Geist der Kleinlichkeit" to strike for an architecture for the individual instead of tamely recognizing senility in the guise of a new invention ... the so-called international style.

No unusual vision is required to see in this alleged invention an attempt to strip hides and horns from the living, breathing organism that is modern architecture of the past twenty-five years and, by beating the tom-tom, try to make the hide come alive, or, in despair, tack the "skin" on America's barn-door for a pattern.

Such, I believe, is the nature of this ulterior "invention."

Architecture was made for man, not man made for architecture. And since when, then, has the man sunk so low, even by way of the machine, that a self-elected group of formalizers could predetermine his literature, his music, or his architecture for him?

I know the European neuter's argument: "the Western soul is dead; Western intelligence, though keen, is therefore sterile and can realize an impression but not expression of life except as life may be recognized as some intellectual formula."

But I think such confession of genital impotence, while valid enough where this cliché is concerned, a senility that healthy youth North, South, East or West is bound to ridicule and repudiate.

Youth is not going to take its architecture or its life that way.

*****

Form, and such style as it may own, comes out of structure industrial, social, architectural.

Principles of construction employing suitable materials for the definite purposes of industry or society, in living hands, will result in style. The changing methods and materials of a changing life should keep the road open for developing variety of expression, spontaneous so long as human imagination lives.

The imagination that makes a building into architecture as mathematics is made into music is not the quality of mind that makes a professor of mathematics or makes a building engineer or makes short cut æsthete. *Nor is it ever a matter of "style."*

Mass machine-production needs a conscience but needs no æsthetic formula as a short cut to any style. It is itself a deadly formula. Machinery needs the creative force that can seize it, as it is, for what it is worth, to get the work of the world done by it and gradually make that work no less an expression of the spontaneous human spirit than ever before. We must make the expression of life as much richer as it is bound to be more general in realization. Or, by way of machine worship, go machine mad.

*****

Do you think that, as a style, any æsthetic formula forced upon this work of ours in our country can do more than stultify this reasonable hope for a life of the soul?

A creative architecture for America can only mean an architecture for the individual.

The community interest in these United States is not communism or communistic as the internationalists' formula for a "style" presents itself. Its language aside, communistic the proposition is. Communistic in communism's most objectionable phrase: the sterility of the individual its end if not its aim and ... in the name of "discipline"!

Life needs and gets interior discipline according to its ideal. The higher the ideal, the greater the discipline.

But this communistic formula proposes to get rid of this constructive interior discipline's anxieties (and joys) by the surrender that ends all in all and for all, by way of a preconceived style for life—conceived by the few to be imposed upon all alike.

Such communistic "ism" belongs to inverted capitalism. Some good, undoubtedly, the inversion if only to demonstrate the cruelty of both. capitalism and such communism. Out of any sincere struggle, something comes for the growth of humanity. But, for a free democracy to accept a communistic tenet of this breed disguised as aesthetic formula for architecture is a confession of failure I do not believe we, as a people, are ready to make.

Centralization (a form of every man for himself and the devil for the hindmost) is what is the matter with us. We are suffering from an abuse of individuality in this virulent form, instead of enjoying the ideal of integration natural to democracy.

We are sickened by capitalistic centralization but not so sick, I believe, that we need confess impotence by embracing a communistic exterior discipline in architecture to kill finally what spontaneous life we have left in the circumstances.

As for discipline?

Do you know the living discipline of an ideal of life as organic architecture or architecture as organic life? Those who do know the interior discipline of this ideal look upon surrender to any style formula whatever as dead exterior discipline. Imprisonment is impotence.

"Besonnenheit?"

"Entsagung?"

Well, ... if an effort is produced at all in organic architecture, it must proceed from the interior of the work. It must be of the very organism created.

Try that for discipline in our democracy!

It is an inflexible will, bridling a rich and powerful ego, that is necessary to the creation of any building as architecture or the living of any life in a free democracy. Call it individual. And it is ever so.

And any great thing is too much of whatever it is: it is a quality of greatness.

"Excess of contrast, in genius, brings about a mighty equilibrium."

But "Geist der Kleinlichkeit" will take the excess and capitalize it as a "style". Never will it take the principle or its essence. But it will take the excess and prescribe a *pattern*. In this case an excess of the original protest.

Styles are anterior, posterior or ulterior.

Humanist Philosophy 1928 – 1973

Why should pretentious formalizers worry about the disciple of a "style" for Americans before either they or America yet know style?

The methods, materials and life of our country are common discipline to any right idea of work. Allowed to exercise at our best such whole-souled individuality as we may find among us, the common use of the common tools and materials of a common life will so discipline individual effort that centuries forward men will look back and recognize the work of the democratic life of the Twentieth Century as a great, not a dead, style. The honest buildings from which this proposed internationalist style is derived were made that way. We can build many more buildings in that same brave, independent, liberal spirit.

So we need no "Geist der Kleinlichkeit" touting a style at us. No, Herr Spengler, we are not yet impotent.

We will, given our own principle, with no self-conscious effort make a great one.

*****

By force of circumstances freely acting upon what is great and alive in us—and that is our democratic principle of freedom—we will make our own.

It is true that we understand imperfectly our own ideal of democracy, and so we have shamefully abused it.

We have allowed our ideal to foster offensive privatism that is exaggerated selfishness in the name of individualism. Selfish beyond any monarchy. But do you imagine communism eradicates selfishness?

It may suppress it or submerge it.

Nor can socialism eradicate selfishness. It gives it another turn. Democracy cannot eradicate it. No, but democracy alone can turn it into a noble, creative selfhood.

And that is best of all for all.

So out of my own life-experience as an architect, I earnestly say: what our country needs in order to realize a great architecture for a great life is only to realize and release a high ideal of democracy, the ideal upon which the new life here was founded on new ground, and humbly try to learn how to live up to its principles.

I am sure, too, that the work of an organic individual, had gone so far in the work of the world before this self-seeking propaganda came up, as to enable anyone with ordinary vision to see it coming naturally as our future architecture, propagandists aside. So why, now, as self-appointed committee on a style, do promoting propagandists imagine they can steal the hide and horns of this living, breathing, healthy, young organism and vaingloriously parade the hide and shake the horns to make Americans think it is the living creature?

Granted they are sincere: having confessed impotence, do they urge others to confess too?

Granted they are ambitious: they wish to be inventors as a eunuch might wish to be a father.

Granted they are impecunious: do they wish to get work to do under false pretenses?

Granted they are aesthetes: they are superficial and ignorant of the depths of nature.

Granted they are as intelligent and hard and scientific as they think they are: they are miscarriage of a machine-age that would sterilize itself, if it could, to avoid continuing to propagate the race.

Youth asks for life, and this "Geist der Kleinlichkeit" would hand out a recipe in the form of a pattern of itself?

The letter is more than the spirit only to artists of the second rank.

It is the thing said that is more important, now, than the manner of saying it.

Our pioneer days are not over.

One Humanism, Not Two

John M. Morris
The Humanist, September-October, 1961

Western intellectual culture is split into two non-communicating camps, according to C. P. Snow's recent much-discussed *The Two Cultures and the Scientific Revolution*.

In one are the scientists, optimistic, confident, "the future in their bones"; in the other, the literary men, tradition-oriented, "wishing the future did not exist." The two cultures exchange little more than hostility and suspicion. "The non-scientists have a rooted impression that the scientists are shallowly optimistic, unaware of man's condition. On the other hand, the scientists believe that the literary intellectuals are totally lacking in foresight, peculiarly unconcerned with their brother men, in a deep sense anti-intellectual, anxious to restrict both art and thought to the existential moment."

Although a number of recent discussions of the book have pointed out the over-simplification of Snow's basic division—a criticism that Snow has already admitted—these discussions have also shown that the breakdown in communications is, if anything, more serious than he describes. For example, while Western scientists maintain fairly good communications with Soviet scientists, American literary people are almost totally unaware of the work of their Russian counterparts. In a recent conference sponsored by the Colorado branch of the Adult Education Association, one teacher described the "typical Russian novel" as altered around the theme of "boy loves girl loves tractor." Obviously the teacher did not know that a major Soviet literature has been created around somewhat different themes.

But the breakdown that interests Snow primarily is the division among the intellectuals of our own nation, the breakdown which makes it easier for the American physicist to talk to the Soviet physicist than for either of them to talk the literary man who occupies the office next to him.

The word "humanist" occurs from time to time in discussions of Snow's book, but in two very different contexts. At times it refers to the literary men, the students of the "humanities." At other times, it means the scientists, the "secular humanists," who are not connected with a religious tradition.

While both these usages are sanctioned by custom, it might be well to emphasize another more inclusive meaning of the word "humanist." It was stated by one of the participants in an all-day conference centered around Snow's book, as members of the group were groping for a resolution of the conflict that he describes. Somehow, it seemed to members of this group, there is a more inclusive goal, in the search for which both scientists and literati can unite. This is "The life of the intellect in the service of man."

This was the aim of the classical humanists who brought Europe out of the dark ages and into the dawn of the Renaissance. It is an aim that includes both the sciences and the humanities, without establishing an artificial division between them.

The rifts that divide our culture are wide and deep. In bridging them modern humanists have a job to do. We are concerned with *both* science and the humanities, and with their interactions. We can act as a cohesive force, uniting "the two cultures" in a common task.

John M. Morris, Associate Editor of The Humanist, *is minister of All Souls Unitarian Church of Colorado Springs.*

Science and Humanities: Two Branches of One Trunk

Lucile W. Green
The Humanist 21:6, 330-335 (1961)

A cold war between science and the humanities is as intolerable in the atomic age as the cold war between sovereign nations. The separation of culture into two independent camps, each with its own method, personnel, and world view, has produced intellectual "isms" as provincial as the political ones which almost engaged us in a world civil war.

The two camps are, unfortunately, entrenched in institutions of education, fortified by administrative procedures, and propagated by hypostatized myths about "The World of Nature" versus "The World of Ideas." The academic separation into "Division of Sciences" and "Division of Humanities" was originally for the convenience of instruction and administration. But it has brought about the idea that a real separation exists—as if life itself could be divided into two worlds (and then subdivided into compartments of subject matter of fifty-minutes each, measured in point-hours of "credit!").

Thus science and the humanities have developed into rival world views, encamped against each other over false issues of fact *versus* value, objectivity *versus* subjectivity, observation versus creation. C. P. Snow's much discussed article, "The Two Cultures and Scientific Revolution," describes the situation:

The non-scientists have a rooted impression that the scientists are shallowly optimistic, unaware of man's condition. On the other hand, the scientists believe that the literary intellectuals are totally lacking in foresight, peculiarly unconcerned with their brother men, in a deep sense anti-intellectual, anxious to restrict both art and thought to the existential moment. Anyone with a mild talent for invective could produce plenty of this kind of subterranean back chat. On each side there is some of it which is not entirely baseless. It is all destructive. (*Encounter*, Vol. XII, No. 6, June 1959, p. 18.)

"COEXISTENCE?"

Some of the more liberal minds on each side have proposed various degrees of coexistence. In some, science and the humanities continue to live side by side but keep out of each other's territory. In others, they may even perform vaguely complementary functions of means and ends (though it is not generally agreed which performs which!). And there are people like Dr. H. J. Muller, who declared not only that education of scientists should include knowledge of humanities, but also that the deep changes needed "'from the inside out' will not be possible before humanity attains a truly scientific and humanitarian background, including a more realistic *understanding of man's place in nature*." (*Bulletin of the Atomic Scientists*, April 1959, p. 150.)

The thesis of this paper is that science and the humanities are not merely coexistent or complementary, but organically connected and, like two major organs of a living body (head and heart), have a necessary interrelation. Either is inadequate without the other. Facts without reference to values are meaningless; values without reference to facts are superstitious. To consider either independently from the other is artificial, for it presents a false view of life. Yet, from the junior high school on, these subjects are usually taught in isolation. The intention of this paper is not to deplore specialized training in either science or humanities. More specialization, not less, is needed in the atomic age. But it should not be acquired at the expense of *falsifying* life. The problem is to present the real-life interweaving of facts and values as the ground from which specialization can richly grow.

A solution to this problem could be attempted in the general education program for the first two years of college. Unfortunately, too often this program has degenerated into surveys of departmental subject matter, still conceived in isolation. Relationships, without which knowledge at best is superficial, are surrendered to another body of subject matter, now watered down to the contemptible level of the "non-major." On the other hand, general education can be a strenuous and vital program in which *thinking itself* is the content, and this is *fed* by material from both science and the humanities. This type of education does in no sense replace or compete with subject matter courses given by the departments. They are essential branches of the tree of knowledge, and an educated person should be at home in several of them. The point is that the tree does not start with branches but with a trunk and the trunk alone contains the unity from which the branches derive their relationship to each other and to the whole. Without an understanding of the trunk, the details of the tree—no matter how minute—are superficial. With it, the tree is an organic whole unfolding with increasing order and meaning. Kirtley F. Mather, professor emeritus of geology at Harvard, wrote:

> Even so, it is my opinion that the kind of unity we academicians ought to seek is more likely to be found by stressing the fundamental, integrating concepts or near the roots of the tree of knowledge rather than by perfecting the multi-disciplinary techniques that tie together the tips of the branches of that tree. (*Daedalus*, Winter 1958, p. 137.)

FACTS AND VALUES

Two of the vital components "near the roots of the tree" are facts and values, categories which later branch out into science and the humanities. General education at its best is a kind of relativity theory in which these categories are hyphenated, like space-time, in their real and necessary relationships.

What are some of the necessary fact-value relationships? In the first place, both are inseparable from the same source—man. It is an inescapable fact that both in his perceptions and preferences man is the agent. His faculties are the condition of his ideas. Past experience largely conditions his values, and values shape his experience. The very act of perception implies subjective images which prepare him to "see" what he is looking for— otherwise there would be no selecting from the welter of meaningless possibility, and experience would remain a misty stream of consciousness. If relativity means anything, it implies the importance of the point of departure, which is man. The eminent physicist, P. W. Bridgman, put it eloquently in his article, "Quo Vadis":

> Since we cannot get away from ourselves, we must find our springs of action within ourselves, a task which the human race has been shirking since the beginning of recorded history. We have to find what admirable motivation is left when we repudiate the almost universal and irrepressible urge of men to get away from themselves, something that we are coming to realize simply cannot be done. (*Daedalus*, Winter 1958, p. 89.)

Later Bridgman says, "Perhaps we have here a worthy candidate for the first law of mental dynamics, namely the law that we cannot get away from ourselves."

A second necessary relationship is that both science and the humanities depend on some symbolic medium such as language. Dr. Philipp Frank, who succeeded Einstein as professor of physics at Prague, said in the same issue of *Daedalus*:

> Non-scientists often believe that science consists in making observations, in accumulating experience. But this image misses the point. At every moment of our life we perceive data of experience, yet by recording them we do not get science. Science begins only when we invent a system of symbols which can bring order into our experience. For building up science, the creation of words and their syntax is as important as experiments. A part of our science is contained in the vocabulary and syntax of the English, French, and German that we use. ("Contemporary Science and Contemporary World View," p. 66.)

Professor Bridgman goes into some detail as to how the grammar of the Indo-European languages conditions some of our basic ideas and logic:

The realization is growing that the grammar of a language may almost compel certain attitudes. For example, reification is almost inevitable in a language with a structure of English and in other European languages. One cannot say "I do" without implying "I do *something,*" and the something becomes reified. The situation is carried over into physics, where the almost universally accepted identity of mass and energy is the result of an unnecessary and illogical reification of energy (p. 88).

His conclusion applies as much to humanists as to scientists when he says:

I would place as the most important mark of an adequately educated man a realization that the tools of human thinking are not yet understood, and that they impose limitations of which we are not yet fully aware. As a corollary it follows that the most important intellectual task for the future is to acquire an understanding of the tools, and so to modify our outlook and ideals as to take account of their limitations (p. 92).

OTHER SYMBOLS

To escape the "tyranny of words," other systems of symbols may be invented. Science relies more and more on mathematics, and logic on nonverbal symbols. Paralleling this development is increasing use of abstraction in art, surely an attempt—perhaps unconscious—to free art from the materialistic chiaroscuro "vocabulary" of the Renaissance. The new symbolic forms—whether they be the mathematics of Einstein or the visual relations of Mondrian or the twelve-tone scales of Schoenberg or surrealistic images of Joyce—are the abstractions with which men are exploring frontiers of thought and feeling. The tools may differ in shape and precision, but the task is a common one, and the frontiers meet in great men of both science and art.

A third necessary relationship is an historical one: breakthroughs in each area sooner or later affect the other. Copernicus' proof of a heliocentric universe eventually penetrated the armor of the church, as did Darwin's theory of evolution. But equally important, the Reformation's breakthrough to an individual relationship with God carried over into the British empiricism of Bacon, Hobbes, and Locke. It is difficult to distinguish cause and effect between the industrial development of the 18th century and democratic ideas of natural right to life, liberty, and pursuit of happiness. In the 19th century the concept of light as energy vibrations found its way into the frivolous field of impressionistic painting, and we have already seen how the abstract, mathematical world of 20th-century physics finds its counterpart in the non-objective reflections of modern art. It is possible that the cumulating influence of oriental thought on western culture today may, sooner or later, develop a major breakthrough in religious concepts, and that this could, in turn, affect the scientific world-view. Of course, education, with its departmentalized thinking, can always slow up the process.

Finally, neither science nor the humanities can be isolated from the culture that bore it, and neither is immune from social manipulation. Great works of literature from *The Bible* to *Dr. Zhivago* are conceived in a context of particular human problems. They may be used by people for even more particular aims of propaganda, good and bad. The cultural exchanges of Bernstein, the Bolshoi Ballet, and "Satchmo" are undoubtedly constructive. The utilizing of scientists by the state in peace and war is generally accepted; but nowhere is it more ironic than the application of discoveries of Einstein, gentle man of peace, to the ultimate weapons of war.

In short, science and the humanities in isolation are fragmentary, hollow, and easily manipulated into unwitting means to unscrupulous ends.

Humanist Philosophy 1928 – 1973

A PROGRAM OF STUDY

When a house is on fire the least needed are people running around shouting "Fire!" Most needed are cool-headed and warm-hearted ones who know what to do and how to do it. Scientists who are politically naive or humanists who are ignorant of facts are more likely to aggravate than to alleviate the problems of the atomic age; or both may be brushed aside like the ineffectual intellectuals of Huxley's *Brave New World*, while the power is taken over by a third group—the hot-headed and cold-hearted, for whom the fire is not a tragedy, but an opportunity.

If general education is to be truly organic, then its integrated courses should show the relativity of fact and value. What, specifically, should be included from the natural and social sciences in a, say, lower division course? Surely the scientists themselves could best answer the question, their opinions would be more valuable than that below. But as a starting point, the following is one humanist's opinion of what a humanities course ought to include:

1. Scientific method—understanding of and practice in reasoning from evidence to generalization.
2. Some knowledge of the basic concepts of modern physics—for example, by reading Lincoln Barnett's *The Universe and Dr. Einstein*.
3. Some knowledge of basic ideas in biology—for example, by reading from Darwin's *Origin of Species* and Edmund Sinnott's *Biology of the Spirit*.
4. Some knowledge of the psychology of the subconscious and its relation to creative thought—for example, by reading Carl Jung's *The Undiscovered Self*.
5. A basic knowledge of semantics—for example, by studying Hayakawa's *Language in Action*, or otherwise supplementing what is studied in the freshman English course.

Surely this company of ideas and men would not seem strange to Aristotle the biologist, Leonardo the inventor, Shakespeare the psychologist, Kant the astronomer, or Whitehead the mathematician.

The Best of *The Humanist*

In the Atomic Age a coherent civilization is impossible without a real integration of science and the humanities. The threat of incineration dangles ominously in the balance. To paraphrase Adlai Stevenson's famous paraphrase: Eggheads of the world, unite—or we may fry!

Dr. Lucile Green is Professor of Philosophy and Humanity at Oakland (California) City College where she has developed a new Humanity program based on the concepts in this article.

Escape into Reality

Isaac Asimov
The Humanist, November-December, 1957

Of all branches of literature, science fiction is the most modern. It is the one literary response to the problems peculiar to our own day and no other.

The literature of the main stream is, at its best, virtually timeless. It deals with the tensions within the human mind and soul, and with the interrelations of man and man. Presumably, while human biochemistry and psychology remain essentially unaltered, penetrating studies of this nature will keep their value over the generations. Certainly, Homer and Shakespeare show no signs of decay. It is not with this main stream that I intend to deal.

In the more time-bound realm of the specialized literatures, the writer finds his inspiration in a more or less stylized world of the present or past. The mystery, the sport story, the adventure story, the romance, are all played off against a contemporary background familiar to the reader. The historical novel and the western are set against patterns of the past which are somewhat less familiar but can be quickly accepted.

In each case, the background is "true." It may be dismissed as possessing little intrinsic value for that reason; as being of importance only as the setting against which the particular human drama is performed. It has all the unimportance of the painted backdrop in the theater or the property armchair set in place so that a character may reach it in a fixed number of steps designed to fit smoothly into the action of the play.

In a completely different class fall those examples of specialized literature in which the background or setting has as little relation to reality as do the characters themselves. Less, sometimes. In such literature (so used are we to the tameness and good behavior of the background and to the fictitiousness only of the characters) there is actually a tendency to let the setting itself assume first importance. It is this which gives this kind of literature a completely different "feel" from the more usual kind.

There are three main types of such "false-background literatures" which, in order of decreasing age, are: (1) fantasy, (2) social satire, and (3) science fiction.

Fantasy is probably as old as speech. In a primitive world, where most of the aspects of nature and of conscious life were unknown and, apparently, unknowable except by direct revelation, man's attempts at explanation led straight to fantasy.

A dream of a person already dead would give rise to stories of ghosts. The ruinous effects of storm and drought would serve as inspiration for tales of malevolent spirits. Dimly-known facts would distort to wonders, so that rhinoceri became unicorns, sea-cows became mermaids, and skulls of prehistoric Sicilian elephants became one-eyed giant cannibals.

For that matter, was fantasy really fantasy until the dawn of our own sophisticated age? Is a ghost story a fantasy to one who believes firmly in ghosts? The background, which to ourselves seems to have no relation to the "true" background, *was* the true background to our ancestors. In that respect, fantasy before our own age was simply another aspect of literature against a familiar background.

To be sure, modern fantasies are written against a background now known to be unrelated to reality, and are read by readers just as aware of that. Yet the neo-fantasy still finds its inspiration in the past. The tales still deal with ghosts and vampires, with witches and demons, with the uses of charms and the dangers of the devil. Such stories, nowadays, are most successful when written lightly and with the intent only to entertain. They no longer frighten.

***

Social satire is, on all counts, more sophisticated than fantasy. Whereas fantasy is a universal type of folk-literature, social satire is the work of an advanced intellect trapped in a society that does not welcome criticism. (One might almost say, simply, "trapped in a society" without the qualifying clause, for what society welcomes criticism?)

In its earliest form, social satire found shape in animal fables like those made famous by Aesop. In such fables, talking animals, with a human society imposed upon their animal characteristics, behave so as to expose man's follies and crimes. The audience laughs and nods in agreement, not at all annoyed at finding animals foolish and criminal; enjoying their own superiority, in fact.

It is on the after-taste that the satirist depends—the second thoughts later on, that after all there is an application close to home in that fable. And because the listener has been seduced into accepting the moral of the tale, since it points the finger of disapproval upon an animal and not upon himself, he is less able now to cast it off.

The parables in the Bible and the funny stories told by Lincoln were designed to make their points indirectly and slowly, and to drive them the deeper for that.

Social satire graduated from the anecdote to the treatise, and the most famous example is Sir Thomas More's *Utopia*. That book deals with the society of a fictitious island. (The word "utopia" means "no place" in Greek, just as Samuel Butler's similar *Erewhon* is "nowhere" spelt almost backward.) Thomas More uses his fictitious society as a whip upon the back of his own society. Utopia is praised as just and virtuous for those aspects of it which were most conspicuously lacking in More's own society. The reader could not but agree with More that here indeed was an ideal society. Then later, slowly, the reader finds himself dissatisfied with his own world just because it is not a Utopia.

Gulliver's Travels by Jonathan Swift is an example of a book that satirizes in both styles. The Lilliputians of the first book and the Laputans of the third are ridiculed for follies (drawn to excess) common to the society of Swift's day. The Brobdingnagians of the second book and the Houyhnhnms of the fourth are praised for those virtues which Swift's own society conspicuously did not possess.

It is possible to mistake social satire for science fiction simply because a society different from the real one is described. It is particularly easy to do this because occasionally in their description of fictitious societies, satirists may include details of a science or technology more advanced than their own. For instance, in *Utopia*, More describes the use of incubators to raise chicks; and in the third book of *Gulliver's Travels* Swift describes a fictitious discovery of two fictitious moons of Mars (all of which later turned out to be coincidentally correct in amazing detail).

Nevertheless, it is important to realize that social satirists were not primarily interested in their fictitious societies as such. The satirists kept their eyes fixed firmly upon their own societies and used the creations of their imaginations to point moral lessons. Their fictitious societies were not what *might* be, but only what *should* be or *should not* be.

In the last century, social satirists have deliberately turned to scientific advance as a tool in their trade. There have been Edward Bellamy's *Looking Backward*, Aldous Huxley's *Brave New World* and George Orwell's *1984*, to name the best-known.

It is almost inevitable that these be considered as science fiction, and yet they are not primarily so. The author's intent is entirely moral. Bellamy praises his society and Huxley and Orwell denounce theirs, each with the desire to work some change, by this praise or blame, upon matters they find deplorable in their own society.

It is social satire, still, for all its science.

***

What then *is* science fiction?

Science fiction, like fantasy and social satire, deals with a background that is not "real." Unlike fantasy, however, its backgrounds are not completely unrelated to reality, but represent a more or less plausible extrapolation of reality. Unlike social satire, the unreal background is dealt with for its own sake, not for its moral application.

Science fiction may be defined as that branch of literature which deals with the response of human beings to advances in science and technology.

Actual change in science and technology, occurring quickly enough and striking deeply enough to affect a human being within the course of his normal lifetime, is a phenomenon peculiar to the world only since the Industrial Revolution (with some temporary and local exceptions). That is, it is a phenomenon that has existed

Humanist Philosophy 1928 – 1973

in England and the Netherlands since 1750; since 1850 in the United States and Western Europe; and since 1920 in the world generally.

The first well-known writer who responded to this new factor in human affairs by dealing regularly with science fiction, studying the effect of additional scientific advance upon mankind without placing primary emphasis on moral judgments, was Jules Verne. In the English language, the early master was H. G. Wells. Between them, they laid the groundwork for every theme upon which science fiction writers have been ringing variations ever since.

It was not until 1926 that a special market was set up intended exclusively for the products of the science-fiction writer. It was in that year that Hugo Gernsback first published *Amazing Stories*. By 1930, three other science fiction magazines were on the newsstands.

Slowly, it became possible (economically) for a young man to decide to make a career out of science fiction writing, but it took ten years for enough writers to be developed to enable the field to attain maturity.

The period of mature science fiction is dated most frequently from the moment when John W. Campbell, Jr., took over the editorship of *Astounding Stories* (which he quickly retitled *Astounding Science Fiction*). That was on October 6, 1937.

To Campbell, science fiction was essentially as I have defined it above. He turned the emphasis of the science fiction story from that of adventures with new inventions or adventures on other worlds (a kind of super-western with spaceships replacing horses and ray-guns replacing revolvers), and made it into an increasingly mature consideration of possible societies of the future.

After the dropping of the atomic bomb a new, hindsight respectability fell upon science fiction. Many who had thought stories about atomic warfare (printed in reasonably accurate detail as early as 1941) ridiculous—or even pathological—revised their thoughts hurriedly. The audience increased. The "slick" magazines published occasional science fiction. Book publishers (notably Doubleday and Company) began to put out lines of science fiction novels. New magazines appeared.

The Best of *The Humanist*

By 1950, *The Magazine of Fantasy and Science Fiction* (edited by Anthony Boucher and J. Francis McComas, later by Boucher alone) and *Galaxy Science Fiction* (edited by Horace L. Gold) had made their appearance. Together with *Astounding Science Fiction*, they are commonly considered the "Big Three" of the field.

The editorial policies of the "Big Three" offer an interesting contrast. All publish science fiction, but *Astounding Science Fiction* adheres most rigidly to science fiction in the pure sense, as here defined. As the name implies, *The Magazine of Fantasy and Science Fiction* adds a generous helping of modern fantasy, while *Galaxy Science Fiction* adds as generous a helping, of social satire. In this way, each of the three major branches of "false background literature" is represented.

***

I rather suspect that a number of readers who have followed me thus far are rather nonplussed at my serious attitude toward science fiction. Can anyone, they may be thinking, really attach importance to such material?

The answer is decidedly yes!

That the question can be asked at all is the result of the fact that the forms of "science fiction" most familiar to the general public are the comic strip adventures of individuals such as Flash Gordon and Superman, and the movies dealing with various types of "monsters."

Neither comic-strip nor Hollywood version is really science fiction. Therein lies the confusion. Rather, both are the result of adding a thin veneer of scientific-sounding mumbo-jumbo to a very old type of literature, the adventure-fantasy. Substitute for the dragon that is slain by Siegfried the equally fabulous monster slain by Flash Gordon, and there are few other changes of any consequence that need be made. The Chimera that devastates the countryside and must be slain by Bellerophon on his flying horse, Pegasus, is much like the monster that rises from twenty thousand fathoms in the black lagoon and must be slain by a movie hero and his flying aeroplane.

Humanist Philosophy 1928 – 1973

For adult science fiction, for real science fiction, it is to the magazines that one must turn, and to the novels which have usually first appeared as magazine serials. Even there, not all stories are "good." (But, then, come to think of it, why should anyone expect all of science fiction to be good, or even most of it? One of the best of the science-fiction writers recently said to an audience of avid science fiction fans, "Nine-tenths of science fiction is crud." The audience sat stunned and disbelieving, and then the writer added, solemnly, "Nine-tenths of all writing is crud.")

Embedded in the crud, however, are stories that are entertaining, well-written and exciting—but, more than that, thought-provoking in an odd way that is duplicated in no other form of literature. Here you will find strange, new societies: societies oriented primarily toward advertising and its psychology; societies hidden in underground cities that can no longer face the open; societies faced with the discovery of new intelligent life-forms, or their discovery of us; societies faced with the depletion of resources or repletion of population; societies in which telepathy and all of its implications are commonplace.

Is this important? Of course it is. Good science fiction is fun, and good science fiction is important. It does something that no other form of literature does: it consistently considers the future.

We are living in a society which, for the first time, must consider the future. Until 1750, the average man was certain that, short of the Day of Judgment, the essential way of life would proceed much as it always did and always would, except for changes in the actual cast of characters playing out the human drama.

After 1750, more and more men became increasingly aware that society was changing in odd and unpredictable directions and would continue to do so; that what was good enough for the father would turn out to be not good enough (or perhaps too good) for the son; that as things had always been, they would not remain.

After 1945, men further became aware that even the mere fact of continued existence of human society in any form was by no means to be assumed. The possibility of a new kind of Day of Judgment grew big.

Science fiction is based on the fact of social change. It accepts the fact of change. In a sense, it tries on various changes for size; it tries to penetrate the consequences of this change or that and, in the form of a story, it presents the results to the view of the public.

It is this which has always made it seem rather ironic to me that science fiction is continually lumped under the heading of "escape literature," and usually as the most extreme kind, in fact. Yet it does not escape into the "isn't" as most fiction does, or the "never was" as fantasy does, but into the "might very well be." In its best phases, if science fiction escapes, it is an escape into reality.

The writers of science fiction are themselves not always aware of what they are doing. Many of them might swear in all earnestness that they are interested only in turning out a craftsman-like story and earning an honest dollar. To my mind, however, they represent the eyes of humanity turned, for the first time, outward in a blind and agonized contemplation of the exciting and dangerous future, not of this individual or that, but of the human race as a whole.

Isaac Asimov is a professor of biochemistry who thinks of his writing as teaching in other forms—from science books for youngsters to science fiction for adults, as well as professional articles and textbooks.

CHAPTER 11
Humanism Comes to Value Other Life Forms and Nature

Early Evolution of Humanist Environmental Consciousness

Warren Allen Smith wrote an essay publishing perceptions of naturalistic humanism on the part of prominent people he had surveyed (*TH* 11:5). However, Smith's definition of "naturalistic humanism" was not the consensus view in 1951, the year of his essay's publication. He defined it as "a set of beliefs born of the modern scientific age and centered upon a faith in the supreme value and self-perfectibility of human personality."

Smith's definition exemplified the waning strain of humanist thought criticized as excessively anthropocentric by many respondents and others. Algernon D. Black's included essay argues strongly against human-centeredness in humanism. He obviously thought the anthropocentric view was much too strong, given his warning against the idea of humans as gods.

Horace J. Nickels's 1933 essay in Chapter 4 states that humans cannot be the sole concern of the philosophy of humanism, because "the human organism seems to be wholly a child of the earth." Lloyd Morain and Oliver Reiser's essay in Chapter 2 asserts the importance of abiding the interconnectedness of things. "The scientific humanist always recognizes that every 'thing' or 'event' exists or happens within a context or framework, here on earth with a planetary framework." In Chapter 3, Curtis W. Reese likewise calls humanism "a planetary-centered movement." But does Reese include more than all humans on earth? Linus Pauling clearly does, as seen in his 1961 essay in Chapter 5 that explicitly one-ups Schweitzer with "reverence for the world."

Despite these brief mentions of concern, Rachel Carson's *Silent Spring*, published in 1962, was a turning point in humanist as well as popular consciousness of the environment. Writings discussing solely environmental issues began appearing in *TH* after the publication of Carson's book. C. E. Busby's essay in this chapter really addresses only conservation of nature. His emphasis on not wasting natural resources points to the conservationist view that nature is for human use. He ignores the distinction between preservation and conservation. For conservation is the word of those, beginning with Gifford Pinchot,[1] who want to actively manage natural resources for future human use. Busby argues for a broader acceptance of conservationist principles by humanists.

Interestingly, Busby's essay includes the text of AHA's first statement on the environment, adopted in 1962, perhaps in reaction to Carson's book. The AHA is much more balanced between conservation and preservation. By calling "for preservation of natural beauty" and support for "wilderness, natural and wildlife areas," the statement encompasses the preservation of nature for its own sake, a la John Muir.

Eleanor Woods's included 1964 essay takes a clearly preservationist point of view. Woods argues against self-love as the center of humanist philosophy. Instead, humanists must, like Muir did,[2] assign intrinsic value to nature. A key concept for Woods is the "life-cycle," which harkens back to Morain and Reiser's interconnectedness. Woods invests humanism not merely with human development, but the "Furtherance of All Life." She argues that humanism must include preservationist principles at its core. She even suggests that reverence of nature is a logical extension of the furtherance of all life. Woods shows that those principles fit well with humanism's overall view of humans within and part of nature itself. In sum, she argues for valuing the environment and other life forms on par with the value of humans, as the basis for life in harmony with the environment.

Humanist Philosophy 1928 – 1973

Hyman G. Rickover wrote in *TH* that "Keeping our small planet habitable is a matter of utmost importance and great urgency." He asserted the need to control technology. Citing Barry Commoner, he echoed the need to preserve the "balance of nature" and the ecosystem from destruction. Rickover took a preservationist view in recognizing environmental science as the key to controlling technology to limit its negative effects on humans and the environment.

Miriam deFord's essay in Chapter 2 emphasizes that "Man must either learn to exercise a high ethical policy toward the earth on which he lives, toward the multitudinous plants and animals inhabiting it with him, toward his fellow humans — yes, and toward himself as well — or cease to survive." Corliss Lamont likewise argued around the same time that naturalistic humanism values nature and natural beauty, and called for conservation, ecology, and protection of wildlife (*TH* 31:5).

The HMII shows the extent to which humanism adopted ecological principles by 1973. It sets forth a number of principles not stated in the 1933 HMI. HMII refers to the danger of ecological damage, and calls for cultivation and conservation of nature as a moral value. It insists that social conscience must factor into exploitation of resources and handling of waste. Thus, it adopts only a conservationist view of the environment.

Environmental consciousness grew in humanist circles to the extent that the year after the publication of HMII, Victor Ferkiss advanced the idea of "ecological humanism" (*TH* 34:3). Ferkiss's analysis and later *TH* essays on environmental issues are beyond the scope of this volume. Through 1973, values of protecting the environment from pollution and managing resources useful to humans received consistently strong support. In contrast, writers in *TH* were on the whole slow to embrace preservationist environmental values. A few individuals argued for them, but the wider statements did not see much improvement. While HMII does not encompass the preservationist view of Woods and Rickover, the newly added principles nonetheless exemplify humanism's core principle that humanist values will and must evolve with improved knowledge of the universe.

Notes

1. See Pinchot, Gifford, *The Fight for Conservation* (N.Y.: Doubleday, Page & Co., 1910), available digitally at http://catalog.hathitrust.org/Record/001312819.
2. See Muir, John, *A Thousand Mile Walk to the Gulf* (Boston & N.Y.: Houghton, Mifflin Co., 1916), available digitally at http://babel.hathitrust.org/cgi/pt?id=nc01.ark:/13960/t5fb5zd5x;view=1up;seq=4.

Can Humanism Meet Man's Spiritual Need?

Algernon D. Black
The Humanist, July-August, 1959

In trying to answer this question much depends on our definitions of "spiritual need" and "humanism." Our purpose here is not to offer tight and neat definitions or to make a simple answer of yes or no, but rather to open out the problems involved.

In approaching the meaning of spiritual nature we may refer to certain tendencies in man. Is it not true that most men at certain moments in their lives are aware of a need within them for something more than the satisfactions that they derive from eating, drinking, sleeping, breeding, and the satisfactions of immediate desire? Is it not true that most men want to think of themselves as more than animal? For many, that extra something beyond physical satisfactions and beyond animal levels may be satisfied by intellectual or aesthetic experiences. But most men appear to hunger for something that goes beyond even these.

Another aspect of man's spiritual nature is evident in the widespread tendency in man to seek and believe in a reality deeper than and beyond the reality that he knows through his senses. Through sight and hearing, through touch and taste and smell, man perceives his world. But man is not satisfied that he can rely completely on the external sources of his perceptions, nor is he satisfied that he can trust his own sense organs completely. There is a transient and temporary aspect to the reality he knows through his senses. He longs for something more permanent and changeless and less subjective and less subject to his own errors.

Every man shares the external world, the world he experiences and lives in with other men. He may share and agree with his fellows that together they live in the same world. But every man lives also in a personal private world, the world of his own imagination, the world of his personalized experience, his wishes and dreams—and with it his vision of the world that is his own personal projection of the self he would like to be and the life he would like to live and the world he would like to live in. Indeed, as the earth turns, the two and a half billion human beings, whether sleeping or waking, live both in the shared world and the personal world of imagination that each envisages. For every man one aspect of his spiritual struggle lies in the effort to relate his dreams to those of his fellows, to combine the personal visions and the hungers of individuals into a realistic idealism expressive of life's possibilities.

And man longs for freedom. He has a sense of selfhood free and able to master the forces that play upon him. He hungers for growth and fulfillment of his individual and unique possibilities. But he also longs for security, for a sense of belonging, for identification with some larger whole, some larger reality of which he can be a meaningful part. Out of his passion for freedom he would break the bonds of the chemistry and the instinctive patterns of his own animal nature. Out of his passion for selfhood he would war with the social environment, which at times confines him and forms and conforms him. Yet he would also be part of a larger process. He would gladly bind himself with the values that give life its greatest meaning.

And man longs to know that what he values as good and true and beautiful is grounded in the nature of things, that his values and his struggle for a better life are validated in nature, and that his life has meaning not only for himself and his fellows and the generations to come, but also in the larger context of the universe.

WHAT RELIGION SUPPLIES

These are some of the characteristics of human beings the world over. They are not entirely the product of particular cultures. They appear in individuals and in groups in ways for which there is no simple explanation. They are evidence of something profound in human nature. They are distinctly human. They are aspects of what we mean by man's spiritual nature. They are an expression of deep hungers of the human spirit. They have brought forth wonder and awe and reverence. They have brought forth endless questioning and all the varieties of answers that we know as the philosophies and the religions of humankind.

Humanist Philosophy 1928 – 1973

And it is doubtless true that this aspect of man's life will be evident in his restless spirit and his endless seeking as long as he dwells on this earth.

In part the spiritual need of man has been met by traditional religions. In the Western world the Christian interpretation of life has marked off man's spiritual nature and has emphasized the dualistic approach.

Most of the churches have taught a concept of spiritual reality that has to do with God and the supernatural and another world, a realm of divinity, holiness, sacredness—as over against the natural world, the material and secular realm of being. Just as God is the soul of the universe, so man himself is conceived of dualistically as body and soul, flesh and spirit.

Who would dare to say that men have not been helped in their spiritual need by this approach and this interpretation and vision of life? For it has given men hope and faith that they are more than animal and that there is more to life than the satisfaction of immediate desire. It has given them a belief in a reality absolute, changeless, and eternal. Insofar as men have believed in this, they have felt a personal dignity, a tie to values, a support from a power making for righteousness, an inevitable victory for their vision of a better life and a better world. No doubt it has contributed much to helping men harmonize their dreams and their energies to rise up and transcend the material conditions, the poverty and frustrations, the meanness and pettiness and destructiveness of their own natures, and the evil in the world around them. It has helped them stand up as men in life and it has helped them face death.

WHERE ORGANIZED RELIGION FAILS

Why, then, do we withdraw from the traditional organized religious institutions? With what do we differ?

First, we reject the dogma and the set creeds that claim authority and finality. We cannot accept these with any intellectual honesty and we cannot support them with any integrity. We see the theologies as human creations, projections out of human longing and imagination. We find them in contradiction with one another and often within themselves, and in conflict with science and with the evidence drawn from history and archaeology, from comparative religion and comparative anthropology. We hold that they often constrict men's minds within a narrow rigid framework, whereas it is our sense that man's spiritual nature requires openness and freedom and stimulation to doubt and explore, to think and work out and grow.

Second, we cannot accept the rituals and magic rites by which men invest clergy and material things and ceremonial acts with supernatural powers. Our emphasis on a rational and scientific approach, our analysis of causal relations, makes it impossible to accept a belief in powers that can be invoked by man to interfere with and violate the laws of nature. We see the exploitation of the irrational in man, and the misuse of religious service. Human work and actions can have a symbolic meaning. They are part of our apprehension and our communication of the meanings of the world around us. But we cannot and dare not attribute to these things, which man invests with his meanings and his longings, an absolute power. The forms of expression for human awe and wonder before the mysteries of life, the appreciative thankfulness for whatever is beautiful and good in life, all too often become forms and externals of religious thought and action; men go through habitual motions without the inner experience or meaning from which these were originally born. Thus, men mistake the outer practice for the inner experience, and indulge in the former without the latter. We reject fixed rituals as untrue to our spiritual nature and in violation of man's spiritual need.

Third, the emphasis on absolute truth and absolute authority by each of the major faiths makes for a rigidity and an exclusiveness and a fanaticism that is in itself a violation of the spiritual needs of man. For the passion to share experience and to seek meaning is a social and communal undertaking. The feeling of fellowship and the sense of oneness of all life is an essential part of man's spiritual nature. Thus, the sectarian and denominational divisions and prejudices, the intolerance and bigotry and hate, the conflict and violent destructiveness, are all violations of the relations of men to one another and of man's relation to the larger processes of the universe of which we are all a part. It is tragic enough when men kill one another for bread or land. It is even worse when men kill one another over their definitions of the unknown, their doctrines concerning ultimate authority, revelation, and the possibility of another life and another world. Of all the aspects of man's life, the questioning and the longing and the answers that men make concerning what we call the great mysteries of life—these should unite men with a sense of common destiny rather than turn men against one another.

Fourth, the dualistic philosophy of the Western Christian world has made for confusion and contradiction and hypocrisy. With this men have suffered feelings of guilt and beliefs in their own sinfulness and evil. With this men have been torn by inner conflict. On the one hand they have one life to live and one world to live in; and on the other hand they are told to prize and prepare for the next life and another world. They are taught that the body is inferior to the soul, that the flesh is evil; yet they cannot live without fulfilling the flesh and without accepting themselves as part of the community of organisms who must eat and drink and fulfill their physical desires—and must fulfill these without self-rejection and without guilt. It is taught in word or by implication that the good life, the way to salvation, the perfect life, is the life lived in the image of Christ. But this ideal of life embraces poverty and celibacy, and rejects the defense of one's life.

And at the same time, do the churches that teach this as basic truth really expect men to live this way? If men took this ideal literally and lived it fully, would there be any human life left on this earth? And are the results of this teaching such as to confirm their validity? We think of the vast areas of poverty and ignorance and sickness with which men have made peace, saying that it is God's will. We think of the evils to which the answer has been that these will be made right in the next life or the next world. We think of the effects in terms of inner conflict and emotional disturbance and mental illness. But most of all we think of the withdrawal from the world and the denial of essential realities of human nature—and with it what seems to many of us to be an abdication of life. Granted that many wonderful individuals have achieved great purity and nobility of character and have given themselves single-mindedly and effectively to many good works, we still question the withdrawal from the normal relationships and fulfillments of human life. Granted that many have through asceticism and self-denial achieved unique experiences and powers among men, we affirm that the spiritual challenge of life lies more in working out the problems of man in and through the world than in withdrawal to another life and another world.

THE NEED FOR NEW PERSPECTIVES

It is precisely in the refusal to be engulfed and buffeted and controlled by the material forces, and by living in and through the world, that man is most tested in his spiritual nature. It is by the way man lives with the known that he keeps faith with the unknown powers of the universe. It is by living in the here and now and in the world of nature and man, that man becomes a responsible active agent in shaping his own destiny. It is to save himself from the mysticism and the other-worldliness and the abdication of his distinctive human character that man has had to turn more and more from the traditional dualistic philosophies of supernaturalism. No one can say with finality just what realities may lie in the spiritual struggles of the asceticism of East and West. None should close his mind to the possibility of dimensions to human experience beyond our knowing. But in answer to old faiths it is well to hold one's self tight by the intellect and with open mind prove the new again and again and again.

These are some of the reasons why men have turned from traditional beliefs and have sought new perspectives of philosophy and faith. Some have come to Ethical Culture and to Humanism intellectually through critical analysis and reflection. They see the conflicts and contradictions of religion with science, with the discoveries in history and archaeology, with comparative religion and anthropology. Others have come out of the revolt against the credal and ritual emphasis, continuing the great tradition of the prophetic revolt on behalf of ethical values. In every faith there have been persons who have challenged the priests. Through their efforts the religious practices have been reformed and the religion purified. So it was through the influence of Amos, Micah, Isaiah. So it was through the influence of Jesus and Buddha. But the Ethical Movement and the Humanist Movement, much as they may have had reformist influences on traditional faiths, have gone beyond to new beginnings. For in these fellowships men have sought an ethics independent of theology and a fixed metaphysics; they have sought an ethics that would be part of a larger world view, and a world view and an ethics that would be based upon respect for the integrity of the individual and that would square with the spirit and discoveries of science, would embody the values and aspirations of democracy and peace, and would be inclusive enough to provide a common ground for human beings the world over, no matter what their diverse cultural and religious traditions.

In using the word Humanism we will here refer to the Ethical Movement and the Humanist Association and any fellowships of men that stand for a non-credal faith in man as central to a philosophy and a life perspective. Regardless of the names used, the important question is, do they meet man's spiritual need ? If Humanism is merely a way of shedding old beliefs and affirming a faith in man and man's intelligence, it may be quite inadequate to larger purposes. For man needs a way of life, a way of thought and feeling and action. So also the emphasis on ethics, on man's relation to man, must meet two tests: it must be an effective ethics, one which through education and reform actually changes human behavior; and it must have an over-view, an awareness of man in the larger setting of the universe.

THE CHALLENGES TO HUMANISM

Can Humanism meet man's spiritual need? The question is still open whether Humanism can grow in depth and breadth and grow as a mature and rounded approach to life. There are at least four challenges that Humanism must meet if it is to be adequate and effective as an answer to man's deepest needs.

First, Humanism must recognize that human experience is not one kind of experience. It is many-faceted. It has many dimensions. And in and through the variety of human experience, within the life of the given individual, and different for every individual, and affected by the unique character of the variety of the cultures of man, there are many ways of knowing. Humanism cannot and must not base itself entirely and exclusively upon the intellect and the reason of man. Nor can it base itself exclusively on the truth that comes through science and scientific method.

For man's knowledge and experience are always relative. Man may know much about electricity, its characteristics and its effects and uses, the ways of generating it, etc., but man through science may still be far from knowing what it is. Just so, we know when a man is dead and when he is alive, but we do not know the nature of life-force. Is it some form of electric-magnetic force or is it some form of energy we have never yet identified? With microscopes we see the human brain but not the mind or thinking process. And even though we may learn much concerning the outer manifestations of our world, we may never be able to grasp the realities entirely; we may never be able to grasp them entirely through one method, the method of reason or the framework of logic or the techniques of science. This is not to devalue what we learn through science. Nor is it to encourage in any way the anti-intellectualism of our time. But it is an attempt to urge that the ways of knowing should not be conceived of narrowly. We can know through love and loving. We know through labor and motion. We can know through sensitivities of appreciation and identification both in relation to nature and in relation to human beings. And these, too, are ways of knowing. And as the ways of East and West come into relations of interchange and reciprocity and mutual understanding, we may find that just as we have ways of knowing through our Western ways of life, so the Eastern ways of life may open up new dimensions of experience and knowing for us.

Furthermore, it is quite possible and probable that human limitations are such that man may never know the totality of the universe. Indeed, Humanism, to offer a sound perspective on human experience and knowledge, should display confidence and pride in human achievement through intelligence and reason and science. But it should also make men aware of the unexperienced and the unknown, and aware that man may never experience qualities of being beyond our capacities, or know the whole of cosmic reality.

MAN IS NOT THE CENTER

Second, Humanism must make certain that, in rejecting creeds and final definitions concerning the unknown, it does not mislead man to thinking that he is God, that he created this world, or that he is the center of the universe. We may wonder at the Biblical account and picture of the earth as standing still and as the center of the universe. We may wonder at the self-centeredness of those who thought that man was the special creation and special preoccupation of God. We may wonder how organized religion can still believe and teach as if, despite all we have learned from Galileo and Darwin, man and this earth were still the center of the universe. And in the effort to free man from the thought framework of supernaturalism, it is important that Humanism not go to the other extreme of giving the impression that it holds man to be the source and center of all that is.

For our human race is located on a small planet that revolves about an ordinary sun. This sun, which is the center of our solar system, is one among two billion suns in our galaxy. It is of not more than ordinary brightness among the suns, and we are located on the periphery of our galaxy. We are on the fringe rather than in the center. And our galaxy is only one among billions of galaxies. In other words, if Humanism is to free men from believing in a God made in man's image and man as the center of God's interest, it must not mislead men into a naïve concept of a man-centered universe.

Furthermore, man must be helped to a new perspective of himself in the larger scheme of things. According to astronomers, there is not only a possibility of life in other parts of the universe: there is a strong probability of it. On a strictly mathematical and scientific basis it is estimated that there are many suns with planetary systems—and there are many planets where the existence of carbon, nitrogen, and water, the distance of a planet from its own sun, the temperature range, and the existence of atmosphere may well mean that organic life is present. And it is possible that among the many examples of organic life may exist forms that are capable of experience and knowledge and powers beyond our own. Thus, the universe, instead of being merely a reality of matter and energy and burning suns, may contain far more life and far more of aliveness than we have ever imagined or thought possible. Our efforts to know and master space take on new meaning far beyond the mere gathering of more knowledge or speed or military power. And with it all we must help man see himself as part of a larger process, a being and becoming, a partnership in some larger creativity, a being small and limited but also great in potential and meaning. Humanism must help us feel that we belong and can feel at home in the universe. It must help us feel that our life has meaning for ourselves and possibly in some larger cosmic process. But it must help man to awareness that we are not at the center of the universe.

A WAY OF LIVING

Third, Humanism is not merely a way of looking at life, a philosophy, but it is also a way of life, a way of action. And Humanism must help man survive. Its crucial testing is in its effect on man's ethical life. In teaching that man must believe in himself and must develop his own powers to solve his problems, Humanism must help man master his man-created social environment as it has helped man master so much of his natural world. Today man has the power to destroy himself in nuclear war. Just as dangerous is man's destruction of self and environment in peace. For the nuclear tests now being carried on to make more perfect weapons of war are actually poisoning the air and poisoning man's food and drink. And the increase of leukemia and the possible impairment of the genetic powers of the generations to come are part of an irresponsible use of man's greatest scientific knowledge. If Humanism is to help men survive, it must develop a greater sense of the responsibility toward human beings. Humanism must be ethically effective. It must square with mental and emotional health. It must help bring about relationships in which men do not use their frustrations and aggressions to destroy one another's life or will to live. The intolerance and domination that make for rejection and self-destruction must give way to self-affirmation, self-esteem, a great zest for life. Nowhere is the Humanist faith and vision tested more than in the way man uses or misuses nuclear energy.

In the old Bible story we may remember that two mothers came before King Solomon and each claimed the same baby as her own. And the King said, "I will cut the baby in half and each of you will have part of the baby." And when one of the women cried out that she did not want the baby destroyed, he said, "This is the true mother. She shall have the baby. It is her child." As I think of it, both the U.S.A. and the U.S.S.R. are the two women. But both would risk the destruction of the human race rather than yield on the nuclear tests. Does not one of the great nations have to stop and take the risk and make a sacrifice for the sake of man?

THE WORLD COMMUNITY

But the challenge to Humanism lies not merely in the cessation of the nuclear tests and the prevention of nuclear war; it lies also in the positive challenge to help create and fulfill the dream of the "world community." Ethics has been thought of as a matter of moral commandments and rules of relationship between individuals in interpersonal relations. It has become evident that ethics must apply to intergroup relations. In our time it must help bring about the kind of unity and communication that will make possible a world community. For the survival of humanity is threatened by the explosive destructive power generated by the hostility of groups toward one another. Religious bigotry and fear and hatred between large masses of Christians and non-Christians, Hindus and Moslems, and in other inter-religious conflict; racial antipathy between large masses of colored and white human beings; ideological cold war over differences of economic and political institutions and power struggles verging on extreme military conflict—all these are tearing the human race apart, turning men against one another, blinding them to their common destiny and basic humanity. Humanism must find ways of emphasizing the common ground, the alikeness that is more important than the unlikeness, the common purposes and interests, and the possibility of a new age of security for every religious and ethical group, for every nation and culture. Most of all Humanism must help men achieve a level of relations between nations so that they can live together in peace and can co-operate with one another in a security system and in a way of life in which they respect one another and trust one another and are able to benefit and be challenged and enriched by the very fact of their ideological differences. It is no great curse to the world that some men live under capitalism and some under socialism and that some experiment with forms of individualism and others with collectivism. We can all benefit. We can all learn. The important thing is to achieve a valuation of persons in which we can all trust in one another that the basic human values will be respected. It requires that we help men overcome the fear and distrust and hate, the violence to thought and truth, the violence of action against persons, that endanger all.

Humanism must remind us that earth and sun and water are the same for all men the world over. Humanism must remind us that our basic structure of bone and flesh, our needs and capacities are the same. Humanism must teach us that the life cycle of birth, of growth, childhood and youth, of work and love, of sickness and age and death, of human sorrow and human joy, are the same for all men. We share a common destiny. For good or evil we are of it together. We must dare to try to live in the world community. Never before have men had the means of transportation or communication or the actual bonds of interdependence through which a world community was possible. Today it is possible and necessary. Humanism must develop in men this larger inclusive vision of a humanity drawing close to one another in understanding and respect for differences and in increasing global awareness and co-operation in the ways of peace.

TO LIVE WITH INTEGRITY

And finally, Humanism cannot meet man's spiritual needs if it offers man a shallow optimistic faith. There are those who think that all we must do is educate and reform conditions and man's life will be better and better. This would ignore the deep roots of our animal heritage and the instinctive forces in human nature. It would ignore the deep historical and social roots of many of our patterns of human behavior, relations, and institutions. Man has much growing to do before he will master himself. This is true in the personal life, the personal drives, needs, and desires. It is true also in group dynamics, where the relations of the individual to the group and the behaviors of men in groups present problems to individual reason and responsibility. But besides the stubborn difficulty of improving our relationships with one another is the hard reality of man's life within the framework of nature's laws. Life has its tragic aspects. Human life is lived in the midst of forces far beyond man and man's controls. And whether it be the life cycle of the individual, the suffering, frustration, and death—or whether it be the fact that man loses his loved ones, his creations become dust, his civilizations rise and fall, his questions concerning ultimate things go unanswered— there are frustrations and humiliations in human life. Nor are there any guarantees of victory for the values man holds sacred. Nor are there any assurances that what man holds of supreme import is recognized or treasured by any of the forces of the universe. Humanism must help man face his situation honestly. And if it were proved beyond any doubt that there is no higher consciousness anywhere in the universe, and if it were certain that man is the only form of life carrying intelligence and moral values, and if it were true that the universe is indifferent to man, possibly about to crush man and destroy every evidence of human life and thought and achievement, still man would have to be true to himself. Man cannot deny his own intelligence, his moral sense, his experience, his own valuation of his situation. For man must live with dignity and affirm the truth as he sees it. And with it all, man must face the reality that suffering and frustration and death are part of human destiny and must be part of the awareness of any mature religious vision.

Thus Humanism has no easy task. It is not enough to turn from old beliefs. It is not enough to throw off the burden of creed and ritual and sectarian division. It is not enough to be free from error. The task is to be free to seek truth, a sounder more inclusive truth, squaring with the values of science and of democracy and a global community of mankind. Humanism must offer a view of life that recognizes that there are many ways of knowing, that man is not the center of the universe; that more than a way of seeing life, it must be a way of living, an ethic making for survival and for world community. And it must help men face the tragic side of life. In such a perspective man can live with integrity, can be honest with himself and his children. He can face the darkest moments with courage and can lighten his sorrows with the great beauties and joys of human life.

As Prometheus climbed the mountain to bring down the fire of reason for all mankind, so in our faith every man can kindle within himself the fire of truth, the fire of love, the fire that can illuminate every life and bring a new light and warmth and color to all the world.

This is a recent address, given at the New York Society for Ethical Culture by one of its distinguished Leaders, and here published in its entirety for the first time.

Conservation Of Man Together With Nature

C. E. Busby
The Humanist, January-February, 1964

In 1962 the American Humanist Association, convening at Los Angeles, adopted a first resolution on the subject of conservation. Here it is:

> Whereas the appreciation of nature is a significant element in the Humanist viewpoint, and whereas the conservation of natural resources is of great importance to man's well-being, therefore be it resolved that The American Humanist Association actively support movements for conservation and for preservation of natural beauty, as well as those on behalf of national, state and municipal parks, and wilderness, natural and wildlife areas.

Though it is limited in scope, this resolution opened the way for a better understanding of the meaning of conservation as an ideal and as a productive way of life. This initial action deserves thoughtful consideration by everyone interested in both man and nature.

The word "nature" is conspicuous in the resolution. The word "man" is less so but man's wellbeing is the central interest. Here is the crux. Together, these two words, man and nature, are tremendously significant. In the concept of conservation they are brought together.

This has not been fully recognized because conservation has usually been advocated by special-interest groups to express their own concern. Their definitions have been confusing or conflicting, so that the broad concept has been fragmented and diluted in meaning. However, when Humanists bring conservation into their forum there is opportunity for a broader and more comprehensive perspective, unhampered by past limited views. They are, indeed, confronted with this fundamental question:

What is conservation in the light of modern knowledge, conditions and needs?

The Best of *The Humanist*

A Broader View

I do not think of conservation merely in terms of nature study, wilderness areas, or recreation, but rather in terms of the whole complex of man and nature in relation each to the other. This includes the atmosphere, soils, minerals, waters, fish, wildlife, crops, power, industry, forests, wilderness areas, nature study and the beauty of the landscape, and, last but not least, man in all his manifold capabilities and needs. It is man's relation to nature that is more significant in a broader perspective on conservation. Man is a part of nature, yet separate from it. Religious groups through the ages have pondered this riddle.

This article presents one view of the full meaning of conservation in the scheme of things and its relation to topics of other resolutions of the American Humanist Association such as birth control, freedom from hunger, civil rights, nuclear testing, disarmament and the United Nations. They are intimately related, one to the other, and the basis of their relation is conservation. So too a decent regard for conservation of energy and of human resources can illumine even customs, religion, politics, law, scientific discovery and the arts.

To establish the principle of conservation on such a broad basis, one may begin with the soil. Each soil has its own inherent physical, chemical and biological properties which, when combined with climate and cultivation by man, can produce food and fiber for many years. Some soils, naturally, have higher capabilities than others; some respond more to fertilizers and good management than do others. Furthermore, each soil is a natural water reservoir, having storage, replenishment and depletion characteristics all its own. It embodies nature's way of conserving water, but the key to man's management of the soil is to study its capabilities and to make the most of them by supplying its needs.

These principles apply to watershed as well, the land area that drains into a single stream, and the water resource that it holds. The natural properties of the many soils, waters, forests, fish, wildlife, and the beauty of the landscape can yield a broad combination of uses over the years under good management. Some watersheds have higher capabilities than others. But it is man—as a part and feature of the watershed—that is the key to its future and his own.

Conservation of the watershed in terms of man and nature is much more complex than that of the soil alone because water and fish and wildlife are mobile resources. They can contribute both use and damage, depending upon how the watershed is used and managed.

Human Conservation

Applying these principles to the child and the family, it is obvious that nearly every child has inherent natural capabilities which, when combined with the natural and cultural environment, can elicit talents of a high order, provided that the child's capabilities are not impaired and arrested. This is the most complex aspect of conservation, for the human being can also contribute values of both use and damage, depending upon how he or she is treated and managed. The child's full development depends very much upon who does the managing. Authoritarian controls do not permit the fulfilment of the child's capabilities because they thwart free expression.

If the capabilities of these many aspects of nature are to be developed, due regard must be given to their needs. Most soils have need for treatment in terms of fertilizers, cover crops, contour terraces, and other management practices in order to produce at high levels, and must be protected from erosion, exhaustion of fertility, and flood damage. Similarly, the watershed has multiple needs for treatment as a natural reservoir of life.

These same principles apply to human conservation, to the human needs for love and affection, food and clothing, a warm home life, education, freedom of expression and economic opportunity, and medical aid. Human needs are physical, emotional, and intellectual if a healthy, productive life is to be developed. Genuine love and affection are by far the most essential human needs.

Yet there is one further need: the coordination of all other needs. The fulfilment of the combined capabilities of man and nature calls for unity of purpose, unity of organization, and unity of action in man as an essential prerequisite to his wholesome relation to nature. This is by far the greatest challenge of our time. No person can be truly whole and creative without this unity. Neither can the family or the community.

Without unity of purpose, organization and action within the self, one cannot well conserve and wisely use one's energy to prevent physical and mental disease, cannot give others the love and devotion that are so essential to a full and rewarding life nor encourage the full freedom of expression that is needed for the manifold creative capabilities of man and nature.

Unity of Man and Nature

Nevertheless, there are on all sides broken bodies, minds, homes, and communities that testify to the lack of unity in conservation. How long can we tolerate this extravagant waste of human resources? We are outdoing the early exploiters and wasters of our soil, forest, wildlife and water resources many times over. We produce and exploit in order to satisfy false needs, and in the process proudly waste precious resources. But the concept of unity in conservation implies the projection to others and to the natural landscape and the community of the creative and productive genius of man. Genuine regard for all aspects of nature and responsibility for their conservation go together.

Perhaps man's greatest waste stems from lack of understanding of his relation to nature, indeed from concepts of ethics, religion, law and government that are not natural but unnatural or supernatural. This confusion has been passed down from generation to generation through the influence of church, court, and political dogma. Values have been ascribed to artificial beings and achievements that have no true relation to genuine love and affection among productive and creative people.

In modern scientific thought things and events are in a constant process of change that is in vivid contrast with the static and dogmatic precepts of orthodox religions and customs. Our ideas and ways of life, including such fundamentals as sex, morality and justice, develop as research in the sciences leads to better understanding.

The waste of our soil, forest and range resources has been arrested to a considerable extent in America through the efforts of local, state, and national leaders who are genuinely devoted to conservation. This is especially true in the South, for which we can all be thankful. But the pollution of fresh waters and of the atmosphere, the defacing of the urban landscape, and the waste of human resources is all the more serious.

The prisons, asylums, ghettos and slums of our major cities are unsightly with human wastage.

And the waste is not confined to the areas of poverty. It occurs in some sophisticated suburbs also. The vast majority of these wasted people could have been saved had their early family and community life been inspired by the creative ideals of human conservation.

The Challenge to Humanism

If unity in conservation is one key to salvation, how can our culture develop a more productive and creative way of life? And how can a relatively small group like the American Humanist Association take part in the great task of conservation of human and natural resources?

Just talking about it is not enough. Neither is the piecemeal attack by groups interested in one or a few aspects of conservation, be it protection of wildlife, development of water resources, maintenance of the highway landscape, or prevention of hunger and disease. Great as these causes are and satisfying to their devotees, their roots go much deeper and spring from a common source which is dedication to all that is natural, a part of nature, or what Albert Schweitzer has called reverence for life. This is their unity. From this tap root grow science and understanding, the joy of physical action, the expression of emotion in music and poetry, the compassion to cherish all living things, the creative skills of medicine and engineering, and even what are called improvements on nature which are merely the development of nature's resources by the use of man's supremely natural intelligence. It is all this that must be conserved. It is the awareness of this unity that is the essence of conservation.

However deeply any one of us may be engrossed in one or another branch of conservation, its unity must be borne in mind and the leaders of each branch must be motivated by the basic concept, and that concept underlies many of the resolutions adopted by the American Humanist Association though they were adopted one by one through the years, with no reference to conservation of human resources. If respect for human dignity and the love of mankind are fundamental to humanism, then the American Humanist Association should cultivate every aspect of conservation, all culminating in man himself. It should take active leadership in a broad re-education that will eliminate senseless ancient myths, end careless, stupid wastage, and inspire all men with today's reliable knowledge and the accompanying reverence for man-in-nature—as one.

C. E. ("Mike") Busby of Lafayette, California, is a professional conservationist, geologist, and water lawyer, serving as consultant to several soil and water conservation districts in California. He was geologist and conservationist at the University of Nebraska from 1929 to 1934, and watershed planner and water law consultant for the U.S. Soil Conservation Service from 1934 to 1961. He is a member of the Bar of the District of Columbia, the Soil Conservation Society of America and the American Humanist Association.

The Furtherance of All Life: A Vision To Broaden And Strengthen Humanism

Eleanor Woods
The Humanist, May-June, 1964

Today mankind is confronted anew with the old problem of values. Western society, having conquered Nature, is now forced to consider how it should use its ever-increasing leisure and its tremendous power. Should it use its power to help the rest of the world attain its own ideal standard of material luxury? What should mankind then do with its leisure? Is leisure an end in itself? What values would the art of such a world of leisure express? For what purpose beyond idle curiosity would scientific investigation be pursued? Thoughtful people in the West realize that the conquest of Nature has brought neither the hoped-for happiness nor the anticipated moral and artistic development. The rest of mankind, in the East and in the developing countries, though tempted by the materialism of the West, finds something lacking in western values. Moreover, even the conquest of Nature has not eliminated the tragedies inherent in living. To what purpose grief and pain? Having abandoned his own religious explanations for such suffering, Western man has not yet found another answer consistent with the science in which he believes.

The time is ripe for a new moral movement, but Humanism is not yet providing it. The goal of Humanism—the full development of human potentialities—is the very goal that has been accepted in the West, at least in principle, but which is found wanting today. Moreover, Humanism, although not specifically endorsing the crass materialism of the West, has not always made clear the distinction between rationalism and materialism.

But even if Humanism were clearly defined as a rational philosophy, its goal of human development is self-defeating. Conscious self-development ends only in self-conscious paralysis and egotism. Self-development, like love, cannot be sought directly. This is as true for the collective development of mankind as it is for the individual.

The weakness of the humanist movement originates in this basic weakness in its philosophy.

If Humanism is to become a vital movement, it must have a rational goal, and yet it must reflect a value felt by mankind. The new value is, I believe, glimmering under the surface of consciousness.

There are two trends which indicate that western man is beginning to act upon a new value. There is the trend away from the cities. This is a search for a healthier way of life in more pleasant surroundings. And there is a trend toward a growing appreciation of Nature. Even the general public is becoming aware of the effects of ecological destruction. In these two trends together is the clue to the new value: *All Life* rather than Mankind; and to the new goal: *Furtherance of All Life* rather than the Development of Mankind.

By furtherance of all life I mean the maintenance of the life-cycle together with the cherishing of life in all its forms. Life is a process that involves the continuous re-distribution of elements and energy in a dynamic equilibrium. The purpose of man's life, as part of this process, should be to help maintain it, not to let the fire of life go out. Without this continuous re-cycling of the elements between earth and sky, man's life would be snuffed out along with that of all other forms.

The maintenance of the life-cycle should not be done, however, at the expense of the individual forms through which it thrives. To do this would be like glorifying society at the expense of the individual human beings of which it consists. The moral principle of Humanism—the recognition of the right of every individual to pursue his own interests—must be extended to all animals if man himself is to become the moral animal he claims to be.

A Rational Goal

Besides expressing a value felt by mankind, however vaguely, the goal of furtherance of all life is a much more rational goal than is the development of mankind:

1. *It is not inherently self-defeating*. Instead of producing self-consciousness and encouraging arrogance,

the new goal would actually develop the best qualities in man: altruism, moral responsibility, and humility.

2. *It would provide man with something to revere.* Man cannot worship himself without being vainglorious, yet man needs to revere something just as he needs to love someone, for reverence is love made great with awe. To hold all life as his highest value would be to express his wonder, his delight, and his awe at the mystery of Existence and the miracle of Life.

3. *It would be consistent with science and reason.* Reverence for Life or Nature does not necessitate postulating anything supernatural or any Spirit isolated from Matter. It assumes that all matter is dynamic, consisting of both mass and energy, and that organic matter is a particular arrangement of elemental matter.

4. *It expresses a realistic evaluation of man's place in Nature.* Although in his science western man recognizes that man is but a small part of life on this planet and that this planet is but a speck in the universe, he finds it hard to admit this emotionally. Indeed, the image western man has of himself is that of a Superior Being in the Center of the Universe. To recognize all life, rather than man, as having the highest value would be to appreciate emotionally what western man now apprehends only intellectually.

5. *It implies a realistic goal.* The furtherance of all life implies as its specific goal, not the building of an all-good environment for man, but the restoration of the natural ecology. This goal does not pretend, as urbanization does, that man can re-make Nature in such a way that he has good without evil, joy without grief, life without death. Whereas the city structure actually attempts to halt the lifecycle at an assumed level of comfort for man, furtherance of all life recognizes that degeneration is regeneration, that death is not failure but the necessary dark side of life.

Restoration of Nature is the complement of a rational way of life for man. It does not mistake comfort for health, nor confuse simplicity with poverty. It would provide a vital environment in which man could develop all his faculties, in which work would be creative and leisure refreshing. Man would not view the rest of Nature as if it were an inert environment to be manipulated, but as a living partner in the dance of life.

6. *It implies the use of effective means.* Furtherance of all life implies working with Nature, not against her. Instead of the sledge hammer of modern industrialization, it would use the scalpel of biological and ecological knowledge to let Nature herself keep the life cycle going. Instead of man's burdening himself with the hydra-headed problems of mechanization, man would let the living mechanisms of Nature transform one element into another to keep the environment fit for man. Instead of demanding that the rest of Nature feed an ever-expanding human population, man would control his own population to a level consistent with the well-being of all life, his own included. This does not mean doing away with all technological advances; it means using them to the best advantage.

7. *It would make of man the moral animal he claims to be.* Man's collective moral code must be consistent with his individual code. So long as he kills other animals wantonly and unnecessarily, man is acting immorally according to his own moral code. Just as the child must learn to see himself objectively as one among many, must learn to recognize the right of others to live their own lives, so man must recognize the right of other animals to pursue their own ends.

This does not mean that man should sacrifice his own life for that of other animals, but that he should weigh the interests involved in an action objectively and decide in favor of the preponderant interest, whosoever it is. In spite of our stereotyped picture of "tooth and claw" competition, the interests of man and those of other animals do not in general conflict; in fact, man cannot live without other animals to maintain the chain of life. Moreover, not to know other animals as friends impoverishes man's life just as it is impoverished when he confines his friends to people of his own culture.

Like arguments raised against racial integration, the arguments raised against recognizing our duties to animals are illogical ("Your concern for animals shows you hate people"), irrelevant ("Should I give my life for a mosquito?"), based on ignorance ("Animals have no feelings"), or are a projection of guilt feelings ("Animals are vicious; it's kill or be killed"). Such arguments, not being based on reason, cannot be overcome by logic. They require emotional as well as intellectual re-education. This would be part of the business of the humanist movement, just as it is the business of the church to educate its members in the values of its own faith.

A Vital Movement

If Humanist philosophy were strengthened by such a heightening of its aim and widening of its moral base, it could become a vital movement: it would have a positive program to offer; it would be able to replace the good functions of organized religion, and it would attract a wider membership.

At present the humanist movement assumes that its goal of human development can be solved by political and economic reform. It thus has nothing to offer which is not offered by a political party.

While Humanism should continue to fight for human rights through political and economic reform, furtherance of all life as a goal would give it a unique program which would not only guide its political thinking but which could change the daily life of its members.

Because furtherance of all life permits man to revere something greater than himself, Humanism could replace the good functions of the church: the provision of sanctuaries, an inspiring service which would educate emotionally as well as intellectually, and which would end in action.

Church buildings, particularly the Catholic churches, offer a sanctuary, a place of beauty and quiet in which to take refuge from the rush and noise of city life, a place for contemplation and for solace in time of distress and grief. So also wilderness areas would be the real sanctuaries of the spirit for Humanists, who could, for the sake of those caught in the city, encourage the creation of open- air sanctuaries nearer to the city, like the Lamont Nature Sanctuary, and even within the city in the form of cloistered gardens. Such a garden could be open to all who seek a place of meditation and it could be, or adjoin, the meeting place of the Humanist group.

But the creation of sanctuary gardens is not enough. Instruction in the principles of Nature, in the nicety of her adjustments, in the beauty of her forms, is needed to awaken people to the significance of the life they see about them. Meetings of Humanist groups could become services which would stimulate as well as express reverence for all life. Art and science could for once be truly integrated, for, through science, intellectual appreciation would be awakened and, through art, sensual and emotional appreciation would be aroused.

Depending upon the size and formality of the group, there might be a simple ritual: perhaps no more than a period of silence, perhaps music, lighting of candles, reading of a short poem. This, together with the decor, would help focus attention upon, and imbue with emotional value, the particular element or principle of Nature being studied.

For example, if water were the theme, the biological significance of its unique physical and chemical properties could first be studied, then its meteorological and ecological importance, then the current problems concerning it, such as the lowering of water tables throughout the world, soil erosion, stream pollution. Field trips to unspoiled streams and to their opposite could be made so that the determination to do something concrete might grow.

Projects could involve activity at all levels, from personally abstaining from using foaming detergents, to writing letters to Congressmen, to persuading industrial owners to filter their wastes, to actual physical help with reforestation of a nearby area. This would in no way prevent aid to human beings; it would, rather, get at the root of much human misery and could in most cases be directly combined with helping people to become self-sufficient while restoring natural resources. Aid in eradicating pockets of poverty in this country or in eradicating widespread poverty in other countries would be done on the basis, not of charity, but of working with fellow human beings to solve the common problems of mankind.

Those Humanists who wished to lead a completely rational, healthful life in harmony with Nature would not have to wait to persuade all other citizens of its advantages before putting them into practice themselves. They could, on their own or with others, found intentional communities which would serve as models of the "good life." If they wished to go one step further and share this life with others, they could establish retreats for other members and hostels for strangers in need. In this way, the "gospel" would spread.

If the above program seems too broad for Humanists to undertake, it should be remembered that by making Furtherance of All Life its goal, Humanism would appeal to a much wider membership. It would attract not only conservationists, organic gardeners, believers in natural diet, but also many atheists and agnostics who do not now see what Humanism has to offer as a positive program. From the international point of view, a Humanism which recognized that man is not the center of the universe would be much more appealing to Taoists, Buddhists, Vedantists, and members of other religions of the world—all of whom realize that man is a small, though significant, part of Nature.

FOR FURTHER READING

Henderson, Lawrence J.: T*he Fitness of the Environment, An Inquiry Into the Biological Significance of the Properties of Matter*. Beacon Press, 1958. Paperback reprint of a classic (copyright, 1913).

Krutch, Joseph Wood: T*he Great Chain of Life*. Houghton Mifflin Co., 1956.

Leopold, Aldo: *A Sand County Almanac*. Oxford University Press, 1949.

Nelson, Leonard: *System of Ethic*s. Yale University Press, 1956; translated from the German by Norbert Guterman (1932).

Udall, Stewart L.: *The Quiet Crisis*. Holt, Rinehart and Winston, Inc., 1963.

Eleanor Woods is a freelance writer on philosophical and social topics. She received her B.A. from Mills College, California, and did graduate work at the University of Berlin and the University of London. Her previous articles in The Humanist *were: "Cost What it May" (1961, p.77) and "The Face of Conscience" (1962, p. 70).*

Index

Ames, Van Meter 1, 96, 97, 99, 102, 190
Aristotle 31, 335, 391
Asimov, Isaac 376, 393
Aubrey, Edwin Evart 7, 8, 22
Backus, E. Burdette 7, 11, 96, 100, 373
Bain, Read 99, 100, 129
Barnes, Gerald 96, 188, 189, 193
Barnes, Harry Elmer 125, 254
Bates, Barbara J. 254, 255, 259
Behaviorism 48-9, 87-94, 337-9
Behaviorist humanism 48-9
Black, Algernon D. 11, 150, 151, 256, 257, 401, 405
Blanshard, Brand 1
Brameld, Ted 191, 226
Brooks, William K. 149
Buddha and buddhism 27, 31, 411, 431
Busby, C.E. 402, 419
Buschman, Harold 46, 47, 95, 151, 185
Camus, Albert 63, 64, 374
Christian humanism 45, 126
Christians and christianity 51, 67, 70, 130, 135-6, 170, 179, 181, 186, 194, 199, 234, 242, 245, 250-2, 308, 314,, 335, 407, 409, 415
Compassion 92, 94, 97, 255, 260, 261-4, 423
Comte, Auguste 15, 185-7
Contingency 9-10, 48, 62, 75, 89-94, 96, 98, 148, 152, 158, 189, 226, 272, 326, 360-3
Cultural relativism 11, 332
Darwin, Charles 168, 390, 413
deFord, Miriam Allen 44, 45, 59, 403
Democracy 5, 14, 19, 34, 38, 41, 43, 48, 55, 76-8, 86, 100-1, 105, 115, 118, 125, 131-4, 140-2, 144, 147, 149, 177, 218, 273, 275, 295, 299, 380-1, 390, 411, 418
Descartes, Rene 64, 90
Dewey, John 1, 6, 15, 20, 31, 64, 96, 97, 108, 125, 126, 148, 181, 227, 231, 233
Dietrich, John H. 125
Domhoff, G. William 46, 61
Einstein, Albert 125, 201, 202, 228, 388-390
Ellis, Albert 8, 271, 272, 288
Emergence 7, 12-3, 98
Emotion 35, 45, 55, 61, 66, 69, 88-90, 120, 143, 188, 206, 254-5, 259-60, 271, 289, 309, 313, 331,

333, 344-5, 373, 376, 415, 42, 423, 427-30
Epicureanism 27, 251
Epistemology 145-7, 154, 159, 226, 375
Equality and inequality 41, 77, 99, 117, 128, 130, 132, 140, 263, 278, 299, 307, 309, 311, 313, 315
Ethical Culture 44, 135, 232, 241-4, 410
Ethical humanism 59
Ethical relativism 242
Ethics 8, 48-9, 57, 59-60, 64, 66-7, 75, 91, 96, 97, 113, 124, 127, 131, 149, 182, 209, 219, 250, 252, 263, 270-82, 288-303, 314-5, 316, 329-30, 334-5, 340, 363-4, 370, 403, 410-1, 414-5, 418, 422,
Evolution of life, and Darwinism 5, 12, 16, 23, 24, 26, 59, 87, 97, 101, 113, 124, 151, 157, 168, 170, 176, 180-1, 211, 219, 237, 279, 331, 334-5, 356, 390
Evolutionary humanism 45, 46-7, 65-73, 232
Evolutionary naturalism 14, 19, 47, 151, 186
Existential humanism 46, 80
Existentialism 46, 61-4, 75, 79, 81, 87, 93, 139
Experimentalism 148, 179-82, 189
Eysenck, H.J. 97, 254, 255, 261
Fairfield, Roy P. 254, 337

Feigl, Herbert 1
Fellows, Erwin W. 96, 96, 99, 112, 149
Frank, Philipp 190, 388
Freedoms 8, 19, 34, 48-9, 62, 74-8, 84-5, 93, 100, 105, 117, 124, 134, 143, 171, 195, 241, 244, 288, 291, 300, 311, 319, 323, 326-8, 330-1, 333-4, 348, 349, 359-64, 368, 371, 381, 406, 408, 421-2
Freud, Sigmund 31, 64, 90, 331, 335, 340
Fries, Horace S. 97, 99, 148, 152, 177, 232, 270
Fromm, Erich 31, 33, 46, 63, 64
Fuller, R. Buckminster 147, 161
Green, Lucile W. 375, 385
Hacker, Helen Mayer 8, 272, 304
Handy, Rollo 5, 95, 270-3, 275
Harper, Robert A. 7, 11, 36
Haydon, A. Eustace 6, 42,, 51, 234, 245, 265
Hinduism and hindus 94, 415
Hobart, Alfred W. 232
Hook, Sidney 1, 3
Humanist Manifesto I 1, 4, 6, 7, 13, 44, 45, 48, 99, 100, 145, 146, 148, 150, 231-2, 234, 403
Humanist Manifesto II 1, 4, 7, 43, 44, 45, 48, 99, 145, 148, 150, 234, 403
Humanistic naturalism 6-7, 14-20, 253

Humanistic psychology 1, 47, 48, 93, 254, 325-372
Hume, David 22, 111
Huxley, Aldous 204, 391, 396
Huxley, Julian 10, 45-8, 65, 101, 125, 232
Instrumentalism 15, 233, 236-40
James, William 15, 90, 127, 146, 203, 204
Jews and judaism 220, 251
Justice and injustice 31, 33, 38, 134, 140, 142, 195, 199, 214, 222, 247, 277, 291, 299, 314, 342, 423
Kant, Immanuel 22, 90, 181, 187 229, 243, 391
Kirkendall, Lester A. 272, 273, 292, 303, 316
Kuenzli, Alfred E. 190, 191
Kurtz, Paul ii, 7, 8, 11, 12, 26, 43, 44, 75, 76, 96, 97, 122, 149, 150, 231, 273,, 327
Lamont, Corliss 5-10, 43, 45, 47, 48, 99, 100, 123, 146, 147, 209, 275, 326, 327, 359, 373, 403
Larrabee, Harold A. 97, 149, 327, 365
Locke, John 90, 390
Love 20, 30-2, 61, 129-31, 137, 161, 195-6, 198, 205, 247, 252, 255, 290, 294-6, 298, 300-1, 306, 311, 313-4, 317, 320, 323-4, 333, 334-5, 342, 343, 357, 375, 402, 412, 416, 418, 421, 424, 427

Marković, Mihailo 47, 48, 74
Marcuse, Herbert 74
Marx, Karl 31, 76-8, 81, 83-6, 125, 197, 199, 200
Marxist humanism 47-8, 74-86
Maslow, Abraham 2, 49, 93, 97, 119, 254, 256, 325-7, 337
Materialism 7, 12, 14, 17, 27, 30, 47, 60, 126-7, 247, 389
Metaphysical naturalism 152
Methodological naturalism 6, 11, 145-7, 150, 232
Moore, George E. 150
Morain, Lloyd 44, 45, 53, 98, 99, 256, 258, 326, 401, 402
Morals and morality 8, 24, 27, 30, 34, 38, 45, 48-9, 51, 55-7, 66, 69-70, 91, 96, 102-18, 126, 144, 148-9, 152, 179-81, 183, 195, 199, 203, 206, 212, 219, 232, 270-4, 277, 288-305, 311, 313-4, 316-24, 325, 327, 330-5, 365-72, 396-7, 403, 415, 417, 423, 425-9
Morris, John M. 373, 383
Moslems 359, 415
Nagel, Ernest 1, 126
Nathanson, Jerome 231, 232, 241
Naturalistic humanism 26-35, 43, 44, 45, 99, 101, 145-8, 150, 152, 159, 234, 271, 277, 373,, 375, 401, 403

Nickels, Horace J. 8, 96, 100, 145-7, 149, 151, 152, 154, 401
Nietzsche, Friedrich 31, 32, 64
Otto, Max C. 18, 52, 125
Patton, Kenneth L. 188, 256, 257, 265
Pauling, Linus 97, 99, 101, 190, 209, 401
Peak experience 325, 337-46
Plato 90, 343
Pluralism 7, 8-9, 98, 152, 156, 244, 290, 312, 326, 375
Positivism 95, 151, 185-7, 339-40
Potter, Charles Francis 125
Pragmatism 15, 79, 127, 146, 194, 236,
Probabilism, probabalism 191-2, 226-30
Protagoras 271
Rationalisms 59, 125, 177-83, 230, 254-5, 261, 288, 425
Reason 5, 10, 13, 28, 31-2, 43, 45, 55, 63, 71, 96-7, 123, 124, 131, 134, 137, 147-8, 154, 178, 194, 201, 206, 221, 227, 229, 254-7, 261-4, 268, 275, 288-9, 329, 363, 391, 412-3, 417-8, 427, 429
Reese, Curtis 46, 99-101, 138, 401
Reiser, Oliver 44, 45, 53, 99, 147, 256, 258, 326, 401, 402
Relativism and relativity 9, 11-2, 36-41, 98, 152, 202, 271, 279, 290
Religious humanism 6, 7, 43-45, 47, 60, 125, 146, 150, 231-53
Rickover, Hyman G. 403
Robertson, Priscilla 7, 273, 325, 329
Rogers, Carl R. 2, 49, 326, 327, 347
Russell, Bertrand 31, 46, 61-4, 275, 276
Santayana, George 14, 31
Sartre, Jean Paul 31, 34, 46, 61-4
Schweitzer, Albert 210, 256, 402, 423
Scientific humanism 6, 7, 14, 43-5, 53-60, 125, 129-37, 145
Scientific method 6, 16, 55, 73, 97, 103, 105, 107, 116, 124, 146-8, 151, 155, 181-2, 191, 229, 254, 271, 277, 367, 391, 412
Scientific naturalism 6, 7, 43, 145-6, 148, 150, 154-60, 233, 243
Scott, Harold 233, 236
Secular humanism 44, 45, 231, 384
Self-actualization 93, 119, 255, 325, 330-1, 344
Sellars, Roy Wood 1, 5, 6, 12, 13, 43, 95, 125, 146, 232, 234, 249
Sex 92, 112, 116, 134, 143, 195, 272, 288-315, 318, 322, 342
Skinner, B.F. 5, 48, 87

Smith, Alfred G. 151, 190, 192, 220
Smith, Warren Allen 401
Socrates 259, 327, 343
Sophists 6
Spencer, Herbert 77, 181
Spinoza 31, 181
Spirituality 44, 45, 57, 86, 93-4, 97, 106, 120, 127-8, 199, 205, 220-4, 231, 247, 256-8, 265-9, 352, 374, 405-18, 429
Stoicism 251
Taoism 27, 431
Titus, Harold H. 6, 7, 12, 13, 43, 44, 48, 146, 256, 373
Values in humanism 4, 11, 49, 95-144, 151, 234, 270, 272, 327, 374, 376, 404
Wilson, Edwin H. 125, 185, 186
Woods, Eleanor 402, 403, 425
Wright, Frank Lloyd 373, 374, 378

www.ingramcontent.com/pod-product-compliance
Lightning Source LLC
Chambersburg PA
CBHW060103170426
43198CB00010B/750